FRANCE 1848–1945

ANXIETY & HYPOCRISY

By

THEODORE ZELDIN

Oxford   New York   Toronto   Melbourne

OXFORD UNIVERSITY PRESS

1981

Oxford University Press, Walton Street, Oxford OX6 2DP

London Glasgow New York Toronto
Delhi Bombay Calcutta Madras Karachi
Kuala Lumpur Singapore Hong Kong Tokyo
Nairobi Dar es Salaam Cape Town
Melbourne Wellington
and associate companies in
Beirut Berlin Ibadan Mexico City

First published in volume 2 of France 1848-1945 by
the Clarendon Press 1977. First issued, with additional material,
as an Oxford University Press paperback 1981

British Library Cataloguing in Publication Data

Zeldin, Theodore
France 1848-1945. - (Oxford paperbacks)
Anxiety and hypocrisy
1. France - Civilization - 1830-1900
2. France - Civilization - 1901-
I. Title
944.07   DC33.6   80-41979
ISBN 0-19-285106-3

Reproduced, printed and bound in Great Britain by
Cox & Wyman Ltd, Reading

CONTENTS

1. Private Lives

PRIVATE lives have, on the whole, been an area into which historians have not penetrated, and certainly not systematically. This is due partly to tradition, to a convention inherited from public figures who have mutually conceded each other immunity outside the arena of politics and war. It has been only poets and novelists who have enjoyed baring their souls and their emotional troubles and it is mainly concerning them therefore that the rule of silence is broken. But the silence has been due also to a genuine lack of interest by historians in individuals as such, or at least to a preference for grander, less limited themes. That does not mean that historians have not written about individuals, but rather that they have subordinated such writing to other purposes. This was particularly the case in France. Any approach to a study of private lives must first explain what people's attitude to the subject was, since the facts about them can be seen only through this veil that envelops them. There is no book about biography in France in this period, but it is important to investigate its prestige and its function in the writing of this period. Secondly, one needs to discover the relationship between biography and the way character and personality were interpreted. What, in other words, were the psychological assumptions that biographers made, and how did the development of scientific and medical knowledge alter views about motivation and behaviour? Psychology in the mid-nineteenth century was still largely a branch of philosophy, and philosophy—or at least the 'philosophical approach'—was the principal enemy of biography.

Biography

The number of biographies written in the nineteenth century was quite enormous. If one opens the *Bibliographie de la France*, say for the year 1856, one finds that of the sixty-four pages listing historical works, biography takes up ten, more than local history, which has nine, and twice as much as foreign history, which has four. It is not worth trying to make these very rough statistics more precise, because the titles indicate very different things. The vast majority of publications—and particularly biographies—were only short pamphlets. A historian who examined 400 biographies of bishops of the *ancien régime* found only about ten to be really substantial.[1] But some idea of the accumulating mass of biographies— whatever their quality—can be obtained from looking at the *Catalogue de l'histoire de France*. In 1865 this contained 21,027 individual biographies of persons involved in the French Revolution alone. By 1940 this number had increased to 71,716.[2] This leaves aside the collective biographies, in which the nineteenth century was particularly prolific, produced by men like Michaud, Hoefer, Vapereau and Larousse.

A count has been made simply of the biographical dictionaries devoted to contemporaries. The nineteenth century produced no less than 200 of these, to which should be added another eighty-one begun but never finished. This contrasts with only fifty-two produced in the first sixty-one years of the twentieth century. These figures refer to general dictionaries only, and exclude the large number of specialised regional and professional ones, and the ones devoted to historical figures.[3] These biographical dictionaries, though enormous, were nevertheless surprisingly modest in their pretensions. They were obviously as much financial speculations as contributions to knowledge. Plagiarism was one of their principal methods. Levot, author, with forty collaborators, of the *Biographie bretonne* (1852), did not presume to claim for biography a place more exalted than that of 'History's younger sister'. Rochas, author of the *Biographie du Dauphiné* (1856), saw his function as to collect information 'disdained by the gravity of history'. None of these compilers seems to have developed any independent philosophy to justify his activity. The Court

[1] M. Peronnet, 'Pour un renouveau des études biographiques: approches méthodiques', *Actes du 91ᵉ Congrès des sociétés savantes, Rennes 1966*, ancien régime et révolution (1969), 7–17. This article limits itself to proposing the compilation of biographical index cards.

[2] G. Walter, *Répertoire de l'histoire de la Révolution française. Travaux publiés de 1800 à 1940* (1941), preface.

[3] J. Auffray, 'Bibliographie des recueils biographiques de contemporains au 19ᵉ et 20ᵉ siècles en France', Mémoire pour l'Institut National des Techniques de la Documentation, unpublished, 1963.

of Paris, in its judgement in the lawsuit between two of the
most famous compilers of biographical dictionaries, Michaud
and Hoefer, in which the former accused the latter of plagiarism, ruled that Michaud had shown no 'unity of thought or
of doctrine', and that his work gave no evidence of 'over-all
supervision or direction'.[1] Dr. Hoefer did not even claim that
he was showing that a man's life could have an interest of its
own: he said that his main innovation was that he was remedy-
ing the defect attributed to other dictionaries of biography,
that they gave too much space to obscurities. He said that he
aimed to proportion 'the length of his articles to the importance
of the personality, as exactly as possible'. He accepted, that is,
the criterion imposed by the general historians.

This timidity of biographers was explained by the firmness
with which the most esteemed authors spurned their activities,
when they laid down what was and what was not worthy of
study in the past. Thus Victor Cousin (who, one tends to forget, did not die till 1867) affirmed that a nation was not an
accidental collection of individuals: it could not be 'a veritable
People except on condition that it expressed an idea that, by
passing through all the elements of which the People's internal
life was composed, gave it a special character'. The proper
subject of history was the idea, not the individual, who was
nothing without it. 'The individual by himself is a miserable
and petty fact . . . Humanity has not got the time and cannot
bother to concern itself with individuals who are nothing but
individuals.' It was interested only in great men, who in-
carnated the idea of their time. But the great man was only one
who succeeded and who was recognised as such by his contemporaries. This severely limited the scope of biography.
In any case, in studying great men, one should not concern
oneself with their private lives, with what, i.e., was particular
about them. The private lives of the great, as memoirs revealed,
were perfectly common, like those of all ordinary men, and were
not worthy of the true historian. 'The philosophy of history is
a classical muse; it seeks out in the great man that which makes
him great, and the rest it leaves to memoirs and biography.'[2]

[1] *Bibliographie de la France* (19 Mar. 1853), 118.
[2] Victor Cousin, *Introduction à l'histoire de la philosophie* (4th edition, 1861),
10ᵉ leçon. Cf., for the development of biography in England, from the eighteenth-
century 'character' to the nineteenth-century 'compilation', and for theories about

Guizot took a similar view. 'It matters little to us', he said, 'to know what Constantine's face was like, or what the precise date of his birth was; we do not need to discover what particular motives, what personal sentiments influenced his decisions and his conduct on this or that occasion, nor to be informed about all the details of his wars and his victories against Maxentius or Licinius: these circumstances concern only the monarch and the monarch is dead.' History should be concerned with large and general questions only, such as the results of Constantine's conversion, his administration and his political principles. There were, for Guizot, two parts to the past. One was dead, and was not worth resurrecting: this included all personal accidents. Only the other, the dominating ideas, because of the influence they had on nations and whole centuries, were the proper subject-matter of history. Besides, it was futile to try to penetrate the private motivations of individuals, which were too complicated, obscure and mysterious to understand. 'Man can barely know himself and he is never more than guessed about by others. The most simple person would have a thousand secrets to reveal to us, which we never suspected, if he tried to paint himself.' This perhaps was an honest explanation of why historians did not examine biography: they had no real theory for interpreting the lives of individuals. In his study of Sir Robert Peel (1850), Guizot gave only 8 out of 354 pages to the first twenty-one years of Peel's life. In his books on the English Revolution, his main concern was to collect documents rather than fathom the characters of the contenders. At most he saw them as examples of types, Ludlow as the archetype of the spirit of faction, Fairfax was that of the disinterested dupe, and so on. When it came to writing his own memoirs, however, he claimed to want to tell his 'personal and intimate history, what I thought, felt and wanted', and to describe 'our internal life in our actions'. But that was the function of memoirs, not history.[1]

It is not surprising to find, therefore, that Bishop Dupanloup, the 'dignity of history', Joseph W. Reed, Jr., *English Biography in the Early 19th Century* (Yale U.P., 1966).

[1] F. Guizot, *Mémoires pour servir à l'histoire de mon temps*, vol. 1 (1858), 388–95, 3–4; id., *Études biographiques sur la révolution de l'Angleterre* (1851), 51, 99, 214. Cf. Barante, *La Vie politique de M. Royer-Collard* (1861), which covers the first 22 years of his life in one page.

in his manual on the teaching of history, should have classified biography, with chronology, as that elementary part of
history which was most suitable to be taught to children. He
considered it to involve little more than the memorising of
genealogical and chronological tables.[1]

Despite this condemnation, there was nevertheless a great
deal of curiosity about and interest in biography. The views of
men like Cousin did not go unchallenged. One of his former
pupils, professor of philosophy at Bordeaux, wrote a book to
contradict him on this very question, protesting against the
ruling that only great, representative and successful men should
be studied. This would make it impossible to concern oneself
with rebels, with innovators who were unrecognised by their
own generation; private lives, moreover, were as much part of
such men as anything else, and were deserving of investigation if only to ensure that history did not hold people up to
admiration who were unworthy of it.[2] Sainte-Beuve was
probably the most illustrious of the opponents of the 'high
and philosophical method', as he called it, which linked a
man so closely to his epoch and background that all was
foreseen and inevitable in his career. Sainte-Beuve claimed
that at any rate artists and poets who did not represent a
whole epoch should not have their lives complicated from the
start by 'too vast a philosophical apparatus'; it was enough
'to confine oneself, at first, to the private character and domestic liaisons, and to follow the individual closely in his interior
destiny, and only then, when one knew him well, to bring
him into broad daylight and to confront him with his century'.
In his biography of Proudhon, for example, he declares his
aim to be 'to show the man as he was, to draw out his moral
qualities, the core of his sincerity, the form of his talent, in
short his personality'.[3]

The biographer Levot was another who protested against the
'abusive extension' given to the philosophy of history. The

---

[1] Mgr Dupanloup, *Conseils aux jeunes gens sur l'étude de l'histoire* (1872), 49.

[2] C. A. Sainte-Beuve, *Proudhon* (1872), 12; A. G. Lehmann, 'Sainte-Beuve and
the Historical Movement', in *The French Mind, Studies in Honour of Gustave Rudler*
(Oxford, 1952), 256–72; J. Bourdeau, 'La Psychologie et la philosophie de Sainte-
Beuve', *Séances et travaux de l'académie des sciences morales et politiques* (17 Dec. 1904),
354–74.

[3] Ladevi-Roche, *Variétés philosophiques* (1867), 1. 84–5.

individual, he insisted, could only rarely be regarded as the 'personification of the various passions that are active around him. By more or less idealising characters and by creating types, writers have too frequently condensed disparate or irreconcilable things into a single humanity, and the real man has disappeared to give way to a conventional man.'[1] First, there was the approach of the 'philosophers of history', who were concerned to show general trends and the large forces that dominated mankind. Mignet had been the principal initiator and exponent of this attitude.[2] Secondly, there were the romantics, who were sometimes interested in other people's emotions as well as in their own. Michelet gave considerable thought to the problem of biography: he agreed with Rousseau that Plutarch 'excelled by using those very details into which we no longer dare enter'; but when he embarked on his national history he was really more interested in penetrating the 'interior of the national soul' than in going deeply into that of any particular individual.[3] The romantic hero usually got lost as the personification of an abstraction. Renan cloaked this approach in a new scientific garb, but his best-selling *Life of Jesus* was basically a self-portrait, with a thin veneer of scholarship placed over it.[4] Taine's view that political doctrines were the result more of a special kind of sensibility than of pure intelligence meant that he was keen to study the heart as much as the mind. 'Political or religious fanaticism,' he wrote, 'whatever the theological or philosophical channel along which it flows, always has as its principal source an avid need, a secret passion, an accumulation of profound and powerful desires to which theory gives an outlet.' His application of psychology to history of course also led to very broad generalisations about what individuals typified, and usually presented a static view of them, in that they tended to remain under the domination of the same psychological state all their lives.[5]

[1] P. Levot, *Biographie bretonne* (1852), avant-propos.

[2] Y. Knibiehler, *Naissance des sciences humaines: Mignet et l'histoire philosophique au 19e siècle* (1973).

[3] On Michelet, see below, pp. 35–7.

[4] P. Alfaric, *Les Manuscrits de la vie de Jésus d'Ernest Renan* (1909).

[5] H. Taine, 'La Psychologie des Jacobins', *Revue des Deux Mondes* (1881), 44. 536–59; id., *De l'intelligence* (1870), i. 7–9; Paul Lacombe, *La Psychologie des individus et des sociétés chez Taine* (1906).

The uncertainties and hesitations of biographers may be illustrated by some instances. Gaston Boissier, professor at the Collège de France, made something of a name for himself with his study of the public and private life of Cicero. He thought the latter worth investigating, even though he came to the conclusion that 'The feelings which are the basis of human nature have not changed and they always produce more or less the same consequences.' But at the same time Ernest Bersot, director of the École Normale, was moralising that 'There are details of our lives which occur behind the scenes: I demand, in the name of decency, that they should be left there.'[1] Napoleon III's *Histoire de Jules César* shows best of all the variety of contradictory attitudes towards biography, which he —as one could expect—tried somehow to reconcile. On the one hand he said that the aim of biographers should be to discover 'the predominant idea that makes a man act in the way he does', but on the other hand he insisted that great men were simply the instruments of Providence and it was wrong to explain the actions of 'superior men' by 'mean motives', egoism or cunning. On the one hand he wished history to teach moral lessons, to inspire love of justice and progress, but on the other hand he also paid lip-service to erudition. It is no wonder that his 'portrait' of Caesar is so brief and superficial.[2]

The bulk of biographical writing during the Second Empire was monumental, that is, it served to commemorate and extol the virtues of the dead. The largest proportion of biographies were *éloges*. This genre was not necessarily the antithesis of analytical biography. A. L. Thomas (1732–85), whose *Essai sur les éloges* was still regarded as the best guide on how to write these essays, had provided extremely acute and subtle precepts, which, if they had been followed, would have produced historically very interesting results. But since *éloges* were the speciality of Academicians, who were restrained by their *esprit de corps*, they did not emphasise criticism. One function of the *éloge* was to defend the choice the particular academy had made in electing the dead man as a member, proving, as Vicq d'Azyr of the Academy of Medicine had said, that they

---

[1] G. Boissier, 'Ciceron', *Revue des Deux Mondes* (1865), 56. 73; E. Bersot, *Études et pensées* (1882), 'De la médecine en littérature', written in 1860, 102–33.
[2] Napoleon III, *Histoire de Jules César* (1865), preface and 1. 410.

had chosen 'only persons, praise of whom the public could applaud'. The *éloge* had the moral purpose of holding up good examples to stimulate virtue, which was the function of history too, as some saw it. The *éloge* was also considered as a source of 'materials for history', a recording by friends of facts which would be lost unless enshrined in this way. The vast mass of these *éloges* would repay study, for it was not all simply secular hagiography. Some specialists made very interesting contributions; and there was a continuing debate about what ought and what ought not to be said about the dead.[1]

The clergy were probably the largest single category of whom biographies were written—followed by soldiers. Now hagiography, like the *éloge*, had a long tradition behind it. But this laid stress not on showing up the individuality of the subject, but rather on showing the virtue he represented. It was common to claim that the hero possessed all his future qualities and his vocation at birth. Hagiography was thus a discourse on virtue more than a biography. Great precision of detail was not infrequently attempted, and massive documentation collected in the tradition established by the Bollandists, but the aim was to edify rather than to explain.[2]

The main exception, in this period, to this attitude was that of Lavisse, who wrote two books on the early life of Frederick the Great, exceptionally lively and readable ones too. Lavisse concentrated on the struggle between Frederick and his father, which he saw as reflecting the struggle of opposing forces in society, from the fusion of which Prussia emerged. His subtle analysis stressed the influence of Frederick's mother who 'on every single point thought differently' from his father; and of Frederick's tutors, who gave him ideas directly contrary to those of his father; but he concludes that the rebellion of the young Frederick was really only a protest against excessive paternal demands, and that the resemblance of father and son,

---

[1] A. L. Thomas, *Œuvres* (new edition, 1773), 'Essai sur les éloges'; cf. the *éloges* by François Arago (1854), Flourens, Dubois d'Amiens, Mignet, etc. For the survival of these ideas, Georges Picot, *Études d'histoire contemporaine* (1907), ix, and Henri Dumeril, 'Éloge des éloges', *Mémoires de l'Académie des sciences, inscriptions et belles lettres de Toulouse* (1912), 131–48.

[2] René Aigrain, *L'Hagiographie, ses sources, ses méthodes, son histoire* (1953) and compare the works of Mgr Paul Guérin, *Les Petits Bollandistes* (1st edition 1858–60, 6th edition 1866–9), and Mgr Crosnier, *Hagiologie nivernaise* (Nevers, 1858).

which the son always tried to conceal, made itself evident as soon as he succeeded to the throne. This was in effect an intellectual as well as a political biography, based on the view that 'our philosophy always obeys our instincts'. But neither Lavisse nor his pupils developed these ideas.[1] It was André Maurois, a novelist, who became the country's most successful biographer, and it was popularised, fictionalised, superficial biography that was most favoured. The large quantities of this kind of writing that were published led to stern expressions of disapproval and contempt from those who regarded themselves as the guardians of the nation's good taste. In 1927 the *Revue des Deux Mondes* had an article complaining that the new reading public was demanding 'pure biography', meaning biography which served no purpose beyond satisfying idle curiosity about the doings of famous people, skimming on the surface of things, recounting amusing anecdotes. The author argued that this was a sign of the country's general decadence. 'Tired epochs have, in common with young epochs, the taste for fables. The essay, the maxim, and direct reasoning which demand meditation and the exercise of the understanding are reserved for vigorous periods.' The cinema was derided as a manifestation of this corrupting taste for a rapid succession of images. In Ancient Greece (which, for such men, was still the model) everybody who went to the theatre knew the plot of the play, and what mattered was the skill with which it was developed, and how character, passion and ideas were portrayed. Nowadays, by contrast, it was information unknown to the reader that was valued, revelations of scandals, so that most biography was reduced to stories of passion. This was acceptable to many readers because they themselves had experience only of passion, and they had done nothing that mattered beyond their own lives. For this classical critic, the theatre and the novel were acceptable forms of art, because 'they had their laws'. But biography 'is a more uncertain genre'. His conclusion was that its worth was determined ultimately by the qualities of the author: the best biographers would therefore be poets or literary critics, who could make out of the biography either a poetic creation, or an essay in philosophy or morals. 'The painter

---

[1] E. Lavisse, *La Jeunesse du grand Frédéric* (1888), 47, and *Le Grand Frédéric avant l'avènement* (1893), ix.

matters more than the model.' Historians could continue to devote themselves to laboriously collecting the facts, but only they were modest enough to place the hero in the forefront, for that meant that they themselves, as authors, would be forgotten.[1]

This is not to say that polemical biography was not also very much in demand. The success of men like Eugène de Mirecourt, whose hundred little volumes on *Les Contemporains* set unbreakable standards in scurrility and inaccuracy, may be linked with the new opportunities being opened up by the popular press.[2] Biography as a serious art was probably discredited by the sensationalism and anecdote-collecting to which journalists usually reduced it. It is not surprising therefore that few professional historians thought biography worthy of their attention, and remarkably few doctoral theses have been written about individuals. Even in very recent times, now that this tacit taboo has lost its force, historians who have written biographies have felt it necessary to apologise and justify their eccentricity, and all the more so because, now that class and economic forces are fashionable, the individual is held to 'make history' even less than before.[3]

Psychology

Biographers were faced by a whole variety of psychological ideas, which they had to choose between when they embarked on their task. The most academically respectable method of discovering the springs of human action continued to be introspection. Psychology was in the mid-nineteenth century above all a branch of philosophy, and so it was a theoretical study, whose principal activity was to classify and define human faculties and passions. The leading expert then was probably Adolphe Garnier (Tocqueville's successor at the Académie des sciences morales et politiques), whose *Treatise on the Faculties of the Soul* was highly esteemed as a 'complete survey, a vast

[1] André Chaumeix, 'Le Goût des biographies', *Revue des Deux Mondes* (1 Dec. 1927), 698–708.
[2] Alexis Giraud, *Monsieur Eugène de Mirecourt* (1856); for an example, E. de Mirecourt, *Fabrique de romans: Maison Alexandre Dumas et compagnie* (1845).
[3] See the prefaces to P. Guiral, *Prévost-Paradol* (1955) and P. Sorlin, *Waldeck-Rousseau* (1966).

compendium of the behaviour of the soul'. Its principal originality was that it increased the number of faculties; but it was still very much an abstract exercise, since it offered no means of discovering which faculties were predominant in any particular person, in what proportions and why. Thus Garnier states that the instinct for power represents a desire for intellectual pleasure, and fortunately nature distributes this desire very unevenly, so that only some people have a strong desire to dominate while most have an inclination for submission and docility. Otherwise, society would be impossible. Heads of state, with a taste for domination and talents necessary to exercise it, are thus a natural phenomenon, explicable not in personal terms, but by the foresight of Providence. Garnier concluded that human nature was in any case so complicated that it was difficult for men to judge each other: his study had led him only to 'the dogma of indulgence and mutual charity'. Professor Paul Janet, who belonged to the same school, accepted that psychology was 'condemned, for a long time to come, to being simply a descriptive science'.[1] The type of biography that followed logically from this kind of psychology was one which attributed individuals to particular predeter-mined categories in a more or less random fashion. The constant arguments about how many faculties there were and what their exact nature was, however, made this kind of psy-chology, as the Premier Président de la Cour d'appel de Paris was to put it, 'a clever game or pedantic fantasy', of little use to practical men: its uncertainties discredited any pretensions it had to being a science, and all the more so because it gave little help in understanding the problems of ordinary be-haviour.[2] Nevertheless, this is what was taught in the schools.

More popular was the theory of temperaments, which of course originates, like that of the faculties, in ancient Greek ideas. It is too readily assumed that this brand of psychology was no longer acceptable in the age of positivism; but Littré and Robin, the positivists who in 1855 revised Nysten's standard *Dictionary of Medicine*, wrote that 'the doctrine of temperaments is no longer accepted, now that it has been recognised that it is

[1] A. Garnier, *Traité des facultés de l'âme* (3rd edition, 1872), with a preface by Paul Janet; id., *La Psychologie et la phrénologie comparées* (1839).
[2] Alphonse Gilardin, *Considérations sur les divers systèmes de psychologie* (1883), 1–2.

due to particular variations in the brain that inclinations or
affections, passions, intellectual faculties and moral qualities
must be attributed'. But it was only the humours which were
completely discredited; and the theory of temperaments was
modified rather than overthrown. Littré and Robin still thought
it significant to talk of the sanguine temperament, attributed
now to men with large blood vessels, and the nervous temperament, which meant an irritable nervous system. Michel Lévy,
Napoleon III's medical consultant and sometime president of
the Academy of Medicine, still kept, in the fifth edition of his
standard *Traité d'hygiène* (1869), the theory of temperaments as
his preliminary explanation of human character and disease.
He said that there was disagreement about its formulation, but
'only truth survives the test of time and we want no other
testimony in favour of the doctrine of temperaments than this
universal agreement about it'. Its strength was that it was
easily capable of being adapted to suit the changing and almost
equally vague ideas of the new science. Thus Professor
Becquerel, in his treatise on hygiene, was satisfied that by
renaming them the vascular, nervous and muscular temperaments, the theory accorded perfectly with modern discoveries.
The *Moniteur des hôpitaux* ran a series in 1857 on the temperaments, in very conservative form, illustrating the bilious type
from the medical history of Napoleon, and sub-categories like
'obstinate dogmatics' from that of Bossuet. These examples
were regularly copied in the textbooks.[1]

Claude Bernard[2] himself—the physiologist who was famous
as the exponent of the experimental method—was believed to
have given his support to the theory of temperaments when he
published an article on the physiology of the heart. In this he
went out of his way to insist that 'the sentimental role that has
in all ages been attributed to the heart' was not disproved by
modern discoveries and was not 'purely arbitrary fiction':

---

[1] P. H. Nysten, *Dictionnaire de médecine* (10th edition, 1855), 1240–1, 156;
Michel Lévy, *Traité d'hygiène publique et privée* (1844, 5th edition 1869), 46–71;
A. Becquerel, *Traité élémentaire d'hygiène privée et publique* (1851, 3rd edition 1864),
77–88. Contrast F. V. Raspail, *Manuel annuaire de la santé* (e.g. 1879), which while
condemning temperaments, recommends camphor and blood baths. Armand de
Fleury (de Mansle), 'Du type bilieux', *Le Moniteur des hôpitaux* (4 Apr. 1857),
321–5.

[2] On Bernard, see above, pp. 581–2.

science was not destroying the ideas of art and poetry.[1] As late
as 1895 the philosopher Fouillée revised the temperament
theory in the light of that of evolution, but using protoplasm
to replace the humours. Fouillée argued that the sanguine
temperament 'long admitted and whose reality it is impossible
to doubt' was caused by a highly oxygenated blood supply,
and that it produced all the usual traits of character, in the
description of which he invoked a host of traditional authorities.[2] Dr. Michel Lévy's chapter on temperaments, originally
written in 1851, was reproduced in the textbook of Bouchardat,
professor at the Paris medical faculty, published in 1881; but
Bouchardat, who was an expert on nutrition, added a new
twist by incorporating his discoveries, while keeping the basic
framework. Thus he concluded that the English, who ate a lot
of meat, were therefore energetic and 'keen on work', whereas
the Chinese, who did not, were therefore 'weak and timid'.[3]
As racial theories came to acquire great favour, the temperament theory was given a new lease of life by being united with
it. Fouillée's book was hailed as an important contribution
because it skilfully combined the two.[4] Nor were these ideas
confined to specialist circles. Charles Letourneau, one of the
most successful popularisers of science, was writing in favour
of the theory of four temperaments in 1878, saying that the
microscope had revealed differences in the blood between
sanguine and bilious people.[5] When applied to biography, the
temperaments of course produced a static psychology, even
though considerable thought was given to how they could be
modified.

Perhaps the greatest change that occurred in nineteenth-
century popular psychology was the transfer of the source of
the emotions from the stomach to the brain. This created a new
determinism but also new uncertainties, because knowledge of
the brain was still pretty elementary. The first important break-
through in its dissection was made by Gall (1758–1828, a
naturalised Frenchman of German origin), who instead of

[1] Claude Bernard, 'Étude sur la physiologie du cœur', *Revue des Deux Mondes*
(1 Mar. 1865), 236–52.
[2] A. Fouillée, *Tempérament et caractère, selon les individus, les sexes et les races* (1895).
[3] A. Bouchardat, *Traité d'hygiène publique et privée basée sur l'étiologie* (1881),
25–9, 215.   [4] *Mercure de France* (Feb. 1896), review of Fouillée's book.
[5] Charles Letourneau, *Physiologie des passions* (1878, 2nd edition), 350–9.

cutting through it in a symmetrical and arbitrary way, pulled
it apart, into its natural sections. It was a simple step to
attribute to each of these independent functions. Phrenology
offered a coherent and clear explanation of behaviour, and it
carried all the more conviction because it was based on the
work of a man who was universally recognised (for his anatomical work) as one of the greatest scientists of the day. A
history of phrenology has collected abundant documentation
to show that this enjoyed great prestige under the July Monarchy, even if it lost it under Napoleon III. A lot of distinguished people nevertheless still remained faithful to it. In
1865 there was a vigorous debate about phrenology in the
Academy of Medicine. The discoveries of Dr. Broca, who had
made the first genuine localisation in the brain shortly before,
were used as additional support by the phrenologists, even
though Broca's conclusions did not accord with Gall's, but at
least they seemed to suggest that the basic idea of localisation
was tenable and promising.[1] The great attraction of phrenology
was that it was simple to understand. As developed by men like
Broussais, it produced a psychology of common sense in plain
language. Instead of subtleties and abstractions, it offered a
series of twenty-seven human characteristics (later increased),
whose importance in any particular individual could be
physically discovered by simple examination. The inexplicable,
and the element of pure chance, thus seemed removed from
psychology. In the popular view, phrenology appeared to be
scientific and based on observation: if thirty musicians were
got together, they would all be found to have the same bump.
Talent could thus be linked with physique. Gall did not mean to
be as determinist as his simpler followers interpreted him. For
him, the bumps simply denoted predispositions or potentialities,
and the individual remained free to choose between them. He
insisted that criminals should not be regarded as irresponsible.
But all the same his theory was much misinterpreted, and was
condemned not only for being arbitrary in its attribution of
qualities, but above all for being atheist.[2]

[1] Jules Soury, *Le Système nerveux central, structure et fonctions: histoire critique des
théories et des doctrines* (1899) places Broca's work in its context.
[2] G. Lanteri-Laura, *Histoire de la phrénologie* (1970) has a good bibliography.
For physiognomy, and the related theory of 'cineseologie', see Prof. P. Gratiolet,
De la physionomie et des mouvements d'expression (1865).

It might have been thought that the positivists would have produced a new psychology for the modern world. But, by their own admission, they did not. Littré lamented that this was a great gap in their doctrine. In his *Cours de philosophie positive*, Comte had based himself on Gall, on whom he wrote a brilliant chapter hailing him as the man who had shown the right approach. The metaphysical unity of the personality must be abandoned, and psychology must become a branch of cerebral anatomy. But then in the *Système de politique positive* he forgot all this and invented an arbitrary 'positive classification of the eighteen internal functions of the brain'. The originality of this was that it made the emotional faculties most important and most numerous. Both Comte's theories were anathema to Littré, the first because it kept so much of Gall, whom Littré considered old-fashioned, and the second because it was anti-intellectual and subjective. Littré had nothing to propose instead. But Dr. Audiffrent, one of Comte's religious disciples and his link with the medical world, wrote a book at the end of the Second Empire to make good the defect. This was not simply traditionalist: it amalgamated the ideas of the Montpellier school, Gall, Bichat and Broussais with the theory of temperaments, declared that the world was heading for nervous collapse, that 'névrosisme' was developing into an epidemic because of the lack of any generally accepted beliefs; that physical illness was simply a symptom of this inability of the mind to offer any resistance. This was—despite many interesting ideas—too much a political programme and a universal condemnation to be widely accepted.[1]

A great new body of detailed observation of human behaviour and emotion was meanwhile becoming available through the work of the psychiatrists. The law of 1838 on lunatic asylums, for all its defects, had provided a great stimulus to the development of this new specialisation, and much research and publication of an original kind followed, which has been unjustly neglected. It is too often assumed that between Pinel (1745–1826)

---

[1] A. Comte, *Cours de philosophie positive* (2nd edition, 1864), vol. 3, 45th lesson, 530–89; id., *Système de politique positive* (1851–3), 1. 724–5; E. Littré, *Auguste Comte et la philosophie positive* (1863), 677; G. Audiffrent, *Des maladies du cerveau et de l'innervation d'après Auguste Comte* (1875, enlarged edition of the 1869 book); Dr. Eugène Bourdet, *Des maladies du caractère: hygiène, morale et philosophie* (1858); cf. Charles Robin, *L'Instruction et l'éducation* (1877).

and Esquirol (1772–1840) on the one hand and Charcot (1825–93)[1] on the other, there was not much that was happening. In fact the ideas of Esquirol were quickly challenged in many respects by his pupils, devoted though they were to him, and a succession of methodological innovations were attempted to penetrate the causes of mental disturbances. Reacting against his 'moral' approach, some of his pupils devoted themselves to the autopsy of the brain, seeking physical lesions to explain abnormal behaviour—as was already fashionable in Germany. Others studied all the organs of the body, believing that the malfunctioning of any one could be responsible for mental troubles. Others, seeing, as Esquirol had done, the difficulty of making definite attributions of this kind, returned to the study of normal psychology; and finally, in reaction against all of these, some advocated the clinical approach, the most distinguished of whom was J. P. Falret. His method could be called the historical method, because he urged doctors to go beyond the facts of the case as they were presented to them: 'Instead of writing one's observations at the dictation of the lunatics, instead of making oneself the secretary of these sick people and simply noting down the most striking facts noticed by all those who have dealings with them, one should penetrate more deeply into the intimacy of their intellectual and moral characters; one should study the general dispositions of their minds and hearts, which are the basis of these predominant ideas or sentiments; one should go into the past of these lunatics, follow their affection in its development, from the most distant origin to the present.' He stressed the need to study all moral and physical symptoms in their chronological order, and he pointed out that 'negative facts', what they did not do, were as important as what they did do.[2]

From the layman's point of view, the discoveries of these psychiatrists which were of particular interest were those concerning mental troubles to be found, in various degrees of mildness, among the 'normal' population as a whole, as well as in the asylums. Thus there were new ideas about melancholy. The theory that it was caused by atrabile no longer stood. The melancholic temperament survived in traditional circles.

---

[1] On Charcot, see below, pp. 93–8.
[2] J. P. Falret, *Des maladies mentales et des asiles d'aliénés* (1864), xv–xvi.

Esquirol had tried to make the concept more precise, renaming it *lypémanie*, but he had regarded it as caused by a defect of the intellectual faculties, brought on by moral causes—though noting also the influence of heredity, temperament, puberty and the menopause. The important development came in 1854 when almost simultaneously Baillarger and Falret discovered the link between melancholy and mania. Baillarger called this form of melancholy *folie à double forme*; Falret named it *folie circulaire*. The discovery had a surprising result. Whereas, as separate troubles, melancholy and mania had each been considered curable, this new manic-depressive form was declared to be almost never curable or even capable of durable amelioration. Heredity was considered to be its principal cause, though traumatic experiences and physical diseases like syphilis could contribute to starting it. The only hope of a cure was to change it into either pure mania or pure melancholy, which could then be treated. Baillarger thus tried to get rid of manic symptoms by prolonged bleeding. Michéa used massive doses of stupefying drugs. There was still disagreement as to whether melancholy was a symptom of other troubles, or a morbid entity in itself. Provincial doctors, combining the various theories, became even more puzzled, declaring it to be 'the disease of an epoch, a family, a temperament', and felt more helpless than ever. The most significant result of the new discovery was that it confirmed melancholy as a highly serious disease, which should be treated in an asylum.[1]

In 1852 the *délire des persécutions* was isolated by Professor Charles Lasègue. His findings were the subject of an article in a medical journal, but they became known also to the new generation of medical students through his lectures and through those of Dr. Legrand du Saulle, who in 1871 published an impressive book containing their combined observations. They calculated that about one-sixth of patients in mental hospitals had this form of trouble. All the usual causes were invoked to explain it, but it was interesting to the world outside the asylums that Legrand du Saulle considered that illegitimate

[1] Dr. Antoine Ritti, *Traité clinique de la folie à double forme* (1883); Dr. Michéa, *Du traitement de la lypémanie ou folie mélancolique* (1860); *Bulletin de l'Académie de Médecine* (31 Jan. and 14 Feb. 1854); E. Du Vivier, *De la mélancolie* (1864); Dr. P. F. Gachet, *Étude sur la mélancolie* (Montpellier, 1858).

birth was probably one of the most frequent factors responsible for it. He laid a lot of stress on unsatisfactory relations between parents and children, leading to lack of confidence developing in the latter. There was also a certain amount of discussion about the effects of political and social revolutions as causes of insanity. The statistics were not very convincing, particularly because life became too chaotic—for the asylums as well as for everybody else—for comparable figures to be produced. But interesting case studies are available of the delusions of legitimists on the one hand and advanced radicals on the other who were locked up because their nostalgia or their ambitions appeared excessive; and the reactions of at least some people to the German invasion and occupation can be seen in this same kind of source.[1]

It was during the Second Empire also that hysteria ceased to be regarded as being produced by troubles of the uterus, or as being exclusively a female complaint. Charcot's work on this subject has caused the revolutionary work of an immediate predecessor, Dr. P. Briquet, to be forgotten. Briquet's book on hysteria, published in 1859, with detailed observations on 396 cases and much statistical analysis, argued that it was a nervous, not a physical complaint, produced by women's peculiar 'mode of sensibility', but that men could suffer from it too. Heredity played a major role in its transmission: so that whereas there was one hysteric to every sixty-six normal inhabitants, in hysterical families there was one hysteric in every four. He dismissed the idea that sexual continence had anything to do with it; and suggested instead that it was hysterical mothers who passed it on to their daughters. Marriage could no longer be recommended as the cure. Legrand du Saulle, who also wrote a book on hysteria, estimated that there were 50,000 hysterics in Paris alone: he urged that they should be studied no longer as isolated cases, but with reference to their social background. Shoplifting from the department stores by

---

[1] Charles Lasègue, 'Le Délire de persécutions', first published in the *Archives générales de médecine* (1852), reprinted in his *Études médicales* (1884), 1. 545–66; H. Legrand du Saulle, *Le Délire des persécutions* (1871); C. A. Claude, *De la folie causée par les pertes séminales* (Paris medical thesis, 1849); Dr. L. Lunier, *De l'influence des grandes commotions politiques et sociales sur le développement des maladies mentales* (1874); Paul Schiff, 'L'Évolution des idées sur la folie de persécution', *L'Hygiène mentale* (1935), 1–56.

otherwise respectable women was one of the new fashions of the
Second Empire which was explained by hysteria.[1]

Hallucination was an especially controversial subject, because doctors were bold enough to apply it to the supposedly
normal world. Among the important works on it, was a long
and thorough study by Dr. L. F. Calmeil, who was head of the
Charenton Asylum for most of the Second Empire, of mass
hallucination and 'great epidemics of delirium' between the
fifteenth and eighteenth centuries. This was both a history of
ideas about madness and an investigation of the pathological
elements in many historical movements of the *ancien régime*.
There was a great scandal when Dr. Lelut argued that psychology could study not just the mental troubles of the poor (and of
course patients in the asylums were mainly poor), but also the
great men of history, that it was possible, as he said, to apply
psychology to history. He claimed that Socrates, Pascal and
Luther suffered from pathological states of hallucination. The
politician Eugène Pelletan replied that ordinary men could
perhaps have mental eclipses of this kind, but he refused to
accept that the great could be diagnosed in this way. 'We are
willing to abandon the body of Pascal to the doctors' autopsy,
but we do not abandon his intelligence to ther . . . Illness,
which among the vulgar is but a collapse or failure of one or
more organs, is, among great men, seeking new ideas, only a
natural predisposition to the sublime.' The Société médico-
psychologique had long debates on hallucinations in 1856
which showed that the doctors were much divided about them.
Dr. Brierre de Boismont, who particularly specialised in them,
refused to allow medical science to destroy historical reputations: 'We cannot but feel profoundly saddened by the efforts
being made to bring down from their pedestals the most noble
personifications of human genius.' He accordingly invented a
special theory for the great creative minds which enabled him
to call their hallucinations 'intuitions'.[2]

[1] Dr. P. Briquet, *Traité clinique et thérapeutique de l'hystérie* (1859); Dr. H. Legrand du
Saulle, *Les Hystériques* (1883), 3, 450. On the later history of hysteria, see below, p. 93.

[2] L. F. Calmeil, *De la folie* (2 vols., 1845); L. F. Lelut, *Du démon de Socrate,
spécimen d'une application de la science psychologique à celle de l'histoire* (1838, new
edition 1856), 45–6; *Annales médico-psychologiques* (1856), 126, 193, 300, 434;
A. Brierre de Boismont, *Des hallucinations* (3rd edition, 1862); id., *Études médico-
psychologiques sur les hommes célèbres* (1869).

This raised the question of who was mad and who was not.
It was a matter of urgent concern because a new category of
madness, *la folie lucide* or *manie raisonnante*, began to be written
about, suggesting that people who appeared quite normal might
in fact be mad. Dr. Ulysse Trélat, better known perhaps for
his political role, was specially interested by this in his capacity
as a psychiatrist at the Salpêtrière. He argued that this kind
of disturbance revealed itself mainly in private life, within the
intimacy of marriage, and that the way to learn about it was
to talk to the families of patients more than with the patients
themselves. This made some people protest that the experts
were now arrogating to themselves the right to pronounce
anybody mad, though he behaved perfectly normally to the
outside world. The great increase in the admissions to the
asylums seemed to lend substance to these fears.[1]

One may relate attitudes to madness to new attitudes to pain,
which the discovery of analgesics and anaesthesia in the early
nineteenth century encouraged. When in 1847 the Academy of
Sciences discussed the subject, the famous physiologist Magen-
die asked 'What interest can the Academy of Sciences have in
whether people suffer more or less?'[2] But now things changed.
It took some time for chloroform, which was independently
discovered by chemists in the U.S.A., France and Germany
in 1831, to be widely used, for between 1855 and 1875 the
amount prescribed in Paris hospitals only doubled. In the
same period however, the amount of ether used trebled; in
1869 chloral was introduced, and by 1875 they were already
using more of it than of chloroform. The consumption of
bromides rose from only 3 kilogrammes in 1855 to 730 kilogrammes in 1875;[3] and of morphine from a quarter of a kilo-
gramme in 1855 to over 10 kilogrammes in 1875. In addition
the traditional pain-killers continued to be employed, especially
opium (about 150 kilogrammes a year throughout this period).
Though alcoholism was making rapid progress, doctors vastly

---

[1] Dr. U. Trélat, *La Folie lucide, étudiée et considérée au point de vue de la famille et de
la société* (1861); Dr. Campagne, *La Manie raisonnante* (1869); Dr. H. Thulie,
La Manie raisonnante du Dr Campagne (1870); *Statistique des asiles d'aliénés 1854–60*
(1865), xvii.

[2] Victor Robinson, *Victory over Pain. A History of Anaesthesia* (New York, 1946),
162; M. A. Armstrong-Davison, *The Evolution of Anaesthesia* (Altrincham, 1965), 135.

[3] Cf. Dr. Georges Huette, *Histoire thérapeutique du bromure de potassium* (1878).

increased their use of alcohol and wine as a treatment of fever and as a tranquilliser: in 1855–75 the consumption of alcohol in Paris hospitals rose from 1,270 to 37,578 litres and that of red wine from 17,000 to 163,000 litres—though the number of their patients remained the same. It is symbolic that Napoleon III stuffed himself with drugs to kill the pain of his diseased kidneys. The Second Empire witnessed an enormous increase in drug-taking as well as a recourse to the asylums.[1]

The practical consequences of the new attitudes may be illustrated from a double murder committed in Marseille in 1853. The illiterate peasant, aged twenty-three, who was responsible, was an epileptic. Esquirol had laid it down that epilepsy led sooner or later to madness; and the psychiatrists who examined the criminal accordingly certified him as mad and incurably so. But the peasant appears to have committed the crime because he was highly superstitious, believed in witchcraft and had become convinced that his epilepsy was caused by a spell cast upon him. Not far from him lived a widow of seventy and her grandson aged seventeen who had received some primary education and who used to copy from religious books, which the epileptic interpreted as signifying that he had supernatural powers. When asked why he murdered them, it was he who volunteered the explanation: 'I was mad'.[2] The court accepted the medical explanation and seems to have given no weight to the social one. It is in such cases—which form an almost inexhaustible source, still untapped, in the criminal archives—that one can see particularly clearly how people opted between alternative interpretations of human behaviour.

What is striking in all this psychological writing is the emphasis given to heredity. Dr. Prosper Lucas's book on the subject became famous but Zola greatly simplified Lucas in making him popular. Lucas did not claim that heredity was the decisive factor in either behaviour or illness. On the contrary he argued that nature acted through two principles:

[1] Prof. Ch. Lasègue, *Études médicales* (1884), chapter on 'La Thérapeutique jugée par les chiffres', 492–542, reprinted from *Archives générales de la médecine* (1877); for later developments, cf. A. Martinet, *Thérapeutique clinique* (2nd edition, 1923), 151–202, on medicines for nervous troubles.

[2] H. Aubanel, 'Rapports médico-légaux sur deux aliénés accusés de meurtre', *Annales médico-psychologiques* (1856), 191–248.

imitation, which meant heredity, and creation, which he
rather confusingly called *innéité*, meaning that certain qualities
were innate to an individual as opposed to inherited from his
family. But there was much controversy as to what characteristics could be inherited, and what accounted for the
differences between individuals in the same family. One school
attributed these to the uterine experiences of the baby, under
the nutritional and emotional influence of the mother. Another
school stressed the state of mind of the couple at the time of
coitus and many books were published advising parents on how
to procreate children with desirable qualities. The third school,
which claimed that education and example could have an
overriding influence, thus had to battle against considerable
opposition. These disagreements were of course politically and
socially important. When Dr. Moreau de Tours developed his
theory that 'psycho-cerebral vitality is essentially innate', that
the taste for work, for example, could not be inculcated, that
genius was to a certain extent a variation of madness, which
was largely hereditary, he by implication attacked the whole
philosophy of meritocracy. He was aware of this and said that
his opponents exalted the value of education only because
they had reached their positions in the world through education. The conflict of the doctors and the educators was never
an obvious or open one, because they were never clearly
separated; but the educational philosophy of the republicans
needs to be seen in this context. When Paul Bert (a physiologist
who became Gambetta's minister of education) claimed that the
men who had control of education could reshape the world, he
was arguing in the face of a contrary opinion, that man was
threatened with degeneration. Statistics were produced to show
that crime was rising in precisely those areas with most education. The case for education was not clear cut.[1]

The question arose therefore of just how much free will was
left by psychology, how determined was the course of history,
how much individuals could do to alter their own characters,
and education to modify the destiny of nations. This was an old
controversy, but what was notable about its conduct during the

[1] Dr. Prosper Lucas, *Traité philosophique et physiologique de l'hérédité* (1847–50);
Dr. J. Moreau (de Tours), *La Psychologie morbide dans ses rapports avec la philosophie
de l'histoire* (1859), 1–13 and appendix.

Second Empire was the moderation of the determinists, who did all they could to leave some room for free will, and the vigour of the partisans of free will in defending their case. The question was complicate i by the uncertainty as to what will was. It may be recalled that for Balzac it was a 'nervous fluid' or 'the soul-substance in the blood', or, after his conversion to magnetism, a form of electricity.[1] Since it was believed that people had only a limited quantity of this fluid, its use in any one direction, to develop any one faculty or skill, meant that other parts of the character might atrophy. That was one reason why it was believed that intellectuals, who used their brains excessively, were liable to have a host of compensating defects: cerebral effort was considered dangerous.[2] Some people claimed that will was something you either did or did not have, but since this had disturbing moral implications, alternative doctrines were available: first that will could be cultivated by moral influences, as physical exercise could strengthen the muscles of the body, and secondly that its apparent limitations were due to social causes, which could be altered. Thus a feminist argued that women had just as much will-power (potentially) as men, but were restrained from using it by convention, habit and repression. The idea that certain forms of anti-social behaviour were caused by repression of instincts was already current. Those who, against the partisans of heredity, believed in the infinite perfectibility of man, and in the power of education to eradicate laziness and drunkenness, appealed, for their part, to comparative anthropology, which they thought could show how different peoples had approached nearer that goal.[3]

The contrast between the relatively static nature of the biographical art and the rapidly changing views of human

[1] Moïse Le Yaouanc, *Nosographie de l'humanité balzacienne* (1959), 131.
[2] See e.g. the classic works of Réveillé-Parise.
[3] Mlle J. Marchef-Girard, *Des facultés humaines et de leur développement par l'éducation* (1865); cf. C. Sedillot (prof. de médecine, Nancy), *Du relèvement de la France* (1874); P. Foissac, *De l'influence des climats sur l'homme* (1867); Dr. Cerise, *Des fonctions et des maladies nerveuses dans leurs rapports avec l'éducation sociale et privée, morale et physique* (1842). For later ideas, see J. F. Richard, 'La Découverte du fait des différences individuelles comme obstacle dans les premières expériences de mesure en psychologie', *Douzième congrès international d'histoire des sciences, colloques, textes des rapports* (1968), 369–82; and M. Reuchlin, 'La Psychologie différentielle au XIXᵉ siècle', ibid. 383–400.

personality developed by the psychiatrists—who, during the
Second Empire, were almost as revolutionary as the financiers
and industrialists were in the economic sphere—has an
important significance. There were, it is clear, strong forces
which inhibited the development of biography as a major
historical activity: first there was the preoccupation with
histoire philosophique, and the desire to deal only with very
general subjects; and secondly, there was the strong tradition
which saw biography as a means of praising the dead. It is true
that against this, a number of writers urged that individuals
should be studied for their own sake, in the greatest possible
detail, but they did not always carry out their own precepts,
being caught up in the advocacy of more general causes.
Biography thus remained on the whole a minor genre.

The fact that it was a genre of its own was perhaps another
reason why it did not get caught up in the investigation of the
mind and the emotions which the psychologists were pursuing
so actively. Biography had its own rules, its own purposes and
its own preoccupations. It was therefore largely to the novelists
that the task of taking up the suggestions of the psychologists
was left. This has a social significance which deserves to be
stressed. The more organised a particular form of writing was,
the less likely was it to be influenced by other forms. Biographers and psychologists thus on the whole worked side by
side in separate worlds. There were occasions when these
barriers were broken, but whenever this happened, there were
usually hesitations and always loud protests. No simple influence by psychology on biography was possible in any case,
because the psychologists were so divided in their views.

It might be maintained therefore that the best biographers
of this early period were often not those who were ostensibly
engaged in the genre, but rather the psychiatrists and the
medico-legal experts. Their reports of cases are extremely
impressive. They often reveal very exceptional ability, clarity
of mind and powers of exposition. These doctors deserve to be
regarded as important witnesses of their age: they have left a
mass of biographical material which still awaits investigation.
Historians today rightly lament that they cannot get the poor
in the past to speak, that evidence about the most numerous
class is exiguous in the extreme. Police reports have often

been used, despite their obvious, but not insuperable, defects. Medical reports also have their faults, but they contain information about aspects of life—personal and domestic in particular—which historians are now coming increasingly to value. Succeeding chapters will examine one of these aspects, anxiety, and attempt to show that it has a history which is no less important because it was played out in obscurity.

People willing to talk about their private lives were above all of two kinds. First, there were the novelists and other writers who were fascinated by emotion and by themselves. Their evidence will be examined in the following chapter. The second type, which will be considered after that, were odd, sick and mad people. This chapter has tried to show that their behaviour should not be immediately classified as completely abnormal. 'The philosopher', wrote Esquirol in his classic work on *Mental Illnesses* (1844), 'will find in an asylum the same ideas, errors, passions and misfortunes as in the world, but in more marked forms and in more lively colour, because man is found there in all his nakedness, because he does not dissimulate his thought, because he does not give to his passions the charm that seduces nor to his vices the appearances that deceive.'[1] The number of people who were declared to be insane rose about fifteenfold during the period covered by this book:

Number of Madmen treated[2]

1838	8,390	1910	98,477
1844	16,000	1920	92,541
1864	34,919	1930	119,154
1871	49,589	1940	150,265
1880	63,600	1945	62,786
1890	73,641	1950	85,659
1900	87,428	1970	262,060

It was in the Second Empire that this rise was most rapid. When the first major law on the insane was passed in 1838,

[1] J. E. D. Esquirol, *Les Maladies mentales* (1844) is one of the most interesting social commentaries of the period. Cf. T. Owsianik, *De la conception de l'aliéné* (Paris medical thesis, 1941).

[2] Jacques Prévault, *L'Échec du système 'administratif' d'internement des aliénés* (1955), 37. For 1970, patients treated in psychiatric hospitals.

there were under 10,000 people so classified. By 1871 there were
about 50,000. To this should be added 'madmen living at
home', a difficult category to be accurate about. Altogether
this makes two per 1,000 insane in 1861. In the Second Empire,
17 per cent of those who went to asylums spent less than a
month there, and 26 per cent between one and six months.
So over a generation, the number of people who had been
classified as mentally ill, however briefly, must have been very
considerable.[1] As the numbers continued to increase during the
Third Republic, they reached the point when there were eight
times more people suffering from mental illnesses than from
tuberculosis.

Of course, not everyone in an asylum was mad. In the U.S.A.
(which had twice as many people so classified, proportionately
to its population, as France) it has been argued that the
increase in mental illness should not be attributed to the increased strains of life, because the major portion of the increase was due to people over fifty going into asylums: it was
a problem of ageing.[2] It is not clear whether the same could be
argued of France, and similar studies have not been carried
out there, but it was certainly the case that the asylums
contained many sane old people, because it was easier to get
into an asylum than into an old people's home. A critic of the
asylum system claimed in 1955 that about 60 per cent of the
inmates of asylums should not have been there.[3] Stories about
people being wrongly locked up are never easy to check and the
publicity given to a few cases of obvious injustice may perhaps
give a false impression.[4] But the law in France established two
methods for locking people up: they could either be sent to
asylums by the medical authorities, or they could go as voluntary patients: but a voluntary patient was not necessarily one
who himself volunteered to enter an asylum; anyone, whether a
relative or not, had the right to request that another person
should be confined to an asylum, and if the prefect and the

---

[1] *Statistique des asiles d'aliénés, 1854–60* (1865).

[2] George Rosen, *Madness in Society* (1968); H. Goldhamer and A. Marshal,
Psychosis and Civilisation (1953). For the old, see below, p. 211.

[3] Prévault, op. cit. 136.

[4] This is the view taken for England by W. L. Parry-Jones, *The Trade in Lunacy.
A Study of Private Madhouses in England in the Eighteenth and Nineteenth Centuries* (1972),
290.

doctors gave their consent, then he became a 'voluntary' patient, destined to remain there indefinitely. This allowed plenty of scope for people to get rid of their enemies. The case that particularly deserves to be recorded is that concerning Colonel Picard, head of the army's historical department, who had a feud with Jean Lemoine, librarian at the ministry of war. Lemoine, for his part, had a feud with his wife over their inheritance from her mother. Picard used this to get the wife to apply for the voluntary internment of Lemoine, who was accordingly locked up for eleven years, until he was let out following a press campaign run by the Abbé Trochu: in 1925 Lemoine (shades of the Dreyfus Affair!) was restored to his post in the ministry of war and his wife was condemned to pay him damages.[1] Jules Vallès is famous for having been locked up at his father's instigation for being unorthodox. At the time, there were better-known cases, like Napoleon III's minister Billault's locking up a barrister of Limoges who was black-mailing him over some compromising letters.[2] In 1920 Veuve Becker, daughter of the founder of the Bazaar de l'Hotel de Ville, was seized at the instigation of her sons-in-law and forcibly sent to a lunatic asylum, as a way of stopping her remarrying. How one fared in an asylum depended on how much money one had. Those who paid for their keep had their rooms cleaned by those who did not. Some asylums, in the 1930s, were still likened to barracks, and some inmates still slept on the floor.[3] But there were private asylums with several different classes of comfort, and the very rich, by paying six times more than those at the lowest rate, could get a private chalet.[4]

In the Second Empire, a calculation was made showing that, proportionately to their total numbers, soldiers went to asylums most often, followed by members of the liberal professions.[5] A doctor's study in the same period showed that these classes came fairly low for the frequency with which they committed suicide;

[1] J. Lemoine, *Les Dessous d'un internement arbitraire* (1937).
[2] N. Blayau, *Billault* (1969), 386–7 shows how difficult it is to be certain about the rights and wrongs of such cases.
[3] Th. Simon, *L'Aliéné, l'asile, l'infirmier* (Cahors, 1937); Georges Imann, *Voyage au pays des déments* (1934), 82; but cf. Henry Bonnet, *L'Aliéné devant lui-même* (1866).
[4] See advertisements in *L'Aliéniste français* (1934) for Villa Lunier à Blois, founded by Dr. Lunier in 1860; and the 'chambre meublée avec luxe' at the Château de Suresne clinic, founded by Magnan.
[5] *Statistiques des institutions d'assistance* (1854–60), xxix.

it was artisans, by contrast, who committed suicide most.[1] In the 1850s, men and women went into asylums in roughly equal numbers, but women increasingly outnumbered men there, especially after 1920.[2] The growth in the population of the asylums did not, however, make the country a safer place. In 1932, 94 people were murdered by 'lunatics' and 116 gravely injured.[3] All this raises difficult problems which have still to be elucidated. Public opinion remained throughly confused about them. But the causes given by the asylums to explain why their inmates collapsed—'intellectual overwork', 'domestic sorrows', 'loss of fortune', 'loss of a person dear to them', 'frustrated ambition', 'remorse', 'damaged honour', 'jealousy', 'pride', 'nostalgia', 'excessive religiosity', drink, the menopause, poverty, disease, etc.—provide an almost complete catalogue of the private stresses and sorrows of ordinary living that is the subject of the following chapters.

[1] A. Brierre de Boismont, *Du suicide* (1856), 91.
[2] E. Toulouse, R. Dupouy and M. Moine, 'Statistique de la psychopathie', *Annales médico-psychologiques* (1930), 2. 390–404.
[3] Henri Claude, *Psychiatrie médico-légale* (2nd edition, 1944), 81.

2. Individualism and the Emotions

For most of this period, France was distinguished among nations for the personal freedom enjoyed by the individual and for a considerable amount of mutual tolerance. 'The notion that a resident in France', wrote a British journalist in 1898, 'is the prey of constant official vexation is exaggerated, and there is no country where under normal circumstances life can be enjoyed more tranquilly.'[1] Private liberty was one of the most fundamental features of this society, as was the variety of thought and action that has attracted admiration ever since. This liberty was a recent acquisition, however, and needs explanation, because though France had had its Revolution, the institutions and many of the administrative methods of the *ancien régime* had not been shaken off. There were three reasons why the power of the centralised government no longer seriously threatened the individual. The first was that the administrative system was not as efficient in practice as its formidable organisation and size should have made it. A succession of revolutions had filled it with men of opposing opinions and traditions; vested interests had entrenched themselves at the local level; it was too large and too slow to move effectively. Secondly, it was held in check by parliament and by a multitude of pressure groups, which were diverse enough to ensure that most people had some kind of support against authority. The political system was so complex that it became self-defeating, and though reform was its avowed purpose, the control, limitation and diffusion of power became its main function. But perhaps the most important reason was that the rights of the individual were established as a dominant creed, thanks largely to the continuous efforts of a whole succession of writers, journalists and polemicists. Writers and intellectuals were, inevitably, infinitely divided, but the right to give and hold their opinion was what they all valued very highly.

[1] J. E. C. Bodley, *France* (revised edition, 1899), 104.

They were far from agreed that tolerance was a good thing, and most of them indeed attacked their enemies with great violence—the bitter struggle between clericals and free-thinkers disposes of any suggestion that this was a genuinely tolerant century—but liberals of different kinds were in a majority among them and France was on the whole a free country, because the individual's dignity was respected.

This was the conclusion of many centuries of argument. The idea that the individual is an autonomous entity, with a right to act by his own judgement, subjecting authority to independent and critical assessment, was enunciated by various writers, by Luther and by Kant before being taken up by the *philosophes*. The right to privacy, 'liberty of tastes and pursuits, of framing the plan of our life to suit our own character', had deep roots in Christian mysticism before being glorified by the Renaissance, the American and French Revolutions, Benjamin Constant and J. S. Mill. The declaration of the rights of man of 1791 was the culmination of a battle of many centuries to defend the dignity of the individual against claims that the public good should always have priority over him. It is inaccurate to see individual liberty as simply a conquest of the Revolution. The cult of reason, of which the Revolution was one expression, had established itself as a French tradition before then. And the full implications of individualism were only drawn out after it.[1]

It was the romantic movement that finally entrenched the independence of the individual in an unassailable way, by greatly expanding the idea of what an individual was. The romantics were writers, and it was the influence of writers therefore that must explain the greatly increased sense of individuality that developed in this period. From the point of view of literary history, romanticism flourished mainly in the early nineteenth century, but its teachings were incorporated into virtually all subsequent thought. Any account of the way people have thought and felt since then must give an important place to them. Romanticism was more than an episode. It left a permanent sediment above the classicism or conformism described in a previous chapter. It constituted an important layer in popular mentality.

Romanticism was not an organised movement with a

[1] Steven Lukes, *Individualism* (1973).

coherent doctrine. It was revolutionary, in the sense that it involved the overflowing of all boundaries, as Kierkegaard defined it; but it overflowed them in different ways. Maurras and Pierre Lasserre at the turn of the century argued that romanticism was the literary or moral counterpart of the great revolution of 1789, that both came from Rousseau. Others, like Taine, have argued on the contrary that the Revolution was the product of the classical, rationalist tradition. The romantic poets and writers were looked on by the bourgeoisie as revolutionaries, if only because they dressed and behaved to flout respectable conventions. In 1871 Thiers said 'The romantics, *c'est la Commune*'. The romantics were first of all liberators of forms of expression and communication. They began as pioneers of the emancipation of literature from the rules and styles established by classical authors. They rejected the view that only certain words, poetic forms and subjects were proper in art. They addressed their writings to all men, not simply to the educated, and they took an interest in the sufferings of the masses. They sought inspiration no longer just from Greece and Rome, but from the Celtic, Germanic, medieval and oriental worlds. They drew material for their art from every class of society. They were revolutionaries also in the sense that they refused to allow their conduct to be determined by the sole guide of reason, and even less by prudence. They were declared enemies of the bourgeoisie, whom they vituperated as grocers and philistines; they abhorred compromise, materialism, sobriety, thrift. Their hero was the artist who flouted society and who by his special powers offered men a new faith or new experiences. The nineteenth century, said Stendhal, 'has a thirst for strong emotions'. The romantics rehabilitated the passions, cultivated sensibility, gave free rein to the imagination. They praised love and gave themselves up to it with lyricism. They sought less to understand reality than to idealise it, so that they quickly got confused in their fantasies and had difficulty in distinguishing their dreams from reality. They replaced self-control by caprice. They developed a new kind of morality. The good and the beautiful were confused in a new way: the value of an individual was determined by the nobility of the sentiments he expressed, the elegance or grandeur of his emotions, irrespective of what he actually achieved. Originality thus acquired a moral value. The criterion by which beauty was judged was revolutionised. What mattered now was not the reflection of a preordained ideal, but the impression or emotion the reader or spectator felt. The artist sought to establish a personal relationship with his audience, and since both could change with time, so his art would change. There was thus often great diversity in the production of artists—which did not favour the founding of any coherent school. But it led, because the romantics were concerned with finding an echo in the masses, or with being themselves echoes of the masses' frustrated, unspoken aspirations, to a stress on harmony, music and colour as a means of reaching a wide audience, to the use of incantation, aiming at winning through the heart, without necessarily passing through the mind.

The romantics were unhappy. Their dreams could not be realised; they disliked the world as it was, their passions consumed and tormented them; they saw themselves in tragic roles. Their founders were 'ardent, pale, nervous', as Alfred de Musset described them in his *Confessions d'un enfant du siècle* (1835), born during the wars of the empire, the children of anxious mothers and absent fathers, doomed to a *mal de siècle*, which he attributed to the collapse of the old world, a nostalgia for its glory, an inability to rebuild it, an uncertainty about the future, doubt, paralysis of the will. 'For thirty years', wrote Taine, 'every young man was a little Hamlet, disgusted with everything, not knowing what to desire, believe or do, discouraged, doubting, bitter, having a need for happiness, looking to the toes of his boots to see if by chance he might not find there the system of the world, juggling with the words God, Nature, Humanity, Ideal, Synthesis. . . . Men were sceptical, idealists, mystics, Indian, pagan, Christian, humanitarian, Manichaean, in stanzas and in verses. . . . Except in the first two centuries of our era, never has there been so strong and continuous a buzzing of metaphysical dreams.'[1] The romantics were often interested in improving the world, but there was also an element of escapism in their outlook. They were constantly searching for new pleasures, exotic countries; they tired of Paris and longed for the East, but they were more excited

[1] H. Taine, *Les Philosophes français du dix-neuvième siècle* (1857), 292–3.

by the camels of the Holy Land than by the wonders of modern science. They gave themselves up to fantastic mental adventures. Berlioz longed to be a brigand in Sicily and 'see magnificent crimes'. Flaubert as a schoolboy slept with a dagger under his pillow. Madame Lafargue, who can be taken as an example of an 'ordinary woman', wrote in her memoirs: 'I habituated my intelligence to poetise the most minute details of life and I preserved it with infinite solicitude from all vulgar or trivial contact. I added to the mistake of embellishing reality so as to render it pleasant to my imagination, the even greater error of feeling the love of the beautiful perhaps more than the love of the good, of carrying out more easily excesses in duty than the duties themselves, of preferring in all the impossible to the possible.' Public prosecutors complained that fictional criminals were becoming popular heroes; that young romantics came to the courts wearing 'the contemptuous smile of an unrecognised superiority', victims of a 'fatal mixture of unbridled egoism and powerless pride, of sombre melancholy and active energy which leads to despair or revolt, suicide or crime'.[1]

Romanticism was far from being of one type. In appearance there were the hirsute bohemians but also the elegant dandies; what they had in common was their desire to be different from the ordinary bourgeois. The romantics proclaimed the rights of fantasy and originality against conventional social morality; they appear as individualists. But they were also advocates of social conscience and pioneers of social reform. They quickly abandoned the theory of art for art's sake, to replace it by one of social art. Some looked back to Christianity and to the middle ages; others were utopian and builders of new religions, but all disapproved of the present. The qualities they stressed, such as passion, or love of liberty, were not peculiar to them, but eternal characteristics of man, and this is why romanticism is difficult to define; but they gave a new prestige to these qualities and greatly expanded their significance. They did much to widen the sympathies and horizons of men, even if they also clouded their outlook and obscured their view.[2]

[1] Louis Maigron, *Le Romantisme et les mœurs* (1910), 381, 384.
[2] Roger Picard, *Le Romantisme social* (New York, 1944); H. G. Schenk, *The Mind of the European Romantics* (1967); Jacques Barzun, *Classic, Romantic and Modern*

To document the effect of romanticism on conduct one must look in detail at biographies. When Rousseau said: 'I am made unlike anyone I have ever met . . . I am like no one in the whole world' he was, by implication, denying the subjection of the individual to class and family; he was making the revolutionary statement that a man had a right to be different from his father. The whole history of France could be presented in terms of that rebellion. But to see how romanticism worked in practice, as well as how it developed, one should look at the lives of some of its principal advocates. This approach has the advantage of showing at the same time how the generalisations about romanticism need to be modified every time one particular individual's experiences are analysed, and also of showing in more precise detail the ambivalence of romanticism on the subject of the individual. Just as conformism was not conservatism, so individualism did not necessarily involve either originality or egoism. Here, some of the varied aspects and problems of individualism will be illustrated from the biographies of seven writers who have left particularly instructive accounts of their personal rebellions.

Jules Michelet (1798–1874), author of a *History of France* in seventeen volumes and a *History of the Revolution* in seven more, throws light on the complex relations between individualism, emotion and sociability. Michelet was an intensely lonely and an intensely emotional man. 'My childhood had no feasts.' It was in the study of history that he found the means of escaping from his intolerable solitude, while yet remaining alone. That is why he was able to put so much into his work and to give it such new dimensions. He made history the crowning science, claiming as much for it as Comte was simultaneously claiming for sociology. He did a great deal of research in archives; he interviewed survivors of the Revolution; he took an interest in all aspects and particularly the social aspects of history, with a stress on the lives of ordinary people; and he adopted a highly imaginative interpretation of his facts, which he sought not to report but to relive, as an

(1962, revised edition of book originally published in 1943); P. Van Tieghem, *Le Romantisme français* (1966) and *Le Romantisme dans la littérature européenne* (1948); M. Levaillant, *Problèmes du romantisme* (special number of the *Revue des sciences humaines*, 1951).

'integral resurrection of the past'. He used a poetical style, full of emotion, passion and colourful imagery. The writing of his books was an intense experience for him—he was ill when his heroes died, he was in ecstasy when the Bastille was taken, he fulminated uncontrollably against the men he disliked and was lyrical in praise of the liberal ideas he championed. Not only the individuals of the past were real for him, but he gave life to collective entities, like the provinces of France, the different social groups, and above all 'the people'. His books were a hymn in praise of the people, whom he saw personified with a clearly defined character and with an independent soul.

Michelet was proud of being a man of the people—the only important romantic writer who genuinely was and who could therefore feel a fraternal rather than an outsider's sympathy for them. His father had been a printer, his mother was of peasant stock. He deliberately clung to his artisan origins; even though he rose very rapidly to the top of the academic hierarchy, becoming professor at the Collège de France at forty. He denounced embourgeoisement: 'Those who rise [in the social hierarchy] lose by it . . . they become mixed, bastard, they lose the originality of their class without gaining that of another.' In the masses he saw a 'new, living, rejuvenating sap', less culture perhaps but more 'vital warmth'. This desire to 'plunge into the living sea of the people' fitted in with Michelet's fear of loneliness. Their life was made up of 'work and family', which meant co-operation with their fellows. Sociability was the way to progress. Michelet rebelled with terror against the pure theories of individualism. Man, he insisted, was a social being and history was the supreme science because it studied him as such. He found support for his views in Vico, whom he translated; in the Scottish philosophers and in Lamennais he found proof of the common sense of the people as equal in value to the theories of philosophers; in Rousseau he discovered the general will. From these and others (Maistre, Voltaire) he developed what he considered his crowning idea, that each nation has a real personality, a collective being, endowed with a will and intelligence. Patriotism was one of the highest virtues, it ought to be a dogma and a legend, 'the first gospel of the people'.

Another virtue closely linked with it was love, from which he expected the emancipation of man. The evil of his time was 'paralysis of the heart' which causes 'unsociability'. Michelet had a desperate craving for affection, for complete union with his wives and mistresses; few men have recorded so carefully, and been so torn by, their need for sexual satisfaction and also their search for spiritual communion with women. Michelet's ideal of love was that his wife would be at once his mistress, his daughter, his sister and his mother. That is why he wrote not only books about history, but also others on women and on love. Love in the family, co-operative association in work, love of the fatherland—the creation of a great 'amitié de France'—were his goals. Michelet thus placed his hopes in sentiment and a return to traditional, partly Christian virtues. He deplored industrialisation which, he thought, caused men to 'co-operate without loving each other, to act and live together without knowing each other'. He wanted France to stick to artisan production, so as to safeguard good taste and the dignity of the worker. He urged the bourgeoisie to marry peasant girls or they would decay like the old nobility. He denounced as vain the ambitious who sought jobs in the civil service or in commerce, which were corrupt. He urged the poor not to get rich, not to aspire to enter the bourgeoisie but to be themselves, to keep their popular instincts. This was their best chance of originality. The people did indeed need a hero to guide and enlighten them, but this hero only gave them a voice: Michelet's real hero was the people as a mass. Michelet founded, as he said, 'a religious philosophy of the people'. Individualism, in him, can be seen already to have met emotional difficulties because of its social implications.[1]

The individualist could claim to be unique, and yet claim to understand ordinary people better than they could themselves. Victor Hugo (1802–85) tried to be the kind of hero Michelet described, giving expression to the ideas of his century. 'Every

[1] The complete works of Michelet are in the process of being brought out in an excellent new edition, with full introductions and notes, by Paul Viallaneix; seven volumes, out of the twenty projected, have appeared since 1971. See also Paul Viallaneix, *La Voie royale: essai sur l'idée du peuple dans l'œuvre de Michelet* (1959); G. Monod, *La Vie et la pensée de Jules Michelet* (1923); Jeanne Calo, *La Création de la femme chez Michelet* (1975); J. Cornuz, *Jules Michelet, un aspect de la pensée religieuse au 19e siècle* (Geneva, 1955).

true poet', he wrote, 'independently of the thoughts which come to him from his own system and those which come to him from the eternal truth, must contain the sum of the ideas of his time.' He believed he was 'the voice of Humanity',[1] and he was indeed probably the most widely read poet of this period. It is important to know what link he established with his readers. Many commentators, in the years following his death, acknowledged, despite their hostility to him, that he did achieve this aim of being the representative of his readers. Paul Lafargue explained this by saying that 'Victor Hugo clothed the ideas and sentiments supplied to him by the bourgeois in a stunning phraseology calculated to strike the ear and provoke bewilderment, in a grandiloquent verbiage, harmoniously rhythmic and rhymed, bristling with startling, dazzling antitheses and flashy epithets. He was, after Chateau-briand, the greatest window-dresser of the words and images of the century.' Taine called Hugo 'a national guard in delirium'.[2] His *Misérables* was hailed as 'the gospel of the nineteenth century [because] everybody understood it'. Only when he published *L'Homme qui rit*, with its monstrous symbolism, did he admit that 'a separation has taken place between my contemporaries and myself'.[3]

Hugo aimed at producing a popular literature. 'Hitherto', he wrote, 'there has only been literature for the educated. In France especially . . . to be a poet meant almost to be a mandarin. Not all words had a right to be written . . . Imagine botany declaring to some vegetable that it did not exist . . . Civilisation has now grown up and needs a literature of the people.'[4] Hugo deliberately avoided Greek and Roman subjects. His greatest achievement was to democratise poetry by using ordinary language, to enrich it enormously by introducing into it every type of word, sound, image, to make verse as free as prose, apart from a few rules, like hiatus and rhyme. Everything in nature was a fit subject for art, which should concern itself not just with the sublime, but with the grotesque too. Rules and fixed taste were obstacles to genius. It

[1] Jacques Roos, *Les Idées philosophiques de Victor Hugo* (1958), 7.
[2] Tristan Legay, *Victor Hugo jugé par son siècle* (1902), 565, 567.
[3] J. B. Barrère, *Hugo, l'homme et l'œuvre* (1952), 191–2.
[4] V. Hugo, *William Shakespeare* (1864, 2nd edition 1867), 257–8.

is not the beautiful but the characteristic that the artist should capture. Hugo had the imagination of a visionary and he used this to create a dazzling world—to evoke splendours in picturesque and moving detail, of countries and places he had never seen. He imagined emperors and sultans, monsters and phantoms, crowds and battles, the East and the middle ages with dithyrambic intensity. He was no profound thinker and he wrote above all about the universal commonplace feelings: love of children, the home, the fatherland, nature, compassion for the poor, sorrow, pleasure in life and hope for progress mixed with a nostalgia for the past. But he succeeded in dressing up these ideas in highly emotional and richly coloured language. Today it might be complained that his verse is static, with words leading only to yet more words, repeating the same things in varying forms, with no development in ideas. However he continued to fill his readers with the same excitement that the repetitive beat of pop music did for a later generation, because he carried imagination to the point of paroxysm. His gift for the epic form gave his writing greater power still. The world he created has been compared to that mixture of the miraculous and the real recorded by Homer.

Hugo was popular partly because he was in sympathy with a primitive facet of the century which is too often forgotten by those who stress industrialisation and scientific progress as its principal characteristics. Hugo believed in the survival of the dead, their frequent intervention in the present world and the successive migrations of the soul. There was an invisible world, not in the sky, but mixed up in the same space as the material world. Hugo communicated with the dead—he had talks at séances with Socrates, Christ, Luther, Shakespeare, Byron and the lion of Androcles. He had visions and presentiments which often terrified him. But he was not just a dabbler in spiritualism and the occult. He believed he was a prophet, called by God, and the founder of a new religion, to succeed Druidism and Christianity. His teaching was that there was no hell. God had created the world with an element of evil, and history was the struggle between good and evil. But all men (and all things, for even stones had souls) had a right to forgiveness. This was democracy and progress brought into religion; it was also the peasant's primitive pre-Christian mentality

justified. It was not by reason that truth could be found. Science
and the intelligence could observe facts, but they could study
only the superficial, evanescent phenomena. The imagination
on the other hand created art and attained the infinite and the
absolute. Intuition was the means to achieve supreme knowledge; certainty came from sentiment, i.e. from mysticism.
Science dealt with the relative, art with the definitive. The poet
must replace the priest as man's guide, with three particular
functions: to explain the past, to civilise the present (by
preaching veneration for age, compassion for women, the cult
of natural affections, raising human dignity), and to predict
the future. His audience must be the masses, who had 'the
instinct for the ideal'.

Victor Hugo established himself as a romantic poet in his
twenties, under the Restoration, but it was the works he wrote
during the Second Empire, particularly *Les Châtiments* (1853),
Les Contemplations (1856) and *Les Misérables* (1862), which won
him his greatest popularity. These revealed that romanticism
was very much alive at a time when new literary and scientific
movements were making themselves felt. Hugo was the son of
a general of the Napoleonic army, and he began as a social
climber; he wrote official poetry for Louis XVIII; he was made
a peer by Louis-Philippe and was friends with the heir to the
throne. But as he became increasingly aware of his social role,
he gradually moved towards republicanism. He was still right-
wing in 1848, but his hostility to Louis Napoleon led to his
being exiled in 1851, and he spent nearly twenty years in
Jersey attacking *Napoléon le petit*. He returned in 1870 to become the grand old man of the Third Republic, Senator of the
department of the Seine. He came to represent devotion to
art, to politics, to social progress, to one's family, to one's
mistress and not least to oneself. He showed how individualism
could turn into megalomania, but also how it remained attached
to primitive traditions, and how it could cultivate both dedication and generosity.

Romantics could not stand still: individualists were free
to try every elixir. How they moved from creed to creed,
building up their individuality, like bees in search of honey,
can be seen in the life of Sainte-Beuve (1804–69), probably
France's most admired literary critic. In his youth he was a

disciple of the ideologues, a student of medicine, and he disapproved of romanticism because of its mysticism and early royalism. But he was drawn to it by the charm of Hugo, with whom he was great friends until he fell in love with Hugo's wife. His novels *Joseph Delorme* (1829) and *Volupté* (1834) are important (partly autobiographical) descriptions of the romantic mind. Michelet congratulated Sainte-Beuve on the latter work, as successfully portraying the 'moral psychology of our epoch'. Sainte-Beuve defined romanticism as 'disgust with life, inaction, abuse of dreaming, a proud sentiment of isolation, a feeling that one was misjudged, a contempt for the world and for well-worn tracks, a belief that they are unworthy of one, a view of oneself as the most unhappy of men and yet a love for one's sorrow; the last stage of this evil would be suicide'. He described his own life as a 'slow and profound suicide . . . an inconceivable chaos with monstrous imaginings, vivid reminiscences, criminal fantasies, great abortive thoughts, wise prudence followed by foolish actions, transports of piety after blasphemy . . . and, at the base, despair'. Sainte-Beuve never recovered from this; he never became gay. He turned to Saint-Simonianism in his search for a faith but it did not change the character of his life. He complained to Enfantin, 'Why, in helping me to understand so many things, have you not taught me to *love life*? . . . Sick of the end of the old world and of the beginning of this one, sick you found me, sick you have left me.' Intellectual satisfactions were inadequate: 'I live by the heart . . . the need of love and friendship, that is the basis of my life.' His repeated efforts to find love were unsuccessful: he ended by visiting prostitutes.

He found only slight consolation in his search for knowledge. As a literary critic he pioneered the biographical method, judging works no longer against a precise ideal of taste or morals but as the products of individual lives. He founded what he called 'the natural history of the mind', seeking to show the growth of genius as though it were a plant. He even believed that minds could be grouped into types, as scientists classified the objects they studied—though he never actually attempted to do this. He claimed, that is, to be scientific. This illustrates well how it is impossible to differentiate scientists and romantics. His science came from the ideologues; he was opposed to Taine's scientific criticism. He cannot be classified simply in his politics either: he admired in turn Hugo, Enfantin, Lamennais, Molé and finally Jérôme Napoléon. He became increasingly conservative as he mixed with the great, and he borrowed his ideas almost like a chameleon. The romantics were particularly responsive to changing times, which is another reason why their school is so diverse. Sainte-Beuve stood at the crossroads between individualism, socialism and scientism. The one constant in his life—which was a major legacy of romanticism—was emotional dissatisfaction and restlessness.[1]

The result of this was that romantics could be disillusioned even before they set off on their enthusiastic adventures. Gustave Flaubert (1821–80) is essential reading for anyone who wants to understand this bankruptcy of romanticism and the origins of modern forms of anxiety. Flaubert was not very successful in his own lifetime, and in fact made only about £1,000 from his writings. He was appreciated mainly by a small group of distinguished realist novelists who acknowledged him as their master and who recognised his quite exceptionally brilliant literary craftmanship. He was nevertheless a most acute analyst of his age, and his own life, as revealed by his correspondence, shows in poignant detail the torments contemporary attitudes produced. Flaubert grew up as a romantic; he knew *René* by heart; he was determined to be a writer from an early age and he devoted his whole life to literature. 'I was born', he said, 'with little faith in happiness. When I was very young, I had a complete presentiment of life. It was like a nauseous smell of cooking escaping from a vent. You don't need to eat it to know that it will make you sick.' At sixteen he fell in love with a married woman eleven years older than himself and this remained the great passion of his life (and the inspiration of his *Éducation sentimentale*). He was afraid of life, as he himself admitted: he chose as his ideal woman one so remote that he could not hope to win her. He was unable to enjoy any other love; his spasmodic affair with the poetess Louise Colet consisted in a series of rejections by him. He feared happiness because he expected it to involve

[1] André Billy, *Sainte-Beuve. Sa vie et son temps* (1952); Maxime Leroy, *La Pensée de Sainte-Beuve* (1940); Marcel Proust, *Contre Sainte-Beuve* (reprinted 1954).

pain and ultimately despair. He had the romantics' sense of destiny, believing he was chosen for misfortune, but, even more than the romantics, he thought unhappiness was part of the general human destiny. He hated mankind; he despised and mocked it. He despised bourgeois conventionality, the platitudes of conversation, the hypocrisy of politicians; he saw moral degradation everywhere. 'How tired I am of the ignoble workman, the inept bourgeois, the stupid peasant and the odious priest.' He assiduously collected examples of human stupidity from which he compiled a *Dictionnaire des idées reçues*. He delighted in the discomfiture of the pompous, in the showing-up of false pretensions, in the denigration of all that was respectable. Mockery was his defence against the world. He laughed at everything, but with a bitterness which showed how this masked other emotions; and he was surprised when he found 'nowadays I laugh at things no one laughs at any more'. 'A gendarme', he declared, for example, 'is essentially ludicrous; I cannot look at one without laughing. It is grotesque and inexplicable—the effect this pillar of society has on me, like public prosecutors, justices of any kind and professors of literature.' Disenchantment to him was inevitable; his answer was to seek not happiness but detachment. He shows how romanticism turned into scientific realism not because of the adoption of a new intellectual doctrine, but from lassitude. Flaubert sought satisfaction from the observation of life, but his ultimate aim was not to draw conclusions about mankind, not to establish laws about its behaviour, not to prescribe means for its improvement. He was convinced there was no solution to the human problem; there was not even a problem; the world had to be accepted as it was. He had no ideals in politics. 'The whole dream of democracy', he wrote, 'is to raise the proletarian to the level of stupidity attained by the bourgeois ... The great moral of this reign will be to show that universal suffrage is as stupid as the divine right of kings, though slightly less odious.' He was not even patriotic. 'I am as much a Chinaman as a Frenchman, and I derive not the slightest pleasure from our victories over the Arabs.' He abandoned the search for experience at the outset of his life; he spent it brooding about emotions he had felt in his youth. He is a good example of the obstinate survival of youthful

ideas for many years after they had been thought up—a characteristic very frequently encountered with politicians in this
period. He denied that he found a goal in the search for
beauty: 'Art', he wrote, 'is perhaps no more serious than skittles.'
But he toiled at his writing with a devotion hardly ever
equalled. He spent days seeking the right word; he rewrote
endlessly; he observed with a fanatical search for accuracy;
he could spend a whole day, for example, looking at the
countryside through coloured glasses, in order to be able to
write one sentence describing such a situation; he claimed to
have read 1,500 books as research for *Bouvard et Pécuchet*.

Flaubert was a universal demoraliser. 'If ever I take an
active part in the world it will be as a thinker and demoraliser.'
It was just that *Madame Bovary* should have been incriminated,
for it was a dangerous work. The public prosecutor, in accusing
Flaubert of writing an immoral book, was right, even though he
was unable to put his finger on what exactly was dangerous
about it. His arguments are an interesting definition, in any
case, of the scandalous. When Emma goes waltzing with her
lover, her dress touches his trousers; 'their legs entered each
into the other, he lowered his eyes upon her; she looked up at
him . . .' 'I do know well that people waltz more or less in this
manner,' said the prosecutor, 'but that does not make it moral.'
He found the descriptions of Madame Bovary's beauty lascivious, provocative; no attempt was made to describe her intelligence. The story of her adultery lapsed into glorification of it;
marriage was painted as being full of platitudes but adultery
as being nothing but poetry. However, the public prosecutor
should have argued that Flaubert was not only undermining society but removing all hope from it. He not only described adultery, but showed how it gave no happiness, any
more than did marriage, or love or any activity at all. He showed
the monotony of passion, which at least the romantics had
believed in, the hypocrisy of religion, the dangers of thinking.[1]
Persigny complained that Flaubert had no ideal. At the end of
the book Emma Bovary's husband pathetically declares, 'It is the
fault of destiny'. This book is a brilliant study of the romantic
attitude—and particularly of that aspect of it which has now
acquired the name of Bovaryisme—the inability to distinguish

[1] 'Il ne faut pas toucher aux idoles'—Flaubert says, but he does.

between illusion and reality. It was more than description. 'Madame Bovary, c'est moi.'

In *L'Éducation sentimentale*, Flaubert was again partly auto-biographical: 'I wish to write the moral—or rather sentimen-tal—history of the men of my generation.' He saw it might alternatively have been called *Les Fruits secs*; it is again a book about failure. The hero was devoted to passion: he was en-thusiastic about *Werther, René, Lélia*; he believed that 'love is the pasture and, as it were, the atmosphere for genius'. He loved luxury, women and the life of Paris with its 'amorous effluvium and intellectual emanations'. But he was sad; he had no will-power. 'Action for certain men is all the more impracticable as the desire for it is strong. Distrust of them-selves embarrasses them, fear of displeasing terrifies them; besides, profound affections are like respectable women: they are frightened of being discovered and they pass through life with downcast eyes.' So the men in Flaubert's books spend their lives metaphorically chasing butterflies; one who sought power is dismissed from his prefecture and is in turn an organiser of colonisation in Algeria, secretary to a pasha, manager of a newspaper, advertising agent and finally legal assistant in an industrial company. Another gets involved in turn in Fourier-ism, homoeopathy, table-turning, Gothic art and finally photo-graphy. *Bouvard et Pécuchet* (1881), Flaubert's funniest book, was called by René de Gourmont 'the archive in which pos-terity will clearly read the hopes and disappointments of a century'.[1] This is a caricature of two petty bourgeois who give themselves up to studying every science in turn, but repeatedly meet disaster and failure. Flaubert declared the book had 'immense significance'; some critics have said it was the culmination of his work. It was an attack on human imbecility and on the absurd consequences of progress, but Flaubert took some pains to make it difficult to see what his point was beyond this: he enigmatically wrote in the preface that its purpose was to praise tradition and order, so that it would be unclear whom he was making fun of. 'I wish to produce such an impression of lassitude and boredom, that in reading the book people could think it was written by an idiot.' Voltaire's

[1] D. L. Demorest, *A Travers les plans, manuscrits et dossiers de Bouvard et Pécuchet* (1931), 154.

conclusion, 'cultivate your garden', was also Flaubert's. The romantic Flaubert ended by preaching something not very different from the classicist Anatole France.[1]

When individualists reached this kind of despair, they sometimes tried to exorcise the pain by renouncing their independence. This was shown most strikingly by Bourget and Barrès. The novels of Paul Bourget (1852–1935) are largely forgotten today. They cannot be read for pleasure, which is perhaps not surprising, for he believed that the trouble with the world was that it sought pleasure. But his novels were acclaimed by a wide and loyal audience in his own day; he wrote no less than seventy-three volumes. He edified a whole generation seeking moral guidance and in the prefaces to his works of fiction he made clear exactly what the moral of each story was. His celebrated *Le Disciple* (1890) was the manifesto of a new code of behaviour. In subsequent works, he specialised in stories about the domestic problems of the bourgeoisie. He devoted himself above all to defending the middle-class family as an institution. He attacked divorce, adultery, irreligion, democracy. He praised the cult of ancestors, the respect of family tradition and property, moderation in social ambition. Yet Bourget began life as a literary critic of rare perception; he was in his youth a positivist and a pupil of Taine. His career is worth examining, because it shows how the worship of science failed to satisfy him, and men like him, and how the Catholic reaction of the end of the century was born. Hitherto the problem was why writers lost their religious faith; now it was why an increasing number returned to it.

Bourget claimed that he remained a positivist all his life. One of the sources of strength in his writing was that he did not deny all value to scientific investigation, but only defined its limits, and incorporated it into a wider philosophy of life. Bourget was thus not so much disillusioned with science, as emotionally unsatisfied by it. He did not abandon positivism for Christianity but combined them. The result was perhaps unorthodox but no more so than his early adherence to positivism was superficial. He made his name with a collection of essays on the psychology of his generation, which turned the positivist

[1] Philip Spencer, *Flaubert* (1952); R. Dumesnil, *Gustave Flaubert* (1932); B. F. Bart, *Madame Bovary and the Critics* (New York, 1966).

method against its creators.[1] Bourget had a very unhappy childhood. It was dominated on the one hand by the loss of his mother when he was five—a loss to which he attributed his permanent inability to love or to be loved, and which may possibly explain his admiration for family life, which he was never to experience. On the other hand, he felt himself to be a child without roots, whose parents came from different parts of the country, whose father, a professor, carried him around France as he was transferred from post to post. He lived with books; he read the whole of Shakespeare, Scott, Dickens and George Sand before he was ten; then all the romantics and positivists in adolescence. This reading filled him with an 'irremediable despair'. The collapse of France in 1871 gave him a desire for action, but the determinism of the positivists discouraged him in advance. The Commune, after a short period of enthusiasm, terrified him and in 1890 he still recalled with horror the fusillade of May 1871. His trouble, he decided, was that 'there was a complete divorce between our intelligence and our sensibility'. Most young men of his generation were equally torn, and his essays were an attempt to lay bare the causes of their anxieties, to be a document, as he said, for future historians studying the moral life of the second half of the century. The essays were a brilliant attack on five leading writers who had, he said, formed the outlook of his generation. They were effective because they attributed one principal characteristic to each author, as his *idée maîtresse*, in the manner of Taine, studying above all mentality and attitudes, rather than biography or events. He used the latest methods of science to show the bankruptcy of all the intellectual system-building and emotional adventures of the century. He argued that literature had become one of the principal influences in life, now that traditional and local influences had diminished. Baudelaire had spread 'decadence' among young men— which was a state in which individuals were 'unfit for the tasks of ordinary life'. Renan had made dilettantism fashionable, 'a state of the mind, at once very intelligent and very voluptuous, which inclines us in turn towards various forms of hope and leads us to lend ourselves to all these forms without giving ourselves up to any one . . . It transformed scepticism into

[1] P. Bourget, *Essais de psychologie contemporaine* (1885).

an instrument of pleasure.' The result was that 'thirty volte-faces, in politics, literature, religion and general thought have cast into the current of ideas all sorts of formulae of taste, aesthetics and belief'. Flaubert preached a virtual nihilism, that 'every human effort ended in failure', that ambition was useless because its fulfilment did not yield the expected pleasure. Taine argued that wisdom was to be found in the acceptance of what was inevitable and that man, far from being good, was 'carnivorous'. Stendhal's hero is a man at war with society; his conclusion is pessimistic, a desire for death. These five masters of modern times, Bourget concludes, are thus all tired of life. They could not offer hope. In his subsequent books, Bourget applied the same method. In reaction against the realist novel, he wrote psychological analyses not of manners and events but of the state of the soul. He became 'an analyst of the disorders of the heart', a student of the revived *mal de siècle*. He had no talent for description; he could remember visual impressions only with difficulty; but he was fascinated by emotions and obsessed by memories of his own. Though he could occasionally invent dramatic twists and surprising end-ings for his novels, they always remained moral essays rather than stories.

The severest criticism Bourget levelled against the authors whose writings had dominated his youth was that they had deprived him of all sense of identity.[1] This is what he tried to regain through his writings, and this is why he was attracted increasingly by traditional values, roots and patriotism. His interest in psychology made him feel the overwhelming im-importance of the unconscious: this, more than anything, he later said, was what made him a traditionalist.[2] His long investigation of the moral ills of France—and their study, he thought, was the principal business of literature—led him to the conclusion that the conservative doctrines in which Balzac, Le Play and Taine had ended were the only ones which could serve as a remedy. In *Le Disciple* he told the story of a fervent disciple of positivism who comes to a tragic end. This book caused a considerable stir: 20,000 copies were sold in six weeks,

---

[1] Lettre Autobiographique, printed as an appendix to V. Giraud, *Paul Bourget* (1934), 195.

[2] V. Giraud, op. cit. 107, quoting letter in *Revue des revues* (1 May 1904).

Anatole France and Brunetière led a violent controversy on
its moral message, a controversy which was in some ways a
rehearsal of the Dreyfus Affair. Taine accused Bourget of
caricaturing his teaching, but he admitted sadly: 'Taste has
changed, my generation is finished.' Bourget again aroused a
furore with his novel *L'Étape* (1902) which argued that class
differences and heredity were so fundamental that it was
impossible for people to *bruler l'étape*, to skip a rung in the
ladder, without grave danger; the doctrine of personal merit
was false.

What Bourget had wanted originally was hope, and a cure for
the doubts of his generation. 'Who will give us back the divine
virtue of joy in work and hope in struggle ... Men do not need
leaders who make them doubt.' He did not quite achieve his
aims. He learnt to hate a great deal in modern society, to
castigate the *machiavellian Italian* Gambetta, the *abominable*
Ferry, the *hideous error* of having a republic, the *stupid* Declaration of the Rights of Man and *ignoble* democracy. But he never
succeeded in getting beyond agnosticism, even when he
preached Christianity: the absolute for him was the unknow-
able; he never quite found faith. His conclusion was that 'the
laws of human life, discovered by the purely realistic observation of facts, are identical with the laws promulgated by the
Revelation'.[1] Too much reading had been the bane of his
youth; too much thinking was as dangerous as incautious use
of noxious chemicals, so he ended up as a critic chastising
criticism, while still believing criticism had its uses. He reconciled science and religion because he could not be entirely
happy with either alone.[2]

Maurice Barrès (1862–1923) was even more significant,
because the philosophy he offered was not that of a disillusioned
middle-aged man, preaching to his juniors, but that of a young
man spontaneously rebelling against his elders, and acknowledged by many of his contemporaries as their representative.
He rebelled first of all against his school: he hated its 'vie de
ménagerie'. He was humiliated by two years of German occupation after the Franco-Prussian War. He was frustrated by
the contrast between the romantic ideals he found in Walter

[1] Charles Baussan, *De Frédéric Le Play à Paul Bourget* (1935), 177–8.
[2] Michel Mansuy, *Un Moderne: Paul Bourget* (Besançon, 1960).

Scott, Balzac and Fenimore Cooper and the mediocrity of his life. He was incensed by the doctrines he was taught. His philosophy teacher Burdeau (a disciple of Ferry, a brilliant graduate of the École Normale Supérieure, who soon after entered parliament and later became president of the Chamber of Deputies) represented the successful modern man approved of by the previous generation: he was a good speaker, well read, self-made, had fought in the war. But Barrès saw him as his enemy because he preached the fashionable Kantian philosophy, universally applicable, which Barrès regarded as hostile to individual whim, and because he sought to cut his pupils from their roots, from their families and provinces, and drive them to seek success in Paris, in a standard mould. Barrès did at first follow his master's teaching and at twenty-one went to Paris. There, however, he published *Sous l'œil des barbares* (1892) which stated his hostility to society and his belief that the world was barbarous and brutish to sensitive men like himself, but he offered no positive answer to what could be done about this. Paul Bourget gave the book a long review and Barrès became famous. The Latin Quarter in 1889 elected him *Prince des Jeunes* and member of parliament— where he sat on the extreme left as a Boulangist, symbolising protest. *Le Culte du moi* (1888–91) defined his position. This trilogy was both a portrait of the new type of young man becoming increasingly numerous, as he said, and of which he was the representative, and a guide to this new type. He aspired to winning their attention by accurately describing their difficulties and by offering them, at last, a solution. 'Our malaise', he wrote, 'comes from our living in a social order inspired by the dead and in no way chosen by us. The dead are poisoning us.' Let the young cast off these shackles. 'Let each one of us satisfy his ego and humanity will be a beautiful forest, beautiful because everything, trees, plants and animals, will develop and rise according to their nature.' Abandon guilt, which is the enemy of love and of enthusiasm. Seek every kind of experience, use up your youthful energy. He summarised his creed in three formulae: 'First Principle: We are never so happy as when we are in a state of exaltation. Second Principle: The pleasure of exaltation is much increased if it is analysed.' Even humiliating emotions, if analysed, can become voluptuous. 'Conclusion: We must feel as much as possible and analyse as much as possible.' This meant cultivating the ego, freeing it from the influence of the barbarians, from German metaphysics and Latin compartmentalisation. He quoted Ignatius Loyola, Benjamin Constant and Sainte-Beuve as models of this art. 'The religious orders created a hygiene of the soul, seeking to love God perfectly. A similar hygiene will lead us to the adoration of the ego. It will be a laboratory of enthusiasm.' But what should young men be enthusiastic about, apart from themselves? Barrès had nothing to offer as yet in these first books. 'Dear modern life,' he wrote, 'so ill at ease with its hereditary formulae and prejudices, let us live it with ardour, and hell! it will certainly end by working out for itself a new moral code and new duties.'

The cult of the self, on its own, was not enough. Barrès found the ego too ephemeral an object for adoration, he wanted to worship something eternal; and so he came to see the ego as part of a larger whole. 'I saw that I was only an instant in a long culture, a gesture among a thousand others of a force that preceded me and which will survive me. I became conscious of the essential of my ego, of the element of eternity of which I have custody.' The cult of the ego thus turned into the cult of his native province, and of the French nation. His rebellion against the dead ended with a worship of the dead. He decided the ego had no permanent reality on its own, that it was the product of tradition, past forces, the nation. 'To save ourselves from a sterile anarchy, we wish to bind ourselves to our land and our dead.' Analysis and introspection, which he had urged in his youth, now failed to satisfy him. Intelligence was only 'a small thing on the surface of ourselves'. So Barrès became a nationalist, and one of the principal writers responsible for its revival in this period. He now said that men's thoughts were not their own, but the result of racial and hereditary influence: 'our fathers and our ancestors speak through us'. Nationalism meant the acceptance of this influence of the past, but also it was a means of discovering the best in each individual, for it was this eternal voice that was the best in him. In 1894 Barrès founded *La Cocarde* to preach this doctrine, coupled with anti-Semitism. His *Roman de l'énergie nationale* (1897–1902), of which *Les Déracinés*, perhaps the most famous of his works, is the first volume, spread the message in half-fictional, half-autobiographical form. He was a founder member of the Ligue de la Patrie Française (1899). In 1906 his respectability was acknowledged by his election to the French Academy. From that date to his death he sat continuously in parliament, a member of the party of order now, but not fully a member of the right wing, and he refused to join Maurras. In his *Les Diverses Familles spirituelles de la France*, he accepted them all. 'Each group', he said, 'leaves too much outside it.'

But nationalism, again, was not enough for him. It 'lacks the dimension of infinity'. So he moved towards Catholicism. His campaign for the preservation of churches after the Separation (*La Grande Pitié des églises de France*, 1914) was one stage in this; his *Colline inspirée* (1913) marked his acceptance of certain aspects of Catholicism. But he never obtained faith; he died before he was sixty and his conversion was never completed. Already in 1909, however, he was preaching an ideal very different from that of his youth. 'Lead a Christian life. Have faith. Take the Sacraments . . . I do not know whether religion is true, but I love it.' Barrès's life was thus a continual flight from abstract ideals and a search for a creed that would appeal to the heart. He could not find any ideal in the future, and so he returned to the past he had once abhorred, with a nihilism as complete as that which he had denounced in his youth. He became obsessed by death, and it is only in death that he ultimately found the peace and conciliation he sought. His traditionalism and rationalism were the cult of the dead. Gide with some justice complained: 'Graves, graves, everywhere and always. To bear wreaths of flowers to graves—it is really only that.'

Barrès was greatly admired in his time and his *Déracinés* has been called one of the ten greatest social novels of the nineteenth century. Its style, with its 'brilliant lyricism, its melody of abrupt beginnings and slow development, its movement, sudden stops and prolonged pauses', has been likened to a combination of geometry and music and the nearest thing in literature to Wagner. The position Barrès held in French society has been well summarised by Léon Blum: 'He was for me, as for most of my friends, not only a master but a guide. We formed a school around him, almost a court . . . To a coldly sceptical society, Barrès brought a philosophy charged with provocative metaphysics and poetry, quivering with pride and domination. A whole generation, reduced and conquered by him, breathed this intoxicating mixture of conquering activity, philosophy and sensuality. It thought it had discovered its master, its model and its leader.' Maurras wrote, 'He was one of the greatest influences, the essential transformer of young intellectual opinion in 1900 and 1914.' For that very reason, and also because the part he chose was rejected by many of his early followers, he was bitterly attacked by the succeeding generation. Gide denounced him as the most evil of educators: all that is marked by his influence is moribund, dead, because he had a taste for death. A few months before Barrès died, a public mock trial of him was held, presided over by André Breton, in which he was accused of damaging the security of the mind. Tristan Tzara gave evidence that 'Barrès is the greatest scoundrel Europe has produced since Napoleon'.[1]

Proust

The analysis of the individual was raised to a new plane by Marcel Proust (1871–1922). His work was for long appreciated by a much smaller audience than was that, for example, of Barrès or Bourget. It was only after the Second World War that he came to be acknowledged as one of France's most original and profound authors. An inquiry by the *Figaro* in 1947, asking people whether he had influenced them, drew largely non-committal answers. But three years later there were twenty theses being written about him in the Sorbonne alone, and the flood of publications about him has not abated since then.[2] Frenchmen did not immediately recognise them-

---

[1] A. Zarach, *Bibliographie barrèsienne 1881–1948* (1951); P. de Boisdeffre, *Barrès parmi nous* (1952); J. M. Domenach, *Barrès par lui-même* (1954); J. Vier, *M. Barrès et le culte du moi* (1958); Z. Sternhell, *M. Barrès et le nationalisme française* (1972); R. Soucy, *Fascism in France: the case of M. Barrès* (Berkeley, California, 1972, controversial); M. Davanture, 'La Jeunesse de M. Barrès 1862–1888' (unpublished Paris thesis, 1975, 2 vols.).

[2] For opinion on him in 1923, R. Fernandez (ed.), 'Hommage à Marcel Proust', *Les Cahiers Marcel Proust*, no. 1 (1927); D. W. Alden, *Marcel Proust and his French Critics* (Los Angeles, 1940); Germaine Brée, 'New Trends in Proust Criticism',

selves in Proust, who must therefore be seen as a precursor rather than as the leader of a generation, as offering explanations before most people had formulated the problems.

Proust's whole life was dominated by his unsatisfactory relationship with his parents. He was the son of a successful doctor and a talented and well-to-do mother; he won high honours as a schoolboy; but though as a young man he published a book of essays and verse (1896), which was a flop, he seemed incapable of doing anything with his life. At the age of thirty-five he withdrew from the world as a neurotic invalid. He spent the rest of his life working out the cause of his troubles and reflecting on his relatively brief experience of society. His conclusions represented an important advance on those offered by his predecessors, but they were also much more complex. Whereas Barrès and Bourget urged men to prop themselves up with the aid of traditional institutions, declaring individualism to be too painful to sustain, Proust argued that this suffering held the key to the solution of the human dilemma. Suffering produced detachment, which in turn made self-knowledge possible. Suffering also produced sympathy for others and that was essential if one was to understand other people too. But Proust had no universal formula for explaining human motivation. On the contrary, he believed that the most fundamental characteristic of men was their instability—like a kaleidoscope—so that prediction of their actions was impossible. His method was to analyse them under the microscope and to reveal the many different sides of their personalities; he saw them changing constantly with time; he excelled in showing the contradictions in them, and the gap between behaviour and intention. The appearance of continuity and cohesion in character was purely superficial: it was partly the result of individuals assuming roles, and partly of those around them creating fixed stereotypes to give them a semblance of stability. The psychiatrist Ribot had recently identified dissociation of the personality as a disease.[1] Proust

Symposium (Syracuse Univ.) (May 1951), vol. 5, no. 1, 62–71; C. B. Osburn, *The Present State of French Studies* (Metuchen, N.J., 1971), 825–36. For the publishing history of Proust, see Zeldin, *Taste and Corruption*, ch. 1. Cf. also G. D. Lindner, *Marcel Proust, Reviews and estimates in English* (Stanford, 1942).

[1] T. Ribot, *Les Maladies de la personnalité* (1885).

argued that it was in fact normal. Ribot thought man's identity came simply from his body. Proust saw much more in individuals; he was fascinated by the sound of their names, by their handwriting, by their every mannerism; but he believed that it was virtually impossible for one person to know another. All that could be hoped for was to know oneself. Proust was a solipsist, for whom man 'is a being who cannot come out of himself, who cannot know others except in himself, and who, if he denies this, lies'.

It took him a long time to accept loneliness and to turn it from an inescapable fact into the basis of a philosophy, for Proust felt a profound need for affection. At the age of seven he had his first presentiment that love and happiness were impossible, when he begged his mother for a goodnight kiss and realised that by asking for it, he had ruined its savour; there could be no consolation for the fact that he could not have enough affection from her. At fourteen he wrote that his greatest misery was to be separated from his mother; guilt, remorse, and a highly developed sensitivity made it impossible for him to resolve the problems of living independently of her, and it was only in late middle age, when he gave his parents' furniture away to a brothel, that he at last resolved his longing for revenge on them. At school, he demanded 'a tyrannical and total affection' from his fellow pupils; as an adult he was distinguished by 'beautiful manners', exquisite politeness and a readiness to flatter which verged on fawning. He quickly lost hope of obtaining satisfaction in love for women, deciding that the desire for possession was both absurd and painful, that jealousy was its necessary corollary, that in any case what one loved was a creation of one's own imagination, and the consciousness of the disparity between this ideal and the reality was more painful still. Love was a poison, bound to create suffering. One could not make a bad choice, because every choice was bad. Later, he found the answer in seeing the suffering love caused as the stimulus that was needed to re-examine oneself and one's motives. But meanwhile he was made to feel even more alone by the realisation, or the decision, that he was a homosexual, and so an outcast, forced into deceit, reduced, after a succession of unsuccessful attempts to combine love and friendship with his equals, to abandon the belief that friendship was a possibility either. His love-affairs with young men of the working class, and his resort to male brothels culminated in his having himself beaten there, and sticking pins into rats, in an effort to come to terms with the haunting image of his parents. Proust became the first famous author to write openly about homosexuality (though Binet-Valmer's novel *Lucien* (1910) and Achille Essebac's *Dédé* (1901) had prepared the way). He defended it against the opprobrium the Church and moralists had laid upon it, but he asserted that it was an incurable malady, and Gide, who was the first author to make public profession of his own homosexuality, attacked Proust for talking of it as deviation, instead of as 'Greek love'. It is wrong to see in homosexuality the basic explanation of Proust's dilemmas. Proust was not entirely in either camp, just as he was not entirely a Jew, that other race of outcasts whose lot tormented him. It was precisely because he stood on so many boundaries that he was able to be so perceptive.[1]

Proust had a strong belief in the importance of heredity. At one stage, he thought he could assuage his desire by being accepted into the most exclusive social circles of Paris. He imagined the aristocracy were able to transcend the limitations of the individual because they were so firmly anchored in the past. It was not quite snobbishness that attracted him to such people; he had no illusions about their stupidity, their inability to appreciate intellectual or artistic worth, even when he was carried away by the suggestiveness and euphony of their historic titles. Proust did come from a family that was only on the first step of the ladder to social respectability; his grandfather had been a grocer, his uncle was a draper who had made his fortune in Algeria; his father had been a scholarship boy, who had risen to be a professor of medicine but who lacked artistic taste; his mother—who was artistic—was the daughter of a Jewish stockbroker and niece of a button manufacturer. Proust in his novel idealised the hostesses and *salons* he frequented. The aristocratic families involved were, like him, on the fringes of their class and so very much more concerned

---

[1] Eugène Montfort, 'L'Homosexualité dans la littérature', an inquiry in *Les Marges* (1926, 176–215); Dr. Robert Soupault, *Marcel Proust du côté de la médecine* (1967); L. Lesage, *Marcel Proust and his Literary Friends* (Urbana, Ill., 1958), 89.

with their status (like the Belgian banker, ennobled during the
Restoration, on whose descendant the duc de Guermantes was
modelled) or else people with titles who had married into money
(like Boni de Castellane, who married the American heiress
Anna Gould, and on whom Saint-Loup was based). Proust
for a time felt he lacked family traditions and admired the
aristocracy who, he believed, were, on account of their ancestry, more than isolated individuals. He also admired professional men who derived substance and stability from their
work, like the doctor Cottard in his novel, who was in his social
life a pretentious imbecile, but who nevertheless was a 'great
clinician', with a 'mysterious gift' for healing. Within a few
years, however, this idol also lost its glitter and the Dreyfus
Affair completed his disillusionment. Proust nevertheless
remained ambiguous in his attitude to class also. He believed
that society would become even more hierarchical as it became
outwardly more democratic. He did not entirely dissociate
himself from the view that the members of each class were
doomed to remain in the one into which they were born, and
that no communication between classes was really possible:
class was a prison, just as individual isolation was; he both
mocked and praised those who were typical representatives of
their class.

Humour was one of the methods he perfected to cope with
the problems of the world. When all his hopes of salvation
through external forces faded, he was thrown back on himself.
He did not see a solution in any positive action, for all action
seemed to him either ridiculous or mean. Life could be either
lived, or dreamt, and he thought those who dreamt it did
better. There are only two pages in his book when he expresses
confidence in the future. He turned rather to the past, and to
introspection. He was no longer afraid of his loneliness, for
he now found his own 'passionate conversations' with himself
to be what he valued most.[1] The key to reality was to be found
in memory, which held together the isolated fragments of
men's existence; not in intelligence, which was only a source of
confusion, providing pretexts for eluding the duties that instinct
dictated. It was not deliberate memory therefore that mattered,
but involuntary memory, unsullied by intelligence, which

[1] M. Proust, *Le Temps retrouvé* (Livre de poche, 1954), 251, 234.

revived parts of one's former self that one had thought dead. In this way one was freed from the domination of time; one glimpsed eternity; the fear of death vanished, because one realised that parts of one were always dying. Proust at last found his vocation, to be an artist, whose function was to translate these visions, to express the truths he had in himself. The artist provided the links between isolated individuals. It no longer mattered that men were alone, once they realised that reality was unique for each one of them. They should not take the behaviour they saw around them as indications of reality, because it was superficial, and needed to be interpreted, as symbols of what lay behind. He was not in favour of esotericism; he insisted that intelligence had its uses; and the artist must use it to clarify what seemed to be obscure. The real world, however, was only partly in the objects surrounding one: it was even more in oneself. The artist therefore led the fullest kind of life, even though he was isolated; literature was the most fulfilling activity, because it enabled men to see beyond the limits of their own vision; books were like spectacles, designed to help the reader see better, and if the reader recognised in himself what the author was describing, then that was truth. What made life worth living, then, was to be an artist who could illuminate the darkness that surrounded all men. The suffering that artistic sensitivity involved was worth bearing, because it was through suffering that one was driven to make the effort from which the discovery of truth could follow. Proust's solution was not self-realisation, but withdrawal, reflection and understanding. He did not aim to offer hope, still less happiness, for he was too conscious of unhappiness everywhere, and 'happy years are wasted years', because they prevented one from knowing oneself. What he felt he could achieve was to 'bring harmony to scattered spirits and peace to troubled hearts'. He believed his method had the power of reconciliation in it, and the victim of internal conflicts himself, this was what seemed most urgent. His detachment, however, had no limits, and he could see the flaws in his own solutions. It was in that way, as much as through art, that he found his liberation.[1]

[1] M. Proust, *A la recherche du temps perdu* (1913–27). Among the several hundred books about Proust and the many thousands of articles, the following are useful

This sample of novelists and moralists, inevitably a small sample, gives some indication of the internal turmoils of individualism as well as of its inextinguishable attractions. The pains caused by individual freedom need to be recorded as much as the principles that made it possible. How ordinary people coped with them, when not sustained by philosophic or religious ideas, or even when they were, may be seen by looking at those who ended up in the consulting rooms of the growing number of doctors treating nervous troubles.

introductory guides: G. Painter, *Marcel Proust, a biography* (2 vols., 1961-5); Jacques Rivière, *Quelques progrès dans l'étude du cœur humain* (1924); Arnaud Dandieu, *Marcel Proust, sa révélation psychologique* (1930); Dr. Charles Blondel, *La Psychographie de Marcel Proust* (1932); Milton Hindus, *The Proustian Vision* (1954); Jacques Nathan, *La Morale de Proust* (1953); E. Czoniczer, *Quelques antécédents de 'A la recherche du temps perdu'* (1957); J. J. Zéphir, *La Personnalité humaine dans l'œuvre de Marcel Proust* (1959); Floris Delattre, 'Bergson et Proust', *Les Études bergsonniennes* (1948), vol. 1, 1-127. See also pp. 88-9. For new attitudes to intimacy, cf. Lion Murard and Patrick Zylberman, *Le Petit Travailleur infatigable* (1976).

3. Worry, Boredom and Hysteria

THE age of fear is as good a label for this century as the age of progress: both labels reveal one side of it. For though there were unprecedented material transformations, it did not follow that there was also increasing hope in all spheres of life, let alone increasing happiness. Opportunities widened in this period, knowledge of the world's workings grew enormously and people, to a considerable extent, became accustomed to coping with far more change. That better things were coming from all this was frequently repeated but perhaps not as often as is assumed: perhaps the optimists talked loudest. For at the same time the whole notion of what constituted an improvement was always a matter of debate and uncertainty. Happiness remained an elusive and controversial ideal. Anxiety, by contrast, may well have increased (though not necessarily in all groups) in the sense that traditional supports of behaviour were weakened, that people were left facing a larger world and a vastly greater range of problems, with far less certainty as to how they should treat them, and often with sharpened sensibilities. To understand this society, one must study it not just in the achievements of its members, but in their loneliness too. One must look into the history, in other words, of personal anxiety—the way people worried, what frightened them and what hurt them.

But this is uncharted territory. It is true that there is no lack of information about the triumphs of science over the great physical scourges of mankind, like smallpox, cholera, tuberculosis and puerperal fever, which were gradually subjugated in this period, though there is still scope for a vast amount of research in this subject. But medical history is inevitably written largely from the point of view of the progress of knowledge; it tells more about the doctor than the patient; and it is more concerned with general demographic results than with the details of how individuals bore their sufferings. This negative side of medical history—the way people reacted to disease, the way they faced pain and death—is far less documented, but it brings out a factor that was crucial in determining people's general attitude to life. The history of mental illness, which has recently attracted considerable attention, can provide clues as to how the strains of existence were met or not met, though again the evidence is twisted by the succession of psychological theories through which it was seen—and it is too often presented as a social problem concerning only a minority. The history of the mental troubles of the vast majority of the population, who were not mad but who had their own—not unrelated—anguish to deal with, falls between two stools, outside the scope of medical history. But it can help to provide the context of obsessions and fears into which all other preoccupations—about work, family, friends and politics—had to fit.

These intimate fears were seldom written down and there is little hint of them in the sources historians generally concentrate on. They come out, however, for example, in the Catholic confessional.[1] One can find traces of them also in doctors' case histories; this is a still untapped source, through which one can eavesdrop on accounts of pain, guilt and an immense amount of suffering. The very same people who, at other times, were busy making money, or protesting vigorously about class repression, the high cost of living, the policies of governments, or any of the other causes historians have recorded, in the privacy of the consulting room give the impression of an overwhelming preoccupation with very different and far less grandiose problems, but ones that generated terror, fury and deep despondency. Their worries were sometimes worries about the human condition itself, but these too have their history, for the unchanging problems of life and death did not always meet with the same response and there was more to them than a variation in the balance of resignation or acceptance.

The diseases people imagined they suffered from are a useful introduction to this, because they reveal imagination and attitude as well as reaction to pain. Hypochondria has the advantage that it blows up into exaggerated forms the

[1] Theodore Zeldin, *Conflicts in French Society* (1970), chapter on 'Confession, Sin and Pleasure'.

kinds of worries that tormented people. And in this period, the advance of medicine introduced severe complications in the way disease was perceived, at the same time as it reduced the incidence of disease. The popularisation of medical knowledge added a whole new dimension to consciousness. In this intermediary stage, between the supremacy of religious and superstitious ideas on the one hand and scientific confidence on the other, a vast number of dangerous possibilities were added to the mere business of existence. As the doctors' nosographies were expanded, many pains were endowed with more terrifying names, and first germs and then viruses invaded a universe previously inhabited only by simple humours and demons. Thus, there had once been an easily understandable explanation of hypochondria: it had been a disturbance of the hypochonder, which caused vapours to rise from the stomach and liver and endocrine gland. Some doctors regarded this as a physical trouble, like Tissot,[1] who attributed it to disturbances in the 'nervous fibres' and 'nervous fluid', or Broussais, who linked it with gastro-enteritis. But in the eighteenth century Sauvages had argued that hypochondria was due to 'excessive self-love, attachment to life and to the pleasures it procures', and that it was therefore an intellectual trouble. In the middle of the nineteenth century these different views continued to be held simultaneously, so there was no generally accepted way of dealing with it. Doctors who received the most varied confessions labelled them as hypochondria when they could find no other explanation. Dr. Michéa, who was one of the national experts on hypochondria at the beginning of this period, stated that hypochondria occurred twice as often among men as among women, and most of all in the liberal professions; it was one of the results of education; the reading of medical books by laymen was both a cause and a symptom of it. But retired soldiers also suffered from it, as though the fear of death only worried them after they had ceased to be confronted with it directly. It may indeed be that as serious dangers to life diminished, men had more leisure to think about less immediate ones, and worry, inevitably, was the principal element in this condition.

[1] S. A. Tissot (1728–97), famous for his best-sellers *L'Onanisme* (1760) and *L'Avis au peuple sur sa santé* (1761).

Four case histories of hypochondria, related by Dr. Michéa, show how the imagination of patients expanded. There was the case of 'an intelligent man of thirty-seven', for whom timidity had been a lifelong problem. He had given up his intention of becoming a notary for fear of 'succumbing under the yoke'. At eighteen he had suffered palpitations of the heart, which gave him a fixed conviction that he had a mortal disease: the doctors he consulted could suggest no remedy. He was overwhelmed by the notion that he was powerless; all work, even reading, became painful; 'the sense of not being like other men towards my wife has always dominated me', he said, though he had one son. After twenty years of suffering, he turned to homoeopathy, and declared himself cured. The obscurity of this case is typical: only a fraction of the truth ever got out and disease was very much a mystery. Book learning could not solve this problem. Many laymen studied medicine—and a flow of medical books catered for them; some later became doctors, because of worry about their own health.[1] A second case illustrates, however, how frightening this new medical knowledge could be. A man, recounting his troubles to his doctor, complained that at thirteen he suffered from 'premature erections' at the sight of a girl. This led him to masturbate; at eighteen he 'obtained a rendez-vous' with a woman to whom he was much attached but 'I experienced so much agitation that it was impossible for me to profit from it'. He was more fortunate the next year, but he then found he had gonorrhoea with inflammation of the testicles. His health deteriorated and he suffered liver and stomach pains. He gave up his plans for a military career and became a medical student instead; but, he said, the cold and humidity of Paris and the sedentary nature of his occupation worsened his condition. He diagnosed that he had a kidney stone, and determined to have an operation; the surgeon he

[1] For example, F. V. Raspail, *Manuel-Annuaire de la santé* (40th edition, 1885); Dr. Jules Massé, *La Médecine des accidents* (9th edition, 1869); Dr. Alexis Belliol, *Le Guide des malades* (10th edition, 1845); Louis Riond, *La Médecine populaire* (5th edition, 1849); Abbé David, *Petit Manuel médical à l'usage des familles, des maisons d'éducation et des établissements de bienfaisances, mis à la portée des ouvriers et des habitants de la campagne* (3rd edition, 1862); E. Barrier, *Médecine des pauvres* (5th edition, 1892). There were over one hundred works classified as 'popular medicine' published between 1846 and 1875.

approached recommended baths instead, which calmed him down. But his hard work for his examinations 'spoilt his digestion and produced frequent ejaculation of sperm'. He had noises in his ears and fainting fits and feared apoplexy. By the time he graduated, he suspected he also had heart trouble and tuberculosis. He returned to the security of his native province, but there he caught syphilis; he treated himself with mercury pills, which 'completed the ruin of his health', and, by producing flatulence, forced him to lead a solitary life. He interpreted this last trouble as being caused by chronic gastritis, which he treated by living on a diet of milk for eighteen months. The work of the once-celebrated German Wichmann then revealed the true cause of his ailments to him as loss of sperm.[1] He learnt the book by heart in his enthusiasm. He cut his sphincters, and had his prostate cauterised to stop the loss. At that point he declared himself cured, sleep and appetite returned and 'my erections had an energy I had never seen before'. That was his own conclusion. Modern readers will immediately interpret his troubles according to doctrines now fashionable, but in his own time this man, a respectable physician in the eyes of his neighbours, had only taken to extremes the spirit of scientific curiosity and the search for explanations. This was the reverse side of progress. When Flaubert satirised it in Bouvard et Pécuchet, he was pointing to genuine and painful dilemmas. And children were particularly vulnerable, as witness a third case, of an eighteen-year-old shop assistant who went to see Dr. Michéa. He admitted to having masturbated since the age of fifteen, until he developed acne: his workmates mocked him for his disfigurement, saying it was masturbation that caused the acne. He read Tissot's book on Onanism, which led him to feeling all sorts of other symptoms that Tissot said followed from the evil practice. The boy was convinced his brain was 'going dry'. So he gave up masturbation in favour of women, but he almost at once caught gonorrhoea. Though he was quickly cured, he remained convinced that 'a venereal element' survived in his blood, which would eventually produce terrible sufferings. A whole succession of pains, vomiting and fainting followed. He imagined that he was going blind, that he had tuberculosis, that he was

[1] J. E. Wichmann, De Pollutione diurna (1791).

going to die. A doctor attributed his troubles to loss of sperm and cauterised his ureter seven times. He felt better after this, despite the appalling pain of the operations, but he was still worried. Dr. Michéa, when consulted, prescribed cold baths and complete abstinence from both women and masturbation; he insisted on his spending at least three-quarters of an hour each day immersed in the Seine; and he claimed this effected his cure.

Finally, worry about the mysteries of disease and death may be illustrated by the case of the Parisian butcher, aged thirty-eight, of generally sanguine temperament, who suffered only from haemorrhoids, until he began to worry that he had a tumour in his stomach, because his father had died of one at forty-two. Every pain he felt, he now interpreted as a warning. He told his family he was dying and constantly lamented that it was sad one so young should pass away. One day, Dr. Michéa was summoned to find him vomiting, with a violent stomach ache, terrified that his moment had come. Dr. Michéa appeased him by placing twenty leeches on his anus and an opium plaster on his stomach and giving him orangeade to drink. Henceforth the man lived on 'calming potions'.[1] Dr. Michéa believed that the basic trouble was materialism and the decline of religion. In his private clinic, he made his patients go daily to chapel, with excellent results, he said. But to his outpatients he gave tranquillising drugs, which, as has been seen, were one of the less discussed alternatives to religion.[2] These various cases show that the history of both science and religion needs to be complemented by that of imagination. The terrors this inspired was another of the important forces that influenced behaviour.

Nervousness

As medical views changed, so worry about one's health, with all that that implied about one's personality and one's functioning, became absorbed into the more general category of nervousness. This was, around 1850, again very much one of the mysteries of life, because opinions on it were also in a

[1] Dr. C. F. Michéa, *Traité pratique, dogmatique et critique de l'hypochondrie* (1845).
[2] Id., *Le Matérialisme refuté à l'aide d'arguments empruntés à l'histoire naturelle, à la physiologie et à la médecine* (1850); see above, pp. 20-1.

state of flux. In the course of the next century a whole host
of novel explanations of nervousness were offered; its manifestations were renamed and subdivided with increasing
complexity, so that it appeared to grow into a problem that
more and more people felt touched by. Since nervous diseases
were, of course, no modern invention, the mid-nineteenth
century preserved the heritage of the ancient world in its
view of them. Nervousness had been explained simply,
though vaguely, by the Greeks (whose statements were still
reproduced respectfully in the French medical textbooks) as
the result of man being endowed with 'passions'. One of the
most popular guides to self-knowledge was still the treatise
entitled *The Physiology of the Passions* by J. L. Alibert, who
had been physician to Louis XVIII.[1] Passion was the
cause of misery, when it was not controlled, and the cure for
this therefore lay in self-mastery. This doctrine could easily
be absorbed into Christian language: will-power was the
answer to temptation. But the issue was complicated by the
association of the different passions with states of the body,
brought about by people's differing constitution and temperament, and by the different conditions in which they lived. Thus
melancholy was brought on more directly by an excess of black
bile, and choler by too much yellow bile; but it was all a
vicious circle, because sorrows 'dried the body', 'consumed the
spirits', exhausted the warmth and moisture of the body, and so
brought about further troubles; blood-letting and purges got
rid of 'the humours'. The ambiguity of the condition was shown
by Cicero translating the Greek word melancholia as *furor*.
Plato had made frenzy a divine gift. Aristotle had combined
melancholy and frenzy to produce the idea of the gifted
melancholic, so that the same physical condition could produce
both madness and genius. Thus whereas the medieval Christian
tradition regarded melancholia as a trial, sent from God, to
be conquered by will, the Aristotelian and Renaissance view was
that melancholy could be a condition of creativity, and that it
was implied in the ideal of the speculative life. One of the
main hazards of intellectual activity thus became nervous
disease; civilisation itself seemed to bring gloom in the wake

[1] J. L. Alibert, *Physiologie des passions ou nouvelle doctrine des sentimens moraux* (2nd
edition, 1827).

of its victories. The educated man sought inspiration in his own independent thinking, but only too often collapsed into despair between his moments of ecstatic self-affirmation.[1]

The whole notion of depression was still very obscure in the mid-nineteenth century. Dr. Du Vivier, a Paris factory inspector and member of the commission on insalubrious lodgings, writing in 1864, declared that it was uncertain whether melancholy was induced by 'an alteration of the intellectual faculties' or by the 'predominance of the liver': 'the precise seat of its cause is hidden from us.'[2] Dr. Lelut, member of the Academy of Moral and Political Sciences, confessed also that man's nature was 'indeterminable' and the 'seat of his passions', which people variously placed either in the 'nervous viscerae or plexus', or in the spinal cord, or in the brain, was really a mystery. Nevertheless, Dr. Lelut insisted that happiness could not be predetermined or accidental, for in that case life would be intolerable. In a treatise on equality, officially commissioned by his academy during the revolution of 1848, he assured his compatriots that all had an equal hope of becoming happy. Some, it is true, had to do disagreeable work, but they were generally not intelligent, so did not mind it. Habit, moreover, could 'soften or annihilate even the most poignant privations' just as it could render luxury insipid. Happiness, he argued, was a habit, or produced by it; inequalities in happiness resulted from people doing work which was not in conformity with the habits they had acquired in childhood. People who did not fit into the harmonious designs of Providence had no cause for despair: education (rather than the redistribution of wealth) would train them for a better life.[3] In such ways, the difficulties of the melancholic enigma were either denied or explained away.

The popularity of novelists came, to a certain degree, from the fact that, even if they could not explain all this,

[1] Jean Starobinski, *Histoire du traitement de la mélancolie des origines à 1900* (Basle 1960, Acta Psychosomatica, no. 3); Raymond Klibansky *et al.*, *Saturn and Melancholy* (1964) for the ancient and Renaissance doctrines; Lawrence Babb, *The Elizabethan Malady. A Study of Melancholia in English Literature from 1580 to 1642* (East Lansing, 1951), on the early problems of intellectuals.

[2] E. Du Vivier, *De la mélancolie* (1864), 65.

[3] L. F. Lelut, *Petit Traité de l'égalité* (2nd edition, 1858), 53, 73, 88, 90; id., *Physiologie de la pensée: recherches critiques des rapports du corps à l'esprit* (2nd edition, 1862), 1. 375, 2. 196.

they did at any rate give it a central place in their description of life. Balzac's world, for example, is one in which the great enemies of health were not physical troubles but strong emotions, unsatisfied or injured passions. His characters frequently died of grief or became ill from a variety of mental causes. Worry was thus not just a side-effect or an inconvenience, but one of the principal torments of life, and what was most frightening about it was that it was an epidemic on the increase, and that intelligence and greater wealth, far from being a safeguard against it, as they were against physical disease, usually brought it on in severer form. Balzac saw man as having a certain amount of energy, a sort of moral capital, which was easily and quickly lost by excessive activity, and above all intellectual activity. He makes his old doctor say in *Ecce Homo*: 'I am convinced that the length of life is determined by the force that the individual can oppose to thought ... Men who, despite the use of their brain, have arrived at a great age, would have lived three times as long if they had not used this homicidal force.' This was in accord with contemporary medical doctrine: education was a form of suicide. Dr. Broussais's treatise on physiology (1822) had a chapter entitled 'How the exercise of the intellect, the emotions and the passions causes illnesses'.[1] Balzac also stressed the suffering that resulted from hereditary traits of character, from the vicissitudes of sexual life, from the unbalanced ordering of people's activity. Women were exhausted by menstruation and childbirth; they were more emotional, but they also needed emotion and, relatively speaking, they bore its trials better. These inner troubles, in Balzac's view, were much more important than natural catastrophes like war and fire, and he criticised painters for simply depicting the superficial contexts of life. Another of his ideas, which was also widespread, was that social relations had noxious effects: he planned to write a 'pathology of social life', to show how men's stock of strength was diminished by too much expense of effort, indeed, of any kind. The division of labour was in particular disastrous; individual professions had their special ailments, and accentuated any disequilibrium

---

[1] F. J. V. Broussais, *Traité de physiologie appliquée à la pathologie* (1822–3), i. 276; S. Tissot, *De la santé des gens de lettres* (1768, new edition 1859); E. Brunaud, *De l'hygiène des gens de lettres* (1819).

that existed in those who specialised. Dr. Cabanis (physician to Mirabeau and Condorcet) had said that 'sensibility is like a fluid whose total quantity is fixed: every time it throws itself in greater abundance into one of its channels, it proportionately diminishes in its centre'. Worry thus brought on additional troubles; it culminated in complete exhaustion—a view which was to survive in a more scientifically sophisticated form.[1]

'Nervous disease' was a subject that aroused increasing attention in the eighteenth century; in the early nineteenth 'neurosis' was the new term for it, coined by Pinel. But when in 1836 the Academy of Medicine offered a prize for the best essay on 'the influence of physical and moral education on the production of overexcitement in the nervous system and the illnesses which are the consequences of this overexcitement', the winner, Dr. Cerise, was not able to offer any clear explanation. He contented himself with satirising the absurdities in all theories that had hitherto been offered, and in particular those of the materialists Dr. Cabanis and Dr. Raspail, who believed that thought was 'secreted by the brain as bile is by the liver'.[2] The study of the mind by doctors involved the invasion of a theological preserve, for the mind, traditionally, was inseparable from the soul, which was the concern of priests. The doctors were conscious of this and for a long time a considerable proportion of them, being conformist Christians, moved rather hesitatingly in this domain. Their invasion, however, had the important result that mental troubles were henceforth studied as illnesses rather than as the inevitable consequence of being human. In 1843 Cerise, together with Baillarger, founded the Medico-Psychological Society whose Annales were to contain a great deal of the writing on this subject. The specialists increasingly concentrated on the obviously mad; the expansion of lunatic asylums gave them the material on which they worked; and their natural inclination was to make those who showed any symptoms which could be linked with madness to come into the asylum, if only for short stays. Dr. Baillarger gave melancholy the status of a morbid entity, thus transforming traditional views of it. For about

[1] P. J. G. Cabanis, *Rapports du physique et moral* (3rd edition, 1815), I. 121.
[2] Dr. Cerise, *Des fonctions et des maladies nerveuses dans leurs rapports avec l'éducation sociale et privée, morale et physique* (1842), 331.

fifty years, his influence continued to be felt, even though the enormously wide definition of melancholy that he gave gradually fell apart, as his successors isolated different diseases from it. Despite all the lip-service paid to the virtues of the clinical approach, stressing observation, the old nosological method survived, in that to find a 'new disease', with a new label, became the ambition of the psychiatrists. Whereas the Church had developed a doctrine for the vast majority, and had exiled the mad as sub-human, the doctors based their theories on the aberrations of their most bizarre patients and left the majority to see their emotional problems as pale reflections of major diseases. The eighteenth-century age of reason may have refused to acknowledge the existence of the human rights of mad people, but the nineteenth-century age of science turned the old-fashioned passions into sources of illness instead of accepting them as the inevitable condition of humanity. When people worried, therefore, or were deeply depressed, they now expected a medical name for their condition, and they got it, though it altered from time to time; when too many people thought they suffered from it, then something more esoteric was needed.

Thus in 1860 Dr. Bouchut, professor at the faculty of medicine in Paris, invented *névrosisme* to describe the condition of people who had nothing physically wrong with them, whose hypochonders and whose uteruses functioned normally, but who were mentally tormented.[1] This was designed to replace all those vague old-fashioned terms like the 'vapours', 'nervous overexcitement' and 'nervous fever'; but it did not have much success, even though it was elaborately subdivided, because there was little perception behind it; it was nothing but a new word, which did nothing new to help those who suffered from it. At the same time as Dr. Bouchut put forward his new theory, however, Dr. Morel developed a more serious threat to the peace of mind of those who felt that theirs was troubled. His theory of 'degeneration' was that madness represented the decay of man from the form originally created by God, as a result of social or physical influences. The main damage was being caused by alcohol (and opium in the East), but

[1] E. Bouchut, *De l'état aigu et chronique du névrosisme appelé névropathie aiguë cérébro-pneumo-gastrique* ... (1860).

industrialisation was also doing harm. Madness was thus not a sign of a primitive mind but on the contrary of collapse, and that is why most madness was incurable. It was increasing and would inevitably continue to do so, unless there was an improvement in moral standards. Meanwhile, vast numbers of people had a hereditary predisposition to it, and the asylums contained only a small minority of those who succumbed. The hereditary fault was usually so ingrained that it could be eliminated only by racial interbreeding, with primitive people who were not yet affected; the most degenerate Frenchmen, meanwhile, should be discouraged from intermarrying.[1] This theory was profoundly influential partly because it fitted in so well with traditional prejudices and Christian doctrines about hereditary influences and moral decay, so that science seemed to be confirming people's gloomiest fears, and partly because it was taken up and developed by Valentin Magnan (1835–1916), one of the most respected of the psychiatrists of the turn of the century.

Magnan, who came from Roussillon (as Pinel, Esquirol and J. P. Falret did also), spent forty-five years living in the St. Anne asylum, looking after his patients with a total devotion that made him eschew all social life, and take only an occasional and very brief seaside holiday. He was an exceptionally gentle, sympathetic, smiling man, who could gain the confidence of his patients and converse even with the most agitatedly mad ones. He was much struck by the influence of alcohol on madness and at the end of his life he calculated that out of the 113,000 cases treated by him, 27 per cent of the male patients had had alcoholic delirium; and if he added also those for whom alcohol was only one of the causes of their troubles, the percentage was 47 (and 20 per cent for women). He saw alcoholism, however, as part of the general problem of hereditary disease, leading to progressive degeneration. He accordingly produced a new nosology of mental illness, which made 'chronic delirium' or 'the delirium of degenerates' into a vast central category. The characteristic of this was that it was progressive: it started with a period of

---

[1] B. A. Morel, médecin en chef de l'Asile des Aliénés de Saint-Yon (Seine-Inf.), *Traité des dégénérescences physiques, intellectuelles et morales de l'espèce humaine et des causes qui produisent ces variétés de maladies* (1857).

incubation, in which only mild symptoms like suspicion, disquiet, preoccupation were visible. The second phase was one of persecution mania, and hallucinations. The third was megalomania and disordered ambition. Finally came 'madness'. This was an easily understandable theory, into which individual cases could easily be made to fit and it acquired considerable popularity. A whole new class of 'degenerates' was thus created. Magnan specified that this could include highly intelligent men, whom he labelled 'superior degenerates', who had 'exuberant imaginations' and 'anomalies in judgement and reflection' combining 'remarkable talents with total lack of certain aptitudes'. Every year he published studies of individual troubles like kleptomania and pyromania, showing the hereditary element in them; he was the first to extend this to sexual perversions, his publications setting off a whole series of research monographs on this subject.[1]

In Magnan's time, the sort of person who might be classified in this way was 'Mademoiselle Lef . . .'. Her father, an intelligent and sober man, had died of pneumonia; her mother had become an alcoholic at the menopause; her brother had died of tuberculosis. She looked after her widowed mother until she was left alone at the age of twenty-eight. She lived in a room by herself and had no social life. At thirty-seven she stopped working in a factory to set up a little business of her own. One of the residents in her block then began to court her; she refused him, and all sorts of troubles followed. The man began spreading rumours that she was the mistress of her former employer; the concierge who 'gossiped all day' repeated these rumours everywhere, embellishing them until she was said to have illegitimate children. She complained to the commissaire de police that she was being slandered. Her obsession with her concierge grew into a persecution mania and she was put into an asylum, protesting her sanity, but developing wild hallucinations as people mocked her. It was up to the doctors to decide when such a person 'whose intelligence seemed intact and who carries out his habitual occupations'

[1] Dr. Paul Sérieux, *V. Magnan, sa vie et son œuvre* (1921); V. Magnan, *Leçons cliniques sur les maladies mentales: le délire chronique* (1890); V. Magnan, *De l'alcoolisme, des diverses formes du délire alcoolique et de leur traitement* (1874); cf. Dr. M. Legrain, *Hérédité et alcoolisme. Étude psychologique et clinique sur les dégénérés buveurs et les familles d'ivrognes* (1889)—case studies by a pupil.

moved from the incubatory to the hallucinatory stage: the decisive factor was often the discovery that he had mad parents, which indicated that there was a disease in germ.[1]

The idea of degeneracy ceased to be so fashionable in the twentieth century, but it still had its adherents. Dupré and Delmas produced a revised version of it under the name of 'constitutional' madness.[2] Kraepelin's dementia praecox was imported from Germany; it carried the implication that hallucinations and delusions were a progressive trouble, leading irreversibly to complete madness; paranoia replaced 'persecution mania' and became a subvariety of dementia praecox. During the First World War, therefore, the psychiatrists found themselves in a difficult position when asked to assess the contribution of the war to the mental troubles suffered by vast numbers of soldiers: they were usually generous, saying that the war was the factor that stimulated madness, even if there were predisposing and hereditary causes of it; but one military psychiatric centre, for example, classified no less than 46 per cent of its patients as 'constitutional psychopaths', 9 per cent as 'organic psychopaths', 11 per cent as neurasthenic, 7 per cent as hysterics; it succeeded in curing about a quarter, it discharged another quarter from the army, it sent a third quarter to convalesce and the rest 'ran away'.[3] These statistics are, of course, ambiguous, for, as two other psychiatrists involved said, 'The whole mental pathology of the modern army is vitiated by the question of alcoholism'.[4]

After the war dementia praecox was often used with great severity in child psychology. Children who misbehaved in various ways were labelled as doomed to madness. The case books of two practitioners in this field contain histories like that of 'André M.', who had been an excellent and normal pupil at the Collège Rollin, until at the age of sixteen he stopped working and insisted on leaving. His father put him into

[1] V. Magnan, Le Délire chronique (1890), 349.

[2] F. Achille-Delmas and Maurice Boll, La Personnalité humaine: son analyse (1922), 40–55; Laignel Lavastine, André Barbé and Delmas, La Pratique psychiatrique à l'usage des étudiants et des praticiens (2nd edition, 1929), 350.

[3] M. A. J. M. Levrault, Étude historique et statistique sur le fonctionnement pendant la guerre du centre de psychiatrie de la 18ᵉ région (Bordeaux medical thesis, 1921). For case studies see Fribourg-Blanc and Gauthier, La Pratique psychiatrique dans l'armée (1935).

[4] A. Porot and A. Hesnard, Psychiatrie de guerre (1919), 49.

commerce, but he gave up that job, for no apparent reason. He was put successively into Félix Potin, the Northern Railway (where his father was chief clerk), the Comptoir d'escompte, but he always left after a few months; he sometimes did not come home for a week, keeping himself by miscellaneous jobs, for example, selling gramophones. Finally in 1926 at the age of nineteen, he refused to work any more. His mother demanded a mental examination, complaining also that he was no longer affectionate to his family. He was put in hospital as a schizophrenic, which was a new development from dementia praecox, advanced by the Swiss Bleuler (1857–1939), whose ideas had been imported into the clinic of professor Claude: this boy was duly sent there.[1] Another rebellious child, 'Aline', the object of a sexual assault at the age of thirteen, became violent, uncontrollable and 'ready to go off with any man who invited her in the street'; she became hostile to her family and complained that her mother was persecuting her. Her doctor diagnosed dementia praecox and she was interned at the age of eighteen. The availability of new diagnoses clearly put a new weapon in the hands of those who would not tolerate the rebelliousness of the young.[2]

The family was thus not simply the pillar of respectability, as moralists claimed, but also a source of anxiety, alcoholism, illness and even madness. Respectability, indeed, was the means by which these difficulties were concealed and the family's dirty linen kept out of public sight. Even if one abandoned the theories of heredity, one was still left with those of environment. It was long recognised that people could suffer all these troubles through the effect of those around them, as a result of demands made on them by those closest to them, and in reaction to parental influence. 'Isolation', or removing nervous patients from their homes, was valued by Esquirol and much used by Charcot. The latter, for example, was once consulted by a Russian Jew, who brought his son, aged thirteen, 'very impressionable and nervous but without any special characteristics', all the way to Paris for treatment. The boy had convulsions every day at five o'clock in the afternoon: the father, who was passionately fond of him, waited

[1] E. Bleuler, *La Schizophrénie* (1926).
[2] Dr. A. Rodiet and Dr. G. Heuyer, *La Folie au 20ᵉ siècle. Étude médico-sociale* (1931), 102, 108.

anxiously for these, watch in hand. Charcot told the father to leave the child alone; he sent him away and after two weeks on his own the child was cured.[1] It was in a development of this tradition that, in 1932, Lacan made a vigorous attack on the family as a source of paranoia: the best condition for its cure was the death of the patient's parents. Lacan argued that there had been too much attention paid to the symptoms of paranoiac crises and not enough to the internal history of the patient's feelings and the influence of his surroundings on him.

'Hallucinations' were now seen as more than a morbid aberration. The poet Paul Valéry said that there was a growing class of people suffering from them—the 'delirious professions': 'I give this name to all those trades whose principal instrument is the opinion that one has of oneself, and whose raw material is the opinion that others have of one. The people who exercise it, vowed to being eternally candidates, are necessarily always afflicted by a certain megalomania which a certain persecution mania ceaselessly crosses and torments.' They were men who wanted to achieve what no one else had done; they both ignored the existence of others and demanded their approval. The writing and teaching professions, said Lacan, were full of paranoia.[2] The progress of civilisation, said the anarchist Charles Albert, was inevitably increasing paranoia, because it exalted self-esteem and the subjective interpretation of social incidents. The reverse side of the sense of personal dignity that democracy cultivated was a greatly increased capacity to be hurt. 'What are today only superficial scratches may tomorrow become profound wounds. A day will come when we shall suffer from the least lack of consideration as cruelly as we now suffer from violent injustice. Social friction is undoubtedly diminishing, but our skin is becoming more delicate.'[3]

If the idea of the individual as a fixed entity, born with definite characteristics, was abandoned, then he became, as Dr. René Laforgue argued in 1941, no longer comparable to a house, built brick by brick, but constantly changing, aban-

[1] *Œuvres complètes de J. M. Charcot*, ed. Babinski (1890), 3. 92–6.
[2] Jacques Lacan, *De la psychose paranoïque dans ses rapports avec la personnalité* (medical thesis, 1932), 282–3.
[3] Quoted from *L'Effort libre* (Jan. 1914) by Paul Schiff, *L'Évolution des idées sur la folie de persécution* (republished from *L'Hygiène mentale*) (1935), 18. Cf. P. Sérieux and J. Capgras, *Les Folies raisonnantes. Le délire d'interprétation* (1909).

doning parts of himself all the time and acquiring new features; and the personality's mobility exposed it to far greater strains of adaptation. Success in a competitive society was no guarantee of serenity. Laforgue quoted examples of patients who came complaining that they could not stand the strain of success.[1] Even the much-lauded virtue of thrift, that basis of social ascension and so the basis of French society, was seen as a cause of 'incurable morbidity'. The Frenchman, wrote the author of a monograph on the psychology of avarice, was peculiarly subject to this pathological exaltation of thrift; 'he is haunted by the spectre of ruin because in our old country ruin is terrible, much more terrible than in a new country like America . . . He who falls is pitilessly stepped on and crushed . . . In France, ruin is shame, social excommunication . . .'[2] The asylums contained many people who could not bear the burden of having transgressed the rules of society, and outside them melancholics, suffering from remorse, must have easily outnumbered the convicts in prisons who had had the misfortune to be caught. Case histories of the disastrous effects of commercial failure could easily be multiplied, and of marital failures also. 'Mme Pauline Ta . . .', a baker's wife, aged thirty-seven, admitted into an asylum in 1893, was typical: she had two daughters and was perfectly healthy until she committed adultery with her brother-in-law. Her remorse made her spend whole days crying, exhausted, hearing voices telling her that she would burn in hell, feeling that everybody knew and was watching her. She finally confessed to her husband, who forgave her, and to all her neighbours; but 'seeing that she was ill', he took her to the asylum to recover.[3]

For much of the nineteenth century, anxiety and melancholy were characteristics one was born with; they were a sign of one's temperament or of one's ancestry. The explanation of their origin corresponded fairly accurately to the attitude that conservatives had towards the social status they occupied, which was generally seen as inevitably unequal: only exceptional individual effort and outstanding moral qualities could change things. But this was too pessimistic for many people, and so, as

[1] R. Laforgue, *Psychopathologie de l'échec* (1941).
[2] J. Rogues de Fursac, *L'Avarice. Essai de psychologie morbide* (1911), 144-5.
[3] J. Roubinovitch and Édouard Toulouse, *La Mélancolie* (1897), 269.

an alternative to neurosis and degeneration, there appeared neurasthenia. This was an American import, though it effectively only systematised ideas that had been in the air in Europe for a long time. The word was invented (or rather launched) in 1869 by Dr. George M. Beard of New York, to describe what he called the most frequent, most interesting and most neglected nervous disease of modern times. Neurasthenia meant nervous exhaustion. 'If a patient complains of general malaise, debility of all the functions, poor appetite, abiding weakness in the back and spine, fugitive neuralgic pains, hysteria, insomnia, hypochondriasis, disinclination for consecutive manual labor, severe and weakening attacks of sick headache, and other analogous symptoms, and at the same time gives no evidence of anaemia or any organic disease, we have reason to suspect . . . that we are dealing with a typical case of neurasthenia.' Beard believed he had discovered a peculiarly American disease, produced by the stresses of modern life. Freud later identified this American peculiarity as the 'undue suppression of sexual life'. But the success of the idea in Europe can be seen from the fact that by 1894 a bibliography of neurasthenia ran to no fewer than fourteen pages; and though Beard's *Nervous Exhaustion* was translated into French only in 1895, there had already been several books on it dating from 1881.[1] The other American influence was that of Silas Weir Mitchell (1829–1914), the inventor of the 'rest cure', whose highly acceptable answer to what he called the inability or the indisposition of Americans to play, was a series of fashionable homes where women patients in particular were put in bed, forbidden movement of any kind, massaged in order to avoid atrophy, overfed with copious meals, so that their weight was raised by as much as fifty or even seventy pounds in six weeks.[2]

---

[1] Significantly Beard's work was translated under the title *La Neurasthénie sexuelle* (1895). Cf. his *Stimulants and Narcotics, medically, philosophically and morally considered* (New York, 1871). Dr. Léon Bouveret, *La Neurasthénie, épuisement nerveux* (1890); Dr. F. Levillain, *La Neurasthénie* (1891); id., *Neurasthénie et arthritisme* (1893); *Essais de neurologie clinique: neurasthénie de Beard et états neurasthéniformes* (1896).

[2] S. W. Mitchell, *Wear and Tear* (1871); *Fat and Blood* (1877); *The Nervous System especially of Women* (1871). Cf. J. K. Hall, *One Hundred Years of American Psychiatry* (1944), 213. Weir Mitchell is only the most famous of the advocates of the rest cure, partly because of his literary talents: he also wrote poetry and novels. Others involved were Samuel J. Jackson and Playfair.

In France neurasthenia was popularised, among others, by two Paris professors, G. Ballet and A. Proust, the father of the novelist.[1] What is striking about their work, undertaken at the turn of the century, is that it shows their patients complaining about those very same things that Balzac had inveighed against, but which were now dignified as causes of neurasthenia. Many patients attributed the vague but distressing physical symptoms described by Beard, to intellectual overwork. Parents worried about the dangerous effects of the long hours of homework done by the pupils at *lycées*. They quoted a German investigator who found that 30 per cent of a sample of 588 middle-class secondary schoolboys had neurasthenic symptoms such as languor, sadness, paleness, palpitation, headaches and sleepiness but also insomnia; the proportion was only 8 per cent in the junior classes but 89 per cent in the top class. Dr. Proust denied that hard work could do anyone any harm: a few days' rest could put any ill effects right: it was rather the poor hygienic conditions in boarding-schools, lack of fresh air, no physical exercise and the habit of masturbation which caused the trouble.

But many adults complained of the same symptoms. Dr. Proust, echoing the general consensus, blamed the competitiveness of life, and 'moral preoccupations, more common and above all felt more deeply in certain social classes'. This meant 'the fear of failure', and worry about one's profession and about passing examinations. Social life 'which left little leisure for rest and for the calm and comforting distractions of the home', overcopious meals, overheated rooms, staying up too late, inadequate and irregular sleep, intoxication, 'the preoccupation with the search for pleasure and the satisfaction of the least elevated and least noble desires'—all this weakened the nerves; and what finally knocked people out was 'the vexations of pride resulting from the inability to realise the fantasies of vanity', and moral (rather than intellectual) overwork, caused by sorrows, disappointments, remorse, anxiety, 'depressive passions'. There were two main types of neurasthenic: the one who complained of headaches, stomach pains and indeed pains everywhere, lamenting that he was tired,

---

[1] Dr. Robert Le Masle, *Le Professeur Adrien Proust 1834–1903* (1936) is a biography, which however makes no mention of this.

weak and could no longer do any work, but who could not give very precise details; and the one who looked perfectly healthy and active, and who gave a fluent account of his troubles, insisting that the doctor should pay attention to every one of them, to the point even of bringing a written list of them with him. Three-quarters complained of headaches— not so much of pain, however, as of pressure, fullness, constriction, what Charcot called the 'neurasthenic hat'. Tiredness when waking up in the morning was also a frequent symptom, as well as 'cerebral depression', weakening of the will, loss of concentration. A few had 'genital neurasthenia', but they were 'degenerates', suffering from congenital debilities, exacerbated by masturbation and sometimes excessive sexual intercourse. 'It is clear', said Dr. Proust dismissively, 'that organic lesions and functional troubles of the genital organs have no specific action on the nervous centres', though he added that very little was known about the chemistry of the nerves. Nevertheless, the cure for neurasthenics was self-evident: it required the strengthening of the physique, by means of exercise. French schools were not even capable of supplying this in their gymnastics classes, because their exercises were too complicated and produced nervous exhaustion: they required pupils to use their heads too much. Old-fashioned French games like ball and leapfrog, and skipping for girls, were best. Then what these people needed was confidence: they should be encouraged and praised in public, and criticised very gently and tactfully; they should be given only tasks within their capacities. Most neurasthenics had inherited 'excessive emotivity': this must be fought, for example, by avoiding telling children terrifying or fantastic stories. Most children, who were troubled profoundly by the awakening of sexual desire, masturbated in an exaggerated way and were frequently nervously exhausted by this. Their attention should be turned away from sex. The very ideals of life, however, needed to be altered if neurasthenia was to be diminished. The businessman thought only of money; work had been turned into an end in itself. War had been replaced by equally exhausting obsessions. 'It is time to move on to the gospel of relaxation.' The strains in life, according to Dr. Proust, came between the ages of twenty and fifty. Occasionally he had seen a 'precocious neurasthenic', usually an adolescent boy who had grown too tall too quickly and who was therefore excessively fragile, 'yielding to the least shock'. Men suffered more than women from neurasthenia, because they had more pressure on them at work; but 40 per cent of them had some hereditary predisposition to it. He had seen little neurasthenia among the working class, which was perhaps explained by the kind of clientele he had, though he attributed it to their not having to use their brains.[1]

But a country doctor in the west of France, in a work published in 1906, reporting on sixteen years of practice, challenged this view. Formerly, he said, it had been thought that neurasthenia was an exclusively urban phenomenon, produced by too many parties, theatres etc., while the peasant was supposed to be satisfied with the little he had. Dr. Terrien claimed that on the contrary there was probably more mental trouble among the peasants than in the towns. For one thing, the peasant normally drank five or six litres of wine a day, and when he got drunk he made love—most conceptions were the result of drunkenness; for another, the peasant was superstitious, his children were overexcited by terrifying stories and sorcery was a constant worry; and not least, peasants were more liable to contract consanguine marriages. 'Psychoneurosis', far from diminishing, was increasing noticeably among the peasants, but it took on different forms. The men were generally hysterical when they were troubled, while the women were neurasthenic. This was because the men normally left it to the women to worry. The peasants had the same symptoms as the townsmen, but they consulted a wider variety of people to cure them, sorcerers as well as doctors. They were terrified of incurability, of death and of madness, as, of course, the townsmen were too. Dr. Terrien published some fifty case studies showing how different forms of anxiety stopped the peasants working and drove them to despair as deep as that of the most refined intellectuals.[2]

It was easy to draw facile conclusions about nervous exhaustion being related to a decadent civilisation; the epidemic of it in America was quoted against this to show that a young nation could suffer from it as well as a satiated one like

[1] A. Proust and G. Ballet, *L'Hygiène du neurasthénique* (1897).
[2] Dr. Terrien, *L'Hystérie et la neurasthénie chez le paysan* (Angers, 1906).

France. The reasons why the theory appealed to doctors were not above suspicion: just as they had at the beginning of the century replaced the chaining of lunatics by incarcerating them in asylums, so at the end of it they completed the abolition of strait jackets by keeping their patients constantly motionless in bed, on the ground that they must have complete rest. Dubois of Berne attacked this, saying that these patients were not really tired, or at least that there was no exhaustion of their nervous system; what was at fault was their defective up-bringing; self-control was the answer.[1] His view received a certain amount of support and some people argued that these complaints of tiredness should be ignored, that such people thought too much about themselves.[2] A. Deschamps, in his *Energy Illnesses*, tried to reconcile the opposing views by saying that some really were tired, while the others were obsessed by being tired, and he built up a whole new collection of illnesses for which rest was the cure.[3] But the psychiatrist who examined this subject in the most detailed way was Pierre Janet (1859–1947), one of the most brilliant students of mental troubles in this period, a remarkably fluent and productive writer also, and for a time France's alternative to Freud. He deserves to be better known.

Fear, Tension and Exhaustion

The richness of Janet's view of human character and anxiety came from a combination of several distinct interests. He was trained as a philosopher and was the nephew of Paul Janet, professor of philosophy at the Sorbonne. His uncle was more a moralist than a metaphysician and encouraged him to study medicine at the same time: he got his colleague Dastre, the professor of physiology at the Sorbonne, to admit him into his laboratory. Pierre Janet, at the age of eighteen, was deeply religious, and indeed said that he always retained his mystical tendencies though he 'succeeded in controlling them'. He was also always fond of the natural sciences, especially botany, and his herbarium, which he increased every year, was a

[1] Dr. Paul Dubois, Professor of Neuropathology at Berne, *Self Control and how to achieve it* (*L'Éducation de soi-même*) (New York, 1910).

[2] Déjérine and Gankler, *Les Psychoneuroses* (1911).

[3] Cf. Dr. P. E. Lévy, *L'Éducation rationnelle de la volonté* (1898, 12th ed. 1925.)

passionate hobby all his life: it was from this interest, he said, that he acquired his love of dissection, precise observation and classification, which found their expression in his very detailed medical case histories. It was his desire to resolve the conflict between religion and science that led him to specialise in psychology, which was then still a branch of philosophy. When he was appointed the philosophy teacher at the *lycée* of Le Havre at the age of twenty-two, he undertook a thesis on hallucination. In due course, he went to work with Charcot and wrote a treatise on hysteria, stressing in particular the mental aspects of it, for he believed that Charcot was too much of a physiologist. Janet became interested in the role of suggestion and auto-suggestion in hysteria and formed a preliminary theory that suggestibility was the result of the weakening of the individual's functions of resistance and synthesis. This led him to study the causes of this weakening, which became the central area of his research. One factor he stressed at first was trauma, the influence of one or more events in a person's past life which had produced a violent emotion and so had absorbed a great deal of energy. He moved on to study various other depressive neuroses, phobias, obsessions, which had hitherto been described independently: he sought to discover what was common to them.[1] He gave the name of *psychasthenia* to a broad range of neuroses characterised by feelings of inadequacy or of emptiness, which he saw at the root of them. These feelings could be explained by exhaustion, whose mechanism he now described in a theory of psychological energy and tension.

Janet's theory owed a good deal to his also being a philosopher. He drew his inspiration from what used to be known as 'functional psychology', which was a revival and expansion of 'faculty psychology'. In the early nineteenth century the philosopher Maine de Biran had put forward a theory of the ego as one force, and passive functions as another, capable of operating independently of the ego. Maine de Biran's friend, Dr. A. A. Royer-Collard (brother of the politician) wrote an article on him in volume 2 of the *Annales médico-psychologiques*, which introduced his influence into medicine. Jouffroy, another philosopher, had developed Maine de Biran's views into a

[1] Autobiography in Carl Murchison, *A History of Psychology in Autobiography* (Worcester, Mass., 1930), I. 123–33.

theory that man had a number of faculties or capacities, that his aim should be to exploit the energies in them, but draining the lower tendencies for the benefit of the higher ones. Janet acknowledged his indebtedness to these thinkers in his theory that mental life had two aspects—the automatic, self-preserving one, and the synthesising and creative one. A weakening in the latter allowed the former to gain the upper hand and so made mental illness possible. Hysterics were prime examples of people who failed to achieve a synthesis of their thoughts and acts; but the split between the automatic and the synthetic was more commonly apparent in dreams. Janet, however, broke away from a number of psychological schools which were more fashionable in his day, like those of Wundt (1832–1920) who sought to discover a chemistry of the mind, and who significantly also talked in terms of a 'creative synthesis' being established among the atoms: in the U.S.A., E. B. Titchener (1867–1927) gave a version of this theory the name of 'structuralism'. Janet was also a heretical rebel against Charcot, whose attempts to find anatomical localisations for nervous troubles he considered off the point. He criticised psychology for having reacted in too extreme a fashion against the charge that it was metaphysics: it had therefore tried to turn itself into physiology; but Janet insisted it must study behaviour; he welcomed the new tendency towards this shown by William James, Baldwin and Bergson, though he rejected J. B. Watson's behaviourism as being concerned simply with external acts, to the neglect of beliefs and thought processes.

Janet's methods can be seen from the case of Marie, a girl who was blind in one eye. Janet got Marie, under hypnosis, to relive her experiences at the age of six when she had gone blind. She had then had to sleep with a child who had eczema on the left side of its face; Marie had developed a similar rash and had gone blind in her left eye. Janet cured her by suggesting to her, under hypnosis, as she relived this event, that the child next to her was healthy; he got her to stroke the child without fear and all the symptoms of the illness then disappeared. Janet aimed to change feelings by suggestion: he offered not abreaction therapy, but integration therapy, getting his patients to incorporate vague memories into the continuity of their personality. He was more interested in the will than in the unconscious. Personality was for him 'a work that we carry out socially to distinguish ourselves one from the other, and in order to assume a role more or less distinct from that of our neighbours'. The idea goes back to Maine de Biran who had had to wage an exhausting battle to overcome his own apathy and depression, and who had seen will-power as the very essence of the ego. Janet refined this, distinguishing energy and tension. He divided activity into nine hierarchically ordered states, rising from the automatic reflex to higher ones in which experience was put to use, finally reaching the creative stage. Energy was needed to produce these activities and to move from the more elementary to the higher levels, but the curing of exhaustion was by itself not enough. The more elevated or complicated an act was, the more energy it required. But in addition 'tension'—or moral energy—was needed to co-ordinate the whole personality.[1] What handicapped most people was not tiredness so much as the inability to rest. Thus trouble often started around the age of twelve to fourteen, and the majority of neuroses began between seventeen and nineteen, usually unnoticed, but explained by the fact that moving into adulthood involved great outlays of physical effort and also enormous moral adaptations. Suddenly all the problems of life—love, work, social relations, religion—were posed simultaneously and the efforts to solve them could easily cause 'fear of life'. Then making friends, passing examinations, could easily increase timidity; even holidays could worsen this, because they involved readaptation, as also did travel. 'Professional occupations are such an evident cause of mental troubles that a special class of professional psychoses have often been admitted.' Women had additional worries from the running of their households and could go into deep depressions when faced with having to order a menu or choose a servant. 'Family life, the reciprocal adaptation of people who live together in the same house' could also be a very important cause of stress.

The importance of Janet's theory was that it tried to explain not only madness and extreme mental collapse, but the strains of everyday life. Accordingly, in the case histories of his

[1] Björn Sjövall, *Psychology of Tension. An Analysis of Pierre Janet's concept of 'tension psychologique' together with an historical aspect* (Stockholm, 1967).

patients, one can see how this strain affected ordinary people. Janet did not try to divide them into distinct categories, because he said 'mental illnesses in our day are not means of classifying illnesses, but stratagems to distinguish the rival psychiatric schools'.[1] At the root of all the different types of melancholy and depression he saw fear, of one kind or another: fear was the word he heard most frequently. Some feared death itself, and were tormented by obsessions which always involved catastrophe. Above all, many worried about the need to act, to take decisions. Some therefore did the opposite of what was expected of them. 'Hermine', a woman of forty, depressed by the death of her two sons in the 1914–18 war, sought consolation in religion and in charitable work, but felt strangely drawn to committing immoral acts: when she prayed at the tomb of her son, she felt she was undressing him; she came to Janet demanding to be watched in order to avoid committing a scandal. 'José' loved his mother but also wanted to kick her and 'this idea', he said, 'makes me mad'. Freud's theory was that it was repressed desire that produced anxiety. Durkheim, giving a sociological interpretation, argued that 'anomie', lack of integration in society, found its extreme expression in suicide. Janet, on the contrary, saw suicide as the expression of the fear of action: to die was a way of stopping action, of getting people to behave towards one as they behave towards the dead. Depression was therefore the opposite of resignation; it was egoism of a special kind, carrying personal defence to extremes. It came naturally with physical weakness, produced by hard work or emotional stress; and it could persist in the way that infectious diseases sometimes continued long after the disappearance of the microbe responsible. It was associated with a feeling of inadequacy or emptiness. The problem therefore was to recover enough energy to overcome this, so as to be able to cope with reality. A whole variety of obsessions concealed this problem, often in the most roundabout way. Janet quoted many cases of people who came to him obsessed that they were too fat or too thin, that they blushed, that they were ugly, that they got writer's cramp. Many women worried about the possibility that they might kill their children, young girls

[1] P. Janet, *De l'angoisse à l'extase. Études sur les croyances et les sentiments* (1928), 2. 302.

had visions of male sexual organs, or felt pushed by Satan to masturbate when preparing for the confession, 'to stop me being saved'. Boys of fifteen ran away from home and travelled aimlessly around the country, hesitating to break completely, however, writing to friends for advice and ultimately returning shamefacedly when they had no money left. 'Byl', a girl of twenty-one, had long refused to go out, being obsessed with the thought that she was ugly. Suddenly she married her gardener, to the horror of her parents, stopped washing her hands in order to place herself on the same level as him, finding expression at last for her self-hate. Ambition, apparently so prevalent in society, found its counterpart in shame: while politicians praised individualism, people worried about every oddity in their appearance, about how they walked, how they stood; while moralists urged virtuous living, virtuous people imagined the most wicked things they could think of. It was often a sense of inadequacy that led people to be conscientious to the utmost limits; precisely because they felt they always did things badly, they forced themselves to read books to the very end, to do homework with great care, and ambition sometimes had its source in this.

Some patients talked of fear; others of anxiety or disquiet, lack of security; others of timidity. Timidity attracted much attention,[1] and doctors heard a lot about it from people seeking reassurance at all hours of the day, or searching for guidance and direction. Wives complained that their husbands did not understand them, and sometimes gave themselves up to lovers who were intellectually their inferiors, but who satisfied their desire to be dominated; some men were so timid that they never spoke to their servants except through the intermediary of their wives, for fear of not being obeyed. One housewife, 'Qi', aged thirty-five, who was obsessed by a desire to cut her hair, to wear it loose, to be called by her pet name Nanette, lamented: 'A child is loved for its pranks, for its good little heart, for its prettiness, and what is it asked for in return? To love you, nothing else. I like that, but I cannot tell that to my husband; he would not understand me. I would like to be a child again, to have a father or mother who would hold me

[1] See a review in L. Dugas, *La Timidité, étude psychologique et morale* (7th edition, 1921).

on their knees, who would caress my hair . . . but no, I am
Madame, mother of a family, I must look after my home, be
serious, think all on my own. Oh what a life!' Inability to
adapt themselves to the real world made some quite similar
people become highly authoritarian, which was just another
way of avoiding having clashes with others, obtaining sub-
missiveness instead of offering it. Janet believed that these
feelings of inadequacy were partly hereditary and partly the
result of early education, which involved humiliations and
frustrations, instilled fear of vices like laziness, stimulated
self-deprecation and a demand for love and direction, but also
partly the result of 'genital auto-intoxication', because three-
quarters of these neuroses started in puberty. 'Nothing was
more common than genital phobias,' said Janet: 'they often play
an important role in people's lives, to the great distress particularly of young couples.'

The most interesting of Janet's cases are those of people
who went about their daily lives in what was apparently a
normal way, and only their close relatives or their doctor knew
of the terrors that tormented them. Thus one could have taken a
cab in Paris driven by 'Gaq', aged thirty-four, who seemed full
of confidence taking his fares to all parts of the city, but who,
once out of his driving seat, was a terrified pedestrian, refusing
to cross roads and clinging to the walls. His father had been
an alcoholic who died in delirium. 'Gaq' had always been
timid, but two events had brought him down: first he had
fallen in the street once when he was drunk, and then his fian-
cée had died shortly before their wedding day. His confidence
disappeared at home, though he could still do his job. 'Bal',
likewise, was a primary-school teacher, but one who worried
endlessly about her work, and increasingly not just about the
morrow or the day after, but even about her husband's health
in ten years' time. She worried about religion and death;
she lost her faith and that made her worry more. She came to
see her doctor, however, only because of stomach pains, which
alternated with her worries and distracted her from them.
People indeed worried when they did not worry. Thus 'Af', a
man of twenty-eight, had always suffered from tiredness,
indigestion, insomnia and headaches and was indeed a typical
neurasthenic; but his really serious troubles started on a day

when a neighbour's wife was killed by her husband, who then committed suicide. 'Af' was the first to find the bodies; he was totally unaffected by the sight; he reported it to the concierge and spent the rest of the day without giving it another thought. But the following morning he read in the *Petit Journal* an extremely vivid account of the crime, in which the anguish of the couple and their appalling wounds were described in highly dramatic style. 'Af' was deeply moved, and horrified that he had been unable to notice anything appalling in the sight itself. This was a typical situation, said Janet. He was one of those who were much more moved by literature and art than by real life. There were women, for example, who never cried in real life, but poured out tears in the theatre: the ablest of them became writers, because they found fiction easier to feel about: real life was too complicated.

Just how many difficulties a simple life could present, and how frightening its ordinary accidents could be, may be seen from the case of 'Ku', aged thirty-seven, of peasant stock and the daughter of an authoritarian and demanding mother. 'Ku' since childhood had had a craving for affection; she used to do everything she could to win a smile; she was always amiable, hated offending people, and was deeply hurt if her friendliness was not reciprocated. When she was criticised by the local park-keeper for allowing her dog to walk on the flower-beds, she made her husband move house rather than chance meeting the park-keeper again. She had a terror of conflict, typical, said Janet, of a class of people who sought situations where everything could be foreseen, where there were never any crises—which they sought to avoid, alternatively by being authoritarian or by being nice and humble. 'Ku' managed in her new house for eighteen months, until another event ruined her life. A young student living across the road was arrested for 'outraging decency, having performed an improper pantomime from his window'. He summoned all his neighbours to his trial to attest the innocence of his gestures. A policeman came to see 'Ku', when, as it happened, her husband was out. She was deeply distressed, did not know what to say, but murmured that she had seen nothing reprehensible. As a result the prosecution was abandoned. But the incident tormented her ever after, because she could not decide whether to reveal the visit of the

policeman to her husband; if she admitted that she had defended the young man, would not her husband think she was
in league with him? Perhaps, indeed, she was in love with the
student: she got worried every time she saw a round hat and
a brown overcoat in the street, such as he wore. The neighbours
would certainly become hostile to her if her feelings were
known; her husband would abandon her: how could she per-
suade him to move again, this time perhaps to America?
After three months of silence, the poor woman confessed
all to her husband, to her concierge and her neighbours: she
was hypnotised, injected with morphine and finally carried
away to hospital—an extreme illustration of a probably not
uncommon situation.

One of Janet's most prized cases was called 'Jean'; he
combined in himself almost every symptom of a 'psychasthenic'.
He was aged thirty-two in 1903 and was described as the son of
a very distinguished man: one is tempted to guess his identity.
Jean was said to have always been timid, so that at eighteen he
was still taken to his *lycée* and brought back by a servant. He
used to be paralysed by the least difficulty. He attributed all
his troubles to his having masturbated from the age of fifteen,
which on one occasion led to a terrifying experience, when
ejaculation was accompanied by the feeling that he was going to
die. At nineteen he amazed his confessor by revealing his
complete ignorance of the facts of sex: he was taught some
elementary ones, but these tempted him instead of reassuring
him and all sorts of obsessions, manias and allergies followed.
Every action worried him because of the prospect that it might
lead to disease: he refused to read out a few lines from a book
for Janet, saying it might make him catch meningitis. He was
obsessed by his childhood maid, who produced erotic sensations
in him; he was a hypochondriac; he measured the temperature
of the water he used, counted his heartbeats, had a mania for
precision, and an astonishing memory for figures and dates.
His most remarkable characteristic was an extraordinary habit
of associating ideas in a most complicated way, as when he said
that he had a pain in his stomach because (1) he ate bread
(2) which came from the baker (3) who was recommended
to his mother by a gentleman (4) whose wife died (5) on
the anniversary of the day (6) on which his obsession

relative to his maid began. He was able to analyse his troubles with great finesse, but every action involved endless preparation, forethought and hesitation. Janet said it would take a whole year to recount all his symptoms. The odd thing is that this man Jean was exactly the same age as Marcel Proust —there is a strange similarity between them.[1]

Janet's solution for exhaustion was to tell his patients to pull themselves together. He did not do this directly, and used infinite tact and much imagination to bring it about, but ultimately he was in the tradition of the moralists who thought that it was up to the individual to master himself by the exercise of will. The difference was that he did not use moral injunctions but treated the will almost as a machine, with the psychiatrist discovering why it was not functioning properly, which parts were damaged and how its activity could be restored. It was in this sense that he called his method analytical psychology, which aimed at discovering what behavioural traits distinguished one individual from another. Freud was to distinguish his method by turning the label round into psychoanalysis.[2] Janet's analysis was directed not to freeing his patients from their past, but to getting them to admit it as part of their experience and to work out an acceptable personality by means that were ultimately rational. He admitted that he studied the abnormal only because it was easier: 'nothing is more complicated', he said, 'than a normal man'.[3] His ideas were to be developed—in combination with those of others—by Jean-Paul Sartre, who stressed the role of the will even more, claiming not only that emotional behaviour was an organised system, but that the passions which composed it were not involuntary. To will to love and to love were one and the same thing. Emotion became with Sartre conscious self-deception.[4] It thus becomes very much the concern of the historian.

[1] P. Janet, *Les Obsessions et la psychasthénie* (1903), 2. 341–51, and *passim*.

[2] Carl Murchison, *Psychologies of 1930* (Worcester, Mass., 1930) contains an article by Janet on his 'analytical psychology'.

[3] For a popularisation of 'will therapy', see Dr. E. Toulouse, *Comment former un esprit* (1908); for a traditional Catholic version, A. Chaillot, *Leçons pratiques de psychologie et de logique spécialement rédigées pour les pensionnats de demoiselles* (1867), 55–6; cf. G. Villey-Desméserets, *Contribution à l'étude des doctrines en médecine mentale* (Paris medical thesis, 1924).

[4] Joseph P. Fell, *Emotion in the Thought of Sartre* (New York, 1965).

Boredom

The strains of living were compounded under the influence of fashion. The spread of education itself, while producing unlimited optimism amongst some, probably the majority, also stimulated the deepest gloom in those who claimed the greatest refinement of taste. Numerous writers described the nineteenth century as the age of *ennui*; 'the sadness of modern times' was deplored by the Goncourt brothers; Paul Bourget defined 'modern man as an animal who is miserable'; Baudelaire, whose poem *Spleen* was to strike chords of sympathy in many successive generations, summarised his outlook (1857) as 'an immense discouragement, an insupportable sensation of isolation, a perpetual fear of a vague misfortune, a complete lack of confidence in my abilities, a total absence of desires, an impossibility of finding an amusement of any kind'.[1] Barbey d'Aurevilly wrote: 'I believe that tiredness and unhappiness decide almost everything in the lives of men.' Melancholy was known as the English malady in the seventeenth century: French writers used a foreign vocabulary to describe it: *morbidezze, schwärmerisch* and above all spleen. Diderot in 1760 had talked of '*le spleen* or the English vapours' and in 1844 the *Encyclopedia of Men of the World* defined spleen as 'formerly little known in France but now spreading only too much amongst us—a morbid affection . . . originating from 'foggy England', characterised by 'a profound disgust for life, a continual sadness and an incurable apathy which, little by little, leads to despair and often ends with suicide'.

The romantics made *ennui* a fashionable literary pose among many of those who read their works. Flaubert, in his *Dictionary of Received Ideas*, defined it as a sign of 'distinction of the heart and elevation of the spirit'.[2] It degenerated at its extremes into what Baudelaire called 'the stupid melancholy of young women'. In the founders of the cult, it had highly complicated origins; it was produced partly by family troubles, and several romantics claimed they had inherited it from their mothers, but it was cherished also as a divine gift which could be turned to

---

[1] C. Baudelaire, *Œuvres complètes. Correspondance générale*, ed. J. Crepet (1947), 2. 108.

[2] *Dictionnaire des idées reçues* (1881), s.v. Mélancolie.

aesthetic ends and it was accepted as a kind of martyrdom. Chateaubriand interpreted it as the result of being over- whelmed by the distance that separated his hopes and what life in fact offered, but it was more than frustrated hope, for he and his successors, led by Sainte-Beuve, added to this feeling introspection and self-analysis. Melancholy could thus turn into self-obsession; and it came to be valued as a form of spiri- tual life, a rejection of materialism. It did not necessarily imply self-hate, though it sometimes involved it. But the end result of this literary fashion was that suffering was adopted as a way of life, even when it was simultaneously idealised and ridiculed (as it was, for example, by Flaubert).

One needs to distinguish between this elitist cult, which later found a philosophical justification in Schopenhauer and fitted in with a whole tradition of decadence, and forms of *ennui* which verged on boredom, and were the mark of people who had too much time on their hands. The development of activities to fill the growing amount of leisure was of course not simply an expression of *joie de vivre*.[1] On the contrary, the frenzy with which they were pursued was seen as a sign of deeper dissatisfactions. Lamartine had complained during the July Monarchy that 'France is getting bored'; and quite apart from the aesthetes, there were more and more people who talked of being bored, in a less sophisticated way than they. 'Sunday boredom', for example, was one of the most painful discoveries of the nineteenth century. A magazine short story published in 1861 begins: 'It was Sunday, the feast day of spleen in Paris . . . It was Sunday and it was raining torren- tially.' Alphonse Daudet complained of 'that terrible day of rest of these poor people'. The upper classes, who had most resources to combat boredom, probably suffered most: as a gossip writer of the *salons* wrote in 1866: 'Paris, and especially the Faubourg Saint-Germain, has a host of bored people who seek out every means of spending their evenings at parties, for bore- dom shared seems easier to bear than solitary boredom.'[2] In 1855 a *Revue anecdotique* was founded, designed, as its prospectus announced, to act as 'a specific against boredom and spleen'. In the sixteenth century, Rabelais used the word

---

[1] See Zeldin, *Taste and Corruption*, ch. 6.
[2] Mme Ancelot, *Un Salon de Paris, 1824 à 1864* (1866), 239.

ennui to mean simply loneliness: in the nineteenth century this timeless feeling might well have been sharper, but it was certainly expanded. There was thus the loneliness and boredom of provincial life, which became an object of increasing ridicule with the growth of towns. Not that towns diminished boredom, for the loneliness of towns was another complaint: the distractions they offered stimulated the need for yet more distraction. Artists interpreted the mania for money-making as a sign of boredom, as well as being boring in itself; the enthusiasm for progress was seen as the product of dissatisfaction with the present, of vulgar American materialism and loss of religious faith. Renan, the ambiguous apostle of scientific progress, warned that 'improvements in the mechanical arts can go hand in hand with a great moral and intellectual depression'.[1] Maxime Du Camp decried photography as marking the triumph of boredom over art. Flaubert enjoyed himself chronicling the absurdities into which frustration and an incoherent search for novelty led the soulless partisans of good causes, the 'fetid mediocracy' with its 'utilitarian poetry' and its 'economic vomit'.

Too much credence should not be given to the accusations that France was losing the capacity to enjoy itself. What is more significant is the repetitiveness with which every generation marvelled uncomprehendingly at the way its successors chose to seek out amusement. The Goncourt brothers claimed that 'the great pleasures of the masses are collective joys. As the individual rises from the masses and distinguishes himself from them, he has a greater need of pleasures which are personal and made for himself alone.' This was to make education and social mobility factors which vastly complicated the problem of enjoyment. It is certainly possible that they brought pressures to bear which altered the character of laughter. Zola declared: 'It is not thus that people used to laugh, when they could still laugh. Today, joy is a spasm, gaiety is a form of madness that knocks one down.' The Goncourts claimed indeed that the coldness of youth was the peculiar mark of the second half of the nineteenth century; good old-fashioned joviality was disappearing. A newspaper, writing on 'the young men of today' in

[1] E. Renan, *Œuvres complètes* (1948), 2. 249, article on 'La Poésie de l'Exposition' first published in the *Journal des Débats*, 27 Nov. 1855.

1859, castigated them for being too serious, sententious, 'scholarship boys'. The condemnation of the scientists as bores does not
mean that they were bored, but it did mean that radically
different notions about what was interesting were developing,
and people had increasing trouble in finding congenial companions.[1]

Hysteria

The way people reacted to these strains varied with time.
One of the most interesting was hysterical behaviour. This, of
course, is a disease as old as man, but France in this period
has a significant place in its history. To see this, one must
look at the work of Charcot, who is, besides, interesting for
several other reasons.

J. M. Charcot (1825–93) was not only one of the dominating
figures of French medicine in the early Third Republic but also
one of the most influential men of his time, because of the new
attitudes to behaviour that he popularised. He was a product
of the petite bourgeoisie of Paris: his father was a coach builder
and his brother took over the family business; he himself married
the daughter of Laurent Richard, a well-known tailor. He was
adopted first by the Bonapartists, when Achille Fould, the
banker and finance minister, made him his family doctor, and
then by the republicans, when Gambetta had a special chair
created for him in the diseases of the nervous system. Charcot
came to be a consultant to royalty from all over the world, and
his lectures to his medical students were regularly invaded by
writers, actors, journalists and fashionable society in general.
Charcot's performances were almost theatrical, not because
he was a great orator, but because of his immense stress on the
visual effect of his lectures on his audience. He wrote out his
lectures in full but then memorised them, and devoted his
energy to getting the best effect from the patients he exhibited:
he would go from one to the other showing how they all suffered from the same disease, pointing out unexpected similari-
ties in posture, gait, deformity and clinical manifestations. He
was one of the first to use projection equipment in medical
lectures; he employed photographers and artists to make a

[1] Guy Sagnes, *L'Ennui dans la littérature française de Flaubert à Laforgue, 1848–1884*
(1969).

record of his patients, and to produce some remarkable portrait studies of behaviour in distress and anxiety, which deserve to be better known as a grim analysis of his generation.[1] Charcot was, as Freud said, above all a man with a visual sense. He was indeed an artist in his spare time, painting mainly on porcelain and enamel, and also sketching and doing carica-tures. He travelled throughout Europe to look at pictures, but his enthusiasms, which started with ancient Greece and came down to Flemish and Dutch painting, seem to have stopped short with Delacroix: he had no interest in the Impressionists. He published a book on *Demoniacs in Art*, with numerous illustrations of epileptics, ecstatics, and other 'possessed' people taken from all centuries, to prove that 'hysteria is in no way, as some claim, a sickness typical of our century'. One of his assistants who did the drawings for his lectures, was simul-taneously professor of creative anatomy at the School of Fine Arts as well as being a member of the Academy of Medicine. But Charcot considered himself not so much an artist as a seer. He was a generally silent man, who seemed shy of human contact and disdained banal expressions of politeness; by contrast, he had a passionate affection for animals, to whom he talked and whom he caressed freely; at table he would play with his pet monkey or with his many dogs. He was a great enemy of fox-hunting and vivisection. He refused invitations to the theatre or to dinner, though he occasionally went to the circus. He hardly ever took any physical exercise. His socia-bility expressed itself only at the dinner and reception he held at home on Tuesdays, when he held court to admiring visitors and amazed them with the brilliance of his conversation. His house was furnished in medieval and Renaissance style; his study was dark, with stained-glass windows. It was here that he saw his patients when he became famous, for he abandoned the practice of going round his wards and had the patients brought to his home from the hospital, one by one. An assistant reported what happened: 'He would seat himself near a table and immediately call for the patient who was to be studied. The patient was then completely undressed. The intern would read a clinical summary of the case, while the master listened

[1] Bourneville and Regnard, *Iconographie photographique de la Salpêtrière* (3 vols., 1873–80).

attentively. Then there was a long silence, during which Charcot looked, kept looking at the patient while tapping his hand on the table. His assistants, standing close together, waited anxiously for a word of enlightenment. Charcot continued to remain silent. After a while he would request the patient to make a movement; he would induce him to speak; he would ask that his reflexes be examined and that his sensory responses be tested. And then again silence, the mysterious silence of Charcot. Finally, he would call for a second patient, examine him like the first one, call for a third patient and always without a word, silently make comparisons between them. This type of meticulous clinical scrutiny, particularly of the visual type, was at the root of all Charcot's discoveries.' When asked to explain his diagnoses, however, Charcot would reply 'I cannot tell you why, but I know it is this disease, I can sense it.'[1]

In the popular view, Charcot's importance was that he was the first man to recognise the role of the emotions in the production of hysteria. This was of course not true, but his predecessors who had seen this had written only weighty monographs for their own profession, and it was Charcot who popularised the notion and indeed thus made hysteria a new kind of almost fashionable nervous disease. Though he stressed psychic factors, he applied the same procedures of analysis to hysteria as he did to organic physical illness: but he established hysteria as an autonomous trouble, separate from any physical causes.[2] Despite Charcot's disclaimer that hysteria was nothing special to his own time, the *Encyclopaedia Britannica* of 1910 declared that 'hysterical fits in their fully developed form are rarely seen in England, though common in France'; and after the waning of Charcot's influence, they were seldom seen in France either. Charcot invented *grande hystérie*, whose symptoms and manifestations he described in enormous detail; he subdivided it into four stages of progressive development, and above all he discovered the *stigmata* by which one could recognise a hysterical person before any crisis occurred. *Grande*

[1] Georges Guillain, *J. M. Charcot 1825–1893, His Life and Work* (English translation, 1959), 52–3; A. R. G. Owen, *Hysteria, Hypnosis and Healing. The Work of J. M. Charcot* (1971).
[2] Cf. Mme G. Abricosoff, *L'Hystérie au 17ᵉ et 18ᵉ siècles* (1897), by a pupil of Charcot.

hystérie was a terrifying performance, resembling an epileptic fit, with fainting, convulsions, and paralysis. Charcot's achievement was to show that all these various symptoms, hitherto studied separately, were all one, and that they followed a predictable pattern. Dr. Briquet in 1859 had described the symptoms with equal care: he had declared that far from being inexplicable, they obeyed clear laws: but he had not formulated these laws. Charcot gave the disease a perfectly homogeneous and apparently powerful theoretical framework.

Everybody is agreed that Charcot was a great doctor, but on hysteria he was in important ways wrong. That he was able to get away with it for so long reveals a great deal about the organisation of the medical profession. Once Charcot had invented his theory, hordes of disciples began writing theses illustrating it in detail and applying it to different parts of the body, and to different groups of people. An immovable vested interest in the disease was the result. Loyalty to Charcot was intense, to a degree remarkable even in a profession ruled by clique, where every doctor knew who his *patron* was. Medical theses always began with fawning expressions of thanks to 'venerated teachers'; Lacan's thesis on paranoia, for example, had no less than eight pages of dedication. Gilles de la Tourette, the professor who codified Charcot's teaching on hysteria into a textbook in three large volumes, worshipped him 'as a God', says his biographer, and his textbook indeed over and over again points out the genius of the great master, seldom mentioning him without an epithet of praise. Long after faults in the theory had been pointed out, respected professors insisted on clinging to it; Gilles de la Tourette himself never abandoned it. (He was a special case, however: following the loss of a son, and after being shot in the head by one of the lunatics in his asylum, he devoted himself to his work of codification with a fury which some considered to be 'ambitious mania'; and he seems to have gone completely mad in old age.)[1]

The attack on Charcot was launched from Nancy, where an obscure professor who was interested in hypnotism pointed out that all the symptoms Charcot considered to be peculiar to hysteria were capable of being reproduced by hypnotic suggestion: there were no symptoms which could not be so

[1] P. Le Gendre, *Gilles de la Tourette, 1857–1904* (n.d.).

reproduced and indeed also cured by suggestion: no hysteric patient's heart stopped beating. Charcot's followers replied that it was the mark of a hysteric that he could be hypnotised: this became a new sign of it. It meant that the category of hysteria was widened enormously; but whereas Charcot's critic Berrheim had had a vast experience of hypnotism, Charcot had never once hypnotised anybody. He investigated hypnotism as a cure, but it was his assistants who did the hypnotising for him; and since they used to rehearse before the great man arrived, the behaviour of the patients not surprisingly took on predictable forms. Now it so happened that, as a result of an administrative reorganisation, epileptics and hysterics—i.e. all those with occasional attacks—had been segregated from the rest of the madwomen of La Salpêtrière into a separate wing, placed under Charcot's direction. The hysterics therefore tended to copy the epileptics' crises.[1] Charcot was well aware of the problem of simulation, but though he invented various lie detectors, he still got what the patients thought he wanted: a few of them put on magnificent performances of incredible violence and drama and their fascinating poses remain recorded in drawings which, incidentally, show how theatricality was generally accepted then as a common form of behaviour. Charcot's scientific efforts to locate the areas of the body most associated with hysteria resulted in his discovering that the region of the ovaries was the key one: pressure on it could start a hysterical crisis and stronger pressure on it would stop it. The breasts could sometimes also be massaged in a similar way and with similar results. In men, it was the testicles that were pressed. Special 'ovarian belts' were made to enable women prone to hysteria to control themselves. But there were several different elements in Charcot's theory, and in his later years he became interested in traumatic experiences as the cause of hysteria, with autosuggestion prolonging the effect of the shock; this was very different from the emphasis he placed on hereditary predisposition to hysteria, which made him an advocate of the constitutional or inborn nature of nervous disease at a time when Pasteur was demonstrating the environmental and

[1] For a detailed description, see Dr. Paul Richer, *Études cliniques sur l'hystéro-épilepsie ou grande hystérie* (1881), with interesting pictures.

infective origins of other diseases.[1] Eventually one of Charcot's disciples, Babinski, cut the Gordian knot by renaming hysteria pithiatism (meaning curable by suggestion); the bitter controversy only gradually died down.[2]

Hysterical behaviour was far from always taking the grandiose forms that some of the prima donnas of the Saltpêtrière hospital gave it; but, in humbler manifestations, it was frequently an outlet for the anxieties of ordinary people. Thus, for example, Jean-Baptiste Tissier, a house painter, who had hitherto enjoyed good health except for some lead poisoning and who was one of the rioters in the insurrection of June 1848, reacted to his arrest by an attack of hysteria, with convulsions, suffocation, headache and local anaesthesia. Then he took to drink, and two years later, after a 'debauching party' he had another attack, and was taken to hospital—where he was quickly cured with electric shocks, sulphur baths and opium. Émile Laroche, a twenty-nine-year-old cook, had no complaints (except for loss of sperm 'even though he made considerable use of women') when in 1849 a friend of his died of cholera in his arms. This resulted in his having hysterical convulsions almost daily for three months, lasting ten to fifteen minutes each. He sought no treatment, but took ether 'which he abused'. Ernest Langlois, a twenty-five-year-old baker, normal in every respect except that he was very romantic, cried easily and was always very moved when he went to the theatre, went into convulsions after a quarrel with his mistress, and then again three years later, after an operation to his ear. On the second occasion, he was kept in hospital for sixteen days, while his loss of the sense of touch, his pains and his low pulse rate were treated. These cases were recorded to show that men could be hysterical and that no sexual, let alone uterine, trouble was needed to spark it off. But the statistics accumulated by Dr. Briquet suggested that women had hysteria twenty times more often than men. Dr. Briquet claimed indeed that half of all women were hysterical or 'very impressionable', though only one-fifth of all women actually had attacks of convulsions in their full

---

[1] Œuvres complètes de J. M. Charcot. Leçons sur les maladies du système nerveux, vol. 3 (1890), 114; N. Baruk, Psychiatrie médicale, physiologique et expérimentale (1938), 322–5.

[2] Auguste Tournay, La Vie de Joseph Babinski (Amsterdam, 1967).

form. About 20 per cent of hysterics were children, 40 per cent
were aged between twelve and eighteen, and there were almost
none after the age of forty. Almost half of the servant girls
who came for treatment to his hospital for venereal diseases
were hysterical—partly because they were young, and partly
because of the difficulties of their lives and of the illicit unions
they were involved in; over half of Paris's prostitutes were
likewise hysterical. In some cases, being hysterical became a
way of life, and poor girls spent many years incurable in
hospital, serving as specimens for the doctors. An example was
Celina Tonnelle, an illegitimate girl who had been in trouble
all her life and finally ended up in hospital at the age of twenty-
two when her illegitimate baby died. Léontine Bellard, likewise,
had been abandoned by her mother at the age of eight, to
which she reacted with her first attack of hysterical convulsions.
Marriage at seventeen cured her, but six years later the
hysterics returned when her sister died: she was taken to hospital: powerful electric shocks under chloroform rapidly cured
her.[1] But hysteria also came to be the 'waste-paper basket
into which all inexplicable nervous symptoms' were thrown.
Princess Marie Bonaparte, for example, hated the worship
of Napoleon that her family forced upon her; at fifteen she
began taking an interest in men, but, as she said, 'since hysteria was fashionable', her disapproving grandmother who
brought her up, declared her to be hysterical, summoned
Charcot's successor to come and examine her, and he recommended that she be sent to a convent.[2] A more curious brand
of hysteria was diagnosed for one Albert D——, born in 1858,
who at the age of twelve left his job in the gas factory of
Bordeaux and ran away from home. He was brought back, but
kept on running away, travelling in due course all over France,
Germany, Algeria and even Russia, whence, however, he was
expelled under suspicion of being a nihilist. Charcot's pupil
Pitres, dean of the medical faculty of Bordeaux, declared that
this man was neither an eccentric who enjoyed travelling,
because in his 'normal' state he lamented with accents of

[1] Dr. P. Briquet, *Traité clinique et thérapeutique de l'hystérie* (1859), 20–3, 123, 197,
701–2.
[2] Marie Bonaparte, *Derrière les vitres closes* (1950), 384; id., *L'Appel des sèves*
(1958), 682.

profound distress the troubles that his travels caused his
family (he had gone off once just before his wedding day); nor
a madman, because when hypnotised he recounted the details of
his adventures with remarkable precision; nor an epileptic, as
the doctors said he was, because his 'crises of deambulation'
were preceded by 'premonitory symptoms' like sadness, headaches, poor sleep, buzzing in the ears and an obsessive desire to
visit some town. His trouble was *vigilambulisme hystérique à forme
ambulatoire*—or, in other words, hysterical double-personality.[1]

Hysteria was not always treated with indulgence. Another
Salpêtrière psychiatrist, Jules Falret (son of J. P. Falret,
also a psychiatrist, who discovered the depressive cycle),
denounced hysteria as 'nothing but perpetual falsehood'.
Hysterical people 'affect airs of piety and devotion and let
themselves be taken for saints while at the same time secretly
abandoning themselves to the most shameful actions, and at
home, before their husbands and children, making the most
violent scenes in which they employ the coarsest and often
most obscene language and give themselves up to most dis-
orderly actions'.[2] So, in contrast to the sedatives that some
doctors prescribed, and to the vaginal camphor pommade that
Dr. Raspail sold (saying hysteria was caused by an insect), a
few angrier doctors cauterised the clitoris and considered
operations to remove it altogether, and the ovaries too, when
patients declared they had an irresistible 'need to overturn
furniture and to utter strident cries'.

On occasion, hysteria ceased to be a domestic drama and
became a problem of public order, when it assumed mass
proportions and whole factories and villages were affected.
Conservative writers claimed that the French Revolution itself
was nothing but neurosis and hysteria: doctors saw a medieval
obsessional fear at the root of it, and sadism as the explanation
of its massacres.[3] In 1848 at least one factory experienced
mass hysteria, starting with one woman and spreading to 115.

[1] Dr. Gilles de la Tourette, *Traité clinique et thérapeutique de l'hystérie d'après
l'enseignement de la Salpêtrière* (1895), vol. 2, part 1, 353; J. M. Charcot, *Clinique des
maladies du système nerveux* (1893), 2. 168–76.
[2] Quoted in Ilza Veith, *Hysteria, The History of a Disease* (Chicago, 1965), 211,
which stresses the international context and the sexual aspects of hysteria.
[3] Dr. Cabanès and Dr. L. Nass, *La Névrose révolutionnaire* (1906), 5–12; Dr. L.
Nass, *Essais de pathologie historique: le Siège de Paris et la Commune* (1914).

In 1861 forty girls at a school in Montmartre went wild in convulsions. The most interesting and best-documented case is that of the village of Morzine in Haute-Savoie 'and everybody knows', wrote the doctor who went to investigate it, 'how common hysteria is in Savoy'. This was a village of 2,000 souls, with 90 per cent illiteracy, deep piety and much superstition, where people 'lied in good faith, so that they ended by believing their own lies as they believed those of others'. In the sixteenth century, sorcerers had been very numerous, and in the nineteenth century the young men who migrated seasonally to search for work regularly came back with magic books, as their most precious booty from the civilised world. In 1857 this village declared itself possessed by demons. It started with a child, who had been badly cut on her leg, going into hysterics, and even more so when it would not heal, saying that the devil was responsible for the wound. The hysteria spread to other children, many women and some men, but half the hysterics were aged between seventeen and twenty-two. The explanation of the villagers was very definitely that the spasms, convulsions and pains they suffered from were due to possession by demons: the municipal council unanimously voted a resolution saying that *natural* remedies were of no use. It was decided that the person responsible might be a former priest who had quarrelled with many in the parish: a band of villagers went fully armed at dead of night to a chapel he had built, where they killed and eviscerated a dog, to the accompaniment of cabalistic curses. It was all in vain, and the village grew increasingly depressed as people feared that they, or their families, would be attacked next. The Parisian spiritualists were fascinated by this case, but the most detailed report suggests that hysteria, in the guise of demonic possession, was adopted as a means of giving expression to family rebelliousness and social deviance. The girls who went into hysterics (and they were the largest group) did so whenever anything unpleasant was said, whenever they suffered any pain, or whenever religion was mentioned. They shouted that they were not mad but damned devils, that they despised medicine, that they should be sent priests to cure them, though when priests came, they insulted them, saying they wanted holy men. They threw furniture around, rolled on the floor, beat themselves, but claimed after their attack that they could remember nothing of this. They refused to eat, but drank a lot of coffee, and demanded good food, butcher's meat and baker's bread. When out of their trances, their main pleasure was to congregate among themselves, playing cards and inciting one another against their parents. One girl entered into the power of the demons after her father had told her to go to bed early: she was hysterical for a whole hour until her normal bedtime, when she went to sleep as usual. Next day she joined the hysterical gang. Another girl began her 'crises' by calling the *curé* a dirty dog to his face. One father cured his daughter by grabbing her by the hair, brandishing an axe and swearing to kill her if her 'crisis' did not stop; and it did. Another cured his by throwing her into an oven, pretending he would roast her alive; another by promising her a new dress. But one father was struck such a blow by his daughter in one of her fits that he never recovered; he stopped eating, saying the devil prevented him, and he died three months later. In the end, the troops were brought in, the most serious hysterics expelled to distant hospitals, and the threat of imprisonment held out as a penalty for hysteria. Sunday mass, which used to be constantly punctuated by hysterical attacks, was, after three years, at last said uninterrupted again. It is curious, however, that the doctor who organised this cure never mentioned indiscipline and always talked of it as an 'illness'.[1] The relationship of hysteria and possession by evil spirits aroused much interest particularly as Charcot's stigmata so closely resembled the diabolic stigmata that medieval inquisitors used to identify sorcerers.[2]

Freud and Sex

It did not need Freud to make the French worry about sex. On the contrary, it might be argued that they became interested in obscure, unconscious and invisible sexual problems only when

[1] Dr. A. Constans, *Relation sur une épidémie d'hystéro-démonopathie en 1861* (2nd edition, 1863); cf. Joseph Tissot, *Les Possédées de Morzine* (1865) and A. Vigouroux, *La Contagion mentale* (1905).

[2] Dr. Henri Cesbron, *Histoire critique de l'hystérie* (1909), 123–54; Joseph de Tonquédec, *Les Maladies nerveuses ou mentales et les manifestations diaboliques* (1938), by the official exorcist of the diocese of Paris; Dr. Jean Camus, *Isolement et psychothérapie, traitement de l'hystérie et de la neurasthénie* (1904).

their directly physical troubles in this connection ceased to be overwhelming. Venereal disease, until it became more easily curable—which only happened in the twentieth century—caused an enormous amount of anxiety, quite apart from the physical suffering it produced. It has been suggested that perhaps 15 per cent of deaths around 1900 were from syphilis, and that half of those who had the disease caught it in adolescence.[1] Syphilis was a subject on which, between 1840 and 1875, no less than 180 books were published, excluding obscure theses, innumerable articles, works on other sexual illnesses, like the even more widespread gonorrhoea, and putting aside the vast literature on female diseases. The sale of these works was very considerable. One unremarkable treatise on diseases of the sexual organs written for 'men of the world' sold 7,000 copies each year between 1853 and 1862; a guide to the *Hygiene and Physiology of Marriage* went through 172 editions between 1848 and 1883.[2] Those who did not have syphilis did not seem much less worried than those who did, for it was a constant menace, with terrifying implications of incurability and ultimate madness and paralysis. At a time when a qualified doctor could warn patients that even constipation could produce lunacy itself, let alone nervous trouble or poisoning of the body,[3] the sexual act was seen as surrounded by innumerable dangers;[4] the use of contraceptives was supposed to produce all sorts of additional irritations, quite apart from the guilt feelings that moralists tried to instil about it: a young man complained to his doctor that contraceptives made him 'confused as though he had committed infanticide'.[5] Coitus interruptus was blamed as the cause of the 'multiple neuroses and bizarre affections that women suffered from', because they found it unsatisfying.[6] Impotence and sterility were much more worrying when their mechanism was barely understood; loss

---

[1] See Zeldin, *Ambition and Love*, 304.

[2] Dr. Émile Jozan, *Traité pratique des maladies des voies urinaires et des organes générateurs . . . spécialement destiné aux gens du monde* (9th edition, 1862); A. Debay, *Hygiène et physiologie du mariage* (1848).

[3] Dr. Félix Bremond, *Les Préjugés en médecine et en hygiène* (1892), 82.

[4] For example, Dr. Louis Seraine, *De la santé des gens mariés* (1865, 2nd edition), 68.

[5] Dr. L. Bergeret, *Des fraudes dans l'accomplissement des fonctions génératrices. Causes, dangers et inconvénients* (18th edition, 1910), 101.

[6] Dr. Antonin Bossu, *Lois et mystères des fonctions de reproduction* (n.d.), 307.

of virility was something that was constantly held up as a danger to young people who masturbated, or who engaged in debauchery; and the terror this inspired can be seen from the varied potions and gadgets placed on the market, apparently with commercial success, to restore virility; massaging, douches, ether, dried Spanish flies, electrical and magnetic shocks, acupuncture, hellebore and strychnine were just some of the remedies people willingly submitted to.[1] A leading authority laid it down that sexual aberrations were 'fatally incurable' when they were produced by both physical and psychic causes, almost so when they were purely psychological in origin, and capable of cure only when they were simply physical.[2]

France was one of the countries which was least sympathetic to the doctrines of Freud, as he himself noted; and the reasons for this are revealing. Freud had close links with France; he had studied under Charcot and had translated some of his writings into German; he had visited Nancy to learn about developments in the use of hypnosis there; and French work on hysteria and hypnosis was a principal starting-point of Freud's thought. The result however was that Freud was looked on in France as a renegade pupil, or more precisely as an outdated one, who continued to develop ideas which had long been discredited in France. The bitterness occasioned by the disputes of Charcot and his rivals meant that Freud had to overcome almost insurmountable prejudices and personal animosities. The people who took up his ideas tended therefore at first to come from outside Paris and outside the top rank of psychiatrists, for these latter had theories of their own. Janet and Freud had a lot of views or attitudes in common; Janet was interested in 'psychological analysis', 'mental systems', 'mental disinfection' and 'contraction of the conscience', which in Freud's language were respectively psycho-analysis, complex, catharsis and repression. But Janet was by temperament the very opposite of Freud, cheerful, optimistic, giving the impression, even in extreme old age, of effortless activity and wide interests; and he considered that Freud was creating a

[1] Dr. Félix Rouband, *Traité de l'impuissance et de la stérilité* (1855), 216, 230.
[2] Dr. Paul Moreau de Tours, *Des aberrations du sens générique* (1887, 4th edition), 287. Cf. Dr. Alexandre Paris, *Folie des femmes enceintes, de nouvelles accouchées et des nourrices* (1897).

closed dogma and carrying his arguments to extremes. Janet said some very harsh things about Freud, which rankled ever after, notably at the London International Congress of 1913: Freud's disciple and biographer Ernest Jones criticised Janet for judging psycho-analysis without even trying it: Janet replied that he had not tried it precisely because he did not believe in interpreting the statements of patients 'to fit a dogma that had been fixed in advance', instead of seeking to find the truth. Janet objected to excessive weight being given to sex and to traumatic memories, though he considered them important, and he thought Freud was promising too much: he was himself very modest about the effects of his psycho-therapy, noting that most cures were inevitably temporary and relapses all too frequent; a long process of re-education was needed to rebuild the personality of the psychasthenic. Nevertheless, Janet knew about Freud's work long before most of his contemporaries; and in his writings he frequently showed his interest in them, though seldom in an enthusiastic way.

The first study of Freud in France was an article on his theory of dreams, published in 1911; in the same year a doctor at Poitiers made him known to general practitioners with a series of articles in the *Gazette des hôpitaux*; and a couple of medical textbooks made references to him. But the first book on psycho-analysis to be published in France appeared in 1914, just before the war, and it passed largely unnoticed. Its authors were Régis, professor of psychiatry at Bordeaux, and Angelo Hesnard, who was the enthusiast behind the project. Hesnard (1886–1969) came from outside the ruling hierarchy of professors. He was the son of an impoverished civil servant; he had joined the navy in order to get a medical education on the cheap and he was now a naval doctor at Bordeaux. His brother Oswald was an *agrégé* in German and founder of the French Institute in Berlin; there he had learnt about Freud from medical friends and, persuaded by Angelo, he was to undertake the first French translation of Freud.[1] Hesnard and Régis were sharply critical of Freud, at the same time as they were fascinated by his ideas. Freud's theory 'had a philosophi-cal allure so manifest that it has justly been likened to certain

[1] He later became rector of the Academy of Grenoble and interpreter to Briand in his conversations with Stresemann.

doctrines of psychological metaphysics'. It was a harmonious
theory which would 'satisfy the dilettante, by freeing him from
the need to engage in detailed researches, the patient accumulation of small facts, which is the current coin of medical
methods'. It was 'purely hypothetical and completely un-
provable', and Kraepelin was right to call it 'metapsychiatry'.
Its ideas on sex had drawn most attention to it and had aroused
most criticism. Hesnard and Régis applauded Freud for dealing
with sexual problems; they agreed they were important:
'Obsessional people instinctively choose sexual things to
motivate their inadequacies, because sexuality is, in the
present state of our civilisation, the most mysterious aspect
of the human personality and because it represents the most
suitable material out of which to create symbols of their inability to act and to think like normal people; in absolutely
the same way as they choose certain social, metaphysical and
above all religious questions to express the constitutional
debility of their affections. . . That sexual troubles are the
rule among neurotics is indubitable, but that the former
are the cause of the latter, we cannot admit.' They argued that
though sexual troubles could cause some of the symptoms of
neurosis, they were themselves effects of more general troubles.
The frequency of sexual obsessions among neurotics was 'a
matter of civilisation and milieu'; and it was just one instance of
obsession with what was forbidden; if society forbade gastro-
nomic satisfactions or making money, they might well be
obsessed by digestion or gold. Hesnard and Régis claimed
neurotics of this kind were 'totally different' from sexual
perverts: these had instincts which were impossible to alter,
they were like criminals, marked men, with damage if not to
their intelligence at any rate to their effectivity; they were
incapable of love, which is what, on the contrary, tormented
neurotics. 'It is imprudent to admit, from a social point of
view, that we are all potentially incestuous or homosexuals.'
'Pan-sexualism' was, however, the only original idea they
attributed to Freud. They quoted French precursors for his
theories of transference, trauma, the unconscious, dreams, etc.
They concluded therefore that Freud's work represented an
advance in only a very slight sense, because basically he was
a delayed survivor of the old German psychological tradition

of the early nineteenth century, of Stahl and Heinroth, which
saw the conflict of morality and reason as the cause of madness.[1]

Hesnard nevertheless remained one of the most important
commentators on Freud in France for a whole generation, being
a fluent and popular writer. His interest was, however, more in
the non-medical side of Freud, in his views on symbolism, art
and religion; he was always convinced that psycho-analysis
would open up great changes in morals. He never underwent
analysis himself and so remained somewhat outside the charmed
circle; he was keen to put Freud to work in the educational
sphere, believing that it was in the bringing-up of children
that guilt and repression were cultivated and the seeds of
much of human unhappiness produced. He urged the Freudians
to abandon 'their isolation into small closed cliques'. But his
Morals without Sin (1954) was placed on the Index by the
Catholic Church. By then, Hesnard, who loved new ideas,
had become interested in Marxism, in phenomenology and in
linguistics. He replaced the libido by love, which he interpreted as joy in life. He turned Freudianism into a humanistic
gospel, which the psycho-analysts could not recognise, stressing
man's ability for infinite sympathy as the link that must draw
him into harmonious living.[2] Hesnard illustrates how the
French assimilated a foreign theory by incorporating it into
their own traditions, taking what suited them, and remodelling
it in their own image.

The early popular reactions to Freud hesitated between
castigating him for being a bad pupil of Charcot and insulting
him for being a foreigner. A doctor who published a book on
Freud in 1925 said that it was France's 'delicacy and critical
sense' that had made most of its medical men turn away from
him. Sexual relations were very different in France and
Germany: in Germany 'they are not discreet and intimate as
in France; they are cynically displayed in all forms, to the
point that perverts have their official journals and meetings';
'German towns were the only ones to have erotic films shown
publicly . . . virgin girls were a much rarer exception in Germany than in France'. That is why Freud was obsessed by sex

[1] E. Régis and A. Hesnard, *La Psychoanalyse des névroses et des psychoses* (1914),
321–8, 341.

[2] 'Hommage au docteur A. Hesnard', *L'Évolution psychiatrique* (Jan.–June 1971),
301–75.

and why also his teachings were most successful in the English-speaking world with its narrow puritanism. France was a Catholic country and the confession 'provided an outlet for perverse thoughts'.[1] In 1934, when a journalist asked a variety of medical men for their views of Freud, reactions had changed only slightly. The director of the lunatic asylum of Toulouse, Professor Maurice Dide, for example, repeated that 'Freudism belongs to the past'; it was based on the study of the abnormal and was no more reliable than Charcot's now-ridiculed stigmata; it had besides never cured anything but hysteria. Its only value was that it had made possible the posing of problems about sex with less hypocrisy. Dr. A. Marie, a leading Paris psychiatrist, agreed that Freud had performed a useful service, in that 'pan-sexualism was a salutary reaction against people whose psychological puritanism caused them to forget and be silent about the important role of sex', but he considered him 'the victim of a verbal construction and of a narrowly exclusive ideology'; the repression of the libido could not be accepted until it was proved by biochemical and anatomical analyses. There was some disagreement, however, as to just how much of a liberating force Freud was. Some doctors insisted that this puritanism was not universal, that the Catholic Church had long been aware of sexual problems and that confessors had been psycho-analysts in their own way. So, while one emancipationist woman doctor hailed Freud for 'helping to liberate humanity from its prejudices', the novelist Jeanne Boujassy protested that his doctrines were 'extremely humiliating: one can no longer go to a fashionable doctor now without feeling immediately scrutinised and undressed to the very depths of one's soul by his inquiries'. Another female novelist, Renée Dunan, was enthusiastic about Freud, as she was also about nudism, but she said he was having no influence on France's way of life or on the literary world: 'no one knows about him except André Gide and me'. The critic Ernest Seillière declared, 'The views of Freud apply above all to the Jews, his co-religionists, who were particularly disposed to a congenital libidinous pan-sexualism by ethnic fatality.' Freud clearly aroused strong feelings: one professor murmured that 'the attitude of his zealots was as disquieting as their rudimentary

[1] Dr. J. Lammonier, *Le Freudisme* (1925), 7–9, 167.

knowledge of biology'. Princess Marie Bonaparte summed it up by saying that the French liked clarity, taste and common sense too much to accept him, but the English were willing to face up to the truth.[1]

It was she who organised the small band of Freudian analysts in Paris. She was the daughter of Prince Roland Bonaparte, a noteworthy explorer and ethnographer, who had added wealth as well as learning to the family's distinctions by marrying Mademoiselle Blanc, daughter of the organiser of the gaming-houses of Monte Carlo, and who then set up a foundation to finance scientific research. Marie herself married Prince George of Greece, whose hobby was collecting snuff-boxes. She was a highly intelligent and energetic woman, who had gone to Vienna to be psycho-analysed by Freud and who then regarded herself as the authentic mouthpiece of his doctrines. In 1926 she founded the Psychoanalytical Society of Paris, with a handful of members; but divisions soon appeared within their small ranks. Some accused her of demanding 'rigorous conformity' from them, and using their meetings 'as simply an excuse for quoting Freudian texts'. In the 1950s the movement split, with one faction remaining loyal to the Freudian International and another claiming independence. In the next decade Lacan, who tried to develop psycho-analysis into the study of language, in turn seceded and founded a dissident *École freudienne*. A number of foreigners participated in the early dissemination of Freud's teaching, and it was above all through Switzerland and through Swiss disciples like Saussure that his works reached France, published by the Éditions du Mont Blanc of Geneva. But even the French university system found a niche for the Freudians. One of the leading Paris professors of psychiatry, H. Claude, the only one to remain faithful to Charcot's organodynamic theory and a pupil of Charcot's successor Raymond, gave teaching appointments to a number of them—to Saussure and Odie from Lausanne, to Madame Sokolnicka, who had no medical qualifications but who was one of the earliest analysts to practise in Paris, but above all to Dr. R. Laforgue, who became one of the major popularisers of Freudianism in readily

[1] P. Vigné d'Octon, *La Vie et l'amour: les doctrines freudiennes et la psychanalyse* (1934).

understandable language.[1] It was only in the late 1950s that a wider range of French doctors, mainly young ones, began to take a serious interest in Freud.

So when in 1961 a sociologist published a report on the attitude of public opinion to psycho-analysis, it emerged that Freud was still considered by the average Frenchman as being above all the theorist of pan-sexualism. Public opinion, in other words, still identified Freud with the first phase of his work, carried out before 1920; it knew virtually nothing of the new directions his researches had taken after that; and there was thus a clear gap between the popular interest in Freud which came after the 1939–45 war on the one hand, and the attitudes of the professional psychiatrists and the leading intellectuals on the other, who were at this very time trying to develop notably different psychological theories on the basis of Freud's researches. The vast majority of the people questioned in this survey thought that psycho-analysis was similar to the confession and to hypnotism. Some 51 per cent of middle-class parents questioned said that they would allow psycho-analysis to be used on their children, and 70 per cent thought it could with profit be used on criminals. Between 58 and 64 per cent thought it helped people, between 9 and 15 per cent thought it did not, 27 per cent did not know. The striking fact was that this large support for it came from the working classes and the least-educated sections of the community. Twice as high a proportion of workers as of intellectuals thought psycho-analysis could cure people. This was not simply because the communists condemned it as charlatanism, for at the same time the right wing dismissed it as a theory of sexuality. Freud became acceptable through popularisation by the mass-circulation press: those who accepted him had not read him. But perhaps he had touched on an aspect of life that meant more than a little to them.[2]

These are just some of the ways that anxiety expressed itself.

[1] A. Hesnard and R. Laforgue, 'Aperçu historique du mouvement psychiatrique en France', in L'Évolution psychiatrique (1925), 1. 11–26; A. Hesnard, De Freud à Lacan (1970). Claude himself had other interests: see H. Claude and P. Rubenovitch, Thérapeutiques biologiques des affections morales (1940).

[2] Serge Moscovici, La Psychanalyse. Son image et son public. Étude sur la représentation sociale de la psychanalyse (1961), 119–21, 138, 421.

How people coped with anxiety is more complicated still. One needs to look at various forms of evasion, like the development of leisure activities, which were not simply an expression of *joie de vivre*, and at different types of palliatives, like drug-taking and alcoholism, which reflected more than a rising standard of living. One must not forget the more elusive readjustments of behaviour, which are virtually impossible to document, like attitudes towards loss of temper. Above all, one must realise that rationalism was, in some small part, a reaction and a defence against emotionalism. But the history of emotion has still to be established as a branch of scholarship.[1]

[1] Judith Devlin has started a doctoral thesis at Oxford on 'Fear in Nineteenth Century France'.

4. Hierarchy and Violence

The Army

FRANCE was an artistic, intellectual, agricultural country, but also a militaristic one. In 1848 it appointed a poet to head its government in a time of crisis and in 1870 it chose a historian to rescue it from the Prussians, but it turned to military leaders more often. The tradition of Napoleon, as the soldier who would save the nation, was continued by General Cavaignac in 1848, by Marshal MacMahon in 1873, by General Boulanger in 1888, by Marshal Pétain in 1940 and then by General de Gaulle. In none of these cases, however, was military government established. The relationship between army and society in France was curious. Even when the country became republican, the prestige of the army was almost as high as it was in despotic monarchies which based themselves on force. France managed to be the apostle of fraternity but also chauvinistic, egalitarian but also accepting a hierarchical military organisation, a parliamentary democracy but one proud of its military virtues. The army united the nation in war but divided it in peace. To be a soldier was a patriotic act, but patriotism was not always fashionable, and to be a soldier could also mean cutting oneself off from society. The army had its own set of values, but it was also regarded as one of the most important instruments of social climbing and also of national unification. These contradictions are important, and they are explicable.[1]

One of the main reasons why the army was the object of so much controversy and violent emotion was that its character changed considerably over time and its significance was therefore difficult to appreciate clearly. The army inherited some of the aura of its *ancien régime* origins. It was associated with the arbitrary discipline that the Revolution had overthrown, with the nobleman's claim to the right to command,

[1] État-major de l'Armée de terre, Service Historique, *Guide bibliographique sommaire d'histoire militaire et coloniale française* (1969) is the fullest bibliography.

with the idea that war was an aristocratic hobby. Famine, pestilence and war used to be the poor man's terror; the press-gang, and then conscription, were the state's most serious attacks on his independence. In the eighteenth century, a soldier was something of a social outcast, often escaping from his village because he had transgressed its moral code, or because he was discontented or disinherited. A large proportion of the army came from the newly annexed provinces of the east of France. The army gave its recruits a sense of belonging; patriotism gave them a sense of mission; *esprit de corps* enabled pride to replace the reputation they used to have of being brutal, lazy and immoral. The army at this time did not have any of the reactionary characteristics which were later associated with it: it was not noted for blind discipline; insubordination and mutinies were not rare; it was not completely devoted to throne and altar, or at any rate it was noted for anticlericalism; and it was not yet isolated in barracks, but was allowed to take civil employment and long leaves in its spare time. The retired soldier came back to his village a non-conformist, speaking French, widely travelled, having lost the taste for hard work but self-confident and capable of dealing with authority and civil servants.[1] There were still notices outside public parks saying 'No dogs, prostitutes, servants or soldiers' and the peasants resisted conscription to the revolutionary and Napoleonic armies with bitter determination.[2] In 1798 the government succeeded in enrolling only one-quarter of the men it summoned to arms; in 1811 no less than 66,000 men were arrested as deserters; but gradually Napoleon increased the success rate of conscription from two-thirds to nine-tenths, and by 1830 conscription was finally accepted, with only 2 per cent defaulting. Two per cent was the proportion of defaulters in 1902 and 1910 also—equivalent to two army corps—but the state had gradually made military service an essential part of national life.[3]

It was successful because it introduced universal conscription slowly. In 1848 only one-quarter of the army consisted of

[1] André Corvisier, *L'Armée française de la fin du 17ᵉ siècle au ministère de Choiseul. Le Soldat* (1964); cf. Richard Cobb, *Les Armées révolutionnaires* (1963), 724–32.

[2] Marcel Baldet, *La Vie quotidienne dans les armées de Napoléon* (1964), 13.

[3] Joseph Vidal, *Histoire et statistique de l'insoumission* (Paris law thesis, 1913).

conscripts. Another quarter were substitutes, for until 1873 the
law allowed those called up to pay someone else to perform
their service for them and there were always poor people, or
soldiers who had served their term and had nowhere to go,
who were willing to sell themselves in this way.[1] (Forty per
cent of the *remplaçants* were former soldiers.) The remaining
half of the army were volunteers. It was thus an essentially
professional army, even though ostensibly based on conscription. It was still so small that it had no use for all the conscripts
who were theoretically obliged to serve in it. Thus in 1847,
304,000 young men were summoned to draw lots as to who
should be called up; 144,000 drawing 'good numbers' were set
free. The remainder were then examined medically, and 48 per
cent of them were exempted either as unfit, or because they
were priests, teachers or students. So only 64,000 had to serve;
but a quarter of these were placed in reserve and were not
troubled any further. Military service was thus a misfortune
that befell only a small proportion of young men, and money
could save those who were determined and could afford
(between 800 and 1,200 francs) to avoid it.[2]

The army, however, had definite attractions for those who did
join it. Almost exactly half of the volunteers were of middle-
class origin, about a third workers and a fifth peasants. One
third of recruits were illiterate, and anybody who could read
and write was immediately considered a potential officer.
Under Louis-Philippe one-third of officer commissions were
reserved for N.C.O.s but by 1848 three-quarters of the officers
had risen from the ranks (80 per cent in the infantry, but
35 per cent in the cavalry). Becoming an officer was considered
a natural continuation of non-commissioned rank, but though
it was thus easy to become an officer, promotion was very slow
after that. One had to wait for vacancies to occur in one's
regiment, so there was a considerable element of chance in the
matter, but generally a N.C.O. who became a sub-lieutenant
at the age of thirty would be promoted a lieutenant at about
thirty-seven and a captain at forty-five. He would be unlikely
to go further. The army was thus an excellent way of making

[1] Bernard Schnapper, *Le Remplacement militaire en France* (1968).
[2] W. Zaniewicki, 'L'Armée française en 1848' (unpublished troisième cycle
thesis, in the Sorbonne library, 1966).

good socially, provided one's ambitions were distinctly limited. A sub-lieutenant was paid only 1,350 to 1,500 francs a year (not much more than a primary-school master), a captain 2,000–2,400. One could not easily get married on such pay and the army was to a considerable extent a society of bachelors —not unlike the Church—enjoying a certain prestige and comfort by sacrificing family life. For the more determined, however, there were two ways of moving up faster. One was to go to the military cadet schools, but that cost about 12,000 francs. Another was to join the colonial army, and seek distinction in the conquest of Algeria; but that involved cutting oneself off from the home country for long periods: that is why the 'Africans' were such a special kind of freemasonry. The colonial army was outside the life of the nation, but the ordinary one was not. There were not enough barracks to lodge its soldiers and these lived as paying guests in the attics of small garrison towns, taking on odd jobs when off duty. In 1848 the army was distinguished by no special political leanings. Its votes in elections showed it was as divided as the nation.[1]

Two new factors altered this situation. First, governments used the army for political repression. In the June days of 1848 and in the Commune, the army spilt the blood of its fellow-countrymen, in civil wars of unforgettable poignancy. Napoleon III destroyed parliamentary government in 1851 with the help of the army and was identified with military rule. Troops came to be regularly used in the breaking of workers' strikes. Secondly, the army became the refuge, in the course of the second half of the nineteenth century, of the aristocracy, who compensated for their expulsion from public office by reviving their traditions of military service. Under the Restoration, the aristocracy used the army as a kind of finishing school; its youth took commissions for a few years as an alternative to a university education; but by the end of the Second Empire they were turning to the army for a life's career. In the early Third Republic, the number of candidates for Saint-Cyr almost trebled; and the proportion of noble names in the officer lists rose enormously. The army therefore came to be considered a danger to the republic, a relic of the *ancien régime* and a bastion of clericalism. Anti-militarism developed in

[1] Raoul Girardet, *La Société militaire dans la France contemporaine 1815–1939* (1953).

close association with socialism. But though the army's character became politically controversial, there were very few who wanted to abolish armies altogether.

All parties placed great hopes on the army for the moral regeneration of the country. The republicans saw in it a way of ending class barriers. Military service forced all young men to mix socially, to undergo the same experiences and to become conscious that their membership of the national community overrode all their petty private interests. The army now took on a new educational character. It ceased to be simply a source of employment for eccentric paupers and fashionable aristocrats. Because it was under attack, it had to defend its discipline and its authoritarianism, and in doing so, it came to reformulate its ideals in a way that gave militarism a new meaning. Sly intellectuals and sarcastic radicals liked to claim that soldiers were stupid, fit only to do what they were told. Renan said that army service was a sure way of losing one's *esprit de finesse*; Clemenceau declared that 'war is too serious a matter to be confided to military men'. But the pacifist movement had been seriously crippled by the disaster of 1870. The idea, enunciated by Condorcet, that war was the instrument of kings to preserve their tyranny, and that it would end when kings were overthrown, lapsed into irrelevance. The Saint-Simonian theory that industry was the enemy of war and that industrialists were bound to replace soldiers as the leaders of society, obtained little support even from industrialists. The suggestion that armies should be put to useful work, building railways and canals to increase national prosperity, and that only thus could service in them be reconciled with democracy, was never followed up.[1] The army was able to draw on a powerful chauvinistic tradition, which gave it something of a sacred function. Even Anatole France had written that 'military virtues have given birth to the whole of civilisation. Abolish them and the whole of society will crumble.' Victor Cousin, the oracle of banality, pronounced that 'a battle is nothing but the struggle of truth and falsehood' and war was

---

[1] See e.g. Captain Ferdinand Durand, *Des tendances pacifiques de la société européenne et du rôle des armées dans l'avenir* (1841, 2nd edition 1844); C. Pecqueur, *Des armées dans leur rapport avec l'industrie, la morale et la liberté, ou les devoirs civiques des militaires* (1842).

therefore 'the terrible but necessary instrument of civilisation'.[1] Popularised science was drawn on to prove that struggle was the essence of life and that force was synonymous with virtue.[2] War was defended by liberals as 'the supreme recourse of the oppressed' and there was a vast literature in praise of military virtues. Captain Danrit's thirty-odd volumes of science fiction urging the need for preparedness against the 'yellow and black menaces' were much read.[3] Army life was held up as the breeding ground not just of patriotism, but of friendship, courage, energy, gaiety, honour, tenacity and dedication to the highest ideals.[4] The distinction between military and civil life was accentuated, so as to counteract the looser morals and manners which were held to be the cause of all France's troubles. Discipline became a military fetish. The army tried to divest itself of its old easy-going ways. Loyalty was demanded no longer to individual officers but to 'the flag', to the principle of 'order'. The chaotic bravura the Algerian army had fostered gave way to passive obedience and the rigid implementation of regulations. Intellectual qualities were discredited and a new formalism developed which was very different from the traditional French military ethos to which it confusedly believed it was dedicated. In Napoleon I's army, a general who had lost his nerve in the battle of Marengo was booed by his troops in the review he held afterwards, and he never showed his face again before them. Such a thing could no longer happen in 1900.

The *N.C.O.'s Manual* illustrates the army's changing values, and the new functions it sought to assume. 'Discipline', said the edition of 1893, 'will be the soldier's religion. . . . The regiment is the school of subordination, of the virile spirit, of male pride. . . . Soldiers resolved to die can always save their honour.' By 1913 the introduction to the manual, dealing with the army's moral role, had grown from two to thirteen pages. The army, it said, developed not only the spirit of patriotism and sacrifice, but also of solidarity and camaraderie; 'though instituted to defend the country against its foreign enemies, it also had the

[1] Maurice Lelong, O.P., *Célébration de l'art militaire* (1962), an interesting anthology.   [2] J. Izoulet, *La Cité moderne* (1895).
[3] Capt. E. A. C. Driant, alias Danrit, *La Guerre fatale* (1903), *L'Invasion jaune* (1909), *L'Invasion noire* (1913), etc. Biography by G. Jollivet, *Le Colonel Driant* (1918).
[4] General Thoumas, *Le Livre du soldat. Vertus guerrières* (1891).

task of instilling respect for the government of the republic and for property, and ensuring the execution of the laws voted by parliament'. It was also 'the school where man learns to live in society, where the citizen is formed,' where different classes got to know each other. The friendships of the regiment, it declared, were the most lasting, but it warned the N.C.O. not to be 'too familiar with his subordinates: he must neither joke, play, drink nor feast with them'.[1]

This rhetoric should not be taken at its face value. The image of stiffness and rigid hierarchy that army propagandists cultivated was not an accurate reflection of what was actually happening. The hostility between militarists and anti-militarists was partly the result of each side exaggerating its position and misinterpreting the realities. Though on the theoretical plane the army came to stand for principles which could not easily be reconciled with those of the Third Republic, or at least with isolated elements of the Jacobin tradition in it, in practice its way of life was much more complex and varied. The influence it exerted on the conscripts that passed through it was not what the manuals prescribed. Though so much was written about the reactionary dangers of the military, there was very little study of the actual effect of national service, of the results of the 'schooling' function of the army. One can, however, learn more about what the army really meant to people—as opposed to what they said about it in their political disputes—by looking at it from this point of view.

In real life, the officer was not a walking automaton, blindly implementing the rules, as playwrights like Courteline, who had a passionate hatred of the army, portrayed him. The first thing officer cadets were taught when they arrived at Saint-Cyr was how to salute and what the gradations of hierarchy were. They were constantly classified in exact order of subordination according to the marks they received; they were taught precisely how to make their beds and every minute rule of discipline and custom. But as the captain in charge of the class of 1863 said, there were two distinct beings in him, the man and the captain. 'If you address yourself to the man, he will try to be as helpful as he can. But if you address the captain,

[1] *Le Livre du gradé à l'usage des élèves caporaux, caporaux et sous officiers d'infanterie* (Toulouse, 1893), 8, and *Le Livre du gradé d'infanterie* (1913), 11.

it is different. The captain knows only the regulations, he
moves only according to the regulations, he lives only by the
regulations.' The cadets soon discovered how to catch him
when he was a man and their life was far more entertaining
than the rules foresaw. The smell of boot polish in the dormitories was often drowned by that of perfume, and 'the fashionable cadets had cosmetic kits far more elaborate than many
girls'. There were artists of every kind among them, and they
spent much time drawing, sculpting, engraving, playing music
or writing poetry. It was true that the richer ones hired the
music rooms simply in order to have somewhere to smoke and
chat at their ease, that those who spent their afternoons off in
museums sometimes did so simply to keep warm, that the school
library was little frequented and that intellectual activity was
not encouraged—the swots used to retire to the infirmary for a
few days before examinations—but the cultural life of the army
officer was not as narrow as his enemies claimed, though it
was not in general bookish.[1] The army was too large an institution, too subdivided into relatively independent units, and too
diverse in its recruitment, to make a uniform type of officer
possible. The military schools were not as influential as was
imagined. They imparted factual knowledge more than a
way of life, and groups of individuals within them created
styles of behaviour and established links of devotion more
powerful than the official programmes. Patronage, and friendship that grew within its networks, was very important. That
was why the Staff College, to which the ablest officers went,
necessarily allowed so much tolerance towards the diversity
of military doctrine. Here, before 1914, while Colonel Pétain
taught the importance of fire-power, Colonel de Grandmaison
preached all-out offensive: there was almost as much doctrinal
disagreement in the army as in the university, and there were
similar personal animosities. There were seven different
cadet schools—Saint-Cyr, Saint-Maixent, the Polytechnic,
Fontainebleau, Versailles, Vincennes and Saumur—and they
each had their own traditions, and slightly different social

[1] A. Teller, *Souvenirs de Saint-Cyr* (*Esquisses de la vie militaire en France*) (1886,
11th edition), i. 99–114, 147–8. P. de Pardiellan [pseud. of Lt.-Col. P. G. A. Veling],
*Grains d'officiers. Scènes de la vie dans les écoles militaires en France, en Russie, en Allemagne
et en Autriche* (1895).

mixtures. French officers did not form a distinct caste, as the Germans were supposed to.[1]

At one extreme, there were the depressed and ageing junior officers, risen from the ranks, dedicated to routine because they had no prospect before them but the retirement they dreaded. At the other extreme there were highly intelligent men who chose a military career because they believed it gave more scope for personal fulfilment and public service than corrupt politics or the static civil service; and indeed in the colonial army such men were able to govern empires with far greater power than civilians enjoyed. Ernest Psichari set out the arguments and the emotions behind this kind of choice in an influential book, *L'Appel des armes* (1913), which explained why he had abandoned philosophy for military service. Lyautey, whose famous article on the 'Social Role of the Officer' became the inspiration of several generations of soldiers and whose career proved that the army could offer as much scope for action and influence as any other profession, typified one kind of ideal. In between these extremes, there were the rivalries of the many varieties of officer, whose different experience and origins gave them barely compatible attitudes. Marshal Juin, the son of a retired soldier who became a lighthouse keeper in Algeria, said he joined the army not because of any taste for the life of the barracks, nor indeed because he felt any desire for revenge against Germany—England was the enemy for him after Fashoda—but because the army offered him a scholarship. In the army, he found a contrast between the smoothly shaven, white-gloved, brilliantly polished officer and the hirsute, bearded one, who liked to fight his battles naked to the waist, wearing espadrilles.[2] There was then the new kind of officer who saw himself as a technician and who frightened the older generation with his talk of ballistics and topography; the arrival of a young sub-lieutenant in a regiment, instead of provoking genial reminiscences from the old officers and admiration for the new sartorial fashions, roused a sense of insecurity; lieutenants now seemed uncontrollable and were therefore given petty duties which sergeants had once per-

[1] General Debeney, *La Guerre et les hommes. Réflexions d'après-guerre* (1937), 9–16, 231–8.
[2] Marshal Juin, *Je suis soldat* (1960), 26.

formed.[1] On the other hand there was the reservist who broke
down the distinctions between civil and military life, and who
inspired horror in the old professionals. The First World War
created a gulf between those who had served in it and those who
were despised as mere novices and theorists of war. The officers
promoted during the First World War 'were fully informed on
points of detail but had no general view of their task. They
could command, but they could not instruct the soldier.'[2]
The increasing number of bureaucratic administrators added
new tensions. It was not surprising that the army's defeat in
1940 was not accepted as an inevitable collapse and that bitter
internecine recriminations at once tore it apart. Only a small
proportion of the army actually had a chance to fight the
enemy, and it felt as betrayed by those who remained in the
rear as by the politicians.

Throughout this period, therefore, to be an army officer
was to occupy an uncertain social position, to be subject to
ideological tensions and to continual pressure for modernisation and reorganisation. The country could not decide what
kind of army it wanted: some officers reacted to the insecurity
this created for them either by grasping at traditional values,
or by entrenching themselves in hierarchical routine. But these
were reactions which concealed much diversity. Partly because
it suffered repeated defeats—in 1870, in 1914, in 1940—and
partly because it was so attacked by the left, the army felt it was
not appreciated by public opinion, and rather than incarnate
the common denominator of French democracy, it withdrew
into its own world, cultivating virtues special to itself. Instead
of seeing itself as a branch of industrial and technological
advance, it confined itself to the cult of individual prowess. The
army's endless difficulties should be seen as a particularly
well-documented instance of the hesitations of Frenchmen in
general before democratic and scientific change, and of the
obstacles that stood in the way both of understanding that
change and of adapting to it. Alfred de Vigny's statement that
the army 'sought its soul everywhere and could not find it'
always remained true. The officers were themselves the most

[1] Marcel Souriau, *De la baïonnette à l'épée* (1934), 96–110.
[2] General Tanant, 'Les Officiers de la guerre', *Revue des Deux Mondes* (1 Mar.
1926).

serious and constant critics of the army, in its organisation and its methods, and it was their disputes which provided the basis for the unending political debates about the army.

That the army was only reflecting national difficulties can be seen from the slowness with which parliament itself modernised it.[1] In 1848, as has been seen, the army was still essentially a professional one, even though some people were conscripted into it. Napoleon III, instructed by the astonishing defeat of Austria by Prussia in 1856, determined to increase the size of his forces by making universal conscription a reality; but he met with almost universal opposition and the law of reorganisation passed in 1868 simply instituted a reserve militia which remained a largely paper organisation. After the catastrophic defeat of 1871, public opinion could no longer resist the arguments for universal service, but the law of 1873, while adopting it in theory, allowed the old system to survive. The main reason why this happened was that Thiers—who was proud of his knowledge of military history—was a firm believer in the superiority of professional armies, and he was able to carry the day because a larger army would require more money, which parliament was unwilling to raise. So though five years' military service for everybody was what the new law prescribed, financial constraints prevented this from being implemented. Some men were called up for five years, but let out after four years, while others were simply given basic training for six months (later increased to nine and then twelve months). The system of buying a replacement was abolished, but equality was still not achieved. Those who wished to ensure that they would not fall into the five-year category could volunteer just before their call-up. They then served a definite term of one year only. This was in fact a piece of class favouritism, because the volunteer had to pay 1,500 francs to cover the cost of his clothing and equipment. In fact, only some 6,000 people a year took advantage of this system, but it became a symbol of the undemocratic character of the army—as too did the exemption of priests and schoolmasters. Only in 1905 were these variations abandoned and two years' service for all instituted.[2] The size of the peacetime army in 1872 was half a

---

[1] J. Monteilhet, *Les Institutions militaires de la France 1814–1924* (1926).
[2] Payment for the students' one-year volunteer system was abolished in 1889.

million; in 1900 it was 600,000; and the law of 1913 raised it to over 800,000. Had a war been declared in 1872 only 1,250,000 could have been mobilised, but by 1914 this figure had been raised to over 3,500,000.[1] Between 1800 and 1814, only 1,600,000 Frenchmen had served in Napoleon's army. In the four years of the First World War, 8,400,000 were mobilised. It was only gradually that the full militarisation of the nation was achieved. But this still did not mean that the military experience of Frenchmen attained an egalitarian uniformity, any more than did their educational experience at school.

Young conscripts sometimes found their first year of service a terrible strain. On arrival they might be expected to sleep four in one bed, and if there were still not enough beds, they might have to sleep on the floor. Their work was fixed for them in a programme that covered twelve hours a day, so that they barely had time to wash or keep their clothes clean. They exercised in all weathers. What struck them most painfully was the discipline, the foul language of the N.C.O.s, the mania about polish, the endless parades, the arbitrary punishments. A conscript, writing in 1894, complained that a trivial offence like arriving late for a class, or borrowing a colleague's arms for parade, would be punished with two days' detention, mislaying an item of equipment with four days', impoliteness to a superior with fifteen days'.[2] There were some who complained that the food was disgusting, and indeed the government seems to have budgeted for only one franc a day to feed and clothe a soldier, but to boys from really poor origins, like Marc Bonnefoy, who joined up in 1859 when he failed to gain admission into a teacher training college, meat and white bread every day were a marvellous treat: conversation in his company centred around food and how they could get hold of wine to complete it.[3] Once the initial training had been accomplished, however, the conscript's main problem was boredom: 'after the first year', wrote a captain who had served during the Second Empire, 'the soldier of the period spent three-quarters of his

[1] Richard D. Challener, *The French Theory of the Nation in Arms 1866–1939* (New York, 1955), 47.

[2] Victor Monmillion, *Trois ans au régiment* (1894), 132.

[3] Marc Bonnefoy, *Souvenirs d'un simple soldat en campagne, 1859* (n.d., about 1871), 21–5.

time in complete physical and intellectual idleness'.[1] That used to be one of the attractions of military life; but as soldiering came to be taken more seriously and as bureaucracy expanded, spare time was increasingly filled in with futile administrative chores and exercises of doubtful value.

In the process, the rigour of discipline increased, though in the course of the twentieth century it was relaxed again. Discipline had been fairly loose in the army of the *ancien régime*, even if punishments were savage. Complaints against 'the spirit of independence and insubordination' and laments that 'authority no longer exists' were already being made in 1775; insubordination was doubtless far more frequent than it was a century later, despite the advent of democracy. However, the army increasingly differentiated itself from society by building up rules and regulations which defined with growing precision the rights and privileges of every rank. The main achievement of the first half of the century was to give predominance to promotion by seniority, and the punctual execution of the rules therefore grew into a fetish. A Russian general argued that France was defeated in 1870 partly because of the complicated disciplinary rules it had evolved, which inculcated 'an inveterate habit of blind and inert subordination, erected into an absolute principle and having the force of law at all levels of the hierarchy'. It used to be considered improper to talk about promotion, but this now became a principal topic of conversation among officers, who therefore concentrated on the maintenance of appearances, on standing up straight and carrying out the regulations precisely.[2] The obsession with saluting correctly, dressing in exactly the right way, went hand in hand with an increasing stress on differences in rank and condemnation of excessive familiarity between them.[3] The regulations gave the soldier no rights to time off: leave was a rare concession. N.C.O.s decorated with the Legion of Honour could return to barracks at 1 a.m., other N.C.O.s and decorated soldiers had to be back by 11 p.m., but the ordinary soldier

[1] Capt. Pringent, *Les Permissions dans l'armée. Leur influence sur l'instruction, la discipline et l'esprit militaire* (1896), 7.

[2] A. Lambert, *Étude sur l'état moral de l'armée française et de l'armée allemande en 1870* (1908), 13, 42.

[3] Capt. Édouard Gillon, *Le Nouveau Soldat du service obligatoire* (1873), 53. Cf. Capt. d'Arbeux, *L'Officier contemporain: la démocratisation de l'armée 1899–1910* (1911).

was confined after 9 p.m. However, under pressure from electors and influential parents, the army became more lenient at
the end of the century in the granting of leave, and soon
weekends, public holidays, harvest time and family feasts were
accepted as an excuse for absence. A new pattern developed,
of soldiers being busy during the week and then going home
on Sunday, returning exhausted in the early hours. The old
officers complained that all the discipline instilled during the
week was forgotten in the riotous, noisy and often drunken
behaviour on leave days.[1]

Having first tried to drill independence out of the conscript,
the army, in its new regulations of 1905, began appealing to his
spirit of initiative. But at that date, there was little possibility
of his profiting morally from his military service, and even after
it, the 'often brutalising and sometimes revolting life' the army
offered, 'duty rendered painful by unintelligent and malicious
N.C.O.s', could hardly inspire patriotism. 'There is perhaps
no place where ideas of liberty, initiative, responsibility, dignity and duty are more ignored, more outrageously flouted
than in the barracks.'[2] A general writing in 1901 admitted that
the efforts of some idealist officers to win the affection of their
troops had had little result: 'the soldiers do not like their
officers, they only fear them'. Too many officers still thought
that their task was to snarl, to criticise, to appear to be constantly in a state of fury.[3] However, with the spread of anti-
militarism and communism, it became clear that simply
punishing soldiers for singing the Internationale would not
help the army's effectiveness. A new school of thought urged
the application of 'psychological' techniques to win over the
unruly conscript, or to get him discredited by his own peers.
Orders would be badly executed, it was now said, only if they
were badly given; conscripts should no longer be discouraged
as soon as they arrived by being boringly forced to memorise
the names of different parts of the rifle and a multitude of
orders and prohibitions, but shown that a soldier's life could
be fun.[4] Already in the first decade of the twentieth century the

[1] Capt. Pringent, op. cit.

[2] *Vers une armée démocratique. Trois réunions militaires* (1907, Au Sillon).

[3] Gen. Cremer, *Éducation du soldat et principalement du fantassin* (1911) (written
in 1901).

[4] Lt. Vaillant, *L'Âme du soldat. Essai de psychologie militaire pratique* (1910), 9, 35.

officers had yielded to the soldiers' hatred of drill and had greatly reduced it.[1] After the First World War, it appeared that the whole notion of military authority was in crisis: 'too many young officers doubt their right to command'. The army began to have a more modest view of its role, and to fall on to the defensive against society. 'The army', wrote an officer in 1919, 'does not demand to be the sole élite. But it must be one of the élites, and officially recognised and treated as such.'[2] Some officers now took to shaking hands with their men, though most stuck to the old ways. Some of those who had risen out of the ranks during the war were uncertain of their status, feeling, as one said, 'like *nouveaux riches*'.[3] 'Prussian-style' discipline was discredited. It was now said that it was impossible to 'radically transform the mentality' of conscripts who served so briefly, so all that should be aimed at was their 'adaptation'; but even this should take account of the peculiar character of Frenchmen. Frenchmen liked talking, so officers should let them talk and should make speeches back. They were democratic, and so it was no use trying to get obedience by being dignified, contemptuous or haughty.[4] Soldiers who persistently rejected discipline were now therefore treated more leniently, classified as 'unadapted' or 'degenerate', and declared unfit for military service. But this influence of psychology was slight: little more than a thousand men were freed in this way each year. Most recalcitrant conscripts were declared perfectly sane but 'fond of liberty' or 'fond of drink', and punished for it.[5]

Those who expressed the hope that the army would instil discipline into the nation were countered by others who accused the army of being a major instrument of demoralisation, of instilling more bad habits than it cured. It is impossible to decide between these arguments, neither of which could be proved. It is even uncertain whether the army did anything to alter the hygienic habits of the nation. The army's sanitary arrangements were very slow to change. A parliamentary

[1] Capt. Jibé, *L'Armée nouvelle. Ce qu'elle pense, ce qu'elle veut* (1905), 296.

[2] Capt. M., *La Crise de l'autorité et l'armée future*, reprinted from *Études* (20 Oct. 1919).

[3] Marcel Souriau, *De la baïonnette à l'épée* (1934), 110.

[4] General A. J. Tanant, *La Discipline dans les armées françaises* (1938), 232, 334; id., *L'Officier de France* (1938), 30, 156–9, 195.

[5] Capt. Ch. Pont, *Les Indisciplinés dans l'armée (normaux et anormaux)* (1912), 203.

inquiry of 1914 revealed that the barracks built after 1885 had
no drainage system, and were even less satisfactory than the
older ones because, owing to financial stringency, they crammed
too many soldiers into too small a space. The older barracks
usually had small rooms with eight or ten beds in each; the
new ones had between twenty and eighty beds in each dor-
mitory and as the size of the army increased, beds were placed
so close that there was no room at all between them. Refec-
tories were abolished in most barracks to be turned into
dormitories, and it was there that the soldiers had to eat.
There were not enough clothes to go round: in 1913 every
conscript was issued with one new pair of shoes but these
were not to be worn except for inspections; he also got one
pair of old, unwearable shoes and one half-worn pair. There
were only 24,000 hospital beds for the whole army and only
1,518 doctors.[1] It is probable that the army did more to cure
venereal disease than to spread it.[2] In 1869 19 per cent of
soldiers in hospital were there for venereal disease; but during
the First World War a very active campaign greatly reduced
this scourge.[3] The evidence however is somewhat contradictory
as to whether the cause of cleanliness, as opposed to that of
polish, was advanced. An official manual was in 1926 still
warning recruits never to wash their feet in water, but only to
grease them, never to divest themselves of their flannel vests and
to beware of draughts, not to sleep with their boots on and to
spit only into spittoons.[4]

The hopes that the army would unite the nation spiritually
and destroy or diminish class divisions, were equally over-
optimistic. The army was a democratic institution in the sense
that it gave poor people the opportunity to rise in the social

[1] Lachaud, député, *Enquête sur les moyens propres à améliorer les conditions matérielles
d'existence et d'hygiène de l'armée. Rapport* (Annexe au p.v. de la séance du 23 mars
1914, Chambre des députés), 432, 516.

[2] *Statistique médicale de l'armée 1869* (1872) claims the incidence of V.D. was
halved in the second year of military service. This series, published annually,
is an important source which has been little used hitherto.

[3] Philippe Avon, *Contribution à l'histoire des maladies vénériennes dans l'armée française* (Lyon medical and pharmaceutical thesis, 1968), 28, 44; cf. Sigisbert Cassin,
*Contribution à l'étude des perversions sexuelles et des maladies vénériennes au cours de la
vie de campagne* (Paris medical thesis, 1964), showing 8 per cent homosexuality in
one unit.

[4] Lt. T. Zuccarelli, *Comment on se débrouille au régiment. Livre moral et technique
du jeune soldat* (5th edition, 1926), 14, 18–19.

scale, but that made it all the more attached to hierarchical distinctions and susceptible to the charms of wealth and birth. It was the last institution to maintain elaborate controls on the marriage of its members. Until the very end of the nineteenth century, even an N.C.O. could not get married unless his bride had a dowry of at least 5,000 francs, or an annual income of 250 francs, but her earnings could not be included. For officers, long inquiries were set in motion to ensure not only that their prospective brides had adequate dowries, but that these were securely invested; full details of their shares and mortgages were required and only state and railway bonds were acceptable; real property which yielded no income was disregarded; if they had siblings, similar details had to be provided about them, so that the position after the parents' death could be guaranteed; a report from the gendarmerie had to be provided to attest their good character.[1] The paradox was that the levels of income required were pathetically small: the officer was a poor man, even if he was obsessed by these monetary considerations. It was not surprising therefore that conscripts from well-to-do families were, in the nineteenth century, treated with more consideration than poor ones. When René Vallery-Radot, of good bourgeois stock, was called up just after the Franco-Prussian war, his hair was cut off and he was set to work at 6 a.m. like everybody else, but the colonel and lieutenants addressed him gently and he was segregated from the masses, together with other bourgeois 'volunteers'. He was allowed to keep his flannel waistcoat, his own shirts and socks. The sergeant amused him by shouting defensively, 'It's me what gives the orders. Well, what's got into you, why are you looking at me like that? Am I not speaking French?'[2]

The attitudes of the N.C.O.s were one major factor in the maintenance of class divisions. They were, as one of them described them in 1882, the 'military bohemians'.[3] They had made the army their life, or at least they dared not leave it when their seven-year term was up, because they had nowhere

[1] Capt. E. Renault, *Du mariage des militaires* (1895).

[2] René Vallery-Radot, *Journal d'un volontaire d'un an au 10e de ligne* (1874), 37.

[3] F. M. J. Dutreuil de Rhins, *La Bohème militaire ou de l'avenir des sous-officiers de l'armée* (Saint-Étienne, 1882).

else to go. They thought a lot about promotion, but they seldom got it. Like artists who never painted the masterpiece they dreamed of and who never won appreciation, the N.C.O.s could barely live off their pay, contracted debts and then joined up for a further term in order to get the 1,000 francs' bounty this brought. If they managed to become sub-lieutenants, they considered themselves worse off than daily labourers, because of the obligations a commission brought. If they retired at forty-five or fifty, they were fit for nothing else, and were as old as civilians of sixty. Some consoled themselves in café life, some in artistic hobbies; later some were to find distraction in sport; few could afford marriage. However, until 1914, the N.C.O.s enjoyed a certain autonomy. The officers kept to themselves, were seldom seen and the adjutants were left in charge. Corporals used to have wide powers of punishment, which required a captain's confirmation only after the reforms of 1905–13. The N.C.O.s were firm believers in hierarchy; discipline restrained them from criticising their officers; but they reflected national attitudes enough to respect a titled officer no more, and no less, than they respected an officer who could ride a horse well. Those who accepted their own limitations looked on the sergeants preparing for entry to Saint-Maixent (with a view to winning commissions) as their intellectual superiors even if they were junior in rank. There were many who did not want to become officers, because they did not feel at home in the officers' world ('it would involve making love to the châtelaine instead of the farmer's wife'). They were content to be instructors, with no pretensions to being educators. They were proud of being masters in their own sphere and relished their power to give or refuse leave. Those who had no academic qualifications enjoyed showing intellectual soldiers their place, to make it clear that intellect was not enough. However, this segregation of ranks was somewhat diminished between the wars, and a certain resentment built up against subalterns who thought they could do the N.C.O.'s job better. The army called this new relationship 'team-work'. A conscript army meant that most officers had to participate in the training of soldiers, rather than leave this task to specialists. There was therefore more contact between different ranks, but not necessarily more social mixing.

The First World War provided those sections of the community which felt unappreciated with a chance to prove their worth. The aristocracy, in particular, saw in it a chance to revive their tradition of military prowess; many of them joined the air force and their bravery was noted; but many ordinary people were equally brave. This equality in the face of danger is said to have ended what remained of the peasants' humility towards the aristocracy, but the change was probably not so fundamental. The relation of peasant and noble was tied up with economic factors which reappeared as soon as they were demobilised; what was probably more important was that the peasant often found himself richer after the war, and the nobleman poorer. The clergy likewise made a reputation for themselves by their spirit of martyrdom and their disregard of danger and death: they won respect on an individual basis but the anticlerical quarrels were too firmly built into the political system to vanish as a result. The intellectuals, for their part, did not emerge as natural leaders in this war. The ordinary soldier showed considerable suspicion of intellectual superiority, and it was the intellectuals who were impressed by the qualities of endurance and humour that the uneducated masses showed. The level of conversation was not generally raised by their presence in the trenches: rather they came down to that of their fellows. They discovered that if they wanted to maintain good relations they had, as one of them put it, to return to the fold, to abandon their aloofness. The war brought to the surface forces in favour of greater egalitarianism, but it also showed that they were by no means all-powerful. There was bitter animosity against those who obtained jobs away from the danger of war. Nevertheless men from the industrial and commercial worlds were largely ill at ease in the army, and many did their best to escape quickly from the front, either back to industry, or into commissions, or into safe jobs in the rear. Those who fought as officers at the front established a tacit pact with their soldiers, by which they got complete obedience in battle, but then withdrew into a sort of reciprocal indifference or broad mutual tolerance. They did not generally make friends with the workers and 'after the storm, these four years of confraternity in arms did not prevent them from resuming their respective places in civil life, each on opposite sides of the barricade'.[1] Two psychologists who studied the effects of the war on individual soldiers claimed that the worker likewise was not basically changed as a result of his military experience. 'Despite the wall that for four years isolated the soldier from his original surroundings, despite his continual impregnation in a new and persistent atmosphere, every *poilu*, with his opinions, attitudes and speech superficially modified, preserved intact his fundamental characteristics.' It was generally city workers, and more especially wine sellers and small shopkeepers, who established themselves as leaders in the little groups of which the army was composed. They gave expression to the spirit of opposition to authority and to the sense of egalitarianism that the soldier felt, which balanced his obedience; their ability to be witty at the expense of the army, to find ways of getting round regulations, but also to work with others, created much of the sense of solidarity that made the co-operation of people of different backgrounds possible. However, 79 per cent of the soldiers at the front were peasants. The war experienced by the peasants and by the rest of society was not entirely the same one. The peasants seem to have borne their war with patient resignation. They were said to have remained as suspicious, egoistical, independent and solitary as ever. They were more respectful of authority than the workers were, but whereas the workers ultimately gave way, the peasants could be obstinate with unshakeable serenity. The peasants consoled themselves with the deep satisfactions they derived from the small items of property they collected and above all from their meals, 'bringing food out of his pockets in every moment of leisure and eating it slowly, religiously, with voluptuousness and concentration'. Soldiers, of whatever class, thus sheltered themselves from the horrors that surrounded them by developing automatic reactions to it, a professional behaviour, escaping with irony, hobbies or physical pleasures whenever they could. Emotion was gradually mastered by distraction and humour.[2]

Few people thought better of the army after 1919 simply because they had served in it. At Saint-Cyr, the first piece of

---

[1] Dr. Louis Huot and Dr. Paul Voivenel, *La Psychologie du soldat* (1918), 44.
[2] Jacques Meyer, *La Vie quotidienne des soldats pendant la grande guerre* (1966). For the more general consequences of the First World War, see chapter 9.

advice young cadets were given was to wear civilian clothes whenever they went into certain districts of Paris, to avoid incidents. 'Among the masses, we were considered the enemy, *les payots*. In bourgeois circles, we were considered imbeciles.' And since officers' pay fell drastically with inflation, some even took on night work as taxi drivers to keep their families and some ate only one meal a day.[1]

There was an obvious lack of concordance between public attitudes to war and state expenditure on it. The army and navy were by far the most expensive items in the budgets, which shows that though politicians talked a great deal about educational and social reform, their priorities were not really altered.[2]

Budget Expenditure (in million francs)

	1852	1872	1891	1910	1913	1930
Military	461	712	1120	1520	1787	15110
Education	19	34	194	279	309	3790
Social Services	—	—	—	93	204	2140
Public Works	63	109	244	268	269	5180
Fine Arts	—	6	8	20	?	?
Public Debt Interest	274	1075	1127	1121	1165	27000
Total	1525	2735	3304	4265	4800	61710

Now France was of course not unusual in utilising its taxes above all for defence; but the figures illustrate that the nature of its political system made comparatively little difference. Having won universal suffrage and control over their own destinies, the French people exerted no real pressure to diminish this expenditure. Pacifism was preached only by small minorities, and without much practical effect. The reason was that, despite the attractions of peace, force was not discredited. Despite all the hardships of the Napoleonic wars, and all the opposition to the dictatorship they involved, the victories won in those years very quickly turned into a glorious legend, which even liberals like Thiers admired. After the Revolution of 1848, when a new age of fraternity was expected, the republic was strongly

---

[1] Robert Darcy, *Oraison funèbre pour la vieille armée* (1947), 49–51.

[2] See *Annuaire statistique* (1878 ff.) for budget summaries, but these involve many complications. Cf. Pierre Baudin, *L'Argent de la France* (1914) on some aspects of this; M. Block and Guillaumin, *Annuaire de l'économie politique et de la statistique pour 1857*, 50–1.

attracted by the idea of a war of liberation.[1] Napoleon III, who had an acute understanding of public opinion, at once launched into a series of wars, though he took care to keep them short. His victories in the Crimea and Italy undoubtedly increased his prestige. A writer like Flaubert could protest that these triumphs left him completely cold, but he did so precisely because they excited nearly everyone else. The way the war of 1870 was declared shows how even those who most sincerely desired to put an end to violence in international relations could not escape their atavistic sense of honour, which overrode their utopianism. Émile Ollivier, who was head of the government in that year, was a man of genuinely cosmopolitan culture, passionately fond of Italy, where he frequently travelled, a great admirer of Wagner, husband of the daughter of Liszt, well read in the literature of all Europe, and a firm believer that all peoples have the right to decide their own fate without interference from their neighbours. He rejected the idea of the balance of power as a defensible principle of foreign policy; he insisted that the 'true principle of foreign policy is the principle of non-intervention, precisely because it is the policy of peace'; he denounced all plans for the territorial aggrandisement of France, saying that he wanted his country to be influential 'because it is loved and not because it is feared'; and he looked forward to a Confederation of Europe 'in the manner of the U.S.A.'. But when he was faced with the ambitions of Bismarck, exceptions to his policy of peace revealed themselves. 'The honour of France' had to be preserved and if it was slighted, war was necessary to avenge it. A war was legitimate, he also said, 'when it is desired by a whole nation'. For all his idealism, in the end he gave way to 'popular pressure', or what he judged to be that: his democratic system contained a basic and unavoidable contradiction.[2] For all his pacifism, he also believed that governments should be 'firm'. Militarism was sustained by a much deeper and wider tradition that associated virility with physical strength or brutality.

[1] L. C. Jennings, *France and Europe in 1848* (Oxford, 1973).

[2] Theodore Zeldin, *Émile Ollivier and the Liberal Empire of Napoleon III* (Oxford, 1963), 168–84. On public opinion on the army in this period cf. J. Casevitz, *Une Loi manquée: la Loi Niel 1866–8* (n.d., about 1960) and Gordon Wright, 'Public Opinion and Conscription in France 1866–70', *Journal of Modern History* (Mar. 1942), 26–45.

A peasant who served in the 1914–18 war recorded that when he left home, his mother expressed satisfaction despite her sorrow at his departure, saying 'When one has not been a soldier, one is not a man'.[1] This tradition ultimately overrode all that the economists wrote about war being disastrous for prosperity.[2] The war of 1870–1 was economically disastrous, but after that of 1914–18 it was realised that, if one survived the carnage, one could also make extremely large profits from it.

Under the Second Empire the republicans, having been repressed by Napoleon III's troops, abandoned their original bellicosity, attacked militarism and the 'military spirit' and demanded the suppression of permanent armies. The League for Peace and Liberty, which published a journal called *The United States of Europe* (1867), had as one of its principal organisers Ferdinand Buisson, whom Ferry later appointed director of primary education. Only defensive wars, using the *levée en masse*, were now acceptable. But after 1870 the recovery of Alsace and Lorraine became an essential aim of the republicans, who never quite resolved the contradiction in which this placed them. On the one hand they encouraged military training, even in schools, but on the other they were suspicious of the army, or at least of professional soldiers. One strand of republicanism poured scorn on the 'bandits' whom history had glorified for their barbaric conquests, but another was intensely patriotic, and urged the people to keep their eyes fixed on the frontiers of the lost provinces.[3] It is difficult to be sure how public opinion in general, as opposed to the politicians, felt on this issue; the rhetorical platitudes should not be too easily accepted as expressions of genuine consensus. The hesitations of military reform reflected a wider uncertainty.

In the Third Republic the main advocates of pacifism and anti-militarism were the socialists, who maintained that the army was simply a tool used by the capitalists to keep the proletariat under their yoke; no war was worth fighting, it would only increase the suffering of the masses and involve them in issues which were of no real concern to them. If a war did break

[1] J. L. Talmard, *Pages de guerre d'un paysan 1914–18* (Lyon, 1971), 10.

[2] E. Silberner, *The Problem of War in Nineteenth Century Economic Thought* (Princeton, 1946).

[3] Georges Goyau, *L'Idée de patrie et l'humanitarisme 1866–1901* (1903); H. Contamine, *La Revanche 1870–1914* (1957).

out, the workers should declare a general strike and paralyse the state before it could cause any trouble. But though socialist congresses continued to repeat these principles, there were two difficulties: first, that a general strike had little chance of being effective, because French workers were barely unionised; and secondly that the problem of self-defence against invasion was not tackled. It was only Jaurès who finally developed these woolly ideas into a practical programme. He accepted patriotism, provided it was not offensive; and he accepted the need for a policy of defence. He wrote a major work urging the creation of a 'New Army' which he hoped would be a new instrument of national cohesion.[1] Instead of a professional army, which he regarded as inevitably an instrument of aggressive wars, he urged the formation of a citizen army, for which everybody would be trained from the age of thirteen, but which would involve only six months of actual conscript service. Such an army, he thought—and he had the support of a number of officer theoreticians—would be far more formidable than a much smaller professional one. The flaw in this reasoning was the expectation that 'the nation in arms' would necessarily be pacifist. In 1914, at any rate, there was almost no resistance to general mobilisation, and even the socialists found themselves reluctantly and agonisingly compelled to abandon their opposition to the idea of using force.[2] After the war, Léon Blum wrote that the old idea of honour was finally abandoned and that Frenchmen no longer felt the need to fight, in the way they used to, rather than face dishonour.[3] There was some truth in this, but even the socialist party remained divided in its attitude to war.[4] Blum recognised that despite the desire not to repeat the widespread mistake of 1914, 'a dangerous fatalism is in the process of re-establishing itself in the public mind'.[5] The idea of a professional army was abandoned at the very time when Colonel de Gaulle was arguing that technical developments had made any other kind useless, because highly trained technicians were needed to man the new engines of war: the outcome of any struggle, he claimed, would be

[1] Jean Jaurès, *L'Armée nouvelle* (1911, reprinted 1915 and 1932).
[2] Actes du Colloque, *Jaurès et la nation* (Toulouse University, 1965); H. Goldberg, *The Life of Jean Jaurès* (1968), 385-9, 417-74.
[3] Léon Blum, *Les Problèmes de la paix* (1931), 206.
[4] Richard Gombin, *Les Socialistes et la guerre* (1970).   [5] Ibid. viii.

decided by their skill in the first few weeks.[1] Nevertheless
military service was reduced to one year and Jaurès's idea of
a defensive army was virtually adopted as official policy. The
result was that in 1940 France was incapable of meeting the
challenge from Germany other than defensively.

In 1914–18, there was no serious threat to the idea of
national loyalty in war: the army mutinies of 1917 affected only
30–40,000 men and only 629 soldiers were found guilty in the
subsequent courts martial; at no stage did the mutineers stop
fighting the enemy; the revolt was against incompetent leadership, not against the war itself.[2] In 1940–4 the idea of collaboration with Germany in the interests of peace was, as will be
seen, quite widely accepted as an inevitable necessity, and in
some cases even with enthusiasm. But that did not mean that
there was a general disillusionment with violence as a political
instrument. On the contrary, violence now became more
frequent and more brutal than it had ever been in this period.
In the wars of 1854–6 and 1859, there was virtually no anger
among the soldiers against their enemies. In 1870, there was
very little until the Prussians occupied the country; only then,
under Gambetta's leadership, did the war, as a German officer
noted, 'gradually acquire a hideous character' and atrocities
reminiscent of the Thirty Years War were perpetrated, particularly by the volunteer *francs-tireurs*.[3] In 1914–18 for the first
time the government applied itself to stimulating hatred of the
Boche in a propaganda campaign which, however, was more
noticeable in print than in conversation. There were some
soldiers who derived deep satisfaction from killing Germans,
but there were not many who still believed that to die for
one's country was the highest good. On the whole, prisoners
of war were treated decently and the most common comment
on them was that 'they are men like us', *pauvres bougres*.[4]
It was only in 1939 that the principle of 'honour' as the basis
of war was replaced by hatred of the enemy. Only then were
nationalism and violence finally married, though it was a
marriage that immediately aroused revulsion.

[1] Charles de Gaulle, *Vers l'armée de métier* (1934).
[2] Guy Pedroncini, *Les Mutineries de 1917* (1967), 308–12.
[3] M. Howard, *The Franco-Prussian War* (1961), 380.
[4] J. Meyer, *La Vie quotidienne des soldats pendant la grande guerre* (1966), 272.

This is a paradoxical conclusion. At the beginning of this period the professional soldier had thought little of death, had accepted the idea of killing others and of being killed himself as simply part of the lot he had chosen. He fought duels on the most trivial pretexts, and it was only in 1857 that, for the first time, an officer was reduced to the ranks for killing another in a duel—though he was recommissioned a year later and ended up a general. Till then, thirty days' detention would have been a more usual reprimand.[1] In the conquest of Algeria, French officers showed themselves capable of extreme cruelty towards their enemies. But as peace descended on Europe, the officer became more and more a bureaucrat and organiser, and as weapons became more complicated, he was increasingly a technician. He ceased to glorify violence and regarded himself essentially as a guardian of peace. But at the same time war became an increasingly murderous business.

The army was indeed united by *esprit de corps* and there undoubtedly was a 'military type' of individual, who could be instantly recognised. This should not cause one to forget that the army was also a microcosm of society at large and, as such, infinitely varied beneath its uniform appearance. It was no accident that Marshal MacMahon, who became the first president of the Third Republic, had hesitated in his youth between becoming a priest or a soldier.[2] There was a great deal in common between these two apparently opposed professions: both were based on a sense of dedication and service to the community and both tended to adopt conservative attitudes. But it should not be surprising, either, that Marshal de Saint-Arnaud, who helped Louis Napoleon carry out the *coup d'état* of 1851, and who therefore has the reputation of a brutal reactionary, should have been an opera singer in his youth, an able musician and a master of four foreign languages. Saint-Arnaud turned to the army as bankrupt authors have turned to novel writing. He had spent his early manhood dissolutely, moving from job to job, falling increasingly into debt. He found in the conquest of Algeria an opportunity to make good, and to restore his fortune. He had nothing to lose: he exhibited extraordinary courage in battle and within

[1] P. Chalmin, *L'Officier français de 1815 à 1870* (1957), 63.
[2] J. Silvestre de Sacy, *Le Maréchal de MacMahon, duc de Magenta 1808–93* (1960).

fourteen years he had risen from the rank of lieutenant to that
of general.[1] His was a career that had once been common,
under Napoleon I; and under Napoleon III it was still possible
for a trooper like Bazaine to become a marshal. Most generals,
under the Third Republic, had careers indistinguishable, in
the regularity of their promotion and in the obscurity of their
services, from those of civil servants, but the army did offer
opportunities for very diverse talents. General André, who is
remembered for assisting Combes to purge the army of clericals, was a distinguished scientist, who had been top graduate
of his year at the Polytechnic, and later its director; he had
assisted Littré in the preparation of his dictionary and had
many contacts with the scientific and university world.[2]

Eminence in the army could therefore be a qualification for
political power, even in the bourgeois Third Republic; generals
liked to make names for themselves also as authors, and they
were often elected to the French Academy. Philippe Pétain,
who had only just scraped into Saint-Cyr (403rd out of 412
admitted), had by the age of fifty-eight reached the rank of
colonel and would have retired into oblivion but for the war
of 1914. His promotion had been prevented not so much by
a lack of distinction—many dull men were promoted above
him—nor by his easy morals and his lifelong devotion to women,
which made him conclude, in extreme old age, that 'sex and
food are the only things that matter', but because he refused
to see war as any longer a heroic matter, in which *furia fran-
cese* could override all obstacles. He had argued that the experience of 1870–1 had shown that an enemy with superior
fire power could not be made to retreat by a heroic offensive,
and that far more attention should therefore be given to
teaching accurate shooting and to protecting soldiers against
enemy guns. When traditional French methods failed in 1914–
16, Pétain was given the chance to prove that he was right, and
he became the most popular of all generals, because he was
regarded as caring about the survival and welfare of his troops.
There was in fact nothing specially sentimental in his theory:
he was simply adapting old doctrines in the light of technical

---

[1] Quatrelles l'Épine, *Le Maréchal de Saint-Arnaud* (1929), 1. 39, 107.
[2] Anon., *Les Généraux de l'armée française* (1904) gives the careers of nearly 500
generals then living.

changes. That did not mean that adaptability was what always
distinguished him. From 1920 to 1936 he was the dominant
influence in defence policy, and throughout that time he
continued to reiterate his old ideas, formulated at the end of
the nineteenth century, failing to appreciate the revolutionary
changes created by the tank and regarding the air force only
as an instrument of defence. It was left to a radical politician
(Daladier, minister of defence 1936–40) to take the initiative
in ordering more tanks; but though France (with England)
had more tanks than Germany in 1940, its army was still not
trained to use them. Pétain's ambitions inflated as he got older.
He arranged for subordinates to write books and articles under
his name, giving them an individual stamp by a meticulous
correction of style. His breach with Charles de Gaulle dates
from 1934, when de Gaulle, who was one of the bright young
admirers he employed for this purpose, broke the rules and
insisted on claiming personal credit for what he had written:
their political estrangement began as an authors' quarrel.
Pétain came to believe that as Europe was taken over by military dictatorships, he was better suited than politicians to deal
with them; he claimed to be above politics, but did nothing to
dissuade the right-wing press from seeing in him the dictator
the country needed to end the chaos caused by the politicians.
In 1935 *Le Petit Journal* organised a referendum amongst its
readers asking them whom they would best like as a dictator.
Pétain came top with 38,000 votes, Laval second with 31,000
and Doumergue, the caretaker prime minister, third with
23,000. Pétain's advent to power in 1940 was the result of a
long-organised campaign, which he did nothing to discourage.
It was later said that he was essentially an actor, who adopted the
role of the severe, fatherly old man with calculated ambition.[1]

In Charles de Gaulle, the notion of military service as the
highest form of dedication to the country found its fullest and
most extraordinary expression. De Gaulle was quickly spotted
as an officer of exceptional character and intellect. He was
selected to lecture at the Army Staff College while still very

---

[1] On Pétain's Vichy regime, see below, chapter 8. Cf. Richard Griffiths,
Marshal Pétain (1970), 173; Henri Amouroux, *Pétain avant Vichy* (1967); D. B.
Ralston, *The Army of the Republic: the Place of the Military in the Political Evolution
of France 1871–1914* (Cambridge, Mass., 1967); Judith M. Hughes, *To the Maginot
Line, The Politics of French Military Preparation in the 1920s* (Cambridge, Mass., 1971).

young, but his superior there, though describing him as brilliant and talented, commented that he 'unfortunately mars these indisputable qualities by his excessive self-confidence, un-willingness to listen to the opinions of others, and his attitude of a king in exile'.[1] This was in 1923. De Gaulle had early decided that 'nothing great can be done without great men, and they are great because they have willed greatness'. He could 'see no other reason for life save to make [his] mark on events'.[2] The most noble cause was to give glory to France, which he regarded not as simply a nation, or a race, but a person, in the way Michelet had done, and he liked to talk of *notre dame la France*. The French army, he said, was 'one of the greatest things in the world'. He had an overriding sense of his own mission and of his own uniqueness. If Pétain took to acting the role of an elder statesman, de Gaulle cultivated his own individuality, so as to become 'destiny's instrument', with a consciousness that leadership was a form of artistry. Neither of them had any original ideas in politics; both had been mildly influenced by the Action Française; but de Gaulle was an intellectual as well as a soldier; he filled his military lectures with quotations from Bergson, Comte, Goethe and Tolstoy; he was acutely aware that power depended on 'charisma', and that 'prestige cannot come without mystery'. Instead of seeking popularity by charm, he distinguished himself by his aloofness. He was concerned not with happiness—which he dismissed as a frivolous ideal—but with distant goals of grandeur and honour. He raised soldiering into an almost religious activity. But if people came to see a national saviour in him, as they did also in Pétain, it was because these soldiers were both out-siders to the political system, rather than because they were soldiers; they were men who refused to compromise, rather than representatives of the army. So the national movements of which they became the head were neither of them militarist.[3]

The history of the army provides a warning against the dangers of 'influence' as a historical idea. It is easy to assert that, because universal military service was established, this had

[1] J. R. Tournoux, *Pétain and de Gaulle* (1966) (French original 1964), 46.

[2] C. de Gaulle, *Le Fil de l'épée* (1932).

[3] Stanley Hoffmann, *Decline or Renewal? France since the 1930s* (1974), especially 187–280; A. Werth, *De Gaulle* (1965).

an important effect on the nation; but influence of this kind is very difficult to prove. The army was too complex a body to leave a distinct imprint on those who passed through it. On the contrary, the interest of the army to the historian is rather that it acts as a magnifying lens revealing aspects of national problems, and of personal tensions, more clearly than they can be seen in civil society. Hierarchy and violence were essential features of life in this period, not just of the army. The army helps to show their character. The army, like the criminal courts, enables one to get a glimpse of these forces at work. It shows how Frenchmen had not co-ordinated every side of their behaviour. It is indeed their contradictions that make up their character.

Crime

How safe was one, and how safe did one feel, when one walked alone at night in Paris in this period? How many people thought it wise to own a fire-arm? How likely was a man to come to blows if he had an argument with a stranger, or with his wife? So much was talked about reason and fraternity, that one needs to ask also what place violence still had in this society, what were the acceptable limits of cruelty, and to what extent there was agreement about what was right and what was wrong in the use of force between persons, and in disputes over property. Was the popularity of crime and detective stories a compensation for an increasing docility of manners?

In the late eighteenth century, Sebastian Mercier wrote that 'the streets of Paris are as safe at night as they are in the day-time, apart from a few accidents'. But he added that 'all the scandalous offences and all the crimes, which could frighten people and suggest lack of vigilance by those appointed to guard the security of the capital, are hushed up'. There were thus very few court trials for murder; but in four months in 1785, no less than forty-two bodies were fished out of the Seine, and only three were identified. People were thus able to feel safe, because crime was not widely reported; they were probably not as safe as they thought.[1] A century later a senior police official

[1] E. Petrovitch, 'Recherches sur la criminalité à Paris dans la seconde moitié du 18e siècle', *Cahiers des Annales*, no. 33 (1971), 187–261; cf. R. Cobb, *The Police and the People* (1970).

showed that precisely the opposite situation prevailed. In the month of October 1880, no less than 143 nocturnal attacks were reported by the Paris press. So worried did people become that in 1882 Paris cafés were for a time forbidden to stay open beyond 12.30 at night.[1] In 1911 the conseil général of the Seine passed a motion complaining that armed crimes were becoming so frequent that 'to carry a revolver is becoming a habit; men, women and young people carry this arm in the same way as they carry a purse or a bunch of keys'. Between 1880 and 1907 indeed prosecutions for illegally carrying fire-arms increased tenfold, to over 3,000 a year.[2] However, the police claimed that public opinion was quite simply being unduly alarmed by the sensationalism of the press. Of those 143 nocturnal attacks, it said, over a half, on investigation, proved to have been invented by husbands coming home with empty purses and excusing themselves to their wives with dramatic stories. It was quite safe to walk in the streets at night, at least in central Paris. It was only on the external boulevards, in the slummy outskirts of the city, round Clichy, Saint-Ouen, Pantin and Aubervilliers, that it was dangerous, and most of the victims, who were often cab drivers, waiters or bus conductors coming home late, had courted trouble, because they were not sober. Professional criminals haunted these areas, often pretending to be drunk, starting brawls with genuine drunks and then robbing them; by working in groups they had little difficulty in avoiding the police. Because so much more was expected of the police, because there were more offences of which one could be guilty, and because there was now a press to report every incident, people talked constantly about increasing crime rates.

It is uncertain what the truth behind the statistics was, for criminal statistics are notoriously difficult to interpret; changes in the law make comparisons between different periods impossible. What seems to have happened was that the number of people accused of crimes (rather than misdemeanours) fell constantly, and between 1865 and 1927 they fell by more than half:

[1] L. Puibaraud, *Les Malfaiteurs de profession* (1893), 12.
[2] Edmond Debruille, *Le Port des armes dites prohibées* (Lille law thesis, 1912), 70, 65; Paul Renard, *Les Armes au point de vue pénal* (Paris law thesis, 1911).

Numbers accused of crimes

1851	7,071	people, i.e.	19·7	per 100,000 inhabitants
1865	4,154	,,	10·9	,,
1874	5,228	,,	14·3	,,
1900	3,278	,,	8·4	,,
1921	3,541	,,	9·4	,,
1927	1,844	,,	4·5	,,
1940	714	,,	1·8	,,
1946	1,834	,,	4·5	,,

This fall, however, is largely to be explained by the leniency
of juries; the police increasingly tended to charge people with
misdemeanours rather than crimes, in order that they could
be tried by judges instead. Altogether the number of people
convicted of misdemeanours rose from 237 to 375 per 100,000
inhabitants between 1835 and 1847, and to 444 in 1868.
After having thus almost doubled, the figures settled down to a
remarkably constant level for the next century. Apart from the
two World Wars, the total number of convictions was generally
between 490 and 610 per 100,000 inhabitants. This meant that
in the course of this century, the total number of offences
against the law did increase considerably.

The character of crime, however, altered significantly in
these years, so that these total figures conceal much change.
In the early 1830s, an average of 135,000 people were charged
each year with stealing from forests; in 1835 the state embarked
on a policy of settlement out of court, so that in 1855 there were
only 75,000 such prosecutions; in 1859 a law gave people the
right to settle out of court and these offences greatly diminished.
On the other hand the offence of drunkenness, invented in
1873, produced 4,000 accusations in the following year and
over 60,000 in 1880 (but this was only one-third of the number
of similar prosecutions in England). In 1850, theft was the
main offence with which people were charged, but by 1860
fraud had overtaken it. Between 1830 and 1880, thefts rose
by 238 per cent, frauds by 323 per cent and 'abuse of confidence' by 630 per cent.[1]

[1] André Davidovitch, 'Criminalité et repression en France depuis un siècle
1851–1952', *Revue française de sociologie* (Jan.–Mar. 1961), 30–49; Michelle Perrot,
'Délinquance et système pénitentiaire en France au 19ᵉ siècle', *Annales* (Jan.–Feb.
1975), 67–92.

The criminal statistics give a limited and confusing picture of the dangers of crime. What was probably more influential on public opinion was the growth of the idea of new classes of criminals, who could be seen as concrete and frightening threats. Attention was diverted from the normal violence of ordinary people by the rise of uncontrollable minorities who flouted the very rules of society. In the eighteenth century, there was no idea of criminals in the permanent sense, as a distinct group of people. Much crime was the result of family disputes, and the stronger family ties were, the larger the proportion of murders and assaults that took place within the family.[1] In the course of the nineteenth century, women, who used to play an important part in the violent settlement of disputes of family honour and property, gradually withdrew into a more passive, or at any rate verbal, role: the percentage of prosecutions against women fell by 28 per cent. Women were no longer as dangerous as they had once been, and as they occasionally still were in war and revolution (when their crime rate roughly doubled). Instead there were two new bogies—'the criminal class' and youth.

Balzac in his *Code for Honest Men* warned that 'Thieves form a republic with its own laws, manners ... and language. Theft is a profession ...' He estimated that in Paris, with a population of 120,000, there were no less than 10,000 thieves. This was not surprising, he said, because every morning about 20,000 people woke up in Paris not knowing where their next meal was coming from. He pointed out that the garrison of Paris consisted of exactly 20,000 soldiers—and the forces of order and violence thus just held each other in check.[2] During the July Monarchy, crime was considered to be closely associated with poverty and the hordes of immigrants into the slums, suburbs and industrial towns arose as a growing menace.[3] Then elementary applications of anthropology and psychology were invoked to argue that criminals formed a distinct physical type, mentally deficient and physically marked, more brutal

[1] Nicole Castan, 'La criminalité familiale dans le ressort du parlement de Toulouse 1690–1730', *Cahiers des annales* (1971), no. 33, 91–107.

[2] Louis Chevalier, *Classes laborieuses et classes dangereuses à Paris pendant la première moitié du 19e siècle* (1958), 59–60.

[3] H. A. Frégier, *Des classes dangereuses de la population dans les grandes villes* (1840).

than normal.[1] The theories of the Italian criminologist Lombroso gained credence because they fitted in with French belief in degeneration, the accumulative influence of heredity, alcohol and disease.[2] The criminologist Quetelet argued that people were more violent in the hot south than in the north, but another criminologist, Tarde, pointed out that the difference in behaviour could also be explained by the different degree of urbanisation. Society was therefore held to be to blame for crime, which was increasingly seen as the result of social factors. Durkheim said that crime was a 'normal' rather than a pathological phenomenon, produced by the transformations brought about by the division of labour, which were dissolving old moral ties and leaving individuals without adequate support.[3] Tarde claimed that the majority of murderers and thieves had been abandoned by their parents during childhood, had learnt the criminal way of life on the streets and had found in crime a trade, which they practised in gangs.[4] The question arose therefore of whether criminals were really responsible for their acts and whether society was right to punish them. Public opinion was divided on this. In the nineteenth century juries were very indulgent and tended to acquit as though they felt that only good fortune or accident had saved them from facing trial themselves; but, just when the criminologists were developing theories of diminished responsibility, juries became much more severe and the rate of acquittals fell from 31 to 8·9 per cent between 1901 and 1952. Legal reformers and public opinion were seldom quite in step. The percentage of sentences of over one year's imprisonment fell continuously during the nineteenth century and remained roughly steady till the Second World War. They then climbed back almost to the same rate as during the Second Empire. The outcries against crime were thus largely independent of the real variations in its incidence.

The government, for its part, tied to solve the problem of the criminal class by two different policies. On the one hand it tried to expel hardened criminals from the country; on the

[1] Dr. Charles Perrier, *Les Criminels* (1900).   [2] See chapter 3.

[3] E. Durkheim's articles on crime, published in the *Année sociologique* between 1896 and 1912, are reprinted in *Journal sociologique* (1969).

[4] G. Tarde, *Études pénales et sociales* (1891), *Philosophie pénale* (1890), *La Criminalité comparée* (1890).

other hand, it reduced the length of prison sentences, so that the total number of convicts seemed smaller. France persisted in the policy of transportation of criminals almost throughout this period. In 1854 it stopped building new prisons and passed a law for the transportation to New Caledonia and Guyana of criminals sentenced to hard labour, just when Britain abandoned transportation to Australia. Recidivists were thus systematically got rid of (40 per cent of those coming before the courts were recidivists between 1870 and 1914, but only between 20 and 30 per cent in the interwar years). As a result, the number of convicts in metropolitan prisons fell from nearly 50,000 in 1850 to under 20,000 in 1940. Conditions in the colonies were appallingly inhumane, as Albert Londres's sensational book *Au bagne* (1923) revealed, but it was only in 1938 that transportation was abolished. The apparent decline of the criminal class was, however, due not just to transportation but also to the courts imposing shorter sentences and to the liberation of convicts by amnesties, conditional discharges (instituted in 1885) and suspended sentences (1891). The number of people who were sentenced to imprisonment in fact trebled during the nineteenth century (from 40,000 to 120,000 a year).[1]

Progress thus did not make men more law-abiding, or more reasonable. The crime rates contradicted the faith in education that was the basis of this society. The real crime rates were of course much higher than the statistics suggested. Criminologists pointed out the existence of the 'dark figure of crime', offences not known to the police, and one has estimated that this may be several times higher than the official figure. The proportion of people guilty of an offence against the law undoubtedly increased dramatically, as the number of regulations that could be broken mounted, and public opinion considered infractions of many of them—like tax avoidance and motoring offences—to be venial. Society did not therefore become more honest either. An Italian criminologist, Poletti, argued that the crime rates should be compared with the development of business activity, and he worked out that the increased opportunities for crime were in fact not quite matched by the rise in the crime rates.

[1] Jacques Léauté, *Criminologie et science pénitentiaire* (1972), 698 and *passim*—an excellent general guide.

Attitudes to crime were so emotional because its cause was so uncertain. It was never satisfactorily proved that crime was produced by any of the major trends of this period. Thus though many criminals were alcoholics, there was no direct correlation between crime and the increase in alcohol consumption. Dechristianisation had no effect on crime rates. Victor Hugo had declared that one needed only to open schools in order to close the prisons, but the spread of education made no difference, and the effect of the mass media has not been proved. Drug addiction was also an independent phenomenon. In the 1920s there was a great increase in it: Paris is said to have had 80,000 cocaine addicts in 1924, but these were not otherwise criminals. The consumption of drugs fell drastically after that (80 kilogrammes of heroin was the official estimate in 1939, 12 kg in 1950) without obvious results. After analysing all the evidence, one criminologist recently concluded: 'Criminals are probably not subject to influences different from those which affect non-criminals.' What remained mysterious was the particular combination of factors, shared by criminals and by others, which somehow became an explosive mixture in the former.[1] The trouble with all investigations of these is that they have been based on criminals who have been caught. It is uncertain whether the roughly constant figures of crime meant simply that the police, with their fixed numbers, could deal only with a constant number of cases, or whether crime did reach some kind of saturation point. Thus since 1900 there has been a steady annual murder rate, or at any rate between four and fourteen convicted murderers per million inhabitants. The suicide rate—which is independent of police action—has been similarly steady since 1890. Crime thus had its own laws, which remained impenetrable to the community at large, part of the mystery of human nature. The ministry of justice in 1871 claimed that 28 per cent of crimes of personal violence were due to 'accidental quarrels', 25 per cent to 'hate against individuals', 17 per cent to domestic dissensions, 13 per cent to 'cupidity', 9 per cent to adultery and debauchery, 4 per cent to hatred of the police and 3 per cent to fights in drinking-shops and to gambling. These were causes which could hardly be dealt with by legislation. Human nature did not seem to

[1] Ibid. 410.

be improving. There was no less violence as the country became more educated and more prosperous; at least, more people were accused of violence. In 1846 15,742 people were brought before the courts for 'coups et blessures volontaires'; by 1934 there were 44,942.[1]

The idea of the criminal class was a confused one. It certainly had a basis in truth. France did have its professional gangsters who, in the nineteenth century, showed remarkable cohesion: they formed a number of private militias, membership of which lasted for many years. Later, however, the 'bands' became only temporary alliances, formed from the 'underworld' which was, in the twentieth century, a much looser phenomenon. Already in the 1880s there used to be large teams of burglars specialising in the complete removal of property from unoccupied houses. There were still 'anarchist' gangs after that movement had lost its political importance; in 1912 robberies of banks by men armed with revolvers and explosives and escaping in motor cars became a new form of terror. The motivations of these criminals were a cause of much puzzlement. A journalist who wrote the biographies of one gang of seven showed them to be individualists, vegetarians, fond of reading, quoting Schopenhauer, playing Chopin and doing Swedish exercises, completely contemptuous of the institutions they were robbing.[2] On a humbler level and in smaller groups were the pickpockets, busy in department stores and at the fashionable resorts like Deauville (on which English pickpockets used to descend in large numbers, for a three months' season); there were the professional beggars (often they used to hire babies so as to make their plight appear sadder); in 1892 one man was revealed to have in his employ fifteen children, each of whom earned him thirty francs a day by begging; the young florists on the boulevards were similarly organised, partly as beggars and partly as prostitutes, by prosperous entrepreneurs. But on 1 January and 14 July, the professionals of Paris were swamped by all the maimed and sick from fifty miles around, and even from Brittany—which specialised in diseases of the skin—coming in

[1] Léauté, op. cit. 289.
[2] Émile Michon, *Un Peu de l'âme des bandits. Étude de psychologie criminelle* (n.d., about 1914).

cheap excursion trains, knowing they could earn as much as fifty francs in a day. Beggars were, by tradition, particularly frightening, because superstitition endowed them with evil powers; though the terrifying beggar hordes of the *ancien régime* had vanished, there were still a large number who survived on regular alms, obtained by ambiguous pressure. There was the corporation of dog thieves, with their market on the boulevard de l'Hôpital, who were said to exercise one of the most lucrative illegal professions, and to have a flourishing export trade to England. There were the usurers lending at 25 per cent per day (the barrow boys and women selling garlic, onions, apples and raw herring along the pavements of the rue Saint-Antoine were enslaved by them, borrowing 20 sous in the morning to buy their goods and having to repay 25 in the evening). There was a whole world specialising in confidence tricks, fake marriage bureaux, false employment agencies. Though forgery was punished by hard labour for life, and four or five gangs were convicted every year, it was endlessly popular and one per cent of French silver coins were estimated to be counterfeit; a forger was even discovered inside a prison, using prison cutlery. Crime was a way of life for such people, but all efforts to explain why they had chosen it, or to associate criminality with particular social or psychological circumstances, were unconvincing. In Germany, between the wars, theft and economic depression were shown to go hand in hand; but in France the opposite was proved, as though there was less theft when there was less around to steal. The widely held belief that the poor working class was the most prone to crime was false; peasants, or at least agricultural workers, probably had a higher crime rate, though it was often when they wandered from the land that they got into trouble. In proportion to their total numbers, however, the liberal professions were even more criminal. Crime should rightly have been associated less with urbanisation as such than with travel and movement: in 1877 only eight out of every 100,000 people who still lived in their place of birth were brought before assize courts, but twenty-nine out of every 100,000 who had moved to another department, while no less than forty-one out of 100,000 foreigners suffered the same fate.[1] In 1952

[1] H. Joly, *La France criminelle* (1888), 56, 7.

North African immigrants were arrested and charged roughly one and a half times more frequently than French inhabitants of Paris, but this did not make them, or foreigners and migrants in general, anything like the blacks of the U.S.A., who were prosecuted three times as often as whites.

Juvenile crime was a particular source of concern. Minors constituted between 15 and 18 per cent of persons brought to court.[1] It was established as early as 1831 by Quetelet that the tendency to crime started early, reached its height at the age of twenty-five and then gradually diminished. The law, however, never quite caught up with the implications of this fact. Its principle was, first of all, that minors were not responsible for their offences unless they knowingly intended to do wrong (acting with 'discernment').[2] This distinction between wicked and unfortunate children was a symptom of the law's hesitation between severity towards nascent evil and faith that education could reform the wayward. The apostles of education gradually won the day, on the theoretical plane, but the tradition of severity survived in practice. In 1906 the age of penal minority was raised from 16 to 18; in 1912 all children under thirteen were declared irresponsible and in 1945 this was raised to eighteen years and the question of *discernement* ceased to be asked. Originally children were sent to the same prisons as adults, but there was increasing hesitation about sending them to prison or punishing them at all. Thus the rate of convictions of minors under sixteen rose between 1840 and 1855 but then fell steadily. In 1854 11,026 minors between eight and sixteen were convicted; a century later only 7,066 were. The increase in juvenile crime concerned the sixteen- to twenty-year-olds. In 1831 only some 7,000 of these were convicted, in 1854 27,000, and in 1893 37,000; there was a great fall in convictions in the 1930s ,but during the Second World War a vast increase to unprecedented heights, to be equalled only in the late 1960s, when the figure rose to 47,000.

The problem seemed to be that of the adolescent.[3] It was

[1] Y. Y. Chen, *Études statistiques sur la criminalité en France de 1895 à 1930* (Paris thesis, 1937), 41.

[2] Gustave Mabille, *De la question de discernement relative aux mineurs de seize ans* (1898, Paris doctoral thesis).

[3] Maurice Levade, *La Délinquance des jeunes en France 1825–1968* (1972, 2 volumes of graphs and tables); Jacques Siméon, 'L'Évolution de la criminalité juvénile

established in the 1960s that one-third of juvenile recidivists were orphans: whether the proportion was even higher in the nineteenth century is unknown, but quite likely. The courts had only two rather blunt instruments to meet this situation. The law of 5 August 1850 ordered that convicted children should be detained separately from adults and above all that 'moral, religious and professional education' should be the principal purpose of their detention. Children would not be deported but instead would be sent to 'penitentiary colonies' within France. This law was put into effect very unequally and imperfectly. Fifty years later there were still articles of it which had not been applied. France then had twenty-nine 'colonies' with 6,000 children in them: England had 203 comparable reformatories with 22,000. The French 'colonies' had originally been philanthropic ventures designed to transform young criminals from the slums by rearing them in pastoral surroundings, but compulsory agricultural labour did not instil love of work, and the countryside became more than ever horrible to the children who were forcibly sent there. The 'colonies' became increasingly military in their discipline, and they were twice as expensive as English reformatories because of the superfluity of bureaucrats.[1] They made virtually no contribution to solving the problem of young offenders, beyond isolating them—or rather a few of them—just as adult offenders were isolated in Guyana.[2] The second instrument was the use of private charitable societies to act as guardians for young offenders. The law of 22 July 1912 greatly enlarged the role of these societies, which were the French alternative to a state probation service. They were not particularly successful, and some of them were disguised employment agencies, which exploited the children confided to their care.[3]

The proportion of crimes reported which were followed by prosecution steadily diminished. In 1851–5, only one-third of

depuis 100 ans', in La Prévention des infractions contre la vie humaine et l'intégrité de la personne, edited by A. Besson and M. Ancel (1956), 2. 1–32.

[1] Maurice Langlois, Les Mineurs de l'article 66 du code pénal et la loi du 5 août 1850 (comparaison avec les régimes belge et anglais) (Paris law thesis, 1898), 131.

[2] Henri Gaillac, Les Maisons de correction 1830–1945 (1971); Prosper Compans, De l'exécution de la peine appliquée aux jeunes délinquants (Paris law thesis, 1896); H. and F. Joubret, L'Enfance dite coupable (1946).

[3] H. Donnedieu de Vabres, La Justice pénale aujourd'hui (1948), 65–6.

reported crimes led to no action, but by 1940 the proportion had risen to two-thirds. The police were more successful with misdemeanours,[1] but when allowance is made for acquittals, the over-all proportion of offences going unpunished was still two-thirds. Apart from exceptional periods like the early Second Empire, when the number of policemen was increased and their activity stimulated, or periods like 1870–1, when police control greatly deteriorated, a remarkable stability was established in the ratio between the police's rate of prosecution and the extent of crime, as though it was accepted that the police should be undermanned just enough to give the world of crime a sporting chance. This was one measure of the public's sense of security, or of its ambivalent attitude to crime.

Attitudes to violence were complex in this period and the common, optimistic view, that men were beginning to treat each other more gently, was not entirely accurate. On the one hand, it is true, the rights of man were acknowledged in the prohibition of corporal punishment, for criminals as for schoolchildren. This was indeed a great change, even if the prohibition was not rigidly enforced. The rights of man could of course work in the totally opposite direction, as the Revolutionary Terror revealed; the massacres of June 1848, the Commune in 1871 and the Liberation in 1944–5 showed that the French were still as capable of tearing each other to pieces as in the seventeenth century. Torture ceased to be used by the judiciary, as it had been until finally abolished by Louis XVI in 1788, but the capacity for it was not eradicated. In the Second World War, the French had their own torture brigades, copying the methods of the Gestapo, specialising in immersing their victims in cold baths until they nearly drowned; and in the Algerian war brutality reached new levels of refinement.[2] In the nineteenth century, the one thing the French police were not accused of was torturing their prisoners, though it was claimed between the two World Wars that they had a 'room for spontaneous confessions' in the Palais de Justice, the screams from which could be heard four storeys away. Torture now took on new forms, the most effective of which was soli-

---

[1] 58·5 per cent of misdemeanours reported were tried in 1851 (194,000 people involved) but 31 per cent in 1946–60 (269,000 accused).

[2] Pierre Vidal-Naquet, *La Torture dans la république 1954–62* (1972).

tary confinement; since the cells could be dark and window-less, the food reduced to a minimum, there were instances of suspects emerging from this ordeal, after a year or more, virtually destroyed. In 1897 a law forbade solitary confine-ment for more than ten days, but that was something an examining judge could impose on a suspect without any formal conviction. A standard textbook of police practice, published in 1945, informed policemen that though the law forbade torture, in the sense of violence to the body, there were legitimate forms of it, such as long questioning, forcing suspects to sit in a chair night and day, and depriving them of sleep.[1]

On the other hand, there were forms of violence that large sections of public opinion approved or condoned. The *crime of passion* aroused fascinated and ultimately sympathetic awe. It was at bottom the traditional right to honour and revenge, but given a new twist by the influence of romanticism. Since the jury that tried this kind of crime was asked not just whether the accused had indeed committed it but also whether he was *culpable*, there was ample opportunity for public opinion to express itself. This was a domain in which literature could perhaps claim to have influenced values: Alexandre Dumas is said to have appeared at assize courts, standing behind the presiding judge, as though to ensure that the rights of passion, exalted to the point that they gave the right to kill, should be recognised. Murder thus did not inspire horror if it was com-mitted in the name of the 'right to love', and the phrase 'I shall kill him and I shall be acquitted' became an expletive of daily conversation. Because of the clemency of juries, crimes of passion increased in this period, taking on an almost standard uniformity: the criminal who immediately surrendered to the police, avowing his deed, confessing all his private troubles, invoking uncontrollable emotions, regretting them and weep-ing over them, had a good chance of acquittal. Thus the actress Marie Bière who in 1879 shot a lover determined to break with her was acquitted after only a few minutes' deliberation: she had won sympathy by relating his cruelty to her—his trying

[1] Raymond Aron, *Histoire et dialectique de la violence* (1973); M. Amiot and J. Onimus, *La Violence dans le monde actuel* (Nice, 1968); A. Mellor, *La Torture. Son histoire, son abolition, sa réapparition au 20ᵉ siècle* (new edition, 1961), quoting L. Lambert, *Traité théorique et pratique de police judiciaire* (1945), 209.

to force her to abort their child, his refusal to recognise her—and by admitting the lies she told him so as to have another child by him, when this first one died, declaring 'All mothers will understand me'. The poet Clovis Hugues was in 1878 acquitted of murdering a journalist, whom he shot in a duel to vindicate his wife's honour. His wife, five years later, shot another man who had insulted her; his death was slow and horribly agonising, but in court she declared that she had suffered even more than he, because of his slanders, and she was acquitted. The vendetta survived in Corsica despite all the principles of French law. A certain Antoine Bonelli, condemned to death several times for various murders in the course of family quarrels, took to the hills and avoided justice for about forty years; when he tired of this life, he gave himself up (1892), was acquitted by a jury and spent his old age as a legendary testimony of traditional rights of honour. Between the wars, however, attitudes became somewhat less lenient. Thus in 1934 a prostitute called Nini was given two years' imprisonment for killing her lover, Causeret, the prefect of the Bouches-du-Rhône. She was a remarkable woman: when plying her trade in a cheap hotel in the rue des Archives, she had been visited by the best-selling novelist Pierre Decourcelle, in search of material for his books. He advised her to change her name to Germaine d'Anglemont and to move to the more fashionable quarter of the Champs-Élysées. There indeed she quickly made her fortune, receiving journalists, ministers and politicians, becoming engaged to a Bavarian prince, but going off with a Polish ambassador, then becoming mistress to the president of Mexico and the prime minister of Yugoslavia as well as a spy for the Deuxième Bureau during the First World War. Finally she ended up as mistress to this prefect, whom she shot when he tried to abandon her. She illustrates how, when private lives were made public in the lawcourts, juries hastened to declare that they should not be subject to the ordinary rules. In that sense the right to privacy, even carried to the extreme of murder, was a passionately held principle.[1]

But only certain forms of violence were condoned. The law

[1] Dr. Hélie Courtis, *Étude médico-légale des crimes passionnels* (Toulouse, 1910); Maurice Garçon, *Histoire de la justice sous la troisième république* (1957), 3. 105–35.

indeed made a specific distinction between murders committed on impulse and those involving premeditation: it singled out poisoning as a method of murder that aggravated the seriousness of the crime. Poisoning reached its peak in 1836–40, when the courts judged on average forty-one cases a year: the numbers then declined steadily to eighteen a year by the early 1870s. Poisoning used to be the speciality of the upper classes; it now became the crime of illiterates. Men used to be the more frequent offenders until 1847; since then women have been responsible for 70 per cent of cases. Once the death penalty ceased to be mandatory for it in 1832, juries had no hesitation in convicting, though curiosity about the crime was as great as abhorrence of it. Madame Lafarge, sentenced to hard labour for life, wrote her memoirs and retained her fame for a whole generation.[1] What juries would not forgive was the calculating cupidity that was often behind these crimes. They were indulgent, however, towards sexual offences: out of 592 people accused of these in 1888, 174 were acquitted and 194 were accorded extenuating circumstances, so that only a small number suffered the full rigour of the law. Juries tended to be severe only when a child was given venereal disease by an assault; they were not worried by the moral implications. Cases of rape usually revealed so much violence within the families of the victims, that it was the parents' demeanour at the trial that was often decisive: the honest workman who pleaded that he had done his best to raise his daughter honourably and now a lascivious man had ruined her reputation, could get a conviction against a rapist by appealing to the emotions of the jurors, as one parent to another. There was much subtlety therefore in public attitudes to crime. The feeling that some people could not expect protection from violence was widespread. Juries were merciless to tyrannical or arrogant people; they were easily won over by pretty women, distinction of one sort or another, and appeals to their emotions.[2] Able barristers could sway them from one extreme to another, so that there was inevitably much inconsistency in the way crime was punished. Fashions in forensic oratory introduced several extraneous elements into judgments. The classical style,

[1] Raoul Sautter, *Étude sur le crime d'empoisonnement* (Paris law thesis, 1896).
[2] Bérard des Glajeux, *Souvenirs d'un président d'assises 1880–1890* (1892), 2. 128–33.

in which verbal elegance predominated, could involve speeches lasting several days, to which judges listened as they might to the reading of good verse; the romantic style, which not infrequently meant the barrister ended his peroration weeping profusely, made trials into melodramatic theatrical performances. Frédéric Lenté, who defended Wilson, President Grévy's son-in-law accused of corruption, spoke in a voice smothered by sobs and on finishing 'covered his face with his pale hands and wept'.[1] The 'modern' style, introduced around 1890 by Henri-Robert, brief, logical, simplified, might have transformed the judicial process if it had been universally adopted, but vestiges of the older traditions survived.

Physical violence within the family probably diminished, but it is difficult to generalise about violence in ordinary life, because sensitivity to pain increased very unevenly in this period and the idea of what constituted violence must have changed. Before the introduction of anaesthetics in the mid-nineteenth century, surgeons performed amputations which were stoically borne. The use of analgesics spread only gradually to the poor. It was when men feared pain that cruelty was seen as a vice. Other values could excuse cruelty: the capacity to be cruel was a sign of manliness, and, as *Poil de Carotte* showed, parents could feel virtuous if they made their children suffer. It was said that women led the movement against cruelty to animals, as a consolation for the brutality they endured from men; there was certainly much wanton cruelty to oppose. Maupassant, for example, was proud of his walking-stick, with which, he said, he had killed at least twenty dogs. Flaubert, in *Bouvard et Pécuchet*, describes a man boiling a cat alive, explaining that there could be no objection to this since the cat belonged to him. The penal code concerned itself indeed with the protection of animals only in so far as they were one type of property. In 1850 a law, sponsored by and named after General de Grammont, for the first time made cruelty to animals an offence, but only if the cruelty was public, 'abusive', and the animal domestic; punishment of an animal's refusal to obey was exempted. It was almost impossible to secure prosecutions under this law, and another law of 1898, which ended the need for the cruelty to be public, was useless because no

[1] Henri-Robert, *Le Palais et la ville. Souvenirs* (1930), 103.

sanctions were imposed. Societies for the Protection of Animals
grew up, but they were unable to institute prosecutions themselves, because they had suffered no direct damage; only in
1929 did court decisions allow them more scope. So though the
Third Republic made love of animals one of the commandments it tried to instil into children, the idea that animals
could suffer, or that there was anything wrong with obtaining
pleasure from their suffering, was by no means universal.
Games in which turkeys were made to dance on red-hot plat-
forms; or in which spectators hurled stones at pigeons placed
in boxes, their heads stuck out to receive the blows; brutality
in slaughter-houses, where for example sheep's eyes were
gouged out before they were killed; these practices were ac-
accepted by many, and seemed appalling at first only to rather
eccentric, over-sensitive people. Cruelty remained one form
of voluptuousness; and some sports, as has been seen, were a
way of giving a new significance, new purposes and new controls to older rituals of violence.[1]

Perhaps that is why *ancien régime* traditions of severity
towards accused persons continued to be tolerated. France had
thirty times as many judges as England, because some of its
judges were also investigating and prosecuting officials.
Though judges had security of tenure (occasionally waived,
as in 1883), they were divided into many categories, and their
struggle for promotion made them susceptible to political and
other influences. In 1930 an English county court judge (the
lowest paid in the country) drew a salary higher than that of
the First President of the Court of Cassation, the most senior
in France.[2] French judges were officials more than independent
arbiters. That is one reason why barristers were so often political figures, defending individuals against the state: judges were
not chosen from among the most successful barristers, but were
civil servants, who had opted for state service in their youth.[3]

[1] René Guyon, *La Cruauté* (1927); Léonce de Cazenove, *Considérations sur les
sociétés protectrices des animaux* (Lyon, 1865); Dr. Ph. Maréchal, *L'Évolution de l'opinion
publique sur les courses de taureaux* (1907); Pierre Giberne, *La Protection juridique des
animaux* (Montpellier law thesis, Nîmes, 1931), 91; Bernard Jen, *Le Sport, la mort,
la violence* (1972); 'Comprendre l'agressivité', special issue of *Revue internationale des
sciences sociales* (UNESCO) (1971), vol. 23, no. 1.

[2] R. C. K. Ensor, *Courts and Judges in France, Germany and England* (Oxford, 1933).

[3] Paul Lallemand, *Le Recrutement des juges* (Paris law thesis, 1936).

Until 1898 an accused person was entirely at the mercy of the examining magistrate (the *juge d'instruction*) who could arrest him and keep him in custody while he collected evidence against him. The proportion of accused who were kept in gaol before trial greatly diminished in the course of the twentieth century, but on the other hand the length of time those who were detained spent there increased very markedly: in 1901 only 7·4 per cent of those held in provisional custody spent more than a month in prison before trial, but between the two wars 16 to 25 per cent did, while in the 1950s and 1960s 40 to 50 per cent did. Only after 1898 was the accused entitled to legal aid from the moment of his arrest (as opposed to having the right to it at his trial). Severe limitations on the right to cross-examine meant that trials were simply occasions for speeches by witnesses and advocates. The depositions of the police, if properly drawn up, were accepted as irrefutable evidence of fact.[1] Justice depended therefore a great deal on the judges.

But one should not criticise this system simply because it was not based on habeas corpus and was so different from the Anglo-Saxon model. Frenchmen were protected in their liberties by the very complexities of their judicial system. Rivalry between the officials was one guarantee: if the *parquet* started a case, the *juge d'instruction* would often try to pull it to pieces simply as a matter of pride. Many officials needed to reach agreement before a man was accused.[2] It is true that repeated attempts to reform criminal procedure were not successful in this period.[3] The individual, however, was increasingly able to sue the state for its misdeeds before the Conseil d'État, and in the course of the twentieth century this power was greatly expanded as a result of that court's growing will to be independent. In the 1870s an average of 1,253 cases against civil servants were referred to the Conseil d'État each year. By 1913 this figure had almost trebled to 4,275.[4] The individual

[1] A. L. Wright, 'French Criminal Procedure', *Law Quarterly Review* (1928), vol. 44, 324–43; (1929), vol. 45, 92–117.

[2] C. J. Hamson, 'The Prosecution of the accused. English and French legal methods', *Criminal Law Review* (1955), 272–82.

[3] René Daud and H. P. de Vries, *The French Legal System* (New York, 1958).

[4] Joseph Barthélemy, *Le Gouvernement de la France. Tableau des institutions politiques, administratives et judiciaires de la France contemporaine* (1939), 215–17.

was also protected by the freedom of the press, though this was a double-edged weapon. Newspapers made it possible for the discussion of crime to be a favourite popular pastime; the obsession with its sensational aspects often led to pressure being exerted on juries and judges which, in England for example, would be regarded as gross contempt of court. France retained the death penalty and it was only in 1939 that public executions were finally abolished. It is true that since 1848 these were held at dawn to minimise the danger of disturbance, and that the scaffold was abolished in 1870; but there were still occasions on which executions took place before large crowds—like that of the murderer Momble in Paris in 1869, carried out with medieval publicity. The guillotine ceased to be used in 1905 while parliament considered its abolition, but it was brought back into service in 1909 when the debates had no result, and the first occasion of its revived use—at Béthune—was the scene of appalling savagery in the crowds, whose interest had been aroused by the press, which photographed and filmed the whole proceedings.[1]

So much was talked about reason, and so much faith was put in it, that violence remained largely incomprehensible. The attitude towards it was always to blame it on one thing or another. Perhaps the punishments imposed contributed to its growth. When Durkheim argued that violence and crime were inevitable, normal features of society, most people found this impossible to accept. The main interest of criminal history to the general historian is perhaps that it shows that the variety of human nature is beyond analysis and beyond reform. Why, of two people with identical backgrounds, one should become a murderer, or engage in petty fraud, and the other obey the law, or succeed in evading detection, cannot be explained by any valid generalisation. That, ultimately, may account for the popularity of crime fiction, which, better than the law, freed improbability from the constraints of reason.

The Colonies

The extent to which hierarchy and violence were elements in the French civilisation of this period (accepted, tolerated, or

[1] G. O. Junosza-Zdrojewski, *Le Crime et la presse* (1943), 183.

ignored) may be gauged from a look at the colonies. Their
history has, until very recently, been presented largely as a
glorious epic, because their historians were usually emotionally
involved in them; the oppression and inequality which colonial
administrators imposed on millions of foreigners was not the
aspect that attracted particular attention.[1] The contradictions
between the liberties and values Frenchmen believed themselves to be fighting for at home and the tyranny they imposed
on those they conquered were for long not generally seen as
such, partly because colonial life formed a separate world,
which most people largely ignored, and partly because the
abuses of colonial life simply magnified features of French
society, which Frenchmen had learnt to live with. The countries
conquered by the French were offered various blends of three
different kinds of inequality, all of which existed in embryo
in France: military hierarchy, capitalist exploitation and the
inequality that came from political corruption and favouritism.[2]

The colonies were, first of all, the creation of the French
army and navy. Between the Napoleonic wars and the First
World War, it was in the colonies that soldiers got most of their
experience of battle and a chance to put their ideas into practice. It was mainly there that military reputations were made and
promotion won. A whole edifice of self-esteem was built on the
histories of the glory won in subduing various colonial peoples.
The colonial wars provided many people with deep satisfactions. It was seldom pointed out how inefficiently and bar-
barically the subjugation was achieved, or at what expense the
glory was bought. A great European power, with a formidable
military tradition, able to draw on a population of over thirty
million, took fifteen years to reduce four million Algerians to
subjection. The war of the Algerian conquest was horrific in
its violence. The army's principle was to kill and destroy every

---

[1] For a critique of historical writing on the colonies, see J. C. Vatin, *L'Algérie
politique: histoire et société* (1974), 17–80.

[2] [René Couret] *Guide bibliographique sommaire d'histoire militaire et coloniale fran-
çaise* (Service historique, ministère des armées, 1969), 315–483; S. H. Roberts,
The History of French Colonial Policy 1870–1925 (1929); J. Ganiage, *L'Expansion
coloniale de la France sous la troisième république 1871–1914* (1968); Henri Brunschwig,
French Colonialism, 1871–1914, Myths and Realities (1966, French original 1960);
C. A. Julien, *Les Techniciens de la colonisation* (1946), 55–156; R. Delavignette and
C. A. Julien, *Les Constructeurs de la France d'outre-mer* (1946).

obstacle in its path. It raised this into a technique known as the
razzia, involving the systematic sacking and burning of village
after village. There was not so much fighting as devastation,
and the reward for the soldiers was not just promotion but booty.
The army was a cobweb of cliques and clans, each of which
sought to build up its power over the natives, to extort presents
for protection, to get rich as fast as possible. Tocqueville, who
visited Algeria in 1841, reported (even though he approved the
method of razzias) that it was carried so far that 'we are now
making war in a way that is much more barbarous than that
the Arabs themselves use'. Because the French could not defeat
the Arabs militarily, they reduced them by famine and destruction. After the First World War Marshal Lyautey used
more tact and sometimes succeeded in obtaining submission with
only a show of force, but his methods still included starving the
tribesmen by driving them out of their pastures, machine-
gunning any who tried to work in the fields, and finally burning
their villages.

However, the army did not preach repression as a system of
government. The empire was conquered by soldiers (or in the
case of Indo-China, by the navy), and so for long the military
had a dominant influence on the way the natives were treated.
Their prime aim was to keep the colonies under their own
control. They were the opponents therefore not only of the
natives but also of the Frenchmen who came to settle or to make
money in the wake of the conquest; and as a result, they often
set themselves up as the defenders of the natives against
exploitation by the colonists. Marshal Bugeaud, the conqueror
of Algeria, who started this tradition, was able to give it force
because in his day there were still as many soldiers as colonists
in the province: in 1846 there were 104,000 of the former and
109,000 of the latter. Bugeaud had a profound contempt for the
civilian colonists, whom he considered to be the dregs of French
society: he tried to protect the Arabs against their depredations,
and to use the army instead to develop the country, turning it
in effect into a great public-works organisation, building roads
and clearing land. Bugeaud was of peasant origin and he
appreciated that Arab peasants loved their soil: he was their
ally against the city speculators. He respected tradition and so
maintained the Arab system of taxation. The army thus emerged

not only as conquerors of the natives but also as their protectors against the capitalists and the middlemen who tried to exploit them too. Once the natives stopped fighting, the army became the advocate of paternalism. The colonies provided scope for it to express its belief in hierarchy. This often involved respect for the traditional organisation of native societies, but on the condition that they accepted an inferior status.

Napoleon III, while persecuting his political enemies in France, also set himself up as the protector of the Arabs, but he had a somewhat different vision of their future. He was influenced by Ismail Urbain, the son of a Marseille merchant and a Guyanese, who, conscious of his illegitimacy as well as of his coloured skin, devoted his life to championing oppressed people against racial discrimination. Urbain, who became a Muslim and married an Algerian Muslim girl, published a manifesto with the motto 'Algeria for the Algerians' (1861). Napoleon was convinced by it and so inaugurated a policy which took as its basis that there should be 'perfect equality between the Europeans and the natives'; he declared himself to be Emperor of the Arabs as well as of the French; and looked forward to coexistence between the races, on the principle of the Arabs concentrating on agriculture while the Europeans confined themselves to industry, mines, public works and the introduction of new crops. Free concessions of land would no longer be given to European settlers; the Arabs' right to their property was to be officially recognised for the first time; the Arab chiefs were to be treated with courtesy and respect. But though Napoleon's liking for the Arabs was as genuine as his dislike for the French colonists, what he was offering Algeria was not so much equality as capitalist exploitation. The state would no longer confiscate the land, but it would use private financiers to develop the country. The guarantee of Arab property turned out to be disruptive, because it allowed the transfer of communal property into private ownership; and the Europeans were able to buy up the land cheaply. The Arabs were given only very limited political rights. The legacy of the Second Empire was that it became possible to turn the Arabs from landowners into labourers, as they increasingly fell into debt to the Europeans and were forced or persuaded to sell up. Economic inequalities were thus vastly increased. The colonies were to provide golden opportunities for profiteering at the expense of the natives.[1]

Comparatively few Frenchmen went abroad as colonists, but they nevertheless managed to acquire formidable power, both over the natives and *vis-à-vis* the government of Paris. This was no accident, for it followed from the way the political system worked. The colonists came into their own with the Third Republic. This was at once shown by the way the Algerian rebellion of 1871 was quashed: 70 per cent of the wealth of the 800,000 Muslims involved was confiscated. The impoverishment of the native population now ceased to encounter any barriers. The land laws were so applied that the natives' rights were turned topsy-turvy and colonists were able to buy, in the space of fourteen years, 377 million hectares of land for only 37 million francs. The forests, which in 1851 the government had declared to be state property, had French law applied to them, so that the natives lost their valuable forest rights; collective fines for numerous offences in forest areas were imposed on tribes, which were soon ruined by them; the forests came to yield a larger income from fines than from timber. Parts of the forests were sold, under pressure, to the colonists, for between 1 and 3 per cent of their value. The French took over the Arab taxation system but gradually increased the amounts levied so that the land tax in Algeria came to be about three times higher than that imposed on mainland France. One of the reasons for this was that the corrupt system of collection meant that a great deal disappeared into the hands of officials. French rule for the Arabs brought an effective increase in taxation of 50 per cent between 1860 and 1890: they did not even have the satisfaction of feeling that this made them the equal of Frenchmen, entitled to the same benefits, for they got very little in return and yet they paid special taxes additional to those paid by Europeans. They had no control over how this money was spent, for they did not have a vote in parliamentary elections, nor enjoy the right to stand for parliament. They had, it is true, representatives on municipal councils: but until 1884 these were

[1] C. A. Julien, *Histoire de l'Algérie contemporaine: la conquête et les débuts de la colonisation 1827–71* (1964) contains the best bibliography for this period, and is itself the best book on it.

appointed by the government and after that only 50,000 of the 4,500,000 Muslims were allowed to participate in municipal elections, and they moreover were entitled to elect only one-quarter of the councillors. Until 1919 these Muslim councillors were not even allowed to vote to choose the mayor. In 1870 Émile Ollivier had proposed to give the Muslims parliamentary representation in Paris, but his republican opponent Jules Faure protested in horror against the 'appearance in this house of a Native'. The republican municipal law of 1884, which was the basis of French municipal liberties, in Algeria had the effect of disenfranchising the Arabs still further.

This could hardly be justified on the grounds of education for the Algerians had been literate in roughly the same proportion as the French when they were first conquered. If they were more illiterate after that, it was largely the doing of the French, for the war disrupted the education of a whole generation and then, when Ferry's compulsory primary education law was passed, its effect in Algeria was to hand over the control of the state village schools to the white colonists, who had no wish to enforce obligatory attendance on the Muslims. As a result in 1889 there were only 10,000 Muslim children in these schools, which was under 2 per cent of those who should have attended. Ferry's legislation simply damaged the Arab Koranic schools. Though liberty of religion was proclaimed, the conquest meant the confiscation of religious endowments, and though Catholic priests were paid salaries by the state, only 78 out of 1,494 mosques were accepted as eligible for state support. The religious fraternities were increasingly regarded as dangerous secret societies and attempts were even made to stop pilgrimages to Mecca. The Arabs were entitled to become full French citizens, but only on condition that they abandoned their adherence to Muslim law: no more than a few hundred did so. They were not allowed to maintain their own judicial system. Napoleon III had restored the power of the *cadis*, who had been dispossessed of their jurisdiction in the conquest, but the first work of the Third Republic was to replace them by French *juges de paix*. These posts were the most junior in the French legal service and were generally given to young men of poor families, who could not afford to start their careers as unpaid assistant judges in France (for judges began in an unpaid capacity). They generally stayed only for a few years, and seldom knew Arabic. Thus though Muslim law was recognised, the judges were ignorant of it. In criminal law, the principle of the separation of judicial and administrative power was overridden: the civil service had power to fine and imprison Muslims (until 1928). The gradual extension of the civil territory and the withdrawal of power from the army did not give the Muslims the rights of French civilians: it merely subjected them to the arbitrary rule of the civil service. The French were more favourable to the Kabyls, about whom they created fanciful myths. This was largely because, in reply to Napoleon's glorification of Arab chivalry, the colonists attempted to strengthen their position by a policy of dividing the natives: they declared that the Arabs were an inferior race, while the Kabyls were less religious, less fanatical and therefore capable of accepting French civilisation. The result was that the Kabyls were taxed less and given more schooling. To the Kabyls, this seemed simply a more vigorous attack on their institutions, and the effort to separate Berbers from Arabs was totally unsuccessful.[1]

The imposition of such an oppressive regime was made possible by the skill with which the colonists exploited the French political system. Under Napoleon III, the colonists had been enemies of the government, but that had got them nowhere. Algeria became, however, a nursery of republicanism. It provided safe seats for republicans, and many eminent politicians thus became defenders of the colonists who elected them: Sadi Carnot, Albert Grévy, Spuller, Constans, Paul Bert all represented Algeria. Above all Gambetta became the patron of a succession of local politicians, who through him obtained considerable power in Paris and were thus able to build up their influence in Algeria. Life in Algeria was always intensely political, even more than in the South of France, and it was dominated by personal considerations and organised in clienteles. The man who developed the most successful system was Eugène Étienne (1844–1921), a close friend of Gambetta,

[1] C. R. Ageron, *Les Algériens musulmans et la France 1871–1969* (2 vols., 1968); Vincent Confer, *France and Algeria: The Problem of Civil and Political Reform 1870–1920* (Syracuse U.P., 1966); R. Le Tourneau, *Évolution politique de l'Afrique du Nord musulmane 1920–61* (1962); J. Berque, *Le Maghreb entre deux guerres* (1962); Y. Turin, *Affrontements culturels dans l'Algérie coloniale: écoles, médecines, religion 1830–80* (1971).

as warm and charming as him, always friendly, a florid orator and a master of both political and business negotiations. Étienne, thanks to his boyhood friendship with another influential politician, Rouvier, became under-secretary of state for Algeria (1887 and 1889–92), long enough to fill the Paris administration with well-disposed civil servants. He established a tradition that Algerian affairs should be left to the Algerian deputies, on the tit-for-tat principle. A colonial group was organised in parliament not out of opposition deputies but out of the regular supporters of all governments. The senate, particularly, cemented the link between republican loyalty and colonial interests. Important colonial laws were thus passed through the Paris parliament with only a few dozen members present or voting. The minister of the colonies, when he was not a representative of the colonists, accepted a secondary role: Clemenceau's nominee, for example, took on the portfolio (1906) announcing that he would follow the advice of 'my eminent friend Monsieur Étienne'. In France, the advocates of the colonies were organised into a series of interrelated pressure groups—the Committee for French Africa, for Madagascar, for Morocco, for Indo-China etc.—which were able to exercise great influence by obtaining key positions in the colonies and even by being left to draw up their own instructions when appointed to negotiate with foreign governments.[1]

The colonies were supposed to be outposts of French civilisation, but they developed a civilisation of their own, though it was a long time before the home country realised this. The people who went to Algeria wanted to get away from France. They were not concerned with spreading the gospel of the French Revolution but with having an easier life. They were probably the least intellectual and religious part of the nation. Their pleasures were above all physical: they were devotees of swimming and sun-bathing, of hunting and of dancing. When Gide visited them at the beginning of the twentieth century, they struck him as 'a new race, proud, voluptuous, vigorous', emphasising practicality, money-making, building. Camus, who was born in Algeria, said the Europeans in it

[1] On the colonial party see C. M. Andrew's articles in the *Historical Journal* (1971 and 1974) and the *Transactions of the Royal Historical Society* (1976) (and for the diplomatic angle, his *Théophile Delcassé and the Making of the Entente Cordiale* (1968)).

were 'a people who had placed all their goods in this world'.
These were not Frenchmen seeking security, but gamblers for
higher stakes. They were almost as different from Frenchmen
as the Americans were from Englishmen, and not least because
there were soon more people of non-French origin among the
settlers in Algeria than there were Frenchmen. These were
mostly Spaniards and Italians, who were quickly granted
naturalisation. French nationality was for them above all a
guarantee of privilege. Algerians even spoke their own kind of
French.[1] It was mainly to Algeria that the French went out as
settlers, with the intention of working the soil, though once
there they quickly gathered in the towns: in 1954 only one-
tenth of them were farmers. Algerians of French and European
origin included a sizeable proletariat amongst them, and these
were, not surprisingly, passionately attached to the status that
distinguished them from almost equally poor Muslims.[2]

The administrators sent out to govern the empire were, as the
Governor of Senegal wrote in 1879, largely 'lost children of the
mother country', 'persons who if not compromised at home were
at least incapable of making a livelihood there'. Until 1912
no educational qualifications, not even the *baccalauréat*, were
required of them, and a career in the colonies had none of the
prestige that it did in England. An *École Coloniale* was founded
in 1885 to train administrators, but by 1914 it was responsible
for only one-fifth of those serving. Recruitment continued to be
based on favouritism and accident. It was only after 1920 that
appointments to the Colonial Corps were restricted to graduates
of this school, and only after 1926, when Georges Hardy was put
in charge of it, that its standard began to rise; it was only in
the 1930s that the colonial school could in any way be considered comparable to the other *grandes écoles*. For long the best
graduates chose to go to Indo-China, where promotion was
said to be quicker and the climate better; the worst were sent
to Africa—as was, for example, Félix Éboué who came one
before last in his examinations. For most of this period these
graduates constituted a small élite. The majority of administrators were junior officials promoted from the ranks to highly

[1] A. Lanly, *Le Français d'Afrique du Nord* (1962).
[2] Marc Baroli, *La Vie quotidienne des Français en Algérie 1830–1914* (1967).
Cf. Albert Memmi, *Portrait du colonisé, précédé du portrait du colonisateur* (1966).

responsible positions, despite their acknowledged unsuitability and inadequacy.

These men were allowed to rule the colonies with the minimum of control, either from Paris or from their local governors. Individual initiative was raised into a cult which made the kind of policy actually implemented depend above all on the person on the spot. Gallieni abolished slavery in Madagascar, but his subordinates virtually perpetuated it by developing a system of labour dues. Most administrators kept their superiors ignorant of what they were doing: 'When I am on an expedition', wrote one, 'my first concern is to cut the telegraph line.' Maurice Delafosse, who ended his career as a governor, said that he was unable to keep up with the stream of regulations and circulars he received, so he just forgot about them, 'leaving it to chance to guide me'. Another governor claimed that in his thirty years in the colonial administration, he never even received an instruction from the ministry of colonies, whose function he saw only as 'to receive our requests and transform them into decrees'. Until 1919, there were practically no officials in the ministry of colonies who had ever been in the colonies. The Colonial Corps was kept distinct from the domestic civil service until 1942; it received far fewer honours and decorations than any other section of the bureaucracy (in 1910 it still got no more medals of the Legion of Honour than it had in 1887, though its size had increased twentyfold). Far lower standards of behaviour and of honesty were tolerated: embezzlers, drunkards, rapists were simply transferred to other colonies when they became too inconvenient. It is against this background that the minority of outstandingly able or eloquent governors should be seen.[1]

Marshal Lyautey (1854–1934) was the most famous of these. His career and policies became the inspiration of the idealistic administrators, who saw their role as one of education rather than simply of power or exploitation. Lyautey's most important achievement was the building-up of the Moroccan protectorate as the most attractive part of the French empire, for settlers as

[1] Robert Delavignette, *Les Vrais Chefs de l'empire* (1939); William B. Cohen, *Rulers of Empire. The French Colonial Service in Africa* (Stanford, 1971); D. C. Rigollot, 'L'École Coloniale 1885–1939' (unpublished mémoire, Paris School of Political Sciences, 1970).

well as capitalists. What he did is particularly noteworthy, because his work represented a revised version of French colonial methods. He took it as his basic assumption that the Algerian experiment had been a failure. He tried to cut off Morocco from Algeria, to treat it as a completely separate world, forbidding even the importation of all Arabic newspapers. His declared aim was to make a love match between Morocco and France. To many admirers, he gave the impression that he was successful, first because he was indeed a man of quite outstanding gifts and secondly because he was an incomparable propagandist and charmer. He became the hero and the model for young people seeking to dedicate themselves to a noble cause in a practical way, and not content simply to express themselves by writing novels. Lyautey was the epitome of the man of action, constantly on the move, sleeping only five hours a day, finding everything he encountered interesting, praising hard work and overwork, working too fast, and moved by an undisguised passion for power. The basis of his restlessness was not boredom but, as he himself said, 'moral solitude', which was what he feared most. Action for him, therefore, involved pleasing people; its reward was to be loved as well as to be admired. He needed an *entourage* of ardent followers and he won their devotion not only by his charm but also by the stimulus that his doctrine of individual initiative gave them. He allowed them power to prove themselves as 'chiefs'. He demanded not blind 'soldierly' obedience, but 'team-work' and 'service'. He was an enemy of bureaucracy, *paperasse*, regulations and precedents. He was not interested in the party squabbles of the homeland and lamented that it was so sectarian; and he made friends with people of all parties. He had originally been a monarchist, and always remained one by inclination, but he abandoned legitimism as too narrow. He found in the colonies an opportunity to reconcile his ideas with service of his country: he could spread the principles he favoured more easily in the 'underdeveloped' world. However, instead of trying to stop the clock, he sought to effect a new combination of tradition and modernity. What he despised about France was its bourgeois virtues. He wanted to give new life to the idea of aristocracy by marrying it with capitalism, socially responsible but definitely inegalitarian. Though brought up and dying as a Catholic, he had no illusions about the Church's powers. He was able to attract disciples of many kinds because he was also a man of immensely wide reading and a fluent writer, who liked to patronise the arts, to have poets reading their verses and musicians giving concerts to him in his desert camps. He liked doing things on a grand scale and those who served with him felt that they too were kings, or lords.

This ideal, much-publicised vision of benevolent government made it very difficult for the French to see what they were doing in practice in Morocco. There can be no doubt that French rule did introduce security to the country. Their Roman roads made it possible for people to travel freely as well as safely. Their establishment of markets by the side of their forts stimulated commerce. Ports, railways and public works provided new opportunities for employment. Lyautey claimed that he was seeking the 'common denominator' of France, the policies everybody could agree on, but these great building projects were rather a deceptive façade. Lyautey kept Morocco a protectorate rather than making it a colony, but that was partly to prevent the ministry of the colonies from interfering with him, and as resident-general he was in fact almost an absolute monarch. He treated the sultan and the tribal chiefs with great respect; he forbade the Catholic Church to proselytise; and he preserved the traditional organs of government. He thought he owed his success to the fact that he was respectful of monarchy, aristocracy and religion. In practice he gave French backing for the preservation of traditional corruption, while undermining the traditional economy that had sustained it. Thus he used the *caids* as administrators, tax-collectors and judges, under the supervision and 'guidance' of a French official. The *caids* in 1945 were still nearly all illiterate. They bought their jobs and recouped themselves by extortion, bribery and a commission on the taxes they levied; when the French finally did pay them salaries, these were still too low to alter their habits. The most famous of them, the pasha of Marrakesh, El Glaoui, used his position to obtain a monopoly of the main industries in the city, including its 27,000 prostitutes, all of whom had to pay him a percentage of their earnings; and every new development involved payment of bribes to him and his subordinates. In 1938 his income was

said to be nine million francs a year, and his debts, which his
power made it unnecessary to repay, stood at eighty-four
million. The effect of the French occupation was to increase
inequality, and to stimulate the development of a proletariat.
But by allying themselves with the so-called aristocracy, the
French alienated the middle classes, for whom they did very
little. Even by 1940, only 3 per cent of Moroccan children were
attending school. Lyautey established five different kinds of
school, one for each social category, so that everybody would
in theory be trained for the station in life into which he was
born: but the finances for implementing an educational programme did not materialise, many of the European settlers
being hostile to it. Even the Moroccan notables did not like
sending their children to the school for notables Lyautey
established, and they paid poor children to act as substitutes for
their own. As late as 1952, there were only twenty-five Moroccan doctors (and fourteen of these were Moroccan Jews); in
1958 there were still only 1,500 Moroccans who had had a
secondary education. In 1952 the European settlers had an
average income of about 1,040 U.S. dollars, compared to the
average of 715 dollars for the inhabitants of France. The
average income in the U.S.A. was then 1,850 dollars, and that
was almost exactly what Morocco's European settlers engaged
in agriculture made. The natives' average income was
170 dollars (and in the traditional rural sector it was only
90 dollars). Morocco was the country to which Frenchmen
went to live at a far higher standard than they could at home.
Many, of course, never made their fortunes. Land was not
given away free, as it had been in Algeria; many settlers had
inadequate resources and some lived off public assistance.

But only some 7 per cent of the Europeans were farmers.
About a quarter were civil servants. Despite Lyautey's attacks
on the bureaucratic spirit, Morocco became a veritable breeding ground for the bureaucrats. In 1953 three times as many
Frenchmen were employed to govern Morocco as Englishmen
were used to rule India, with forty times the population. These
civil servants, it was generally agreed, were incapable of
resisting the pressure of the rich settlers, so virtually no social
legislation was enforced which might be an obstacle to the
freedom of the capitalist entrepreneurs. In 1930 there were only

two inspectors to watch over the labour regulations. The settlers accepted administrative rule of the country, with a limitation of political rights, because they got a free hand for economic enterprise. Capital was freely provided by the large banks and firms in France. Morocco became an outpost of the most advanced sector of French capitalism. When the Popular Front disrupted their idyll, the local employers turned to corporatism, and became fervent supporters of Marshal Pétain. Until the 1950s, the idea that Morocco might want independence was regarded, even by liberals, as a distant and barely practical possibility.[1]

What France offered its colonies was thus, ultimately, a certain amount of prosperity, but this distillation of its civilising mission into material improvements was not as attractive as it imagined. It simply replaced one form of feudalism by another, and created needs which could not be satisfied within the imperial scheme of things. Thus in Indo-China, France's engineers did carry out one of their most impressive feats, comparable to the excavation of the Suez Canal, when they drained and reclaimed the Mekong Delta, and increased the area of cultivable land from 215,000 to 2,200,000 hectares (1869–1930). But here again they were unable to control its economic development. Frenchmen showed no interest in farming this land and by 1931 they owned under 15 per cent of it. The land was bought up by native and Chinese entrepreneurs, who put tenants on it, in return for up to 70 per cent of the crops they produced. The largest landowner in this region was a money lender, who by 1957 had accumulated 28,000 hectares. Agricultural wages did indeed quadruple between 1898 and 1930 and to that extent the French could claim to have raised living standards, but by also improving medical care, they helped to cause the population to treble in the same period. In 1930 the land available for colonisation

[1] H. Lyautey, *Paroles d'action* (1927); G. Hardy, *Portrait de Lyautey* (1949); Robin Bidwell, *Morocco under Colonial Rule: French Administration of Tribal Areas 1912–56* (1973); L. Cerych, *Européens et Marocains 1930–1956: sociologie d'une décolonisation* (Bruges, 1964); René Gallissot, *Le Patronat européen au Maroc 1931–42* (Rabat, 1964); Hervé Bleuchot, *Les Libéraux français au Maroc 1947–55* (Aix, 1973); Alan Scham, *Lyautey in Morocco. Protectorate Administration 1912–25* (U. of California Press, 1970); E. Gellner and C. Micaud, *Arabs and Berbers* (1973); G. Spillmann, *Du protectorat à l'indépendance: Maroc 1912–55* (1967).

was exhausted, but the population doubled again between 1931 and the early 1960s. Wages accordingly fell back to the level at which they had started; agricultural yields did not increase; and the conditions for revolution—land hunger and famine— were established.[1] French rule had benefited a small minority, much more than the masses. Those who acted as middlemen between the French and the natives made enormous profits, as too did some of the businessmen who controlled the country's export trade. Even the minority converted to Catholicism participated in the revolt against the French, and the French did not succeed in creating a sense of community above the traditional rivalries. The irony of it was that the exploitation was of so little benefit to the French state: France spent far more on administering or defending its empire than it collected from it in taxes.[2]

What went on in the colonies, and what was said about them in Paris, was so different that the doctrinal debates about the colonial system need to be seen as a reflection of tensions and anxieties in France, rather than as designed to provide administrators with guidelines for actual behaviour in the field. The colonies were not established as a result of any conscious policy. When the French sent their first expedition to Algeria in 1830, they had no intention of founding a colony; and it was only after much indecision that the naval engagements in Cochin-China were backed up by the government and used to lay the foundations of an eastern empire. France was a European power, absorbed above all by its rivalry with Germany. Colonies began to matter to it when military defeat in Europe caused it to worry about its diminishing prestige, when it saw the other great powers expanding overseas and felt the need to keep up, or lose its status as their equal. It was nationalism that was the prime basis of the interest in the colonies that gradually grew up; it was the clashes with England that raised this interest into a question of national honour, and when Germany became a colonial rival too, as it did in Morocco, then the colonies became a matter of life and death. But for

[1] Robert L. Sansom, *The Economics of Insurgency in the Mekong Delta of Vietnam* (Cambridge, Mass., 1970), 18–52.

[2] Nguyen Van Phong, *La Société vietnamienne de 1882 à 1902* (1971); C. Robequain, *The Economic Development of French Indo-China* (1944); D. J. Duncanson, *Government and Revolution in Vietnam* (1968), 72–139.

long there were many who feared that colonial adventures would only waste French resources, distracting attention from Alsace and Lorraine, which remained the main concern of nationalists. France did not have a surplus population that wished to emigrate. There was no economic pressure for colonial expansion, or for the capture of new markets for industry. In 1900 less than 10 per cent of French trade was with the colonies, and less than 5 per cent of its investments abroad went there. The tenfold expansion of the French empire between 1870 and 1900, so that it had a population of fifty million and an area of 9,500,000 square kilometres, represented not a concerted national effort but the achievement of a number of minorities. People excluded from political life, rebels against prevailing conformities, and eccentrics dissatisfied with or ill at ease in the normal occupations of life found an outlet for their energies in the colonies. That is why there was so much idealistic talk about colonies: colonists were dreamers and adventurers inspired by hope which seldom had a sound basis in reality. Thus the soldiers and sailors who laid the foundations of the empire were rebels against the bureaucratisation of military careers, against the boredom of the long years of peace and the slow promotion that went with it: they found in colonial life a way of transforming the significance of military life, of restoring it to a more dominant position, such as it had once held, and indeed of increasing its influence, to include not just the defence of territory, but also the government of men. The army found a new source of self-respect in the belief that it was serving the community in a more positive way, and new opportunities to win admiration, to fulfil the ambition to be heroes rather than symbols of routine and regulation. Likewise the Catholics who flocked to the colonies as missionaries found there the chance to preach and put into practice their faith, to which the home country was becoming increasingly unsympathetic. In its early stages, colonisation was also a dream of the socialists, particularly the Saint-Simonians and the Fourierists, who saw in it a chance to build a new society, and to bring about a union of east and west. The explorers and the armchair travellers who followed their exploits in the geographical societies (which had 9,500 members in 1881) were partly romantics but also businessmen, merchants, engineers and scientists for whom the colonies could open up exciting new opportunities of achievement and research. It is not surprising that there were so many aristocrats involved in the empire, nor therefore that the empire should have perpetuated some of the characteristics of the *ancien régime* whose disappearance they lamented. But what is equally significant is that the men who showed an interest in the empire came also from every other section of society. The political divisions prevalent in France were laid aside when they went abroad. The colonies effected new alliances between formerly opposed types. They provided an alternative society, in which many old European debates seemed irrelevant.

In course of time, as more people were affected by them, the colonies became more generally important. Between the wars, trade with the colonies increased to one-third of all external trade. The colonial armies made a significant contribution to France's war effort in 1914–18 (and even more in 1939–45). To be hostile to the empire increasingly meant to be anti-patriotic. Only the communist party, indeed, came out fully against imperialism, at least until 1936, when even it changed its tune. That meant that to defend the colonies was to fight the Bolshevik conspiracy to undermine western civilisation. The socialist party favoured the ultimate granting of independence to the colonies, but in this period, it did not think that the time had yet come: it was for a reform of colonial administrative methods (and in 1936–7 vainly attempted to introduce some), but it still believed that France's civilisation was superior to that of the peoples it had the mission of guiding. The radical party, having found in the colonies an important source of patronage, reformulated its doctrines to make imperialism an expression no longer of nationalism, but of solidarity, replacing the right of conquest by the right and duty of the powerful to help the weak, and fitting the colonial ideal into its general preaching of international co-operation. The Catholics for their part began changing the emphasis from conversion to ensuring the general well-being of the colonial peoples. The challenge of the iniquities perpetrated in the colonies, and of the nationalist movements that were rising in them, was met by the growth of a new doctrine of trusteeship and community, to which nearly all parties adhered. Even so, however, the colonies did not become a matter of prime concern for the majority of the nation. In an inquiry held early in 1939, only 40 per cent of those questioned said that they believed France should go to war rather than give up any of its colonies, whereas 44 per cent thought not. Paradoxically, it was during the war of 1939–45 that the empire came to be more generally regarded as an essential part of France, when the legacy of contempt and maltreatment had already built up to formidable proportions. It was the slowness with which France took stock of the realities in the empire, and the time-lag in its emotional involvement, that made it unable ever to meet the demands of nationalist movements, moderate though, for a long time, these were.[1]

The long debate about whether France should pursue a policy of 'assimilation' or 'association' was largely a theoretical one, for the assimilation was in practice degraded into bureaucratic uniformity rather than involving any real equality, and association, though supposed to mean indirect rule and the maintenance of indigenous cultures, was in practice difficult to distinguish from direct rule, for native chiefs were made to do what the French told them to do. The theory simply distracted politicians from appreciating the realities in the colonies themselves.[2] Assimilation might have been attractive if it had ever been practised. One can see this from the diaries left by Mouloud Feraoun, an Algerian primary-school teacher and novelist (writing in French), who was killed by the colonists in 1962. He wished to be a Frenchman. 'I express myself in French,' he said; 'I was made what I am in a French school. . . . But when I say that I am French, I give myself a label that all Frenchmen refuse me.' He once exclaimed angrily to a colonial civil servant: 'I am more French than you, you miserable, narrow-minded little Vichyite.' It was with deep reluctance that he became a nationalist: he had nothing but contempt for those who suddenly rediscovered their Muslim faith and sought to re-create an Algerian identity. But he had to reach the conclusion that force must be used to overthrow

[1] Raoul Girardet, *L'Idée coloniale en France 1871–1962* (1972).

[2] Raymond F. Betts, *Assimilation and Association in French Colonial Theory 1890–1914* (Columbia U.P., 1961); and for a good study of what happened, Martin A. Klein, *Islam and Imperialism in Senegal. Sine-Saloum 1847–1914* (Stanford, 1968), based almost entirely on the archives.

the French, even though he abhorred it; French troops raided his village, they showed more respect to the son of his concierge, who was of European descent than, to himself, the headmaster. The presence of France was an affront to human dignity, and the declaration of the rights of man had to be upheld against its inventors. Faraoun wished to be a citizen of the world and he was as horrified by the nationalism he had to adopt, as he was by that of Guy Mollet, who claimed to be a disciple of Karl Marx. He consoled himself with the hope that once the French were defeated, they would at last treat the Muslims as equals, and the two races could live together not in harmony perhaps but at least with dignity.[1]

The history of Léopold Senghor (born 1906) likewise shows how the theory of assimilation was undermined by the very culture into which Africans were supposed to be drawn. Senghor was the son of a Catholic groundnut merchant, but his mother was the daughter of a pagan cattle herder. He was educated in a missionary school, then in a *lycée*, and ended up an *agrégé*, teaching French grammar in a *lycée* in Tours. He tried to become an *évolué* (the privileged status accorded to the small minority that were offered full assimilation) but he always felt torn between his French and his African ties, between his father's and his mother's families. He was fashionable enough, in French terms, to be a royalist in the 1930s. He was deeply influenced by Barrès's doctrine of the need for roots and by Gide's urging that it was through stressing one's uniqueness that one arrived at universality. It was the ethnologists of Paris who opened up his appreciation of Negro culture and it was the surrealists who encouraged him to justify and defend African irrationalism or emotion against French logic. 'France', he wrote, 'opened me to self-knowledge . . . and revealed to me the values of my ancestral civilisation.' His answer to assimilation was that the Africans should assimilate, rather than be assimilated, but it was a symbiosis of African and European values that he sought to create in his concept of 'negritude'. He rejected French colonialism with a concept which had strong French elements in it and which he developed in highly polished French prose and verse.[2]

[1] Mouloud Feraoun, *Journal 1955–62* (1962).
[2] J. L. Hymans, *Léopold Sedar Senghor, An Intellectual Biography* (Edinburgh, 1971).

Senghor's Catholic background is important. The French culture that was propagated abroad was not just the culture of the republic, but also that of traditional, Catholic France. So it was a confused or ambiguous message that was transmitted. Whether France would have won more influence abroad had it abstained from colonial conquest is, however, uncertain. Thus though Egypt, for example, was taken over politically by England in 1882, French missionary schools continued to flourish there and in 1942 55 per cent of the well-to-do Egyptians attending foreign schools in that country chose these French schools. But whereas until 1882 most Egyptians going abroad for their education went to France, British rule at once changed this and henceforth the vast majority went to study in England. French could become the language of polite society, but the jobs and careers that political control offered were ultimately more important.[1]

What the colonies rejected was a corruption of ideals; but that also was largely what they inherited. France exported its national pride in its most arrogant form, undiluted by its universalism and its capacity for self-doubt; it was a similar national pride which rose up to expel it from its colonies. It exported materialism more than its spiritual concerns. The legacy of this century of tutelage did not reflect the values France could have transmitted.[2]

Servants

The status of servants was another indication of attitudes to hierarchy and of the progress of equality. They formed a large and important group, though their character changed. A servant in ancient usage was above all a farm-hand, lodging with his master. In this general sense, the total number of servants fell:

	Men	Women
1866	892,000	1,311,000
1896	160,000	703,000

[1] Raoul Makarius, *La Jeunesse intellectuelle d'Égypte* (The Hague, 1960), 82; Anouar Abdel-Malek, *La Formation de l'idéologie nationale de l'Égypte 1805–1892* (Paris thesis, 1969), 76; and cf. S. Longrigg, *Syria and Lebanon under French Mandate* (1958).

[2] André Nouschi, *La Naissance du nationalisme algérien 1914–54* (1962); David C. Gordon, *The Passing of French Algeria* (1966); C. Micaud, *Tunisia, the Politics of Modernisation* (1964); R. von Albertini, *Decolonisation* (New York, 1971).

However, domestic servants increased as the urban middle classes grew in prosperity and as the peasants migrated to the towns:

Domestic Servants

1891	683,000
1906	840,000
1911	940,000

Paris in 1866 had 100,000 servants, but by 1906 it had 206,000, which was 11 per cent of its population; and in Paris there were then five times more female than male servants. The principle of the career open to talent meant not just equality but also that every successful man wanted to have a servant to show off his status. Thus in the 1890s virtually all barristers, doctors and magistrates kept servants, 71 per cent of pharmacists, 44 per cent of dentists, 12 per cent of midwives, 44 per cent of scientists, men of letters and journalists, 61 per cent of architects and engineers, 20 per cent of artists and 26 per cent of retired *rentiers*.[1]

The French Revolution had attempted to abolish domestic servants as a class, at least in their traditional form, and it sought to give them a new name, *officieux*; but Napoleon's Civil Code reaffirmed their subordination, by laying down that in a dispute about wages, the master was to be believed by the courts simply on his word: it gave the master the right to dismiss servants without the customary eight days' notice in cases of drunkenness, theft, insolence or misbehaviour. It is true it allowed the servant to leave without notice if he was insulted, or refused his wages, but the master had the right to search his baggage before he left, and a crime committed by a servant against his master was held to be aggravated because it involved a breach of trust. A servant could be dismissed without compensation if he fell ill (unless it was of a contagious disease caught from his master) or when he was too old to be of further use.[2] In 1875 a Paris court condemned a lady to pay 2,000 francs damages for having falsely accused her maid of stealing her jewels; after six weeks in police custody the maid's innocence

[1] Viviane Léon, épouse Ayme, 'La Domesticité féminine à Paris de 1890 à 1914' (unpublished mémoire de maîtrise, Nanterre, 1973).

[2] *Manuel des bons domestiques. Droits et devoirs des maîtres et des domestiques* (1896), 8° R 13245.

was proved and she successfully sued her mistress; but a case two years later showed that if an accusation was made against a servant in good faith and not 'maliciously or lightly', there was no redress against it. It was only in 1923 that the 1898 law on accident insurance for industrial workers was applied to them (but governesses, companions and secretaries were still excluded).[1]

The legal inferiority of servants was however less of a worry to them than the way they were treated in their daily lives. Moralists liked to look back to a golden age when servants respected their masters and masters treated them as members of the family. At the end of the nineteenth century, there were indeed still rural employers in traditional regions like Brittany who made little distinction between their children and their servants, who had maids sleeping in the same room as their mistress, and who used to say, not 'Go and work', but 'Let's go and work'. In Tréguier and Cornouailles servants used to call their masters uncle and aunt.[2] There is no doubt that some servants, who worked all their lives in the same family and who had brought up the children, had a respected role which they valued. But already in the eighteenth century there were complaints from both sides which showed that these idealised relations were always the exception. In the nineteenth century there were increasing laments that 'reciprocal confidence barely exists any more'. The Agricultural Inquiry of 1866 noted 'a certain enmity'. In 1867 a play, *Ces Scélérates de bonnes*, showed masters already despairing of their ability to control their servants: it showed a maid, when interviewed by her prospective employers, submitting them to long questioning on exactly what her duties would be, on how much free time she would have, when she would have to get up in the morning, and adding that she drank only Bordeaux wine: the master replied by asking, 'Do you know Greek? Do you know astronomy? Can you paint in oils? Then I am afraid you are no use to us.' This was a verbatim reproduction of the experience of an American author in Paris.

---

[1] Adrien Sachet, *Maîtres de maison et domestiques sous le régime de la législation sur les accidents du travail. Commentaire de la loi du 2 août 1923* (1924).

[2] Jean Choleau, *Condition actuelle des serviteurs ruraux bretons, domestiques à gages et journaliers agricoles* (1907), 94.

The Salon of 1864 showed a painting by Marchal of an Alsatian Servants' Fair, where they could be hired in the traditional way, but these had almost vanished by the end of the century, when there was much talk of a 'crisis' in the servant situation. Too many people wanted servants now. They were much harder to find, particularly *bonnes à tout faire*. Though their wages increased considerably as a result, they had new grievances. The employment agencies, trying to profit from the shortage, were said to extract no less than two million francs a year in fees from servants in Paris alone.[1] The growth of the practice of segregating them on the sixth floor of apartment blocks gave them a sense of being outcasts, but also encouraged them to become more aware of their exploitation, to demand improvements, and to move on to better jobs. A newspaper (*Le Larbin*) appeared specifically for domestic servants, edited by a cook. A Declaration of the Rights of Servants demanded that employers should cease to expect more than the performance of duties for which they paid.[2]

But employers also demanded respect. A servant was socially and educationally inferior, even if he did have the vote, and employers used servants to assert their superiority, either by ostentation, by showing that they could avoid menial tasks, or by trampling on their servants' dignity. One servant, in his memoirs, argued that employers were not worthy of the respect they demanded: maids were seduced by their masters and sacked when they became pregnant, so that they often became prostitutes; Balzac had shown wives, anxious to liberate themselves from their husbands' sexual demands, choosing pretty maids as substitutes; Eugène Sue had complained: 'Nothing is more frequent than this corruption more or less imposed by the master on the servant.' Employers confided their worries to their servants, so 'the vices of Monsieur and the coldnesses of Madame' drained away respect. This servant described his successive employers with great wit.[3] Others had a different way of getting their own back: they compensated for their low wages by stealing. It was a favourite complaint

[1] Jean-Pierre, *Maîtres et serviteurs. La crise du service domestique* (1904).

[2] Emmanuel Chauvet, *Les Domestiques* (Caen, 1896).

[3] *Maîtres et domestiques fin de siècle* par un cuisinier philosophe, ancien gendarme (dix ans de service militaire) devenu domestique de 1875 à 1897 (1898), 8° Li(5)439.

that servants were often thieves; and there was constant squabbling about property. The servants, however, profited from their masters by a tacit bargain with other poor people who served the well-to-do: in the Paris markets, there were two prices, one for masters and one for servants, and other trades- men also generally gave servants a 5 per cent commission on sales. The concierges were brought into the racket, to overlook other forms of peculation, by being given a share of the remains of the food from the master's table.[1] In this way, servants were able to save considerable sums of money, and that was ulti- mately the reason why most of them had chosen this kind of work: it was the easiest avenue by which poor peasants could rise into the petty bourgeoisie. Only a minority of servants married. When they did, they married late, and they very often had only one child. Men servants frequently married women servants, but there were more of the latter and these were often successful in using their savings to marry up the social scale. A sample survey of nineteenth-century Versailles has shown 16 per cent of them marrying artisans, 8 per cent marrying shopkeepers and 4 per cent clerks. Another of Lyon in the 1870s showed only about one-tenth of servants making domestic service a lifetime career. Servants were increasingly literate, because service was one way of learning to read and to acquire manners; they were noted for spending a lot of money on clothes, and Balzac said that a cook could dress as well as her mistress.[2] Domestic service declined when alternative professions arose for poor girls to make their way in the world, with the expansion of shops, offices and factories. The hierarchic character of domestic service survived because servants were often imbued with the same obsession with status that tormented their masters: they maintained inequali- ties amongst themselves—as between valet, cook, chambermaid and scullery maid—and they tried to extract respect from their inferiors, using almost identical brutality. The *Moniteur des gens de maison*, their trade union paper, wrote in 1907: 'They accept social inequalities as one of the consequences of human

[1] Bouniceau-Gesmon, juge d'instruction à Paris, *Domestiques et maîtres. Question sociale* (1896).

[2] Theresa M. McBride, 'Social Mobility for the Lower Classes: Domestic Servants in France', *Journal of Social History* (Fall 1974), 63–75.

existence and they firmly believe that it is above all by faithful duty that they can improve the general lot.'

Fourier, and Vacherot during the Second Empire, had suggested that menial work should be done by children. But that class was rising to independence even faster than the working class. Moralists like Adolphe Garnier and Jules Barni thought, in that same period, that the answer lay in converting domestic service into piece work, so that there should not be anything degrading about it. But in 1925 Madame Moll-Weiss, founder of the *École des Mères*, while urging the mistress to treat her servant with consideration, acknowledged that there was often 'hateful hostility' between them and they just could not understand each other's point of view.[1]

Mutual incomprehension is what all four sections of this chapter have been about. This should not be surprising. The next chapter will show that even in their attitudes to the most basic problems of life, Frenchmen were deeply divided, though in a different way.

[1] Augusta Moll-Weiss, *Madame et sa bonne* (1925).

5. Birth and Death

THE French worried obsessively and increasingly about the slow rate at which their population increased. At least that is the impression one gets from the vast literature that poured out on this subject. These hundred years, when birth-control was adopted in France on a scale hitherto unprecedented and never to be repeated, appear to stand out as a crisis, when Frenchmen became neurotic about their virility and about their capacity to survive as a great power. Their decadence could be measured at every census. But despite the warnings of the population experts, the exhortations of moralists and even the financial inducements held out by governments, the country as a whole steadfastly continued to produce fewer and fewer children, and to act in apparently complete disregard of the opinions of its leaders. The demographic history of France is therefore very revealing not only about the attitudes of individuals towards the most basic facts of life and the status of the family, but also about the clash between their interests and the nationalist aspirations of the politicians. This conflict and contrast between the ambitions of different sections of the community, and the way they could ignore each other, makes the problems of population much more than an exercise in statistics. The reasons why Frenchmen had small families but also deplored them are worth investigating.

The word demography was invented by a Frenchman, Achille Guillard, in 1855.[1] The French have long been highly regarded as exponents of this science; the Institut National d'Études Démographiques, founded in 1942–5, has been the source of a very large body of research; no one can study historical demography without examining the theoretical and empirical contributions of French scholars to it; and even now, when population problems have been attracting a vast amount

---

[1] Achille Guillard, *Éléments de statistique humaine, ou démographie comparée* (1855); for his other interests, see id., *Biographie de J. Jacotot, fondateur de la méthode d'émancipation intellectuelle* (1860). But the word statistics was first used in its modern sense in eighteenth-century Germany.

of attention all over the world, Frenchmen continue to play a
leading role in their discussion (as they do not, for example,
in economics, or most of the natural sciences). However,
this should not blind one to the many obstacles which none the
less stood in the way of the French knowing the facts about
their own population. Officially, French population statistics
are available from 1801. But no uniform method of collecting
data was prescribed in that year and it was a long time before
truly comparable series became available. Only in 1836
were the prefects' estimates replaced by actual counting of
heads; only in 1876 did each inhabitant have his particulars
inscribed on a separate card; only in 1881 was the actual
population present on the day of the census recorded, as
opposed to the 'legal' population supposedly existing in
habitual places of residence. The first complete census of industrial and professional activity was made in 1896; the
analysis of families dates from 1906. The census of 1901 was
the first to satisfy the experts, but subsequent ones have been
criticised, and anomalies appear when these are compared
with statistics produced for other purposes, as for example
those in agriculture. Part of the explanation is that the Statistical Office had a very small staff; it had to use unpaid assistants in the provinces; and it was only after the Second World
War that the collection and analysis of statistics became fully
professional.

However, the deficiencies of French statistics could not
obscure the most striking fact which became obvious in the
mid-nineteenth century, that France was, from the numerical
point of view, losing the predominant position it had hitherto
held in Europe. In 1800 France had 28 million inhabitants.
Great Britain and Ireland together had only 16 million. All
the German states put together totalled 22 million, and those
of Italy 18 million. But by 1860 the Austrian empire had
caught up with France; in 1870 the new German empire had
five million more inhabitants than the new Third Republic;
in 1900 Britain overtook France and in 1933 even Italy did.
So France now came at the bottom of the European league, in
fifth place (Russia always leading). Thus in the years 1800–1940
Germany's population quadrupled and Britain's tripled, but
France's rose by only 50 per cent. Moreover, this small increase

in the French population—of 13 million odd—was not achieved
by natural increase: on the contrary, the rate of reproduction
produced a loss of five millions; and the war of 1914 was
responsible for a loss of a further three millions. It was simply

Population of European nations, in millions

	1789	1815	1860	1871	1910	1920	1939
France	26	30	37·4	36·1	39·6	39·2	41·9
Great Britain	16	20	29	32	45	44	47·5
Austrian Empire	27	29	36	36	51	—	—
Prussia	6	10	18	—	—	—	—
Germany	—	—	—	41	65	59	80
Italy	—	—	23	27	35	38	44
Russia	30	48	67	80	142	120	170

the increase in people's longevity, accounting for an increase
of 16 millions, and the immigration of 5 millions, which
explained the rise. All European nations experienced a check
to their population growth in this period, but the decline in the
French birth-rate began almost a century before that of its
rivals, around 1760, so that the accumulative effect was felt
much longer and more noticeably: the decline in England and
Germany started only around 1875–80, that in Italy (and the
U.S.A.) around 1885. The French regularly produced fewer
babies, proportionately to their population:

Births per 1,000 inhabitants

	France	England	Germany
1841–50	27·4	32·6	36·1
1891–1900	22·2	29·9	36·1
1938	14·6	19·1	19·7

Historians regularly use these and similar statistics to
show that France was losing its hegemony in Europe and to
imply that there was therefore some moral or economic decadence at work to explain what they always see as a silent
defeat. Both of these common generalisations, however, need
to be looked at more carefully. International comparisons are
fruitful only if one is clear about the criterion one is adopting:
to argue that power comes simply from numbers is to use

military and economic criteria: a large nation wins battles
and produces more machinery, but it will be realised by now
that France did not wholly accept these ambitions. The fall in
its population was indeed a challenge to the idea that these
were the principal aims of life. To argue that France was
decadent because it produced few children is to adopt the
theories of a relatively small minority of conservative propagandists, whose motives need to be examined more carefully.
It is too easy to assume that the criticisms these theorists
made of their countrymen were empirical observations of fact,
and to quote them as impartial judgements above contradiction. Nearly everything written about the French population
in these years has looked on its development as manifesting
some weakness or aberration: the assumption has nearly always
been that because other nations were increasing in size, France
ought to have been increasing also. It is worth seeing first,
therefore, just who it was who led the lamentations.

   In the eighteenth century, French economists had become
generally hostile to the traditional belief that the increase
of a nation's population was a good thing. Instead of regarding
the poor simply as material to supply the state with soldiers
and taxes for its own glory, they argued that humanitarian
considerations should determine population policy. They asked
that the rights and interests of the poor should not be overlooked. They wanted the increase in prosperity to benefit
the individual, rather than to be used as a stimulus to make the
poor have more children. Some people said that population
depended on the amount of work available, so that the way to
increase the population was to increase manufacturing. But
others replied that no nation could really be improved by
having large masses of miserable industrial workers. Malthus,
who suggested that men would not automatically gain from
technical progress and that the poor would improve their lot
by reducing the number of children they had, was widely
approved. There was distinct hostility to filling France with
smoky factories. In 1847 the head of the state census office,
Legoyt, wrote that those countries which had the most rapidly
increasing populations, like England, Prussia and Saxony,
'were precisely those where pauperism makes the most redoubt-
able progress'. It was believed that there was a limit to the

amount of food the land could produce, that to rely on imports would be dangerous, that only advances in agronomic science could be looked to for greater productivity, and that meanwhile the stimulation of the birth-rate was wrong. Under Louis-Philippe, ministers and prefects advised the poor to limit their families: in 1866, during debates held on the subject by the Academy of Medicine, the anthropologist Broca insisted that the number of births was 'a false criticism of the prosperity of a population'. France, said Legoyt in 1867, was a 'grown-up country, arrived at maturity': it should concentrate on improving the lot of its existing population.[1] While its population was increasing rapidly, a reaction thus set in against the nationalist attitude that this was an end in itself. At first, no alarm was felt when it was seen that the increase was slowing down, and many indeed applauded.

The first complaint that France was losing its dominant position among the great powers was made in 1849 in a book which went through four editions in a year. C. M. Raudot's *The Decadence of France* claimed that the country was heading for ruin, citing as proof the decline in the height of army recruits. Writers on demographic history who quote him omit to discover who he was—a legitimist public prosecutor who had resigned in 1830 from loyalty to Charles X, and who had written in praise of *France Before the Revolution* (1841).[2] A very considerable proportion of the advocates of a larger population were indeed admirers of a vanished golden age, in which they imagined large families had lived in harmony, ruled benevolently by aged patriarchs. A constant underlying assumption in the debates on this subject was that family life, like religion, was indispensable for the preservation of a hierarchical organisation of society. It is true that this link was by no means always present, nor always in a simple form. Thus Léonce de Lavergne, whose article in the *Revue des Deux Mondes* in 1857 made the facts about the country's declining population known to the majority of educated people interested in public affairs, was a friend of Guizot, an Orleanist politician

[1] J. J. Spengler, *French Predecessors of Malthus. A Study in Eighteenth Century Wage and Population Theory* (Durham, N.C., 1942), 365; id., *France Faces Depopulation* (Durham, N.C., 1938), 111–17.

[2] C. M. Raudot, *De la décadence de la France* (1849); A. Motheré, *Réponse à l'ouvrage de M. Raudot* (1850).

who accepted the republic only in the 1870s. He declared himself to be a 'faithful disciple of Malthus', but he quite correctly said that Malthus was not opposed to increasing population provided it could be achieved without poverty increasing. Lavergne was a great admirer of England and of its agricultural revolution: it was eighteenth-century England, before its industrialisation, that he held up as an ideal; and he urged France to increase its population by improving its agricultural productivity.[1] But the most important source of conservative populationist thought was Frédéric Le Play (1806–82).

Le Play

He has many different claims to notice, and not only because several generations of leaders of the *familles nombreuses* movement owed much to his influence. He was an outstanding sociologist, engineer, traveller, propagandist and also a very curious man. His private and public careers reveal in a striking way the options, and the difficulties, facing men in their attitudes to the family within the context of modern civilisation.

Superficially Le Play appears to be a representative figure of the Second Empire—that much-simplified, easily labelled regime: a scientist, graduate of the Polytechnic, organiser of the International Exhibitions, professor and senator, standing for authority and material progress, but typically divided between religion and science. In reality he was a sensitive, worried man, searching for stability in a world which depressed him but which he studied minutely and indefatigably for the key to happiness. He was trained as a mining engineer, winning the highest marks ever awarded by the École des Mines, but in 1830 he suffered severe burns and permanent scarring following a laboratory accident: 'one of the decisive events of my career. . . . Eighteen months of physical and moral torture produced a transformation in me.' He made a vow to devote at least half of his time to studying society and the family, and to discovering why there was so much animosity and strife in them. For the next fifteen years he spent six months earning his living as an industrial consultant, manager and professor and

[1] A. Armengaud, 'Léonce de Lavergne ou un malthusien populationniste', *Annales de démographie historique* (1968), 29–36.

six months travelling. He covered altogether 175,000 miles, visiting almost every country in Europe, comparing the degree of harmony to be found in different situations, analysing the relationship between technical and social change and investigating above all the organisation of the family in varying situations. He thus developed a new methodology of social study. Whereas the Saint-Simonians, with whom he grew up and among whom he numbered several close friends (Jean Reynaud was often his travelling companion; his son married Michel Chevalier's daughter,[1]), believed that a totally new order must be invented to replace the present intolerable situation, Le Play, breaking away from them, advocated comparative and historical approaches. Foreign countries should be studied for actual examples of possible alternatives; and the past must be looked on not as something to be escaped from, but as a source of wisdom. Denying that progress was infinite and inevitable, he preferred a cyclical view of history, seeing decadence and resurgence alternating; and he thought that the merits of the French past could often be observed surviving in foreign societies untouched by modernisation. He embarked on a gigantic compilation of facts about the different types of families existing in Europe, from Norway to Portugal, arranged according to the amount of 'stability' he detected in them. He wrote monographs on over 300 families, interviewing each for between a week and a month, and using eight languages in the process. The central core of these monographs consisted in a budget, showing the minutest details of income and expenditure, from which, he argued, all else could be deduced, but he added information about the biographies, religious beliefs and social contacts of his subjects. Even if exception may be taken to the way Le Play presented his material, these monographs remain a unique and irreplaceable source for social historians. Le Play's methods prefigure those of social anthropologists: 'The time is not far distant,' he wrote, 'when the fact that an author has not moved out of his study will be sufficient refutation of his theory.' But sociologists have criticised his monographs; Durkheim, who was interested in more abstract argument, dismissed him as of little importance; and

[1] Through Michel Chevalier, he was related to Paul Leroy-Beaulieu, Émile Flourens and Émile Pereire.

he seldom figures among the great names of social science. The explanation of this can be found partly in the inaccuracies and inadequacies of his work, but even more in the political implications he drew from it, which condemned him as a reactionary, a 'reincarnation of Bonald', as Sainte-Beuve called him.

There have been over 160 studies (in books or articles) of him, but these have been almost exclusively by admirers praising him and there is still no full biography available.[1] But one needs to do more than categorise him as a reactionary if one is to understand the origins and significance of his nostalgia. There is probably an almost Proustian story behind it, though more research will be needed before any definite explanation can be offered. Le Play's life was devoted to the search for 'happiness' and 'social peace', by which he meant individual contentment, the absence of anxiety and antagonisms, and satisfaction with the organisation of society. It was this psychological, unquantifiable, element in his ideal that first set the sociologists against him. He believed that social peace could be established by three methods: restoring religious belief, increasing the power of the father and legislating to make the 'seduction' of women more difficult. This kind of brief summary is what usually condemns him, but there was an interesting theory and history behind it. Le Play was no orthodox Catholic and, until just before he died, probably not a practising one either. The religion he was interested in was that of the Old Testament, not that of Christ. It may have been coincidental that strong paternal authority should have been one of the principal panaceas of a man whose father died when he was only six. He at any rate attributed his breaking-away from his Saint-Simonian friends to his having been born in the country (Honfleur, where his father had been a customs official), and to having been sent away to Paris on his father's death, to live with an uncle: 'ever since I have always found the sight of towns distasteful'. His schooling was 'a torment the memory of which has never left me'; later his years at the Polytechnic were 'suffocating'. He longed to return to the fishermen he had played with as a child, whose primitive husbandry,

[1] The nearest approach is M. Z. Brooke, *Le Play: engineer and social scientist* (1970), which provides a useful introductory survey in 140 pages.

living off natural resources, ever remained his ideal. His uncle
was a royalist with a group of counter-revolutionary friends,
who filled the boy with horrific stories of the Terror, but also
with the moral that it was the corruption of the upper classes
and their abandonment of religion that had brought catastrophe to the monarchy. These opinions, he himself noted,
revived in him in later life, after having been temporarily
obscured by the teaching of the schools. What his relations
with his mother, who sent him away, were, and how they
relate to his obsession about seduction, is not known, nor what
feelings of guilt made him place such stress on the virtues of
obedience.

But he based his philosophy on a staunch reaffirmation of
original sin. Children were ignorant and vicious, an endless
barbarian invasion against which society must guard itself.
The spirit of rebellion starts in very infancy, respect for parents
is not natural, and needs to be inculcated by chastisement, to
show children their weakness; but even that is not enough to
quell them, so 'the fear of God and the counsels of reason' must
be summoned in support. Le Play argued for the restoration of
religion, making the practice of the Ten Commandments the
first basis of happiness. He thought this restoration would be
possible if the upper classes set the example in their own private
lives, and made religion fashionable again, if the clergy improved their morals and ceased to interfere in politics (it was
mainly this that had turned people against them). 'The counsels of reason' meant that the father should have the right to
dispose freely of his property, to cut off disobedient children,
contrary to the Napoleonic Code. The most vigorous nations—
Russia and England—were those in which, he claimed, paternal
authority was strongest. The French, by compelling a more or
less equal distribution of inheritance between children, gave
most the prospect of a tiny property, so that modest ambitions
prevailed and the need to show individual initiative was
reduced. Le Play's ideal family was what he called the stem
family (*la famille souche*), meaning that the family property
was transmitted intact from the father to one son, while the
other children left the stem to make their own fortunes and
to establish stem families of their own. This he contrasted
with, on the one hand, the unstable family, which was the

commonest type in France, where the property was divided up between the children, who dispersed rootless, and, on the other hand, the patriarchal family, in which many generations lived together: he saw many virtues in this last form, but conceded that it was capable of becoming too hostile to innovation. The restoration of paternal authority could be easily secured, he thought, simply by changing the inheritance laws, and this became the main demand of his followers.

That such a change would offend the French worship of equality he denied, because, he said, 'France is of all the European nations, the least keen on equality', as was proved by the mania for decorations, and the maintenance of class and other distinctions. France could borrow a lot from England, and particularly 'the just equilibrium it maintained between classes', its religion moderated by tolerance, its hunger for riches balanced by Christian renunciation, hard work balanced by Sunday rest, and temperance societies which spread 'moral influences'. The English loved their past: the French must learn to do the same. The English had preserved an aristocracy which lived on its ancestral estates, set an example of morality and maintained a clergy to ensure obedience to the Ten Commandments. But Le Play found many faults in England too, and above all its *laissez-faire* industrialisation, which gave no kind of security to the workers, and he was no supporter of aristocracies as such. The people who held the key to the restoration of social peace were what he called the 'social authorities'—men residing on their own lands, who won general respect for their wisdom and morals, who 'found in the traditions of their family the origin of the happiness they enjoy and the source of the good they spread around them. Their constant preoccupation is to work for the two fundamental needs of humanity, social peace, obtainable by regulating their thoughts and actions according to the prescriptions of the Decalogue, and the enjoyment of daily bread, by subjecting all the members of the community to the obligation to work.' Le Play had searched all Europe for these benevolent patriarchs: far from modelling them on the English aristocracy, he turned up examples of them everywhere, in the Norwegian fjords and the hills of Saxony, Switzerland and the Basque country. His ideal society was essentially rural, and he wanted industry to

make provision for its workers to have a balanced range of
occupations which freed them from the dangers of unemployment. Though an engineer, he was opposed to technology
providing the model for social planning. He complained that
'the French today are an urban people, as the Gauls and the
Romans were. They must become once again a rural people, as
the Franks were and as the Anglo-Saxons still are.' The great
enemies, therefore, were the bourgeoisie who had despoiled the
countryside and corrupted the masses. More specifically, he
attacked the *lettrés*, who in the eighteenth century had started
the 'universal of contempt for all human and divine authority,
the destruction of all forms of respect and the creation of
insatiable appetites'—all based on hostility towards the past.
Custom, not theories or laws, must be the guide to action.
Royalist decentralisation was no use, because too many de-
centralisers were bourgeois, who would only oppress the rural
populations even more if given power: rural and urban areas
should have separate governments; the parish was the only
real unit; the authority of the 'Voltairian mayor and *instituteur*' must be replaced by that of heads of families. Regulations
must be replaced by rites. The family must be given its autonomy.[1] And to crown all this, chastity, on which he laid great
store as the basis of family morality, must be enforced by placing
the responsibility for its violation entirely on the male; there
must be no truce with the idea that seduction involved consent
by the woman; the family system could not be preserved without
chastity and rigid distinctions in sexual roles.

Le Play does not appear to have been able to implement all
these ideas in his own life. He preached against Malthusianism
but had only one son; he opposed boarding-schools, but sent
his son to one; he extolled the beneficent rule of patriarchs,
but he admitted his grandchildren into his presence only once
a week, when he silently and briefly distributed sweets to them.
But it should not be thought that his ideas were purely theoretical and out of touch with reality. Le Play found numerous—
if odd—examples of patriarchal and stem families in France
and the traditions he wished to restore were far from being
completely dead. A precursor, in some ways, of Maurras, he
was like him an outsider among the conservatives, and his

[1] Charles de Ribbe, *Le Play, d'après sa correspondance* (1884), 403–13.

tragedy was that he was taken up only by the conservatives, when he believed he was appealing beyond the political parties or religious denominations, to what he considered to be universal family values, truths inescapably following from the human condition. Le Play's influence was limited by his refusal to avoid drawing all the implications from his investigations. Montalembert declared that *The Social Reform of France* was 'the most original, useful, courageous and in every respect the most powerful book of this century. It does not have as much eloquence as the illustrious Tocqueville, but much more practical perspicacity and above all moral courage . . . [because it] combated the majority of the dominant prejudices of its time and of France.' Le Play, for his part, thought Tocqueville had produced 'probably the first political and social work of our time', but ended by condemning Tocqueville as a sophist and a coward, because 'he could not see where to go' and did not really dare say what he believed. Le Play himself may well have said too much.[1]

The Myth of the Only Child

It will be seen in due course how the populationist movement reflected these kinds of anxiety, how Le Play was influential as their most systematic exponent, and also how the movement was always very much a minority one. In this subject, one is always dealing with minorities, for though there are broad national trends, these do not result from everybody following more or less the same pattern of behaviour, but are the average produced by adding up quite a wide diversity of situations. This simple fact was too often overlooked because the propagandists were concerned mainly with national totals. The general condemnations also make the simple error that people knew how many children they wanted and procreated accordingly. But French sociologists have recently shown, through opinion polls and inquiries, just how large the gap between belief and actions can be. Public knowledge of demographic

[1] F. Le Play, *Les Ouvriers européens* (2nd edition, 1879), vol. 1 contains autobiographical information, preface, 17–48 and 395–438; id., *L'Organisation du travail* (1870); id., *L'Organisation de la famille* (1871); id., *La Réforme sociale* (5th edition, 1874); Ferdinand Aubertin, *Frédéric Le Play, d'après lui-même* (1906). For a full bibliography see M. Z. Brooke, op. cit. 142–64.

trends, even in the 1950s and 1960s, when these were constantly discussed, was extraordinarily inaccurate; the ideal family size was considerably higher than the average size; and worries about unemployment, overpopulation and housing remained vigorous even while people did produce more children. In 1947 73 per cent of the country appeared to want the population to rise, but by 1965 only 29 per cent did; the proportion in favour of its remaining stationary rose from 23 to 66: and this was during a period of dramatic economic growth. The attitudes of different classes varied considerably: in 1965 15 per cent of the liberal professions and industrial managers were in favour of having larger families, but only 7 per cent of artisans and retailers were, and only 2 per cent of peasants.[1] Another inquiry carried out in the 1960s in Lyon questioned mothers before and after their child was born, as to whether the child was wanted. Fifty-four per cent said, before its birth, that it was wanted, and 60 per cent gave the same answer after birth. When these replies were averaged out, and broken down according to the number of children the mother already had, the replies were:[2]

85 per cent of those whose first child it was said they wanted it
64 ,, ,,　　　　,,　　　,, second　　,,　,,　,,　　,,　　,,
35 ,, ,,　　　　,,　　　,, third or fourth　,,　,,　　,,　　,,
10 ,, ,,　　　　,,　　　,, fifth or more　　　,,　,,　　,,　　,,

These examples may be enough to show how dangerous it is to generalise about broad national trends, and to attribute rational or conscious explanations to them.

In 1906, 11·5 per cent of couples had no children, 42·4 per cent had one or two children, 25·3 per cent had three or four, but 20·8 per cent have five or more. The slogan that France was a nation of only sons was false. Half its families failed to reproduce themselves, but the other half amply succeeded. The proportion of couples with one child (21·1 per cent) was almost exactly equal to that of couples with five or more children. This meant, however, that a relatively small group of mothers produced quite a sizeable section of the nation's

[1] Henri Bastide and Alain Girard, 'Les Tendances démographique en France et les attitudes de la population', *Population* (Jan.–Feb. 1966), 9–50.

[2] H. Pigeaud, 'Attitudes devant la maternité. Une enquête à Lyon', *Population* (Mar.–Apr. 1966), 231–72.

children, as can be seen by looking, for example, at the history
of the half-million women born in 1881. Twenty-eight per cent
of these died before reaching the age of fifteen. Twelve per cent
died unmarried; 6 per cent were still alive but spinsters in 1931;
only 54 per cent married. Sixty per cent of these married women
had either no children, or one or two children, which altogether
accounted for 25·6 per cent of the descendants of this generation of 1881. Only 6·3 per cent of the married women bore
seven or more children, but they accounted for 20·9 per cent of
all the children. The rare couples who had ten or more children
produced almost as many children (7·2 per cent of the total) as
the large number of couples who had only one child (8·5 per cent).
This kind of statistic meant that the Frenchmen of 1880 were
themselves descended from only about 10 or 12 per cent of
Frenchmen who had lived in 1789.[1] The concentration of the
reproductive function is even more marked when one compares
fertility in different regions. The most prolific regions of France
used to be Brittany, the Massif Central, Corsica, the Nord and
Pas-de-Calais. In the course of this period the economically
declining parts of France had a drastic fall in their birth-rates,
while the urban regions increased theirs. The department of
Calvados which in 1906 had the lowest fertility had the highest
in 1953. The regional variations became so pronounced that
some departments had birth-rates twice as high as others: in
1938, the department of Manche had 210 live births per 10,000
inhabitants, Morbihan and Pas-de-Calais 197, while Bouches-
du-Rhône had 102, Corsica and Alpes-Maritimes had 108,
and Ariège 113. The southern coast of France stood in direct

[1] P. Vincent, 'Les Familles nombreuses', *Population* (1946), vol. 1, 148–54;
A. Landry, *Traité de démographie* (1949), 366. The increase in the size of small
families may be seen from the following comparison (per 1,000):

Families with	1906	1931
0 children	115	121
1 child	211	264
2 children	213	236
3 ,,	150	147
4 ,,	103	87
5 ,,	68	52
6 ,,	47	34
7 ,,	32	21
8 ,,	22	15
9 ,,	15	10
10 or more	24	16

contrast to the north and west: Brittany's population density
was, in 1939, twice as high as that in the rest of France's
countryside, making it resemble an industrialised region; but
at the same date the birth-rate of Lot-et-Garonne was less
than half of what it had been a century before. Such enormous
variations were something new, for during the Second Empire
the ten most prolific departments had been widely distributed
over the country.[1] But the histories of different departments
themselves contain very striking internal variations: thus
within Tarn-et-Garonne, one canton's birth-rate fell by about
60 per cent (1800–1930), from 32·6 to 13·6 per 1,000, while
another only a few miles away dropped by half that amount,
from 26·2 to 18·4, which meant that the latter, after having
had a birth-rate below the national average, came to have
one considerably above it. Brittany, despite its reputation for
fertility, had widely differing birth-rates in the interior, on the
coast and in the towns.

Conservatives tried to explain both the decline in the birth-
rate and the regional variations in terms of religious practice.
They claimed that the Church's motto 'Increase and multiply',
and its opposition to birth-control, made it a powerful force
in favour of large families. The north and west, where birth-
rates declined far less rapidly than elsewhere, were outstandingly
pious. But this kind of correlation was flimsy if not definitely
inaccurate. There were other regions, like the Garonne, which
had been no less religious, but which had reduced their fertility drastically. On detailed investigation, departments like
the Hérault have been found to have had small families
equally in religious and in anticlerical communes.[2] It is true
that occasionally statistics could be found to show that the
pupils of church secondary schools came from families with
twice as many children as the average, and that monks and
nuns came from families with three times as many children as
the average;[3] but this is not enough to make religious belief
the determining factor in fertility. The anticlericals were

[1] The most prolific departments in the 1860s were Haut-Rhin, Finistère, Bas-
Rhin, Nord, Pyrénées-Orientales, Aveyron, Loire, Lozère, Corrèze, Haute-Vienne.
The most prolific ones in 1938 were Manche, Morbihan, Pas-de-Calais, Mayenne,
Vendée, Calvados, Sarthe, Ille-et-Vilaine, Moselle, Seine-Inférieure.

[2] G. Cholvy, *Géographie religieuse de l'Hérault contemporain* (1968), 325–7.

[3] A. Cauchois, *Démographie de la Seine-Inférieure* (Rouen, 1929).

vociferous in arguing that in any case the Catholic Church's admiration for celibacy, chastity and continence made its influence ambiguous. Certainly it was not always in pious areas that it preached its sexual code most vigorously. There were, occasionally, regions noted for anticlericalism which stood out also as exceptionally prolific; and the decline in religious belief was not necessarily accompanied by a fall in the birth-rate. As one *curé* of Finistère (which was by no means all pious) said of his parishioners, 'These unhappy people have lost all their religion, but they have not lost their *esprit de famille*.'[1] But of course this was not a century in which 'dechristianisation' was either uniform or universal; and there were other forms of supernatural belief which were far from declining. A taboo on marriages in the month of May, 'the month of the Virgin Mary', which affected only a few departments in the Vendée and Touraine in 1810, spread to 15 departments in 1837, and to 43 departments by the 1930s, and came to affect an increasing proportion of marriages in them. The avoidance of November, 'the month of the dead', by marrying couples started in the Creuse in the 1870s, spread to neighbouring departments in the next twenty years and then into the south, so that by 1945 in most southern departments this new custom was observed by over 20 per cent, and in three (Creuse, Haute-Vienne and Dordogne) by over 80 per cent.[2] The rela-tionship between religious belief, folk superstitions and fertility was too complicated to make a simple generalisation possible, but that did not stop people from asserting firmly that a revival of Christianity would put matters right. The permanent feature of discussions about demographic trends is that they provided excellent opportunities for everyone to mount his favourite hobby-horse. One learns as much about these—about the commonest platitudes on what was going to the dogs—from these discussions as about demography.

The reverse side of the lament about irreligion was the condemnation of materialism and greed. To have few children,

[1] L. Naudeau, *La France se regarde: le problème de la natalité* (1931), 27, 215; Paul Leroy-Beaulieu, *La Question de la population* (1913), 395. Even the distinguished economist A. Sauvy still attributes the falling birth-rate to the decline of religion: in H. Bergues, *La Prévention des naissances* (1960), 389.

[2] J. Bourgeois-Pichat, 'Le Mariage, coutume saisonnière', *Population* (Oct.-Dec. 1946), 623-42.

it was argued, was to be selfish, because it involved ignoring
the interests of the state; and emancipation from feudalism
and traditional constraints meant that people were becoming
more selfish. Translated into liberal terms, people were wanting
to better themselves, to rise in the social hierarchy, to ensure
that their children had a better life than they themselves had
had. They therefore began to have smaller families as soon as
children ceased to be a source of wealth—as they had been
when they went to work at an early age. Now that the state
was forbidding them to work, compelling them to go to school,
but leaving the expense of their upkeep to their parents, they
had become a source of poverty: the larger families were now
the poorest, in terms of what each member enjoyed in con-
sumable goods. The satisfactions to be drawn from children
had to be altered to emotional ones; and since immediate
returns ceased to be provided by children, there had to be
more concentration on returns in the form of prestige and
social climbing. The man who worked this out into a theory
was Arsène Dumont (1849–1902), a most interesting student
of demography whose monographs on eighty different communes enabled him to base his generalisations on an impressive
mass of facts. His works failed to win him the professorship at
the School of Anthropology he had set his heart on: he had
decided, when embarking on his research, to commit suicide
if he did not get it—which he duly did. He invented the phrase
'social capillarity' in 1890 to define what was widely considered the basic cause of depopulation—the desire to enjoy
a higher standard of living, with more luxury, elegance,
pleasure and justice: it was not quite the same thing as ambition, which he thought implied desire for power through
political influence or wealth. Dumont attacked the economists
for trying to explain demographic behaviour in terms of the
subsistence and employment available: economists 'observed
the contingent and proclaimed it necessary'. He claimed that
the age of sociology had arrived to replace these simplistic
explanations, and that it would transform political understanding in the same way as physiology was transforming
medicine. The birth-rate, he said, stood in inverse ratio to
the strength of the desire to climb socially. A strong family
organisation could diminish 'social capillarity' but a strong

centralised state increased it. Power was passing more and more to the civil service, entry into which was becoming an almost universal aim, or at any rate the attractions of the fashions and ideals of Paris were becoming universal. The more egalitarian and homogeneous a country became in its customs, tastes and aspirations, the fiercer would competition between its members be. The rise of individualism intensified people's feelings of isolation and inadequacy, so that they alternated between ambition and melancholy, obsessed by what others thought of them, craving for honour, esteem, knowledge or wealth as compensations. The small family was the inevitable result. Only the industrial working class, which had no hope of rising, did not care and so remained fertile.[1] The economists told men simply to produce more, consume more, accumulate more and it was their advice that was bringing about these catastrophic results. The sociologists, by contrast, should give Frenchmen a national aim, so that the individual would not take his own private concerns as being the ultimate purpose of life, but would see himself as part of a movement of successive generations towards greater beauty, virtue, knowledge, courage. But sociology, of course, never succeeded in propagating any such positive values.[2]

Dumont laid it down as a principle that individuals had families of the size favoured not by their own class, but by the class to which they hoped to belong. In 1908 a newspaper published a list of 445 names, generally regarded as the most celebrated and influential in Paris. Between them, these had only 575 children. One hundred and seventy-seven of these celebrities had no children, 106 had one child and 88 had two children. The great statesmen of the Third Republic included an extraordinarily large proportion who were childless— Thiers, Ferry, Gambetta, Spuller, Challemel-Lacour, Goblet, Floquet, Waldeck-Rousseau. It appears to be an established fact that the merchant-aristocracy of Geneva first set the example of having few children as early as the seventeenth century, and that the French aristocracy, followed by the upper

---

[1] On the expense of bringing up children, see G. de Molinari, *La Viriculture* (1897).

[2] Arsène Dumont, *Dépopulation et civilisation; Étude démographie* (1890); cf. id., *Natalité et démocratie* (1898) and *La Morale basée sur la démographie* (1901).

bourgeoisie, adopted the same pattern in the eighteenth
century. In the nineteenth century, the lower middle class
and the peasantry followed suit. The variations in fecundity
among different classes were very considerable. Thus in 1911
(the year which has the best statistics on this subject), every
100 artists had on average 139 children, journalists and concierges 141, but miners had 289 and metal workers 253.

Comparative fecundity per 100 families in different professions (1911)

	Total	Employers	Clerks etc.	Manual workers
Fishermen	256	..	..	..
Agriculture	230	228	..	238
Mines	280	244	..	282
Industry	216	209	186	222
Transport	198	225	178	203
Commerce	174	183	155	212
Liberal professions	163	165	161	..
Domestic servants	159	..	..	..
Civil service	185	..	165	208
Total	213	216	165	223

In industry, the fecundity of different grades varied thus:

Labourers	237
Semi-skilled workers	218
Foremen	215
Employers and artisans	209
Clerks	174

A survey carried out by Bertillon with a sample of 3,472
instituteurs and road-menders (examples of the lowest-paid
civil servants) revealed that they had an average of 1·15 and
1·04 children respectively. Another statistic showed that
manual workers in state service had fewer children as their
wages rose.[1] But these national figures about professional
variations are shown to be averages with little reality in them
when they are broken down by departments. Thus fishermen
in the Nord had families 142 per cent larger than fishermen in
the Gironde and there were regions where civil servants had

[1] Landry, op. cit. 166; Henry Clément, *La Dépopulation en France* (1910), 118.
Cf. Philip Ogden, *Marriage Patterns and Population Mobility: A Study in Rural France*
(Oxford School of Geography Research Papers, no. 7, 1973, duplicated).

the largest number of children second only to fishermen. A favourite assertion was that the richer you became, the fewer children you had: this was never based on any facts, since incomes were not revealed in this period, but it seemed that though the richer classes set the pattern of smaller families, they also abandoned the practices with which they were associated just when the poorer classes were beginning to copy them. Thus in 1858 half of French dukes had one or two children; in 1878 two-thirds of them had reduced their families to this size; but by 1898 they had already reverted to larger families and only 48 per cent had one or two children, while in 1938 only 40 per cent had that number. In 1938, people with noble titles in general had significantly more children than those without them.[1]

But the idea that comfort, or the desire for it, stimulated sterility had a wide currency. A Swedish statistician produced maps in 1886 to show that those departments in France which had the largest number of savings accounts and of fire insurance policies also had the lowest birth-rates.[2] It was on the basis of such arguments that the responsibility for the declining birth-rate was placed on the law of property. Peasants, interviewed by journalists, professors and doctors, were quoted as saying that their main aim in limiting their progeny was to avoid the division of the plot of land they had laboriously accumulated: their hope was to have a sole heir, who would marry a sole heiress and so continue the process of building up an estate. This may well have been a motive among many, but it must have been associated with other ones, for there were all sorts of alternative ways of avoiding the division of one's land, and there were, as has been seen, far fewer landowners than people imagined.

Prosperity, it was claimed, was even leading to physical degeneration. Dr. Maurel produced statistics to show that the population of the Haute-Garonne had fallen in direct correlation with the rise in the amount of food consumed, which was why the towns, which had started 'overeating' earliest, had been the leaders in having small families. He argued that

[1] Worked out from the *Almanach Gotha* and the *Bottin mondain*.
[2] J. V. Tallqvist, *Recherches statistiques sur la tendance à une moindre fécondité des mariages* (Helsingfors thesis, 1886).

'overeating' caused 'arthritis', which he considered to be a hereditary disease as destructive as syphilis, except that it got worse with each generation, attacking the first one at around the age of fifty, the second at around thirty-five or forty and the third in youth; intermarriage exacerbated it, while reverses of fortune retarded it. He included many symptoms under the heading of arthritis, not just gout, but all sorts of affections of the circulatory, respiratory and nervous systems, culminating in the reproductive organs becoming sterile. His theory should not be dismissed as medically absurd, because there can be no doubt that it reflected worries people had and actual or fashionable symptoms for which they wanted to find explanations. He claimed that overeating was partly due to a new custom, which led people to think it right to eat till their appetite was satiated, whereas formerly it was an accepted rule that you rose from table while still feeling hungry. Parents now made children eat more than they wanted. Maurel estimated that about one-third of the population was affected by 'arthritism', and so only partially fertile; birth-control he considered was used by only about 50 per cent of couples.[1]

The Causes of Death

There can be no doubt, however, that hygiene had a decisive influence on demographic trends. The expectation of life at birth rose as follows:[2]

	Men	Women		Men	Women
1817–31	38	40	1928–33	54	59
1861–5	39	40	1933–8	55	61
1877–81	40	43	1946–9	61	67
1898–1903	45	49	1952–6	65	71
1908–13	48	52	1960–4	67	74
1920–3	52	55			

The significance of this table is threefold. First, the greatest and most rapid rise has occurred only since the Second World War: in the nineteenth century, the expectation of life increased

[1] Dr. E. Maurel, *De la dépopulation de la France. Étude sur la natalité* (1896), 240–1.

[2] G. Calot, 'L'Évolution de la situation démographique française', *Population* (July–Aug. 1967), 629–92 and Landry, op. cit. 232.

by only about eight years; in the forty years 1900–39, by about
eleven years, but between 1939 and 1964 by thirteen years.
However, secondly, the expectation of life for those who survived the hazards of childhood hardly changed at all: in 1861
people aged twenty could expect another 41·40 years of life;
in 1903 they could still expect only 42·81 years; though in
1933 they could hope for 45·38. The death-rate of males over
fifty remained absolutely fixed between 1817 and 1936; and
that of males between thirty-two and fifty fell hardly at all.
Thirdly, infant mortality fell in France more slowly than in
other countries. In the mid-nineteenth century, about 65 per
cent of children could hope to survive to the age of twenty;
in England it was the same; in Holland only 60 per cent. But
by 1930, the proportion in Holland had grown to 91 per cent,
in England to 87 per cent but in France to only 85 per cent.
These differences were not extraordinary, for though France
was considerably behind Holland and Sweden, it was more or
less on a par with England and Germany, and well ahead of
Italy.

However, for a country which produced so few children the
death-rate was catastrophic, and was all the more disturbing
because it could be attributed to clearly remediable facts.
Infant mortality was particularly worrying because certain
types of children were killed off at rates which suggested
almost mass extermination. The French practice of sending
infants out to wet-nurses was, from one point of view, conducive
to a higher population, because it allowed women both to
breed and to stay at work, but on the other hand it was claimed
that the mortality rate of these *nourrissons* in the 1870s was
51 per cent—at a time when infants brought up by mothers
died only at the rate of 19 per cent. Two contiguous communes
of the Gironde, one of which used wet-nurses and one of which
did not, had a death-rate before the age of one of 87 and
13 per cent respectively.[1] The *nourrices*, it was claimed, were
killing 100,000 children a year.[2] The death-rate of illegitimate
children in their first year was even higher, reaching as much
as 92 per cent in the Loire-Inférieure; the death-rate of

[1] Dr. Brochard, *Des causes de la dépopulation en France et les moyens d'y remédier*
(Lyon, 1873).
[2] Edmond Desfossé, *Décroissance de la population en France: causes, remède* (1869).

foundling and other children in the state's care (148,000 of them in 1862, of whom 76,520 were aged under one year) was 56 per cent.[1] Infant mortality fell as follows (deaths in first year per 1,000 live births):[2]

1806–10	187	1931–5	73
1861–5	179	1938	65
1881–5	167	1950	47
1909–13	126	1960	23
1921–5	95	1965	18
1926–30	89		

But these averages conceal considerable difference between male and female mortality, for in 1938 the figures were 73 for boys but 57 for girls; the illegitimate rate at the same time was 105; and the regional variations extended from 52 in parts of Central France to 105 in Brittany.

France was much in advance of the poor countries of the Balkans and the Mediterranean but well behind more hygienic ones in the north.[3] Then Frenchmen in the 1930s had almost twice as high a chance of dying of tuberculosis as other Europeans, and for every one who died of it, there were probably about seven others suffering from the disease. The male death-rate between the ages of twenty-five and forty-five was much higher also because of alcoholism. The decline in the death-rate of different age groups was uneven. Thus between 1856 and 1937 infant mortality was reduced by two-thirds, that of children by 80 per cent, that of young men from twenty-five to thirty-five by only a half, that of men between fifty-five and sixty-four by less than a quarter, while men over eighty had a higher death-rate in 1935 than in 1856. The result of these combined changes was that the balance between the different age groups altered drastically between 1851 and 1936. There used to be 361 children and adolescents under twenty years of age in every thousand inhabitants: but this fell to 302—i.e.

---

[1] Dr. Brochard, *La Vérité sur les enfants trouvés* (1876), 51.

[2] M. Huber, *La Population de la France* (1943), 187; and Calot, art. cit. 641.

[3] Infant mortality under one year, per 1,000 live births, 1937–9:

Romania	179	Germany	61
Poland	138	England	54
Italy	107	U.S.A.	50
Austria	82	Netherlands	36

by 16 per cent. There used to be 102 old people over sixty years
of age in every thousand, and they increased to 147, i.e. by
45 per cent. Fewer young people, many more old people,
accentuated the sense of a vanishing population; even though
very similar trends could be observed in neighbouring countries, France in 1936 had a larger population of old people
than anywhere else in the world.

Age groups in 1936 (per 1,000)

	Under 20 years	20–39	40–59	Over 60
Japan	465	289	172	74
Italy	379	315	197	109
U.S.A.	367	317	225	91
Germany	305	341	235	119
France	302	311	240	147
England	301	323	247	129

Birth-control

There are no certain facts about the extent to which various
methods of birth-control were used during this period. An
inquiry in Lyon in the 1960s revealed that 64 per cent of
mothers questioned said that they had used contraceptives
(in Grenoble the figure was 69 per cent). The most favoured
method was coitus interruptus (about 50 per cent, and 61 per
cent in Grenoble); about 5 per cent used the condom, and
about 12 to 16 per cent used the Ogino and temperature
methods.[1] At the turn of the century, the anthropologist
Jacques Bertillon wrote to 500 doctors in four selected departments of France to ask them the same question about their
patients' use of contraception, and they gave the same answer.
In the countryside, ninety doctors reported that coitus interruptus was 'very frequent', five said douches were much used,
four mentioned the condom, two abortion and one sponge and
pessary. In towns, douches were relatively more frequent, in the
proportion of six to fifteen attributed to coitus interruptus,
but everywhere the condom was little used.[2] It is clear that

[1] H. Pigeaud, 'Attitudes devant la maternité', *Population* (Mar.–Apr. 1966),
241–57.

[2] Jacques Bertillon, *La Dépopulation de la France* (1911), 99.

Frenchmen did not wait for technological innovations and mass manufacture of rubber goods. It is significant that though Dr. Condom, who invented the contraceptive named after him, was a Frenchman, his product was referred to as a *lettre anglaise*, while the English, who used them much more, referred to them as French letters. The problem is why and how these different practices were introduced into love-making.

There are two alternative ways of finding the answer. As has already been suggested, certain changes in people's view of their own interest caused them to reduce their progeny and one can see this as proof of the triumph of enlightenment and forethought over fatalism, as a sign of changing values, of greater interest in education, of a stronger desire for comfort, for the accumulation of wealth, which could be handed over to one's children, of a new view of how to attain immortality. The fact that the death-rate diminished might have reduced people's desire to react against its ravages. These are all factors so imponderable that no amount of quotation from literary, medical or sociological commentaries will ever make it possible to be certain about the relative weight which should be assigned to them. But it is also worth looking at the problem from the point of view of women. They may well have taken more initiative and had more influence than male writers have conceded to them. The desire to have children, which in recent times is considered to be stronger among women, may previously have been much more of a preoccupation among men, intent on preserving their property. Motherhood was considered to involve some risk, even if the statistics did not support this.[1] So many infants died, Madame de Sévigné had said, that there was little pleasure in giving birth to them. She is the woman whose letters are frequently quoted to show the hesitations of French women towards maternity in the seventeenth century. She urged her daughter to keep her husband at a distance, and congratulated her on her success at avoiding pregnancy; she gave the impression that one of the marks of a good husband was that he was not importunate in his demands

[1] The statistics on deaths in childbirth are unsatisfactory. In Paris in 1884, 386 women were registered as having died, when 63,840 children were born. But there is nothing for the rest of the country. In the U.S.A. at the same time, out of 100 deaths of women aged between 20 and 30, 18 were in childbirth and 6 from diseases of the breast or uterus. Levasseur, *La Population française* (1889–92).

for sexual gratification—or, presumably, went elsewhere for these. Père Féline's *Catechism for Married Couples*, published in 1782 and reprinted in 1880, stated that the fall in the birth-rate was due to wives complaining of the great pain motherhood involved, and to husbands becoming increasingly attentive to their wives' wishes.[1] Mgr Bouvier in the 1840s likewise gave as a reason for smaller families the greater concern of husbands for the health and happiness of their wives. It is interesting that in 1969 an inquiry into explanations of family size showed that women with few children stressed above all considerations of their own health, though many also expressed an unwillingness to give up work to have children.[2]

France was long remarkable for the large proportion of its female population in employment: about 28 per cent of the active population were women in 1866, 30 in 1872, 37 in 1906 and that was the figure it remained at. The second half of the nineteenth century was thus the period when the number of women who went out to work increased most rapidly.[3] It was also the period when the ideal of female beauty changed, as Zola observed, from the plump, large-thighed, heavy-breasted mother to a more boyish, sylphlike form. Breast-feeding was a challenge to male sexuality, because it was considered dangerous to copulate when a woman was still breast-feeding. Galien had argued that sexual intercourse induced menstruation and made the milk bitter; and this idea still flourished. Zola describes in his *Fécondité* the prohibition on copulation imposed on husbands for nine months during pregnancy and for fifteen months thereafter. The use of wet-nurses was a victory for the husband, but then the couple were terrified lest the nurse engaged in sexual activity, from which she was rigorously prohibited.[4]

Rather than see a gradual change in women's attitudes, as evolutionists always like to imagine, one should appreciate that an identical situation might be differently interpreted at different times and in different circumstances: breast-feeding

[1] Père Féline, *Catéchisme des gens mariés* (1782).

[2] Louis Roussel, 'Les Mobiles de la limitation des naissances dans les mariages de un ou deux enfants', *Population* (1969), 309–30.

[3] J. Toutain, *La Population de la France de 1700 à 1959* (1963), 152.

[4] E. and F. van de Walle, 'Allaitement, stérilité et conception', *Population* (July–Oct. 1972), 685–701.

could be a sign of a greater prestige for motherhood, but also
a defence against it. It should not be forgotten that this was a
period when medical ideas on reproduction were changing and
surprisingly large problems long remained cloaked in mystery.
In the 1850s debates were still active among doctors as to
whether it was the father or the mother who produced the germ
from which the child developed. The conflicting theories of
Hippocrates and Aristotle, as embroidered by Buffon and
Descartes, still divided them, so that some called themselves
'seminists', some 'ovarists', and other animalculists' depending
on which sex they imagined was decisive, and on how they
explained the physiology of copulation. The modern view of
menstruation was first advanced by a German only in 1835
and by a Frenchman in 1847, but it was slow to gain ground;
and experts continued to say that conception could occur
only in the first eight days after it.[1] Impotence and sterility
were the subject of many theories, and the extraordinary stories
people told their doctors about their sexual difficulties, and the
extraordinary remedies prescribed to cure them, show that the
idea that people now felt masters of their destiny, able to control
birth and postpone death, was far from the truth. The physical
properties of the sexual organs had in 1850 still not been fully
understood, the mechanism of erection was still being argued
about. One doctor, for example, invented a 'mechanical
flagellator' to cure impotence, another a special chair incorporating an 'aromatic fumigator', to be sat upon before jump-
ing into bed.[2] One of the greatest sources of inhibition was the
worry created by masturbation, which was for long widely
considered to induce sterility, and vast numbers of guilty and
impotent people poured out confessions on this subject to
their medical advisers. It may well be that as education and
medical attention spread, these worries also did. A *Medical
Guide for Marriage*, published in 1868, records how many men
feared that their misdemeanours as children, or their debauchery as young men, had rendered them permanently
sterile. A large number, it said, suffered from loss of sperm at
every excitement. Premature ejaculation caused much de-

[1] Dr. F. A. Pouchet, *Théorie positive de la fécondation* (1847).
[2] Dr. Félix Roubaud, *Traité de l'impuissance et de la stérilité* (1855); Lallemand and
Civiale, *Traité pratique des maladies des organes génito-urinaires* (1850).

pression, and women were sometimes found to be virgins years after marriage. Copulation with prostitutes made many men expect the same kind of ecstasy in their wives, and they were disappointed not to find it; wives for their part were lucky if they did not develop a disgust for sex after the exaggerated activity young husbands believed it was their duty to engage in. New fashions in education, which encouraged girls to be 'impressionable and delicate', often filled them with horror for intercourse. Above all, 'our experience, based on innumerable cases, allows us to affirm that the troubles of many couples come not from any real incapacity, but from ignorance of physiological laws'.[1] Among some people, ignorance may well have increased with 'refinement'. There is still a great deal to be discovered about the history of love.[2]

Old Age and Death

Old people like to look back to happier, more ordered times when old age was respected, when the problem of senile parents did not exist, because their children venerated them. There is little evidence that this situation ever existed. Anthropological research has revealed that respect for the aged is not normal in primitive societies, that though the old are sometimes regarded as repositories of knowledge and mediators with the supernatural, the respect they are accorded is usually due to some special asset, and it is rarely continued when they fall into decrepitude. The old are generally saved by their property rights. But there are peoples who kill them off or even bury them while still alive.[3] In France respect for old age has long been ambivalent and by no means to be relied on. There is an old-established literary tradition mocking old age as ridiculous, ugly and stupid. Montaigne at the age of thirty-five was already lamenting that he was slowing down and he could see no sign that he was getting any wiser. Molière

[1] J. L. Curtis, *Guide médical du mariage* (1868), 46, 50, 78, 93; id., *De la virilité* (56th edition, 1856).

[2] See the new insights in J. L. Flandrin, *Les Amours paysannes: amour et sexualité dans les campagnes de l'ancienne France* (1970), which shows how much can be learnt from demographic statistics (but this book is mainly about the eighteenth century) and E. Shorter, 'Différences de classe et sentiment depuis 1750', *Annales* (July–Aug. 1974).

[3] Leo W. Simmons, *The Role of the Aged in Primitive Society* (Yale U.P., 1945).

made fun of old men as suspicious, avaricious, pusillanimous,
grumbling and silly. Parricide was rare: in 1855, for example,
four cases of it were recorded; but the report of the official
commission investigating the state of agriculture in 1866–70
warned landowners not to divide their property up between
their children while they were still alive, because 'the father of
a family, once he has surrendered his goods, is deprived of all
authority. He passes into a state of being despised, rejected by
his children, thrown out of the homes of each of them, sent from
one to the other with a pension which is often not paid, or
promised a house which is not given him.' A newspaper inquiry
in 1885 told the same story of the neglect to which old parents
were subjected. Zola, in his study of the peasantry (*La Terre*),
has left a forceful picture of the terrible clashes that could occur
between generations. In the 1960s, statistics established that
two-thirds of old people received no help from their children.[1]

The concern with the plight of the aged is not the result of
changed treatment, but of three new factors. First, the veil of
hypocrisy has been drawn aside, and a new sensibility has made
people aware of a situation which has always existed. Secondly,
there are now more old people: between 1851 and 1972 the
number of those over sixty-five doubled:[2]

Percentage of population over 65

1851	6·7
1901	8·5
1936	10·0
1954	11·5
1974	13·2

Thirdly, and not least, old people became more vocal about
their plight, and their attitudes also changed. The old became a
national problem when they began to unite, to see themselves
as a class apart, in the same way as the young asserted their
own individuality.

The number of books written about the old increased steadily
in this period, but for long they simply repeated advice culled
from ancient Greek and other traditional sources. They advised
the old to preserve themselves by abstaining from the more

---

[1] S. de Beauvoir, *La Vieillesse* (1970), 17, 189, 209, 254.

[2] From 2,317,000 to 5,184,000—whereas the population as a whole increased
by only one-fifth.

violent pleasures of life, by following the principle of moderation in all things, and by accepting their limitations with
resignation. They attacked modern civilisation and its evils
as sources of the tension and illnesses which reduced the length
of life.[1] These grim warnings continued to be repeated into the
inter-war period. But there were also some doctors who rose
up to protest against the idea of old age being inevitably marked
by decay. The creation of large hospitals, and notably the
Salpêtrière in Paris, which had geriatric wards for between
two and three thousand people, provided opportunities for
closer examination of their peculiar troubles. Dr. Durand-
Fardel wrote in 1854, on the basis of fifteen years of such
research, that it was not one's years that made one old, but
how one functioned: fresh air and exercise could keep one going
efficiently beyond the normal limits. But he still recommended
fifteen leeches on the anus to avert strokes, which he saw as
the worst, mysterious threat to the old, and daily purges to keep
the bowels moving.[2] In the 1860s Dr. Charcot's lectures on the
diseases of old people argued that old age as such was not a
disease, and that each organ deteriorated or ceased to function
largely independently: only a few illnesses were specifically
attributable to old age.[3] In the 1870s Dr. Brown-Sequard
claimed he had succeeded in revitalising himself with solutions
of macerated animal testicles. Hope for women came somewhat
later. In 1923 a woman doctor could still write that those past
the menopause had to accept their situation as inevitable, but
in the 1930s hormonal treatment began to be prescribed.[4]
These new ideas affected a small minority. A recent inquiry
among adults revealed that one-fifth of them thought old
age began before fifty-five. (Another fifth said it started after
sixty-five: one-third placed it between fifty-five and sixty-five
and one-third did not know.)[5] The boundaries of old age have

[1] Dr. Guyétant, *L'Âge de retour et la vieillesse. Conseils au gens du monde* (1870);
Vicomte de Lapasse, *Essai sur la conservation de la vie* (1860); Dr. P. Foissac, *La
Longévité humaine* (1873); Dr. B. Lunel, *Dictionnaire de la conservation de l'homme.
Encylopédie de la santé* . . . (1857).

[2] M. Durand-Fardel, *Traité clinique et pratique des maladies des vieillards* (1854),
xi, 285–7, 325.

[3] J. M. Charcot, *Leçons cliniques sur les maladies des vieillards* (1866–7).

[4] Peter N. Stearns, *Aging in French Culture* (1976), a pioneering historical survey.

[5] William Grossin, 'Les Temps de la vie quotidienne' (unpublished doctoral
psychology thesis, Paris V, 1972), 453.

not been pushed back in general opinion, mainly because for the working classes physical impairment means unemployment, and most managers have come to accept the view, probably pioneered by the Americans, that full efficiency at work cannot be expected after the age of fifty.[1]

But the growth in numbers of those who could afford to retire, or were forced to retire, created a new justification of old age as a period of independence that came as the reward of work.[2] Civil servants were the leaders in this movement, followed by the industrial and commercial middle classes (but excluding members of the liberal professions, who continued to work well beyond sixty-five). At the turn of the century, only a third of workers had retired by the age of sixty-five, compared to two-thirds of the employees of banking and commerce and 95 per cent of state officials. Special journals began appearing between the wars to cater for this new class, either as organs to defend their rights (*Le Cri du retraité*), or to teach them how to enjoy themselves (*La Vieillesse heureuse*). This latter journal reported on youth sports and urged the old to develop similar activities. This illustrates how old and young simultaneously sought to create a way of life for themselves which was independent of that of adults. This does not mean that the old wanted to be segregated into old people's homes: on the contrary, inquiries in the 1950s showed that 80 per cent did not wish to go into these. But exactly the same proportion also took the view that they would rather not live with their children and indeed only a very small minority did live with their children (mainly in the country). In 1954, 30 per cent of people over sixty lived alone, 40 per cent lived in couples and 24 per cent in households of more than two members.[3] The idea of retirement as a Third Age was still very much a utopia in the distant future. Most people did not have adequate cultural or financial resources to profit from their leisure. Retirement, more often than not, meant 'social death', with-

---

[1] W. A. Achenbaum, 'The Obsolescence of Old Age in America 1865–1914', *Journal of Social History* (1974), 48–62.

[2] In 1954 74 per cent of men and 37·2 per cent of women were still at work at the age of 60; at the age of 70, 33·5 per cent of men and 12 per cent of women were still at work.

[3] [Pierre Laroque], *Politique de la vieillesse*, rapport de la commission d'étude des problèmes de la vieillesse (1962), 112.

drawal from contact with the world. Pensions and assistance from social workers, the solution offered by the mid-twentieth century, was not enough, because it concentrated exclusively on the old, ignoring the problem of preparation for retirement.[1]

Just how slowly ideas on this subject came to be formulated, and to move beyond the tradition of charity, can be seen from the development of the insurance industry. Until 1818, life insurance was forbidden by law, on the ground that it was immoral to place a value on something so sacred as life, but also because the state wanted to have a monopoly for its own *tontine* system, which was a form of lottery. This system, however, went out of fashion during the Second Empire, as interest shifted from insurance against death to endowment policies: a mixture of the two, introduced in 1857, became, as from 1895, the most common form of insurance. Insurance companies for long appeared as tainted by fraud, on the part of the speculators who profited from them or the customers who tried to cheat them: of those which mushroomed under Louis-Philippe, only four survived the revolution of 1848, and a sensational poisoning case in 1864, in which Dr. Couty de La Pommerais was accused of killing his wife in order to benefit from an insurance policy worth over half a million francs, made the possibilities of insurance better known, but in a dubious way. In 1874 there were probably about 121,000 people insured. The rise of the insurance business took place only between the wars. In 1942 3,300,000 life insurance policies were in force, and 115,000 people were employed selling and administering insurance. But the proportion of the national income invested in insurance represented only one-half of the amount invested in Britain and a little over one-quarter of that invested in the U.S.A.[2]

This must be linked up with attitudes to death. The current view is that death is a subject people have increasingly become unwilling to talk about, that it has indeed succeeded sex as the most important taboo aspect of human existence. In the middle

[1] Anne-Marie Guillemard, *La Retraite, une mort sociale. Sociologie des conduites en situation de retraite* (1972).

[2] I. Tournan, *L'Assurance sur la vie en France au 19ᵉ siècle* (Paris law thesis, 1906), 73, 180; Jacques Deschamps, *Cent trente ans d'une industrie: bilan des assurances privées en France* (Versailles, 1946), 29; P. J. Richard, *Histoire des institutions d'assurance en France* (1956), for new trends after 1945; Raoul Ménard, *De l'assurance sur la vie: son rôle économique et sociale dans la vie moderne* (Poitiers law thesis, 1908).

ages, it has been argued, people knew how to die calmly and without fear; death was accepted as an integral part of experience, met by all ages; funerals were social events and cemeteries were used also for sports. Praying for the dead was a minor religious industry. But then death became more individual, until mourning itself was frowned on, so that there was no way left to express grief: people tried to forget about death, and the aged were sent to hospitals to die in isolation from society.[1] More research is needed before this general contrast of the present and the past can be made less schematic, for the fragmentary evidence available on the period of transition does not fit easily into either stereotype. A doctor who in 1842 published his observations on some 1,000 deaths he had witnessed recorded that there were indeed ideal deaths, by the old criterion, in which the victim had prepared himself for death all his life and was ready for it, expected it to happen at six in the evening, which was when his father had died, had the church bells rung to help him obtain forgiveness of his sins, and took leave of his family very movingly. But this doctor also recorded a labourer going into delirium at the thought of hell, when told the priest had been sent for: his teeth chattered and he wept profusely and begged for pardon, repeating endlessly 'My God, do not damn me.' The majority of poor people however, were, he said, totally indifferent to the admonitions of the priest and expressed interest only in food: there were those who would also tolerate painful surgery in complete silence if promised a meal at the end of it. There were men who died worrying obsessively about the details of their business affairs, or dominated by jealous thoughts concerning their wives. It was impossible to predict how people would behave in dying: 'the approach of death is the beginning of a new way of thinking and of hoping for all'; ideas on the subject were full of contradictions.[2]

Certainly in Normandy, it is known that fraternities to organise burials survived, even if they fell from 550 in 1843 to a mere 100 at the present day. These fraternities had a vigorous

[1] Philippe Ariès, *Western Attitudes towards Death* (Baltimore, 1974); M. Vovelle, *Mourir autrefois* (1970); Geoffrey Gorer, *Death, Grief and Mourning in Contemporary Britain* (1965).

[2] H. Lauvergne, *De l'agonie et de la mort dans toutes les classes de la société* (1842), I. x, 2. 142–50.

life in the nineteenth century, with increasingly codified and
elaborate rules. The fines for those who made mistakes, like
'for allowing the straw in one's clogs to fall out', or for 'drop-
ping the body because of drunkenness', show that funerals
sometimes remained boisterous affairs.[1] Whether the Association of the Good Death, founded in 1859, achieved anything
in perpetuating or spreading Catholic attitudes is not known.[2]
Anticlericals were not necessarily freed from the emotions that
believers felt. Thus Roger Martin du Gard (1881–1958), who
never had any religious beliefs and whose novel *Jean Barois*
became a symbol of the triumph of free thought, was all his life
terrified by death and obsessed by the thought of it. It was only
after having slaved away for twenty years on his major work,
Les Thibault (1922–40) that he at last felt he would be ready to
accept death, because he had created a monument that would
ensure his immortality.[3] At another extreme, the romantic
attitude involved curiosity about death and even longing for
death, resulting from despair with life, or longing for love too
absolute to be found in this world.[4] Suicide was something
people thought about increasingly as they grew older; its incidence rose steadily with age.[5]

An inquiry by a psychologist in the late 1960s suggests that
France has been left with a variety of attitudes, rather than with
one 'modern' one. Worrying about death seems to be related
not just to religious belief but also to boredom: those who said
they were never bored, seldom thought about death. There
were clear differences therefore between different professions:
thus teachers said they were bored far less often than workers,
or wine-growers for example. For them, old age was something

[1] *La Sociologie de la mort.* Special issue of *Archives de sciences sociale des religions*,
no. 39 (Jan.–June 1975), 83.
[2] Al. Lefebvre, S.J., *La Science de bien mourir, manuel de l'Association de la Bonne
Mort* (1864).
[3] Melvin Gallant, *Le Thème de la mort chez Roger Martin du Gard* (1971). Cf.
Louis Bourdeau, *Le Problème de la mort. Les solutions imaginaires et la science positive*
(3rd edition, 1900) and L. Leblois, *Mort et immortalité. Trois lettres à un rationaliste*
(2nd edition, Strasbourg, 1866).
[4] Malaka Gourdin Servenière (*née* Sedky), 'Sentiment et problème de la mort
chez les prosateurs et les penseurs français de la première moitié du 19ᵉ siècle'
(unpublished doctorat ès lettres, Sorbonne, 1973); N. J. Popa, *Le Thème et le sentiment
de la mort chez Gérard de Nerval 1808–55* (1925).
[5] E. Durkheim, *Le Suicide* (1897); J. D. Douglas, *The Social Meaning of Suicide*
(Princeton, 1967).

they thought of as arriving late. Altogether, 36 per cent of this sample never thought of death, 31 per cent rarely, 17 per cent quite often, 9 per cent often and 7 per cent very often. This had little connection with belief in afterlife, which itself was not always related to religious belief. Thus a public opinion poll in 1947 found that 58 per cent of those questioned said they believed in an afterlife, while another in 1968 found the figure had fallen to 35 per cent, but in the meantime those who said they believed in God rose from 66 to 73 per cent.[1]

These hints are enough to show that the relationship between attitudes to death and behaviour in life, if it is ever worked out with greater precision, is unlikely to be a simple one, which can be stated by reference to a single, or even a few, social variables. They suggest, as do also the statistics on population and family, that several fundamentally opposed forms of behaviour coexisted. France was not all one in the way it tackled birth, death, or anything else.

[1] William Grossin, 'Les Temps de la vie quotidienne' (unpublished thesis, Paris V, 1972), 455, 457, 471. For other statistics on religious belief, see below, p. 264.

6. Religion and Anticlericalism

TWENTY years ago it would have been possible to argue that the anxieties from which people suffered in this period were directly connected with the decline of religious belief. It is now clear that this was not the case, first because it is by no means certain that religious belief did decline, secondly because religion now came to offer new consolations, and thirdly because the Church was itself torn by anxieties of its own. What the ecclesiastical history of this century shows above all is a crisis of communication: churchmen and free-thinkers were so carried away by the bitterness of their disagreements that they became incapable of understanding each other, and hopelessly confused as to what their quarrels were about. The country split into two, but that split concealed a whole plurality of beliefs and temperaments which it cut across in a most misleading way. The dispute about religion was a genuine dispute of fundamental importance but, at the same time as it created new attitudes to life, it also became a major obstacle to self-knowledge and to perception of the complexities of human motivation. Simply to recount the anticlerical battles in terms of the persecution, the legislation and the insults is to miss at least half of what was going on.[1]

In 1961 85 per cent of French people declared themselves to be believing Catholics: 34 per cent claimed to practise regularly; only 6 per cent stated they had no religion. These findings show that lip-service was still being paid, as it was in the century covered by this book, to the idea that France was a Catholic country. The Church itself, however, had no illusions. It realised that its contact with the 85 per cent was often confined to only three occasions: baptism, marriage and burial. Its statisticians stated that the figure of 34 per cent of regular church-goers was in reality 26 per cent. Two-thirds of

[1] A. Dansette, *Histoire religieuse de la France contemporaine* (1849–51); J. McManners, *Church and State in France 1870–1914* (1972); C. Langlois and J. M. Mayeur, 'Sur l'histoire religieuse de l'époque contemporaine', *Revue historique* (Oct.–Dec. 1974), 433–44.

these church-goers moreover were women; the majority of them were middle class; only between 2 and 10 per cent at most of the working class practised regularly; the very rich and the very poor on the whole kept away. The majority of church-goers were not wage earners but children and old people. Most children were taught their Catechism, but between a quarter and a half among the bourgeoisie, and between half and 80 per cent among the working class, abandoned all regular practice immediately after their first communion. Attendance at church varied enormously in different regions of the country; some rural areas had almost totally empty churches; in Paris 15 per cent went to church; in Strasbourg 39 per cent.[1] But these figures do not represent a decline of faith.

Under the *ancien régime* attendance at church was legally compulsory, but it was not in practice enforced. The myth that France was pious and Catholic before the Revolution was invented by modern conservatives idealising the middle ages. In the eighteenth century there was little militant abstention from religion, but only a small and unorganised minority was fervently devout. Most people went to church, but by no means every Sunday; nearly everybody took Easter communion, but though faith was sincere it was frequently passive, induced by social pressure or combined with appalling ignorance of the doctrines of the Church and with much superstition. In church, behaviour was not infrequently rowdy and inattentive. Brittany, then as now, was one of the most religious parts of the country, but as has been seen its religion incorporated considerable elements of pre-Christian origin, and rituals that made it original, which was perhaps why it resisted both Protestant heresy and modern materialism.[2] The study of the different varieties of Catholicism in France, and their relation with local traditions, is still in its infancy; but it is clear that in certain regions the marriage between them was not successful, so that once the pressure for religious conformity was lifted by the revolution of 1789 and then again by that of 1830, the divorce, often latent, became public.

The diocese of Orléans—about which there is detailed information, thanks to the minute inquiries of Dupanloup, its

[1] Philippe Alméras, *Les Catholiques français* (1963), 9–14.
[2] G. Le Bras, *Études de sociologie religieuse* (1955).

bishop under the Second Empire—was by 1850 openly heathen. In its most religious archdeaconry, only 2 per cent of the men took Easter communion, 11·6 per cent of the women, 21·9 per cent of the boys and 56 per cent of the girls—in all 10·6 of the population. In some villages attendance at Easter was 0·5 per cent for men, and 5 to 7 per cent for women. One *curé* wrote contemptuously of his flock: 'They have certain habits, which have nothing to do with religion. They recite the formulae of prayer, but they do not pray; they attend Mass, but they never listen; they believe in a God whom they fashion themselves; they pray to God fervently when they are ill, when they believe they are bewitched, when their animals are sick; they ask God for temporal goods but never for spiritual ones. They pray for the dead but only from habit and custom; and among the prayers for the dead they prefer those which give most glory to the living.' Another wrote 'Faith is lacking in almost every heart; people believe in religion only by a kind of habit.' The regions of highest religiosity in this diocese were not ones of genuine piety: they were regions with high illegitimate birth-rates, exceptional drunkenness, strong superstition. The men who attended church resented the preaching, and made a deafening noise during the services, spitting, slamming doors, coughing and shuffling.[1]

The latest archival investigations reveal that religious practice in some regions continued at virtually unchanged levels between 1850 and 1900, despite the anticlerical battles: in the Romorantin district of the diocese of Blois, for example, the proportion of men taking Easter communion remained at around one-third. In other regions (e.g. Chartres) the proportion fell from 3·8 per cent in 1868 to 1·3 per cent around 1900, but returned to 3·4 per cent in the 1930s and reached 8·3 in 1959.[2] The quality of religion differed so much from region to region and from epoch to epoch that it is virtually impossible to trace the progress of belief as a constant factor: fervent piety, popular religiosity and superstition, conformist attendance at church,

[1] Christianne Marcilhacy, *Le Diocèse d'Orléans au milieu du dix-neuvième siècle* (1964), 302–95.
[2] F. Boulard, 'Aspects de la pratique religieuse en France de 1802 à 1939', *Revue d'histoire de l'église de France* (1973), vol. 59, 269–311; F. Boulard, 'La "Déchristianisation" de Paris', *Archives de sociologie des religions* (1971), vol. 31, 69–98.

membership of charitable, social and militant church organisations each have their own history. It is because there is no easy
method of distinguishing between these that there has been so
much confused argument, and that so many different factors
have been blamed for the supposed decline of faith. France is
not unique in this respect: Victorian England was far less
dominated by the established church than popular novels
pretended, and in 1851 a nation-wide census revealed that
almost half of those free to attend church did not go.[1] But the
absence in France of nonconformist churches (which provided
religion without clericalism) has meant that the anticlerical
battles have been greatly exacerbated, and the issues have
therefore got more muddled. In particular this has meant that
Catholicism has been seen as essentially medieval and irreligion
as a modern liberation from it, which vastly oversimplifies the
problem.

The Church did indeed repeatedly attack modern civilisation, progress, industrialisation, capitalism, socialism, urbanisation and virtually every new phenomenon, as sources of
temptation, degradation and immorality. In the nineteenth
century, papal encyclicals spelt out these anathemas in a form
that showed no desire for compromise of any kind. People who
believed in modernity and progress had every reason to think
that the Church had no room for them. But in practice the
split between religion and free thought was not one of the
backward rural parts of the country against the new towns.
Religion survived in Brittany, which was economically backward, but also in Alsace and Lorraine, which were the very
opposite. The contrast between town and country, from the
point of view of religious practice, was sometimes less marked
than the contrast between two towns, like, for example,
Béziers and Montpellier. New industrial towns were not
necessarily irreligious; far from it. What seems to have been
more decisive was, first, the religious character of the region
in which the town stood, and secondly, the type of immigrants
it attracted. Different areas have had distinct personalities
which have not been totally effaced by demographic movement.
Migrants have sometimes taken their faith with them to the
towns, and they have not always been rebels trying to escape

[1] John D. Gay, *The Geography of Religion in England* (1971), 55.

social constraints. Religious practice could be at an above average level in towns, and on occasion the most religious groups in a town were those whose families had been there longest.[1] Of course, peasants who brought to the towns a view of God as a power to be placated, so as to avoid natural disasters and to obtain good harvests, often came to find alternative methods of advancing their interests and alternative superstitions, in towns where church attendance was not an established practice. Poor industrial workers did indeed often have no religious life at all, and they were not surprisingly regarded by the upper classes as barbarians.[2] The religious sects for the poor that flourished in England and the U.S.A. had no counterpart in France. But this does not mean that the working class as a whole was always irreligious. Apart from local traditions, its beliefs differed from occupation to occupation. The old artisan corporations had had a religious side to them and the workers' funeral clubs showed that they valued the last rites, if not all the teaching of the Church. Non-religious funerals were a well-established custom in the 20th *arrondissement* of Paris before the anticlerical campaigns, but they became no more frequent as a result of these and remained in a minority.

Percentage of non-religious funerals in Paris

	Paris	13th *Arrondissement*	16th *Arrondissement*	20th *Arrondissement*
1884	23	25	6	41
1913	33	31	13	38

The propaganda of the political classes thus had only a limited influence on the behaviour of the masses. This has been illustrated rather strikingly by a detailed study of the effects of lay schooling and the anticlerical press in the diocese of Montpellier. The establishment of state primary schools made virtually no difference to church attendance and the villages where radical newspapers were bought were not made anticlerical by them: there has been a steady continuity in religious

[1] E. Pin, *Pratique religieuse et classes sociales dans une paroisse urbaine, Saint-Pothin à Lyon* (1956).

[2] F. A. Isambert, *Christianisme et classe ouvrière* (1961).

affiliation, despite all the agitation.[1] This diocese is geographically very diverse, and historically different parts of it have built up different traditions towards religion; but it is not the economically most developed areas which have rejected Catholicism. A doctor writing a 'medico-psychological' study of its beliefs in 1868 noted that it was precisely the most advanced areas which were most superstitious, and superstition and religious practice did not always go together.[2] So though it is true that the middle classes today go to church more than the working classes, this does not mean that there are not regions where substantial numbers of workers are religious.[3] Nor was it always the towns which led in 'dechristianisation': Marseille, for example, was in the eighteenth century considerably more devout than many parts of the surrounding countryside.[4] The history of middle-class religiosity is still only a matter of rough conjecture: it is customary to say that irreligion became fashionable in the late eighteenth century, but that the well-to-do returned to the Church in the course of the nineteenth century, frightened by the chaos produced by their revolution, and still more in the twentieth century, when Catholicism ceased to involve monarchism; but the detailed evidence to justify such generalisations is fragmentary: the piety of the rich has been of less interest to sociologists than the problem of winning the masses to the Church.

A study has been made of the time elapsing between birth and baptism in Marseille between 1806 and 1958. The professions of the parents, known until 1871, show that farmers were most religious, if one takes as one's criterion baptism within three days of birth, while doctors, industrialists, merchants and sailors were least so. This is the nearest that anyone has come to providing a statistical comparison of class behaviour, but the criterion is unfortunately not really indicative of belief. Until 1830 75 per cent of infants were baptised within

[1] Gérard Cholvy, *Géographie religieuse de l'Hérault contemporain* (1968).

[2] Gérard Cholvy, 'Religion et société au 19ᵉ siècle. Le diocèse de Montpellier' (Paris doctoral thesis, unpublished, 1972); Dr. Calixte Cavalier, *Étude médico-psychologique sur la croyance aux sortilèges à l'époque actuelle* (Montpellier, 1868).

[3] See figures for 1965, by profession, in F. Boulard and Jean Rémy, *Pratique religieuse urbaine et regions culturelles* (1968), 96.

[4] Michel Vovelle, *Piété bourgeoise et déchristianisation en Provence au 18ᵉ siècle* (1973).

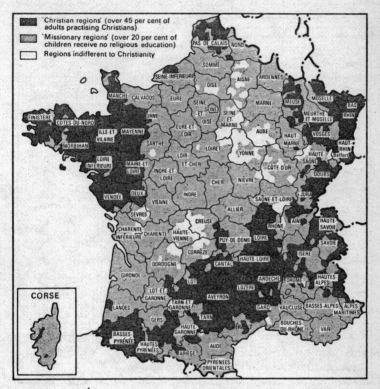

Map 1. Religious Practice (1947). Based on F. Boulard, *Essor ou déclin du clergé français* (1950).

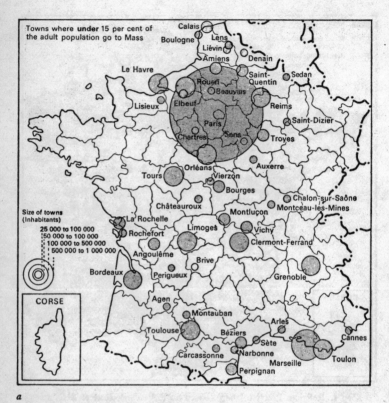

Towns where **under** 15 per cent of the adult population go to Mass

Calais
Boulogne
Lens
Liévin
Amiens
Denain
Le Havre
Saint-Quentin
Sedan
Rouen
Beauvais
Reims
Lisieux
Elbeuf
Saint-Dizier
Paris
Chartres
Sens
Troyes
Orléans
Auxerre
Tours
Vierzon
Bourges
Châteauroux
Chalon-sur-Saône
Montceau-les-Mines
Montluçon

Size of towns
(Inhabitants)
25 000 to 100 000
50 000 to 100 000
100 000 to 500 000
500 000 to 1 000 000

La Rochelle
Rochefort
Limoges
Vichy
Clermont-Ferrand
Angoulême
Brive
Bordeaux
Périgueux
Grenoble
Agen
Montauban
Arles
Toulouse
Béziers
Sète
Cannes
Carcassonne
Narbonne
Marseille
Toulon
Perpignan

CORSE

a

Maps 2*a* and *b*. Religion in the Towns (1960s). Based on F. Boulard and
J. Rémy, *Pratique religieuse urbaine et régions culturelles* (1968).

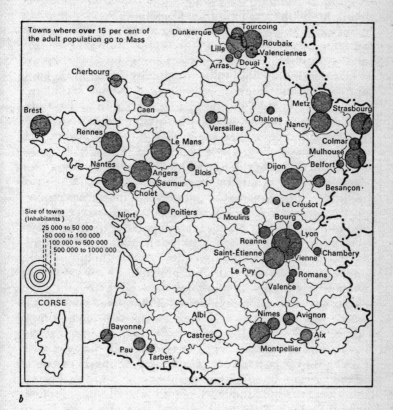

Towns where **over 15** per cent of the adult population go to Mass

Dunkerque
Tourcoing
Roubaix
Lille
Valenciennes
Arras
Douai
Cherbourg
Metz
Caen
Strasbourg
Brest
Chalons
Nancy
Rennes
Versailles
Colmar
Le Mans
Mulhouse
Dijon
Belfort
Nantes
Angers
Blois
Besançon
Saumur
Cholet
Le Creusot
Size of towns
(Inhabitants)
Niort
Poitiers
Moulins
Bourg
25 000 to 50 000
50 000 to 100 000
Roanne
Lyon
100 000 to 500 000
Saint-Étienne
500 000 to 1 000 000
Vienne
Chambéry
Le Puy
Romans
Valence

CORSE

Albi
Nîmes
Avignon
Bayonne
Castres
Aix
Pau
Tarbes
Montpellier

b

three days. There was a significant fall to 70 per cent in 1831–3 and this percentage remained constant during the July Monarchy. By 1870, however, it had fallen to 30 per cent; a further important fall occurred after the Commune; and by 1958 the figure was 0·52 per cent.[1] This suggests that political events had immediate repercussions in religious behaviour, but too much cannot be read into these figures, because they are complicated by the fall in infant mortality which made hasty baptism less important. Politics by itself cannot provide an adequate explanation of attitudes to the Church. Thus 'dechristianisation' in Provence has been traced to the middle of the eighteenth century, and to a wide variety of factors, well before the Revolution. The revolution of 1830 revealed a lot of anticlericalism, but it was followed nevertheless by a considerable revival of interest in religion. The identification of the clergy with the monarchist cause in the nineteenth century and their increasingly active role in politics, however, so confused attitudes to religion, that contemporaries could no longer make sense of the very complex relationships that resulted. It remains very difficult to see clearly through the polemic, quite apart from the fact that probably no historian can be totally impartial in approaching the subject.[2]

Thus one of the main peculiarities of this period was that the Church was more popular among women than among men. This is usually looked on negatively, as implying that the Church was not strong enough to hold the allegiance of men. It could, on the contrary, be appreciated positively as one of the most important ways by which women began to liberate themselves from the domination of men. The Church, of course, never thought of itself as doing any such thing, for it was dedicated to the patriarchal family. But in a world in which the male reigned supreme, the Church in fact provided a haven where women were treated as equals, and given opportunities to lead lives independent of their menfolk, organising and participating in exclusively feminine charities and societies. The anticlericals protested loudly against this, claiming that

[1] F. L. Charpin, *Pratique religieuse et formation d'une grande ville. Le geste du baptême et sa signification en sociologie religieuse: Marseille 1806–1950* (1964).

[2] Cf. René Rémond, 'Recherche d'une méthode d'analyse historique de la déchristianisation depuis le milieu du 19e siècle', *Colloque d'histoire religieuse*, Lyon, October 1963 (Grenoble, 1963), 123–54.

the clergy were using weak-minded women to spread their own reactionary influence. Michelet, for example, argued that, through the confessional, priests were invading the privacy of the home, making the wife spy on her husband and using children against their parents. Michelet claimed that he—and the republican anticlericals in general—were keen to make wives into true companions, but he also made clear that this was to be achieved by the husband instructing his wife and moulding her to conform to his ideal. Michelet talks of confessors 'seducing' wives, 'flagellating' them with 'spiritual rods', arrogating the right to visit them when they pleased, insisting that they confess details of their private lives which they would never dream of mentioning to their husbands; the result was that the husband lost control of his own household and 'the home became uninhabitable'.[1] There was a strong element of jealousy in Michelet's attack on the Church, which he accentuated precisely when his mistress, on her death-bed, turned to her confessor, rather than to him.[2] He claimed he wished to strengthen the 'religion of the home' against the religion of the Church. But, as the abbé Laurichesse replied, the Church provided women with consolation to enable them to bear the sexual and other demands made upon them by men and the subordinate role they had to accept: it enabled them to 'obtain spiritual vengeance while being dependent'; it gave them 'an inner life' and 'an asylum against all the oppression from outside'. In this way it strengthened marriage.[3] There were perceptive women who agreed with this abbé, saying that women went to confession because husbands could not understand their wives; husbands blamed wives for frigidity without seeing that they were themselves the cause of it.[4] The building-up of separate male and female preserves in social life was a reflection of this mutual incomprehension. Anticlericalism was, to a certain extent, a confused reaction to this problem of relations between the sexes; female religiosity could be an emotional escape from it.

[1] J. Michelet, *Le Prêtre, la femme et la famille* (1845, 1875 reprint), 267, 307.

[2] Jean Pommier, 'Les Idées de Michelet et de Renan sur la confession en 1845', *Journal de psychologie normale et pathologique* (July–Oct. 1936), 520–2.

[3] Abbé A. M. Laurichesse, *Études philosophiques et morales sur la confession* (1864–5).

[4] Adèle Esquiros, *L'Amour* (1860); see Zeldin, *Ambition and Love*, 293–4.

There was a great thirst for religion in 1848. Neither republicanism nor socialism was originally hostile to Christianity. But the French Catholic church proved incapable of providing the teaching, the solace or the example that idealistic people asked of it, because the political battles it had engaged in, and the harrowing persecution it had undergone, had left it too aggressive, too frightened, too uncertain of its mission in a changing world. This century was therefore one in which the interests of the Church as an institution and the cause of religion as an attitude to life drifted apart. France was apparently divided by its religious disputes into two camps. But the mentalities to be found in each camp were not as totally opposed as the militants, blinded by anger, believed. Each camp was obsessed by the need to defend itself, and the desire to attack its rival. Clericalism and anticlericalism became probably the most fundamental cause of division among Frenchmen. But it led to another division being forgotten, which was more fundamentally religious: the division between those who were preoccupied by the problems of death, guilt, conscience, the distinction of the valuable from the trivial and the place of the individual in the universe, and those who were not. It is quite wrong to assume that those who attended mass on Sunday represented the religious part of the nation. If one adopts the (over-simple) criterion that it is incompatible to be both religious and materialist, then a good portion of the Sunday communicants should probably not be classified among the religious, whereas not a few of the anticlerical *instituteurs* should. The battles fought about the organisation and power of the Church were a different problem.

The parish clergy

The parish clergy of the Catholic Church were, in this period, in a phase of development which made them singularly incapable of providing a leadership that would be widely acceptable. In the course of the seventeenth and eighteenth centuries, their condition had been much improved: they were no longer ignorant feudal servants, but of middle-class origin, sometimes aristocrats. They received an up-to-date training, which made them, as some have argued, the most efficient clergy in Europe. They held an influential place in society not only because of their numbers (there were altogether 200,000 priests in France) but also because of their intellectual activity: in Périgord, out of the forty subscribers to the *Encyclopédie*, twenty-four were *curés*. There were already areas where they met with resistance; and there were certainly black sheep among them. But in the revolution of 1789 they took a leading part in the movement for the abolition of privilege. The Revolution, however, had three results which destroyed most of the fruits of the Counter-Reformation and had a disastrous effect on the clergy's action. First, it split them into two, and a large portion of them became irreconcilable enemies of the liberal cause. Secondly, it turned them into civil servants, paid by the state and subject to a far more rigorous discipline from their bishops: by losing their independence, they became involved in the variations of governmental policy. Thirdly, it drove many into exile, and it was half a century before every parish had a priest again: the Church ceased to be a universal institution. The status of the priest fell accordingly: henceforth he was usually of peasant origin, often a poor boy who saw in the Church a way of obtaining a free education and a secure life, and who sacrified marriage to obtain it. (In the twentieth century, it was the sons of shopkeepers, artisans and clerks who became priests: these classes provided 55 to 60 per cent of the priests in 1950.) The clergy thus suffered from ambitions and anxieties which did not make them the natural guides of society.

The education they received encouraged them to withdraw into a ghetto, where they could be safe from the pressures of the world.[1] They were trained, first, at *petits séminaires*, which were distinguished by the determination with which these sought to cut off children from the pleasures of the world and to 'instil principles into them'. Prayers before and after every lesson, recreation, meal and exercise; daily mass with communion, and ardent worship of the Virgin, gave the pupils a special stamp. It was only in 1938, in an attempt to modernise the seminaries, that Abbé R. Ducasse, a teacher at the seminary of Montréjean, founded a paper, *Servir*, to urge an end of this dissociation of the budding cleric from the

[1] Joseph Rogé, *Le Simple Prêtre* (1965).

layman and the introduction of more modern methods. But as late as 1955 seminaries could still be found issuing exit passes on which it was specified that the exit must be *en famille* and that a promenade with anyone except a member of the boy's family was forbidden. At the end of this schooling, the boys went on to spend five years at the *grand séminaire* (one year of philosophy and four of theology). At the turn of the century, three-quarters of the eighty-four *grands séminaires* taught no science or mathematics; ecclesiastical history was only a recent addition, and considered of secondary importance; there was very little critical study of the Bible, and no effort was made to introduce the pupils to the modern world. The middle ages were held up as the ideal period of Christianity. The theological textbooks, largely renewed in the course of the Second Empire and then kept till 1940, were still based on ancient models; there was virtually no study of original texts or of modern philosophy. Latin was used as the teaching language.

The methods were no different from those of primary schools. The students' function was to prove to their teacher that they had learnt their textbook. The teacher would ask three or four questions in Latin and they would do their best to answer in the same language. He would then read out a few pages from a textbook, translate them into French, and under guise of commentary, repeat the message in several different ways. Occasionally he would dictate a few sentences to the students. They would go away to précis the pages of the textbook they had just studied, copy into their notebooks the dictation of the professor and prepare the next lesson. Questions were not invited; objections were treated as signs of pride and indocility. In some seminaries there were no tables in the classrooms; the students sat with their books on their knees. The ideal was to put every fact into a pigeon-hole, to memorise all definitions, with the dates or articles of the canon law, to label all heresies in red.[1] It was only in the 1940s that group study was developed or pedagogy (with reference to the catechism) taught.

[1] Émile Baudaire, 'La Formation intellectuelle du clergé de France au dix-neuvième siècle', *Annales de philosophie chrétienne*, 3rd series, vol. 5 (1904–5), 153–69, 267–307; J. Hogan, *Les Études du clergé* (Rome and Paris, 1901)—by a former teacher at Saint-Sulpice who emigrated to America.

The *grands séminaires* were boarding establishments, like the state's *grandes écoles*, but with far more severe discipline. No loud talking was allowed, no singing in the students' cells; silence and solitude were the rule; no one was allowed to knock on a student's door without the Director's permission, and the student then answered not 'Enter', but 'Open', for the visitor had to remain outside the cell. Permanent friends in games or conversation were discouraged; the student was required to mix with the first group he met, but these had to be of not less than three and not more than five students. The directors joined the students in their recreations; when they went for walks, it was in single file. Only after 1945 was this abolished and the compulsory wearing of cassocks ended. In this system, discipline and conformity were more highly esteemed than the development of character and the acquisition of knowledge; memory was cultivated at the expense of reason; obedience at the expense of responsibility; routine and prejudice were inculcated in the name of tradition. A former seminarist recalled how he was forbidden to keep up his hobbies of painting and English, on the ground that they were useless or dangerous for a priest; intellectually, he said, the effect of the seminary was to castrate him. He did only four or five written exercises a year: the education was almost entirely oral. The conflicts of theology and science were concealed from him; in his study of the Bible, he was even forbidden to read certain parts of it, until he was considered ready for them.[1] For many years he read the Bible on his knees, 'a posture not designed to encourage criticism'.[2]

The seminarists dealt with the problem of chastity very efficiently from their own point of view, but with disastrous effects for the relations of their graduates with their flocks. The system of close surveillance and active delation (Combes's *fiches* were regarded as typical of a former seminarist) meant that the weak-willed were soon weeded out; there was none of the homosexuality that flourished in the *lycées*. The seminarists were to become merciless censors of contemporary morals.[3] However, their own lives in their parishes were not always

[1] For example, Genesis 19, 29, 30, 38.
[2] Albert Houtin, *Une Vie de prêtre. Mon expérience 1867–1912* (1926).
[3] Abbé Dolonne, *Le Clergé et le célibat* (n.d., about 1900).

blameless and they were charged with hypocrisy. Today a third of pious church-goers doubt the chastity of their *curés*. Half of the people questioned in an opinion poll gave disappointment in love as their explanation of why men became priests.[1] The young priest certainly often emerged from his seminary hostile to the society he aimed to serve and isolated in it. As a result, he spent much of his time defending the rights of the Church against encroachment, rather than seeking to proselytise. He tended to confine his attentions to those who came to him. He condemned the rest for materialism, egoism and licence, without trying to understand.[2] As late as 1945, *curés* were still indiscriminately accusing progress, prosperity, communications and industry of causing dechristianisation, anathematising the desire for profit in work and pleasure afterwards. They were even then classing dances and cinemas as 'facile or immoral pleasures'. One of the Church's leading pastoral experts reported that 'many *curés* have seen dancing as the principal instrument of dechristianisation between the two wars'.[3] They fulminated against abortions, realising there were about a million of these a year but not trying to comprehend the reason for them; they advocated large families in the face of an almost universal desire for their limitation; they inveighed against sexual licence and observed with horror that young men carried around photographs of their naked girl friends.[4]

It was not only the relics of Jansenist influence but also pressure from the self-righteous faithful that made many *curés* unwilling to admit former sinners to communion, to give them only conditional absolution and to impose exaggerated penances. (The movement for frequent, i.e. weekly, communions only got going after 1898.) Such was the bitterness of their struggle with their enemies, that they usually preferred to be content with their few faithful, to live in a closed, fortified world. One of them acknowledged that, as a result, religion became 'a religion of fear, consisting in defences.

[1] Julien Potel, *Le Clergé français* (1967), 239–50.

[2] Abbé Lagoutte, curé du bourg d'Hem, *Du prêtre et de la société présente* (1868) is a good example.

[3] F. Boulard, *Problèmes missionnaires de la France rurale* (1945), 168.

[4] H. Godin and Y. Daniel, *La France, pays de mission?* (1943) has many instructive quotations from *curés* and laymen.

One would say that God was He who prevents men from being happy.'[1] Certainly, the Judgement of God, hell, sacrilege
and sin haunted them. To examine one's conscience and to
confess therefore seemed the essence of Christian life. In the
mid-nineteenth century at least they were often little less
ignorant than their flocks: the archives show them writing
in bad French, with many mistakes; some were even unable to
fill in a questionnaire and asked the local schoolmaster to
help them. They were suspicious of meetings, markets, fairs,
libraries and newspapers; they saw their function to be the
saving of their parishes from the contagion of change.[2] Preaching was one of their weakest points: there were few sermons
in the ordinary village church in the nineteenth century: 'the
continual movement of people in our vast church', wrote one
curé, 'does not allow one to go into the pulpit'. When sermons
were preached they were based on classical models, with
limited relevance. After 1914, these thirty-minute lectures
were often abandoned for short extempore outbursts of spiritual
fervour distributed throughout the service. Attacks on freemasonry and the enemies of God were for long the favourite
subject of sermons. But by the turn of the century priests
began talking of Christians as the élite; soon they urged
frequent communion; and after the war their concern became
grace, predestination and the mystic body of Christ.

There were learned curés just as there were ignorant ones.
Some had exceptional records for erudition and pastoral zeal,
in the organisation of charities and of religious fraternities. In
the mid-nineteenth century, the model curé was J. M. Vianney
of Ars, made famous in numerous biographies.[3] He sanctified
himself by penitence and self-renunciation, overcame the
persecution of demons to build chapels and orphanages,
organise pilgrimages, multiply services, abolish dances and
cabarets, obtain Sunday observance and leave a cult of himself behind him when he died. In 1858, the last year of his
life, over 100,000 people came to his village, attracted by his
fervent preaching. He was simply the best-known of a vast
number of priests whose human qualities gave them similar

[1] Boulard, op. cit. 66.
[2] C. Marcilhacy, Le Diocèse d'Orléans . . . (1964), 247-58.
[3] For example, Abbé Alfred Monnin, Le Curé d'Ars (1861).

prestige, and whose influence was exerted more obscurely on their communities.[1] The priests did not emerge in a uniform mould from their training. There were those amongst them who wished to marry religion with popular aspirations. At the end of the nineteenth century, there were some remarkable priests who emerged as advocates of social Catholicism.[2] There were 700 priests who met at Reims in 1896, to demand a reform of clerical education, an acceptance of democracy and a new missionary attitude towards the people.[3] There was the modernist movement, which attempted to reconcile the teachings of the Church with recent discoveries, and which according to some won the support of 1,500 priests, and according to others of 15,000; but it was vigorously suppressed by a series of papal decrees and encyclicals. Its adherents were evicted from positions of influence, a rigid censorship was established in reaction against them and a 'veritable terror' of 'ecclesiastical Combisme', lasting till 1914, stamped them out. In the interwar years there was a revived interest in mysticism which deepened, but sometimes also narrowed, the outlook of many clergy. Only after 1943 did the idea of the *curé* as a missionary in an almost pagan country begin to be formulated.[4]

Most parish priests were not encouraged by their circumstances to adapt themselves to change. Isolation was one of their chief problems, isolation both from society and from each other: 'always alone, everywhere', one of them wrote pathetically. Their bishops seldom summoned them to meetings and visited them perhaps once a year, and in the nineteenth century sometimes only once every four or five years. They were required to attend retreats every few years, and they had their seminary old boys' reunions. In 1882 the Union Apostolique des Prêtres Séculiers du Sacré Cœur was founded, issuing a monthly bulletin, and several other similar ones, with dinners and meetings, to increase their opportunities for contact; after the war came the association of Prêtres Anciens Combattants and in 1931 the Automobile Club Saint Christophe.

---

[1] P. Pierrard, *Le Prêtre français* (1969) is a good guide.

[2] Cf. J. M. Mayeur, *L'Abbé Lemire* (1969).

[3] R. Rémond, *Les Congrès ecclésiastiques de Bourges et de Reims* (1964).

[4] See Georges Fonsegrive, *Lettres d'un curé de campagne* (1894); Henri Bolo, *Ce que sera le prêtre du vingtième siècle* (1908); Cardinal Mercier, *La Vie intérieure* (n.d.); Chanoine R. Cardaliaguet, *Mon curé chez lui* (1926).

The bishop of Besançon suggested in 1907 that parish priests should be turned into a religious order; and since then proposals for some sort of communal life have been repeated. It was realised too that their education needed to be made more intellectual: energetic bishops tried to found schools of advanced study and to train seminary professors, whose standard was far inferior to that of the state's *normaliens*; but these efforts had little success.[1]

The world of the parish priests changed considerably in this century. In the parish of Deville near Rouen in 1875, for example, the *curé* had to assist him, in ministering to a population of 4,500, one *vicaire*, two beadles, one sacristan, one organist and one pew attendant—and only the last two were part-time. (Four employees was quite normal, but some parishes had as many as ten.) On great feasts there was lavish decoration of the church and elaborate processions. The world of the church embraced two schools run by the Brothers of the Christian Doctrine and the Nuns of Providence. There was a fraternity of Christian mothers, a Congregation of the Children of Mary, a Maternal Society (i.e. organisations for women and girls only). By 1954 the population of this town had risen to 8,000. The *curé* now had a second *vicaire* with an auxiliary chapel, but all the minor employees had gone, for the low wages offered no longer attracted anybody, and at important marriages or burials itinerant chanters had to be hired. The Sunday services lost their liturgical splendour; the processions of the Holy Sacrament no longer followed their traditional lengthy route, though pilgrimages to Lourdes compensated. The boys' church school was closed down in 1906. On the other hand religious life became active in innumerable societies—Action Catholique, Jeunesse Ouvrière, Jeunesse Catholique, Cercle Saint-Pierre, Ligue Patriotique, with its annual pilgrimage to Lisieux, a Union Paroissiale for men, with varied lectures, a dispensary run by three nuns, a holiday camp for a hundred children every year and 160 outings for the aged.[2] It was this transformation of the Church from a state institution

[1] Abbé Garilhe, *Le Clergé séculier français au dix-neuvième siècle* (1899), 31–43; Anon., *L'Église de France et les réformes nécessaires. Le clergé séculier* (1880), a vigorous and informed attack.

[2] Robert Eude, 'Histoire religieuse du diocèse de Rouen au 19ᵉ siècle', *Études normandes* no. 14 (1955, first trimestre), 165–96.

into a vigorous complex of private societies that was to give it new life.

In 1814 there were 29,076 churches in use. In 1830 there were 36,000, in 1848 39,000 and in 1869 42,000. The Second Empire marked the peak of the Church's physical presence. Between 1830 and 1869 the total number of priests rose by 39 per cent, whereas the population increased by only 17 per cent. In 1870 there were 56,500 priests compared with 31,870 in 1810 and 42,486 in 1950. Napoleon III's government spent twice as much on its religious budget as it did on education; and it allowed the Church freedom to argue its case at a time when every other section of the community was controlled by censorship. However, the Church did not profit from this opportunity as much as it might have done. The clergy were distributed in inverse proportion to where they were needed. Because the system of recruitment was diocesan, bishops jealously guarded the independence of their seminaries, whose graduates were mainly local children and nearly always made to serve in the same diocese. The more a region became irreligious, therefore, the fewer clergy it got, because it naturally found fewer candidates. Thus whereas the religious diocese of Rennes had 19·2 priests for every 10,000 inhabitants in 1904 and 17·3 in 1946, that of more pagan Limoges had only 8·6 and 5·8, and Mende only 3·5 and 3·7. One diocese could therefore have five times as many priests as another.[1] The Church failed to provide for the growing towns. In Paris in 1956 it was calculated that four times more priests were needed to bring it up to the national average: in the suburbs 26,000 people were expected to share each church.[2] All these calculations, moreover, assume that the parish priests were ablebodied; but in 1948 35 per cent of them were over sixty; in the diocese of Carcassonne 50 per cent were over sixty, and in Ajaccio 60 per cent. The towns got more than their fair share of these old men, for the traditional hierarchy of promotion was from *vicaire* in the countryside to *vicaire* in a town, then *curé* in a suburb and finally *curé* in a town. But the income of the priest varied in proportion to the piety of his flock. Until 1905 the average priest's salary placed him on roughly the same

    [1] F. Boulard, *Essor ou déclin du clergé français?* (1950), 40, 78–9.
    [2] Yvan Daniel, *L'Équipement paroissial d'un diocèse urbain: Paris 1802–1956* (1957).

level as the village postman.[1] Donations, fees and the hire of
pews could often amount to more than this salary. In order
to keep alive, the priest had to say as many private masses
as possible; but the more actively pious his congregation, the
less time he had to give to evangelising those who never came
to church. After 1905, priests became wholly dependent on the
support of the faithful, and this further accentuated their
inequality. Some continued to live in the most pathetic poverty,
in crumbling presbyteries.[2]

Paradoxically, however, their professional insecurity, which
had plagued them in the nineteenth century, was ended in 1910.
Only the *curés de canton* (about 3,425) had enjoyed permanent
tenure. The rest were liable to be dismissed or transferred at
will by the bishop; and some bishops in the nineteenth century
made great use of their power. One changed round every
single priest in his diocese. This was a source of bitter humiliation to the parish clergy, for before the Revolution they had
all enjoyed security of tenure; their diminished status was due
to Napoleon's wish to increase his control of them. Many
clergy were very conscious that they had come to occupy
a role in society inferior to that which they had had under the
ancien régime. 'The *curé*'s authority over the people', wrote two
disgruntled ones already in 1839, 'is dependent almost entirely on his personal qualities. Some individuals are still
respected: the order no longer is.'[3] This partly explains why
they had to fight so aggressively to maintain their prestige
against the upstart *instituteurs* and mayors. It explains also
why some of them made such extravagant claims for religion
and refused to compromise with the new society in which they
were offered so inferior a place.[4] It is no wonder that they
became fervent supporters of papal omnipotence, and that

[1] N. M. Le Senne, *Condition civile et politique des prêtres* (1847), 201–3. Most
priests earned between 800 and 1,000 francs, though the first-class *curé* (a tenth of
the total) got 1,500–1,600 francs. The *vicaire* got 350 francs, plus a supplement
from parish or municipal funds, of 300 to 500 francs (but in the diocese of Orléans
in the Second Empire only a fifth of communes paid this supplement).

[2] See the begging letters and descriptions of decaying churches in Guy de
Pierrefeu, *Le Clergé fin-de-siècle* (n.d., about 1895).

[3] C. and A. Allignol, *De l'état actuel du clergé en France, et en particulier des curés
ruraux appelés desservans* (1839), ix.

[4] For example, Abbé A. Martin, curé du Brusquet (Basses-Alpes), *Le Prêtre
devant le siècle* (Guincourt, Ardennes, 1858), 91.

they received their reward in 1910 when the Pope gave back to the *desservants* their security of tenure.

Bishops

The inadequacies of the parish priests may be partly attributed to the often unsatisfactory leadership they received from their bishops. The Church, indeed, was prevented from formulating a coherent policy. The minister of religions gave the bishops no pastoral orders. The bishops were forbidden to meet to co-ordinate their policies, first by the Concordat and, after the Separation, by the Pope. It was only in 1919 that the archbishops began holding meetings twice a year, and only in 1947 that an assembly of all bishops was called: but neither had any power to legislate. In the nineteenth century the bishops were selected by governments anxious to obtain supporters for their regimes. After 1905 the Pope, who was no less keen to secure the subservience of bishops, made appointments which were sometimes just as eccentric. Only two new sees were created in this whole period (Marseille and Lille) bringing the total to eighty-seven; the general idea was that each department should have its bishop (though seven did not and four had more than one). On average a diocese had about half a million inhabitants but the variations were as enormous as they were in the parishes: the Paris diocese came to have over five million soùls, while the smallest, Saint-Jean-de-Maurienne, had only 47,000. Before the Revolution, bishops had been limited in their activity by their cathedral chapters, by their provincial parlements and by numerous lay and ecclesiastical rivals, but after it they became almost absolute, arbitrary sovereigns of their sees, with greatly augmented powers of appointment and decision. The accidents of health combined to vary the kind of administration they provided, for they were seldom appointed before they were fifty years old; they did not retire; and some lasted for thirty or forty years, on occasion leaving their dioceses in complete disarray. There were saints among them, scholars, bureaucrats, preachers, evangelisers, aristocrats, mediocrities, sycophants and recluses; the individual character of each had a profound effect on the way the Church met the changes before it. In the early years of the Third Republic 12 per cent of bishops were noblemen, 33 per cent bourgeois or substantial peasant landowners and 53 per cent of humble origin; in the middle of the twentieth century they came largely from the middle class or petite bourgeoisie; only 10 per cent were sons of workers.[1]

It is impossible to make generalisations about so diverse a collection of men over a whole century. The vigorous Archbishop Donnet, for example, who built 310 churches and 400 presbyteries in his forty years at Bordeaux (1837–82), had little in common with the muddler Fonteneau, Bishop of Agen (1874–84) and of Albi (1884–99) who was absorbed by family worries and accumulated debts totalling 800,000 francs.[2] However, the attitude of bishops in the face of material progress, of increasing agnosticism and of anticlericalism was for most of this century generally conservative. At what was perhaps the most crucial period in the Church's history, the early years of the Third Republic, when it made itself the irreconcilable enemy of modern society, there were indeed a few bishops who had no aspiration to clerical domination. Maret, the most distinguished of these, professor of theology at the Sorbonne since 1841, bishop *in partibus*, and a friend of Victor Cousin, argued that to condemn the Revolution would be to cut the Church off from national life and to destroy its power to combat the evils it admittedly contained. In his major work *Philosophie et religion* (1856), he sought to reconcile human reason and divine revelation; and he urged that state and Church should coexist in a free union, with the former recognising its incompetence in religious matters and the latter renouncing all claim to domination. However, the very large majority of bishops demanded a privileged position for the Church in society, not just freedom to propagate its doctrines. Bishop Dupanloup of Orléans, senator under Napoleon III and a deputy after his fall, the leader of the moderate wing among them, was willing to compromise with modern ideas, and he claimed to accept all modern liberties, but he excluded as intolerable liberty of worship and liberty of the

---

[1] Jacques Gadille, *La Pensée et l'action politiques des évêques français au début de la Troisième République 1870–1883* (1967), i. 27; P. Alméras, op. cit. 122.

[2] R. P. Lecanuet. *La Vie de l'église sous Léon XIII* (1930), chapters 1 and 2.

press. He thought the state should recognise that it would collapse without religion, that it should back the Church's work and suppress its enemies. He linked Atheism and the Social Peril (the title of one of his many forceful pamphlets, 1866), warning the bourgeoisie that it would lose its property—in support of which he quoted the seventh and eighth Commandments—and its privileges, in which he ardently believed. He praised hierarchy and élites, authority, obedience and respect, *laissez-faire* mitigated by private charity, the prohibition of strikes, so that he was a total opponent of republicanism and even more of socialism. Bishop Pie of Poitiers (1815–80), the main spokesman of the less moderate bishops—slightly fewer in number than Dupanloup's followers, but including most of the cardinals and archbishops—frankly and vehemently condemned the French Revolution in its entirety as being dramatically opposed to Christianity. The exercise of reason, he insisted, must be subordinate to the teaching of the Church. The state must implement the divine law, and though he denied that his aim was theocracy, he looked back nostalgically to the thirteenth century, when princes sometimes agreed to be simply the secular arm of the Church. Theology was the crowning science which absorbed all levels of human activity. It was the duty of liberals to realise this and rectify their false ideas.[1] But there were still other bishops who were even more reactionary than he, the neo-ultramontanes who were without qualification keen to return to the thirteenth century. It took a long time for the ambitions of the episcopacy to become more moderate.

The way individual bishops tackled their task in their dioceses will illustrate the resources and energy of some, and the limitations of imagination in others. The diocese of Nantes was an example of a religious area in which the damage of the Revolution was quickly repaired. In 1848 there was very widespread attendance at church. Two active bishops during the later years of the Restoration and during the July Monarchy maintained close links with their clergy by visits, correspondence and frequent meetings. Precisely because it was a pious diocese, Nantes lost more during the Revolution: in 1814

---

[1] For Bishop Pie, see Austin Gough, 'Bishop Pie's campaign against the Nineteenth Century', in T. Zeldin, *Conflicts in French Society* (1970), 94–168.

it had only one-third of the priests it had in the *ancien régime*;
but these gaps were quickly filled. Missions were frequently
used to stimulate zeal. Over a million francs were collected in
gifts and legacies between 1802 and 1850, but then the diocese
had lost ninety million from the sale of its lands at the Revolution.[1] This was a diocese capable of being saved, and it was
saved. But in the diocese of Toulouse irreligion was becoming
increasingly vocal. Around 1830 young people frantically
applauded all hostile references to the Church in the theatre
and attacked religious processions. Archbishop d'Astros (1830–
51) was well aware of the progress of 'dechristianisation'; the
state of his diocese, he said, caused him 'terror'. But he attributed it simply to the perversity of his enemies—to whom he
refused the least particle of good faith in their errors—and to
the 'false doctrines' of the eighteenth-century *philosophes*. He
feared innovation above all else and condemned the liberal
theologian-politician Lamennais largely because of this. His
answer to the challenge of his times was to repeat the need for
faith and prayer. There was no question for him of rethinking
the Church's apologetics or dogma. His remedy was Sunday
observance, the proselytisation of the Protestants, the distribution of 'good books', the spread of religious education, the
extension of charity and the limitation of civil marriages. He
pointed out to the authorities that religion was essential to
safeguard 'the integrity of public and private morals', though
he judiciously kept out of politics. Around 1841 he began to
take note of the social problem but only to urge charity. 'It is
permissible to improve one's condition,' he wrote, 'but provided a Christian moderation is used in this aim.' He condemned 'the passion for lucre so alive in our time' and took
the conservative side in the debate within the Church on usury;
his instructions were obscure or equivocal on this subject, in
which the French church generally was less perceptive than
that in Italy and Germany. Archbishop d'Astros always insisted on the *curé* being made president of any new charitable
society that was formed and on the inclusion of religious
practice among its activities. This excessive zeal turned the
working class away: one of his major blunders was to lose, by

[1] Marius Faugeras, *Le Diocèse de Nantes sous la monarchie censitaire, 1813–1848*
(Fontenay-le-Comte, 1964).

this policy, the friendly societies which were beginning to form. He saw religion as the protector of the *status quo*; it rightly 'repressed passions'; it could not compromise with a society built outside it 'with no basis but pleasure'. He seems to have carefully followed the precepts of Abelly's guide to episcopal conduct, first published in 1668, and reprinted in 1837, which made the maintenance of faith the bishop's principal task: this book might perhaps once have been good advice, but it was barely adequate in the nineteenth century.[1]

Dupanloup, bishop of Orléans from 1849 to 1878, was faced by an exceptionally unchristian diocese. This illegitimate child, brought up by a tailor but then patronised by the families of the aristocratic friends he made in his *petit séminaire*, was perplexed and frightened by the social aspirations of the masses. He saw his task to be to provide them with religious leadership, to contain them. But he made the conquest of the notables his first concern, and he had considerable success, for he was charming and tactful. However, the result was that Catholicism was made to appear a bourgeois religion, and one tainted by nostalgia for the *ancien régime*. Though Dupanloup frequented the Paris *salons*, wrote numerous books and was a member of the French Academy, he did not have the intellectual equipment or curiosity to appeal to the intellectuals and to the new generation of students. He was suspicious of science; though learned in the classics, he was far from being so in theology; his library contained no nineteenth-century books except Chateaubriand's. (Many bishops indeed seem not to have read the books they condemned: another episcopal member of the French Academy, Perraud, bishop of Autun 1874–1906, is said to have avoided reading anything less than fifty years old.) Dupanloup wrote a rival *Life of Jesus* in reply to Renan's, but it was a feeble scissors-and-paste collection of quotations with no attempt at serious exegesis. The religion he offered was above all 'socially useful': it consoled, it preached resignation. The policy he followed with regard to the poor was to conciliate them by charity, to attract them to church by accentuating the spectacular element in services, by having rich ornamentation and pompous processions. He demanded

[1] Paul Droulers, S.J., *Action pastorale et problèmes sociaux sous la monarchie de juillet chez Mgr d'Astros, archevêque de Toulouse* (1954).

obedience, not participation, except in singing, which he encouraged as an incentive to piety. He rebuilt or repaired churches, presbyteries and schools on a large scale, to last his diocese for half a century. He was a boring writer and a poor orator, but he had brilliant gifts as a teacher and he did much to improve the catechism. Whereas previously the children had to answer 'Yes, Sir' or 'No, Sir' to leading questions, he rephrased and simplified the catechism so that they had to learn complete sentences by heart. He did a lot to reduce the ignorance of his clergy, though the ideal he held up to them was a medieval one of asceticism, piety and withdrawal; he castigated them for reading newspapers or even for looking 'imprudently at certain pictures, engravings and statues'; he ordered them to abstain from smoking and to read only religious books. He increased the number of clergy by 24 per cent and used them with a clear sense of strategy, concentrating his best priests in the towns where they could meet the gravest challenges and where they would not be disheartened by rural isolation. He ruled them almost like an army, moving 70 per cent of them to new parishes in his first eight years. After consulting them in synods upon his arrival, he held only one more in thirty years, though it is true a few idiosyncratic clergy remained insubordinate and his cathedral chapter waged a constant war against him, even to the extent of publishing an attack on his administration. Dupanloup was bewildered by the age in which he lived: the last few years of his life, in the 1870s, with its still further diminished church attendance, clearly showed the failure of his approach.[1]

Just how slow things were in changing may be illustrated from the career of Petit de Julleville, bishop of Dijon 1927–36 and archbishop of Rouen 1936–48. On being told by the nuncio of his appointment, he protested his unsuitability on the ground that he had no private income. He then asked the nuncio for advice on how best to perform his new duties: he was told to shave off his beard. Petit de Julleville was the son of a university professor; and he had himself been an energetic headmaster of a church school. He gave much weight to intellectual success—though he never wrote anything of

[1] C. Marcilhacy, *Le Diocèse d'Orléans sous l'épiscopat de Mgr Dupanloup, 1849–1878* (1962). Cf. A. Gough's forthcoming book on the Second Empire clergy.

importance. He was particularly active in trying to reform the
catechism, but he had to drop his proposals after a third of his
episcopal colleagues ignored them and another third opposed
them. He did a lot of visiting, even though for much of his
time as archbishop he was too old to walk unaided. But his control over his clergy was erratic: parish priests ignored his
letters with impunity, or forgot to meet him when he announced
a visit. Petit de Julleville urged his clergy to keep up with
modern ideas but he also warned them that youth's exclusive
interest 'in today and tomorrow' was 'childish'; he forbade the
clergy to *tutoyer* their parishioners, which would be carrying
friendliness too far; he insisted on boys wearing ties and jackets
at dinner, even in his holiday camps. His own reading was
largely in the classics of the seventeenth and eighteenth centuries (including Rousseau), the nineteenth-century historians
and religious authors. He was a man of considerable distinction but by now the traditional episcopal organisation was
no longer the decisive influence on the religious life of the
country. Petit de Julleville was one of the first bishops to urge
his clergy to co-operate with the Action Catholique, and he
was right to see in this the new hope of the Church.[1]

Monks and Nuns

The first sign of the changing nature of piety and the new
outlets for it was the phenomenal expansion of the monastic
orders in the nineteenth century. In 1848 there were still only
3,000 monks; but already in 1861 there were 17,676, in 1877
30,286; in 1901 37,000. There was a slight fall in numbers after
the expulsions of 1902–14 but by 1946 the numbers were back
at 29,500. These figures were lower than those of the *ancien
régime* (about 70,000) but the sudden increase after 1850 made
the presence of the monks powerfully felt. Of nuns, however,
there were soon far more than there had ever been before.
In 1789 there were about 35,000 of them, but by 1877 there
were about 128,000, a figure which remained more or less
constant (125,000 in 1900; 120,000 in 1960). However, in

---

[1] Mgr de La Serre, *Le Cardinal Petit de Julleville* (1955); cf. André Deroo,
L'Épiscopat français dans la mêlée de son temps, 1930–1954 (1955), a collection of
official doctrinal pronouncements.

1900 only some 1,800 men and 4,000 women of these were in contemplative orders. The rest took an active part in providing social services: they taught, it was said, two million children, tended 200,000 sick people, brought up 100,000 orphans.[1] The anticlericals estimated their wealth at a milliard francs; they themselves admitted to about half or a third of that amount.[2] What frightened their enemies was their rapid growth. As against this milliard in 1900, it was said, they had owned only fifty-three million in 1850: the threat of mortmain was menacing France again as in 1789. This was not so. Most of the wealth of these congregations was in houses they inhabited: they claimed they owned only 23,000 hectares, compared for example with the 4,816,000 hectares which were common land in France.[3]

Far less is known about these monks and nuns than about the secular clergy; few historians have examined their archives; no sociologist has studied their lives and organisation.[4] The most controversial among the male orders were the Jesuits. They were expelled or attacked over and over again (1764, 1828, 1843, 1880, 1901) on the grounds that they were politically dangerous, but they returned or survived under one guise or another. There were not many of them—3,085 in 1900—but they ran twenty-nine secondary schools which attracted the sons of the aristocracy and conservative bourgeoisie—9,000 boys at a time—and won them brilliant academic successes. The very close contact between pupils and teachers was said to leave a permanent mark on their products. They were much sought after as confessors. They produced some of Paris's most celebrated preachers like Ravignan and Félix and itinerant ones like Pierre Chaignon, who devoted himself to missions directed at the secular clergy. The Jesuits had a great talent for adapting themselves to changing times, and they exerted far greater influence than their numbers would suggest: they set up religious associations, the Apostolat de la prière and the Association de la Sainte Famille, which had a vast membership; they acted as almoners to numerous lay

[1] Mgr Baunard, Un Siècle de l'église de France 1800–1900 (1912), 150.
[2] Henri Brisson, La Congrégation (1902), 416–17; cf. 304.
[3] Père du Lac, S.J., Jésuites (1901), 185.
[4] Leo Moulin, Le Monde vivant des religieux (1964) claims to be the first book on monks by a sociologist but it is only a very general survey.

organisations; and they fathered several religious orders, since they could not expand themselves.[1]

Their methods were discretion itself compared to those of the Assumptionists, who soon supplied the anticlericals with far more ammunition. They were one of the many new orders founded in the nineteenth century. Emmanuel d'Alzon, born in 1810, was the son of a legitimist deputy of the Restoration, and great-nephew of the vicar-general of Nîmes, who appointed him a canon at twenty-four and whom he succeeded in 1837. He set out at once to capture the young. Already in 1840 he wrote, 'I am more or less master of all the children of Nîmes, from twelve to fifteen, and with time I can hope to extend my influence to the adults.' He founded a secondary school, with the help of *agrégés* whom he had converted. He gave the boys a smarter uniform than the state schools, with a military hat; he led them on long marches to the sound of clarions; he devoted great expense to the celebration of religious feasts; he used frequent communion to save boys from temptation; he produced great emulation among them in pious exercises; he encouraged them to join the charitable societies, like that of St. Vincent de Paul; he got the older ones to lecture soldiers and apprentices; and by his 'inflammatory exhortations' filled them with absolute devotion to the Church and the Pope. In 1845 he took monastic vows, and slowly built up the Assumptionist Order with the explicit aim of fighting Protestantism (important in Nîmes), Voltairianism and the French Revolution. The Assumptionists had aims highly relevant to modern society and a determination to make use of all the resources of modern propaganda to achieve them. D'Alzon slept only five hours a day; he was nervous, suffering from 'terrible migraines and nervous diseases'; he left a corresponence of 50,000 letters, and made about 5,000 public speeches, as remarkable for their histrionics as for their passion. He knew how to make religion an all-absorbing obssession for his converts, and filled them with his own vigorous missionary zeal. He loved crowds; he wanted mass conversions. In 1872 he founded the Œuvre de Notre Dame de Salut, assisted by his successor Picard, to save France by public prayer and by the

[1] Joseph Burnichon, *La Compagnie de Jésus en France: histoire d'un siècle 1814–1914* (4 vols., 1914–22).

moralisation of the working masses; he distributed millions of tracts in favour of a day of public prayer, which he established as an annual event. In the following year he collected 1,600,000 signatures from Christian mothers in favour of sabbatarian legislation. He inaugurated national pilgrimages to Rome, Lourdes and La Salette, which were major financial and organisation feats, as well as occasions for remarkable mass hysteria. He established close co-operation with a parallel female order, whose founder, Mlle Milleret de Breu, took a vow of obedience to him. The Assumptionist Order itself was never very large: there were only eighty monks at d'Alzon's death in 1880; about 700 in 1923; and 1,264 in 1937; but like the Jesuits, it made its impact through its innumerable ramifications. He established many subsidiary lay societies, through which the pious could convert, assist, educate and provide employment for different classes. He was always aware of the need to modernise his methods and to increase the appeal of Catholicism to the young. Shortly before his death he wrote, 'We must capture the young, but the young want new forms. In our part of the world we have now only old methods like the Conférences de Saint Vincent de Paul and the Catholic committees. So we must establish new societies, we must have associations for Catholic youth . . . with two aims, the moral and religious improvement of the young, and leadership for social action.' He was keen to fight revolutionary propaganda with its own methods, and laid the foundations of the great press empire which made the Assumptionists famous and an immense national force. Their press campaigns against the republic led to their expulsion in 1900; they disbanded among their numerous foreign missions. But in 1924 they took over the parish of Javel in which the Citröen factories stood. In 1945 they optimistically sent a priest to Moscow—who was promptly transferred to Siberia.[1]

However, the Assumptionists represented only one type of nineteenth-century monk and by no means the most common type. By 1877 there were 116 different male congregations. The Benedictine monastery of Solesmes, refounded in 1833, sought to re-create the medieval ideal, giving particular

---

[1] Anon. (official history), *Les Religieux de l'Assomption* (Bonne Presse, 1963); Jean Monval, *Les Assomptionistes* (1939).

emphasis to liturgy and reviving plain-chant. The Dominicans distinguished themselves through the writings of Lacordaire and in the mid-twentieth century by their publishing house, Les Éditions du Cerf, which brought out the principal books urging a missionary revival in France, as well as learned biblical studies; their political weekly *Sept* was a significant liberal Catholic journal.[1] New orders devoted themselves to the worship of the Virgin and of the Sacred Heart and the Holy Eucharist. The oblates of Mary Immaculate, founded to revive the faith in Marseille, ran parishes, pilgrimages and some seminaries but directed most of their efforts to foreign missions. This was a field in which there was great activity. The Pères Blancs, founded by Cardinal Lavigerie when he was bishop of Algiers (1869), concentrated on North Africa; but many orders were active both in France and abroad: this enabled them, as it turned out, to find easy refuge when they were expelled, and to return in due course. There was great variety in the organisation of these orders: the Pères Blancs, for instance, took only the vow of obedience: they were never alone, but moved in groups of at least three; each had free use of his private fortune and of the fees he received for mass. The Brothers of the Christian Doctrine, by contrast, were schoolmasters, and highly influential as such in France.[2]

The male orders were nearly always responsible directly to the Pope and independent of the bishops, so that there was a certain amount of resentment against them for drawing off the wealth and potential ordinands of the parishes. The female orders, on the other hand, were part of the diocesan organisation; a far smaller proportion of them had pretensions to national stature. Some consisted of no more than perhaps a dozen members: even in the 1960s there were only four orders with over 2,000 members. One may quote as examples

[1] A. Coutrot, *Un Courant de la pensée catholique, l'hebdomadaire Sept, 1934–7* (1961).

[2] Élie Marie, *Histoire des instituts religieux et missionnaires* (1930); Mgr Landrieux, *La Leçon du passé. Nos congrégations, nos écoles* (1926); Camille de Rochemonteix, S.J., *Les Congrégations non reconnues en France 1789–1881* (Cairo, 1901); H. Marc-Bonnet, *Histoire des ordres religieux* (1968); Mgr Théas, *Livre d'or des congrégations françaises, 1939–45* (1948); A. Belanger, S.J., *Les Méconnus. Ce que sont les religieux, ce qu'ils font, à quoi ils servent* (1901); Édouard Schneider, *Les Grandes Ordres monastiques et instituts religieux* (1917 ff.), a series of volumes, of unequal value, see e.g. Paul Lesourd, *Les Pères Blancs du Cardinal Lavigerie* (1935).

the Filles de la Croix de Casseneuil, founded in 1858 by the *curé* of this parish to educate poor girls; in 1877 they had fourteen members. The Servantes de Marie de Blois (1854) were started by an ordinary domestic, to help other domestics find work and to offer them asylum when ill or old—they dealt with between 100 and 150 cases a year. The Sœurs de la Charité, however, founded in 1662 and authorised by the French government in 1811, had 140 branches in 1877: they ran hospitals, asylums, poor houses, schools, orphanages, adult education classes and workshops. They lived off the produce of these workshops and of the orphanages and off their salaries as teachers. The Sœurs des Prisons, of whom there were about 400 in the 1930s, were founded by a few women under Louis-Philippe, without any private resources. The lay republic removed them from the prisons, which were put on a more professional footing, but it still found a use for them in looking after delinquent and abandoned children; individuals with broken homes brought them others; state subsidies and private fees provided the finances. They helped also in detention centres for prostitutes. All the sisters had a vote in electing the General Chapter of the order, which in turn elected a Superior for six years at a time.[1] These are just a few examples of the many social services performed by nuns. About two-thirds of French nuns were engaged in hospital or other social services and one-third in education (in 1960). It is no wonder the lay republic could not expel them *en masse*.[2]

Catholic Lay Organisations

Side by side with these full-time propagandists of the faith, the Church was assisted by a much larger army of charitable organisations. There was enormous scope for them, since the Napoleonic system of assistance left public charity to the discretion of each commune: the majority of communes had very limited resources; the large towns had a disproportionately large share of very poor people. (In 1829 one in twelve of the Paris population were classed as 'indigent', in 1856 one in

[1] Jeanne Ancelet-Hustache, *Les Sœurs des Prisons* (1933).
[2] See notices on numerous orders in Émile Keller, *Les Congrégations religieuses en France. Leurs œuvres et leurs services* (1880).

sixteen, in 1880 one in eighteen.)[1] The state system, which was itself partly kept going by the cheap labour of nuns (very unequally distributed over the country), counted on being supplemented by private enterprise; and private charity increased considerably in the second half of this period. In 1897 2,700 charitable organisations were counted in Paris alone; in 1904 3,150; in 1912 6,930 (of which 1,330 were public and 5,600 private); in 1921 9,065. These figures are unsatisfactory and imprecise but they suggest a vast and growing activity.[2]

Not all these organisations, by any means, were religious. For example the Fondation Émile Zola assisted 'debilitated wet-nurses'; the French Academy administered awards of 1,000 francs to 'poor but well brought up spinsters, of irregular birth'.[3] The number of neutral organisations was impressive, but the majority seem to have had religious affiliations. They covered every stage of life, infancy, apprenticeship, maternity, illness, old age; there were some that catered for leisure and others that provided work. The Société de Saint Vincent de Paul was one of the most successful. Founded in 1833 by a group of students led by Frédéric Ozanam, its purpose was as much the salvation of the souls of these students as that of those they assisted. The society's principal activity was visiting the poor and sick, distributing alms to them, with the idea that this practical work would keep students pious more effectively than church preaching. The society's meetings were preceded and ended by prayers, but it was decided not to hold these meetings in churches, so as to avoid anticlerical opposition. The society spread so rapidly that by 1852 it had branches in every diocese, usually founded by old student members returning to their provinces. The principal branch in each diocese then set up further local branches, sometimes as many as fifty. Napoleon III grew alarmed by its strength, fearing it might be used for organising Catholic opposition on the political level: in 1861 he dissolved its central council. Only some 600 branches survived the isolation of the next decade but the growth was

[1] Émile Chevalier, *De l'assistance dans les campagnes* (1889), 4, 27, 122; Ferdinand Dreyfus, *L'Assistance sous la seconde république, 1848–1851* (1907), 18, 25.

[2] Office central des Œuvres de Bienfaisance: *Paris charitable, bienfaisant et social* (1921), xxxvi.

[3] Ibid. 39, 45.

resumed after 1870, so that by 1903 there were 1,526 branches, and in 1933 1,670, with nearly 25,000 members. Though visiting was their basic activity, they did much more: they supplied the poor with soup kitchens, cheap food, old clothes, help with rent, warm public rooms in winter, cheap housing, employment agencies, free medical and legal advice, holiday camps, old people's homes, catechist teaching, orphanages, apprenticeships, adult classes, clubs, allotments, libraries and pilgrimages. They had a subsidiary organisation, the Œuvre de saint Régis, which got unmarried couples to regularise their unions in church, at the rate, in Paris, of about 2,000 or 2,500 a year in the 1880s, and 250 to 400 in the 1930s.[1] However, the attitude of the almost exclusively middle-class members of this society was paternalistic and traditional. They were not concerned with curing the causes of poverty. They voted to ignore Leo XIII's social encyclical, *Rerum Novarum*; they even thought state legislation on workers' pensions should proceed 'prudently'.[2]

In organisations like this, enthusiastic Catholic laymen could give practical expression to their religion, but it is doubtful whether they converted many of the people they assisted; their significance lies in what they did to stimulate the zeal of donors. The Social Catholic movement, however, attempted to go beyond this and to win back the masses. It was based on an urgent feeling that the tragedy of the nineteenth century was that the Church had 'lost' the working classes and that entirely new methods were needed to win them back. *Laissez-faire* capitalism, it was argued, contradicted Christianity; and Social Catholicism sought to create alternative forms of social relations and economic organisation. It proposed various solutions. In 1848 Buchez attempted to reconcile Catholicism with the French Revolution, by using the universal panacea of that period, 'association', but only a few bishops were favourable, and the failure of the Second Republic discredited this movement.[3] Under the shock of the Commune, two aristocrats, Albert de Mun and René de la Tour du Pin, founded a Catholic club to establish contact with the workers, the Œuvre des

---

[1] Katherine Lynch is writing a doctoral thesis on this subject at Harvard.

[2] Société de Saint Vincent de Paul, *Livre du centenaire* (1933).

[3] J. B. Duroselle, *Les Débuts du catholicisme social en France, 1822–1870* (1951).

Cercles. This had something in common with the Society of St. Vincent de Paul, but it was organised on a more military basis. It was run by 'councils of war' and 'directors'. By 1878 there were about 10,000 such leaders distributed over the country— in effect the provincial nobility and notables. On joining they all denounced the French Revolution and accepted the Papal Syllabus. They attracted only about 35,000 workers into their clubs, whose aim was to keep these men out of trouble in their leisure hours by supplying them with games, food, club rooms, religious services and feasts to celebrate every possible saint's day, with prizes being awarded for frequent attendance. Their libraries contained practically no modern books except Chateaubriand. This military phase collapsed after 1879, under the combined hostility of the republican government, which forbade officers and civil servants to join, and of the Church, which disliked its non-diocesan organisation.

An attempt was then made to christianise the workers by reviving the medieval corporations and by getting paternalistic employers to take on only Christian workers. The theory for this was supplied by La Tour du Pin, ostensibly a disciple of Le Play and even more of the comte de Chambord, but really a traditional aristocrat brought up to believe in the duty of the feudal lord to his serfs; as he himself said, he had been indoctrinated by his own parents 'to the point of being unable to receive any new imprint'. The political leadership was provided by de Mun, who tried to form a Catholic Party, but he was stopped by the Pope, so that he had to devote himself to rather isolated parliamentary agitation for social legislation. The most practical impulse came from Léon Harmel (1827–1915), a textile manufacturer in Champagne, at once a mystic who conversed with the Sacred Heart and an untiring organiser and enthusiastic propagandist of social responsibility among the employer class. In his own factory he was known by everybody as Le Bon Père, and he was willing not only to provide social benefits for his workers but to discuss management problems with them. He converted perhaps a dozen other employers, but on the whole he found Catholic employers too frightened by the prospect of having to share any power at all with their men or even of holding discussions with them. The socially conscious Catholic employers tended simply to put up crucifixes and religious statues in their workshops, to begin the day with prayers, recited in unison by the workers, and to keep nuns around to 'maintain order and good spirits'. They were willing to offer charity, but they feared to talk of justice, rights or state intervention. The idea of the Christian corporation conflicted with the fact that most workers were not Christian, and men like de Mun could not reconcile themselves to admitting pagans.[1] When Père Ludovic de Besse founded a bank to provide cheap loans to workers, without religious tests, and relying on Jewish financial support, he was scorned. The Catholic social movement failed to obtain much success before 1914 because it underestimated the extent of irreligion, because it preached outdated medieval ideas and because it was able to convert only very few employers from *laissez-faire* capitalism. In the 1890s Harmel tried to go further. He launched a Democratic Christian movement, exclusively working-class, but it collapsed likewise from lack of adequate leaders, from the hostility of the conservative Catholics, and perhaps most of all from the fact that a profound change of attitude by the Church was needed before the workers would be attracted to it.[2]

The *Sillon* movement, led by Marc Sangnier, went further towards democracy. He wrote, 'Our primary aim is not to increase the wages of the workers, nor even to get a little garden for each one in which they can relax on Sundays. It is not simply a question of giving the workers roots in beautiful little gardens, and offering them little houses while their boss rubs his hands and says: now my workers will be good and docile because they have a pretty toy. No, citizens must be themselves responsible for what they do.' He urged a reorganization of industry, the abolition of its monarchical system of management, an end to purely mechanical work which destroyed human dignity, and the encouragement of co-operatives for production and consumption as a first step. But Sangnier was no theorist, and no rival to Marx; he read very

[1] H. Rollet, *L'Action sociale des catholiques en France* (1947–58); Robert Talmy, *L'Association catholique des Patrons du Nord 1884–1895* (Lille, 1962).

[2] Georges Guitton, *Léon Harmel* (1925); J. R. and G. Rémy, *L'Abbé Lemire* (1929); Georges Hoog, *Histoire du catholicisme social en France, 1871–1931* (new edition, 1946); Maurice Montuclard, *Conscience religieuse et démocratie: la deuxième démocratie chrétienne en France, 1891–1902* (1965).

little; he worked out his ideas as he went along. His success came from his physical beauty, his gift for inspiring affection and almost hero-worship in the young. First names only were used in his organisation, which was held together mainly by emotional bonds. He was a brilliant propagandist, orator, and organiser. He formed a Young Guard to act as stewards at his meetings, of men whom he initiated with mystical ceremonial in the crypt of Montmartre, like Crusaders, except that they were dressed in modern gymnasts' clothes. In his discussion groups, he chose delicate topics which added excitement to the proceedings. But he was too narcissistic, too emotional and too tyrannical to produce a movement which could last. He could not tolerate rivals and so trained no leaders. His appeal was essentially to adolescents, and worship of him was a major element of the *Sillon*. He was carried away into political ambitions, formed a party, democratic rather than Catholic, and stood for parliament, though he got in only in 1919–24. Already, however, in 1908 thirty bishops and in 1910 the Pope himself condemned him, for ignoring the ecclesiastical hierarchy and too precipitately seeking to overthrow the traditional bases of society. At this time the Church was not generally ready for modernisation. To extirpate the modernist heresy an oath abjuring its tendencies was required after 1910 of every priest, involving the signing of a document twenty-six pages long specifying them in detail. The French clergy submitted to this without any of the protests which arose in Germany. Only with the election of Benedict XV in 1914 did this repression in the French church come to an end; but though relatively brief, it was enough to alienate many intelligent laymen.

The acceptance by the Church of democracy was an essential prerequisite to its regaining its influence in the twentieth century. This acceptance came only slowly and partially in the 1930s. In 1926 the Pope announced his condemnation of the Action Française but eleven out of the seventeen cardinals and archbishops were favourable to Maurras, and a very sizeable proportion of the clergy. It was many years before the conservatives appointed to the episcopacy died off. The majority of Catholics still remained right-wing. General de Castelnau's Fédération Nationale Catholique, founded in 1924 to oppose the laic plans of the Cartel des Gauches, had 1,800,000 members within two years. A large number supported the Italians in Ethiopia and Franco in Spain, being more conscious of the dangers of communism than those of fascism. The official teaching of the Church on temporal matters became, it is true, increasingly cautious, and abstention from party politics was firmly demanded. However, its approved guide to social behaviour could not be accepted by men of the left. This condemned socialism as materialistic; it argued that men liked being governed; that they needed a leader; that authority came from God, not from the people. Though it recognised the 'substantial equality of human beings', inequalities in 'acquired or justly inherited situations' were legitimate; it accepted the 'inequality of classes', which it hoped would be attenuated by 'friendly accord'. It admitted that wealth was badly distributed but asked no more than that wages should be adequate to maintain life—and particularly family life. The workers should better themselves by saving, which would enable them to acquire property. Profit-sharing was a good thing; private enterprise was preferable to state intervention; corporate activity was best of all. The Church now at last said that all forms of government were acceptable, and that Catholics should accept the government of the day, whatever its complexion. It even allowed resistance to government 'in extreme cases'. But 'simple individuals' should not presume to decide on this by themselves. The Church no longer preached the acceptance of the *status quo*, but its ideal of 'harmony' was rather tame. It warned the young not to engage too hastily in political activity, which required a lot of experience. This book of guidance, with its scholastic tone, its innumerable scissors-and-paste quotations, and its search for carefully guarded definitions, meant that the Church was still hesitant in its attitude to modern problems.[1] Every attempt to found a democratic Catholic party failed, to some extent because the hierarchy opposed or discouraged it, but even more because the mass of the faithful could not be drawn from their traditional attachments. The failures of Jacques Piou and Marc Sangnier were repeated between the wars with the Parti Démocratique

[1] D. Lallement, professor à l'Institut Catholique de Paris, *Principes catholiques d'action civique* (approuvé par l'assemblée des cardinaux et archevêques de France) (1935).

Populaire, which never mustered more than fifteen deputies. It was significant that one member of this party, Georges Bidault, owed his defeat in 1936 partly to the opposition of the Fédération National Catholique.

However, in the 1930s an increasing number of Catholic intellectuals began urging a new attitude which was to transform the situation completely. Emmanuel Mounier ran his journal *Esprit* as a meeting-place for believers and unbelievers and he supported the Popular Front. Jacques Maritain's *Humanisme intégrale* (1936) argued that Catholics could participate in politics without compromising the Church by their commitments. Mauriac took a stand on the Spanish Civil War which showed that Catholics did not necessarily subordinate their political judgement to religious considerations. The Dominican journal *Sept* favoured collaboration with the Marxist parties. During the war, the journal *Témoignage chrétien* showed the resistance of Catholics to totalitarianism and racism. The Vichy regime, to a certain extent, marked the triumph of the Church's traditional aims: the encouragement of the family and of corporations, the recall of the religious congregations and the subsidies to church schools. Most of the bishops supported Pétain, though with diminishing enthusiasm. But the war was far from discrediting the Church. There were also some bishops who were imprisoned or deported by the Nazis. Above all, the important part played by Catholics in the Resistance finally restored them to a central position in public life. In the 1944 election the Mouvement Républicain Populaire won 24 per cent of the votes. Though not a church party, it was dominated by Christian Democrats, and had Marc Sangnier as its honorary president. The post-war Church of France would be as different from that of the Third Republic, and as rejuvenated, as the expansionist post-war economy.

What distinguished the new Church was the active role of the laity, in what was known as Action Catholique. To be a Catholic in 1840 usually meant simply acceptance of a position within a large hierarchical organisation, of which the clergy were the leaders and prophets, so that the layman's function in it was the passive one of attending church, and, at most, giving it alms to distribute to the poor. By 1940 this was no longer so. Membership was much more like membership of a society, like freemasonry. One had to take positive measures to join and it was not just a question of keeping up one's subscription; one became a proselytiser, and, at least in theory, one's way of life reflected one's religious beliefs; to a certain extent one opted out of normal society; one almost became a rebel by being pious. The Catholics now had that enthusiasm that the free-thinkers had shown a century before. Action Catholique, the generic term used to cover the activity of Catholic laymen, began in a series of youth movements. The Association Catholique de la Jeunesse Française was founded as early as 1886 by Albert de Mun, as a student movement, guided by Jesuit almoners, devoted to piety, study of the new role of the Church, and social action. In 1891 it had 5,000 members, in 1904 70,000, in 1914 140,000. It was essentially bourgeois; it expected its members to have enough education to participate in its 'study groups', and for long it was conservative politically. But it became most active in rural areas, where it gave birth to a new élite, founding and leading mutual benefit societies for farmers. In 1927 a similar organisation was founded for workers, the Jeunesse Ouvrière Chrétienne (J.O.C.), which had 65,000 members by 1937. Different movements for different social classes now became the rule, in the belief that the old idea of the upper class converting the poor was hopeless and should be replaced by 'conversion of like by like'. The Jeunesse Agricole Chrétienne, founded in 1929, had 35,000 members by 1935; the Jeunesse Étudiante Chrétienne, founded in 1930, 10,000 members; the Jeunesse Maritime Chrétienne (1932, 7,000 members). The Jeunesse Indépendante Chrétienne, for the bourgeoisie, was founded in 1936. Parallel organisations for women followed. In addition, the Scouts (founded 1920, 55,000 members in 1936) kept Catholic boys separate from the lay *Éclaireurs*. Pope Pius XI encouraged these movements; a central secretariat in charge of Action Catholique was established in Paris to co-ordinate its efforts; each diocese was required to have commissions (half lay, half clerical) to advise the bishop on pious, educational, charitable and press institutions; and efforts were made to co-ordinate the *curés'* parochial work with that of these independent organisations. These arrangements were not successful in this period. The organisations were too vigorous and independent to be co-ordinated by the hierarchy; some, like the workers and agriculturalists, were so keen to get mass class support that they were lax about the religious practices of their members; and the older parish clergy for their part were slow to accept this lay interference. This new enthusiasm of the Catholics brought about a fragmentation of attitudes and policies over a considerably wider range than had existed before. The power of the Church was not directly strengthened, but its stability was, and indirectly, because Catholics now had a wider range of options open to them, they were able to participate more fully in the life of the nation.[1]

Anticlericalism

It was thus only at the very end of this period that the Catholic Church, as a body, began to accept that it could not fulfil its ambition to be universal. Tradition left it with more status than a sect, but its hopes of dominating every aspect of life were now abandoned. Once it acknowledged society to be pluralistic, it was able to respond much more effectively to the demands of its adherents. The conclusion, therefore, is not that there was less religion in the mid-twentieth century than in the *ancien régime*, but that what had previously been spread rather thinly, and often very superficially, over the masses, was now concentrated in smaller numbers, who were more positively interested and satisfied by it. These numbers were probably fewer than they would have been had not the anticlerical campaigns been so bitter, for the enemies of the Church had by no means all been enemies of religion. Religion was discredited quite as much by its supporters as by its own qualities, or by its inability to appeal to all temperaments. Just how powerful the animosities created were may be seen from the fact that as late as 1960 no less than ten and a half million people signed

[1] Charles Molette, *L'Association Catholique de la Jeunesse Française, 1886–1907* (doctorat ès lettres, 1968); Mgr Guerry, *Action Catholique* (1936); Raymond Laurent, *Le Parti démocrate populaire* (1965); Aline Controt and F. Dreyfus, *Les Forces religieuses dans la société française* (1965), with good bibliographies; René Rémond, *Les Catholiques, le communisme et les crises 1929–39* (1960); M. P. Fogarty, *Christian Democracy in Western Europe, 1820–1953* (1957); William Bosworth, *Catholicism and Crisis in Modern France* (Princeton, 1962); A. Achard, *Cinquante ans de J.A.C.F.* (1953); Michel Darbon, *Le Conflit entre la droite et la gauche dans le catholicisme français, 1830–1953* (1953).

an anticlerical petition protesting against state subsidies being given to church schools (which meant about half the country's voters). Many of these, even so, still used the church for baptism, marriage and burial. It is important to be clear about the nature and extent of their anticlericalism.[1]

Anticlericalism was, first of all, political. It was originally a protest much less against religious belief than against the political pretensions of the Church. In 1789 and again in 1848 the Church co-operated in revolutions which destroyed privilege, but on both occasions it quickly abandoned the popular cause, and emerged on the winning, reactionary side. It was rewarded with a reinforcement of its position: Napoleon I made the clergy into civil servants, paid by the state; and Napoleon III allowed them to develop an immensely expanded educational system. It may be argued, with hindsight, that this was an option that was beneficial to the Church only in the short term. The alternative was for it to reform itself thoroughly, in keeping with the new aspirations of the century, as the early socialists demanded of it, to revive the stress on love, rather than fear, in its message. Socialism and Christianity were very close in 1848. But the Church was too deeply instilled with the medieval idea that it should have charge of the souls of all men, that the government of lay and spiritual matters was inextricable, and that the state should lend its authority to the Church to ensure that religious principles were obeyed. The clergy were too depressed to opt for a policy of sacrifice. They were panic-stricken by the changes around them, and exaggerated their demands precisely because they suffered from a sense of inferiority. The failure of their occasional efforts at compromise confirmed them in their determination to resist with obstinacy, and to hurl anathemas at their enemies. As in every war, each side claimed the other had started it; but by the nineteenth century the war had gone on long enough for it to have a hereditary tradition, and that is why it is still not extinct. However, it was a war the Church could not win, using the strategy it adopted, for it had never really converted the masses to Christianity. It sometimes had

[1] For general histories, see R. Rémond, *L'Anticléricalisme en France* (1976); Alex Mellor, *Histoire de l'anticléricalisme français* (1966); G. Weill, *Histoire de l'idée laïque en France* (1925); L. Caperan, *Histoire contemporaine de la laïcité* (1960).

governments on its side, but this merely saddled it with all the animosity governments aroused, for reasons independent of religion. As in all wars, also, second-rate polemicists exacerbated the quarrel with arguments of exactly the same level as those which suggested, for example, that Frenchmen could never live in peace with Englishmen or with Germans, and these arguments gave a very misleading indication of the doubts of thoughtful men on both sides.

Renan said that the Catholic Church had never been tolerant, never would be and indeed could not be tolerant. The *coup d'état* of 1851 was perhaps a decisive date in its modern history, because, for a whole decade, having been given the chance by Napoleon III's government, it embarked on a policy of persecution of its enemies which destroyed most of the sympathy that liberals and republicans may have had for it. Proudhon, whose book on *Justice* was condemned in the courts for 'offending religious morals', complained that 'the tyranny of priests' was worse than ever now: 'their avowed plan is to kill science, to snuff out all liberty and all enlightenment. Their anger increases in proportion to their power.'[1] Louis Veuillot, in the *Univers*, delighted in taking Catholic claims to their extremes, condemning all forms of liberty deriving from the French Revolution, demanding the ending of freedom of the press, insisting that toleration was a menace and lamenting that Luther had not been burnt, for he had caused the damnation of millions of souls. The open alliance of Catholic bishops and priests with the legitimist party, their support of the most absolutist theories and their active participation in parliamentary elections, in the end frightened even the Bonapartist government. By staking all on the restoration of the monarchy, they became the political enemies of the majority of the nation, and they united quite disparate forces against them.[2] For a whole century, Catholicism and democracy seemed incompatible, and the bishops' loyalty to Action Française between the wars confirmed this. When the question of the republic's existence was finally settled, that of education

---

[1] P. J. Proudhon, *Correspondance* (1875), 6. 110.

[2] J. Maurain, *La Politique ecclésiastique du second empire* (1930) is the best guide for this period; G. Weill, 'L'Anticléricalisme sous le second empire', *Revue des études napoléoniennes* (July–Aug. 1915), 56–84.

remained to perpetuate the division: now the Church claimed that it was entitled to freedom to educate Catholic children in its own way; but the left rejected this, as divisive. In 1952, an inquiry among practising Catholics revealed that only 8 per cent of them voted for the left wing (5 per cent socialist, 2 per cent radical, 1 per cent communist).[1] Politics thus made people increasingly reject religion—or in occasional reactions, adopt it—for reasons which were not inherently religious. The socialists originally condemned anticlericalism as a bourgeois quarrel, which simply distracted the workers from the class struggle, and Veuillot had indeed said that he was a clerical precisely because he was of humble birth, instinctively opposed to the bourgeois liberals; but the revolutionary and egalitarian aspects of Christianity were lost sight of by the Church in this period.[2] It was only around the time of the Second World War that some Catholic divines began to be attracted or fascinated by Marxism.[3] On certain issues, they were not as opposed as their political stances suggested. Anticlericalism, however, had left a legacy which made it impossible for them to admit any agreement. Its effect was to perpetuate mistrust long after the causes for it had altered; it made French divisions historical as much as actual. Anticlericalism indeed had often developed as a rationalisation of divisions within villages, started off by the clash of personality and the struggle for power, and then solemnised by principles when *curé* and *instituteur* symbolically assumed the leadership of the two parties. From this point of view anticlericalism fulfilled a political need: it provided a means by which the two-party system was effectively established in France, because everybody had to be either for or against the clergy. But, as with the division of Englishmen into Whig and Tory, the principles were not always what divided them most.[4]

Anticlericalism got mixed up with free thought and the quarrel widened into one of science against religion. The

[1] A. Coutrot and F. Dreyfus, *Les Forces religieuses dans la société française* (1965), 195.
[2] 'L'Église et le monde ouvrier en France', special issue of *Le Mouvement social* (Oct.–Dec. 1966).
[3] 'Les Chrétiens et le monde communiste', special issue of *Christianisme social* (Jan. 1959).
[4] See Roger Magraw, 'Popular Anticlericalism in the Isère 1852–70', in T. Zeldin, *Conflicts in French Society* (1970), 169–227.

number of atheists in France may have been even smaller than
the number of pious believers. In 1952 only 8 per cent of a
sample survey said that the existence of God was improbable
and only 5 per cent that there was definitely no God, though
when divided according to sex, 24 per cent of men and 9 per
cent of women declared themselves to be agnostics or atheists.[1]
There was, however, certainly more positive disbelief of religion
in France than in either the U.S.A. or Britain.[2] Why should
the French, who saw less of the wonders of science than the
Americans or the British, have been more convinced that
science had disproved religion? Perhaps for that very reason,
but perhaps also they were not convinced by science as might
be supposed. Science did of course lead some people to doubt
the accuracy of the Bible, to reject miracles and revelation and
to declare religion to be a conspiracy to keep the masses obedient.
Violent polemics did break out in which science and religion
attacked each other. But France also had a strong movement
of 'concordism' which aimed to show that there was no real
conflict. There were plenty of Catholics who used scientific
discoveries to support their faith, or who simply put the two
in separate compartments of their minds. What was perhaps
peculiar to France was that there was a whole combination
of grievances against the Church, and therefore much more
radical argument. The cause of science was eagerly seized on,
as a result, by the enemies of Christianity. Positivism, for
example, was often raised up as a new flag by people who had
previously been atheists or anticlericals. Until someone analyses
all the histories of loss of faith that can be found, it will be
impossible to say what factors were most influential; but it is
probable that the influence of parents and of friends was
important: the hereditary origin of beliefs and the example
that schoolboys and students set each other (rather than the
doctrines taught by priests or teachers) are frequently referred
to. Science may have convinced above all those who were
ready to be convinced.[3] The early free-thinking philosophers

[1] G. Rotvand, *L'Imprévisible Monsieur Durand* (1956), 199.

[2] A less precise international survey in 1947 showed 95 per cent of Americans,
84 per cent of Britons and 66 per cent of Frenchmen admit to belief in God. Ibid.

[3] Alfred Verlière, *Guide du libre penseur* (1869); Charles Charpillet, *Conflit du
catholicisme et de la civilisation moderne* (1864); J. B. Cloet, *L'Arsenal catholique . . .
réponses aux objections* (1857); Dr. Jean Grange, *La Prêtrophobie. De ses causes et de ses*

believed that their independence of mind was too difficult for
the masses to attain: they considered themselves to be an
intellectual élite (not unlike the pious Christians who thought
God had picked them out). They were generally profoundly
interested by religion, tormented by uncertainty, and sometimes heretics more than unbelievers. The attitude of such
men differed from that of the simply cynical, or of the wits who
poured scorn on religion in what they believed to be the tradition of Voltaire, or of M. Homais, the village pharmacist,
who had no doubts at all and derived considerable satisfaction
from his position as the local philosopher. The party of Voltaire, when it comes to be analysed, will be seen to have
infinite variations in it. Perhaps that, ultimately, is why
religion was able to withstand its onslaughts.[1]

Anticlericalism had a paradoxical relationship with morality.
The regions in which it was most active were often ones where
the monastic orders had had large estates under the *ancien
régime*, where the presence of the Church had been felt particularly strongly and where, above all, Jansenism had been
most widespread. The Jansenists had made Catholicism a much
more demanding, ascetic and rigorous doctrine, insisting on the
basic corruption of man, who was held to be capable of salvation only through severe self-discipline and only if God
chose him out specially, by grace; they maintained that only
the most holy were worthy of receiving communion and only
after submitting to severe penances; absolution should be
given by the priest only when the habit of sin was thoroughly

remèdes (1871); Abbé Isoard, *Le Clergé et la science moderne* (1864); A. F. F. Roselly de
Lorgues, *Le Christ devant le siècle ou nouveaux témoignages des sciences en faveur du catholicisme* (1835, 18th edition 1856); François Russo, S. J., *Pensée scientifique et foi chrétienne*
(1953); W. C. Dampier-Whetham, *A History of Science and its Relations with Philosophy and Religion* (Cambridge, 1931); Dr. Louis Fleury, *Science et religion* (1868);
C. C. Gillespie, *Genesis and Geology* (Harvard U.P., 1951); M. Ladevi-Roche,
Le Positivisme au tribunal de la science (1867); E. Boutroux, *Science et religion dans la
philosophie contemporaine* (1911); F. L. Baumer, *Religion and the Rise of Scepticism*
(New York, 1960).

[1] L. A. Prévost-Paradol, *De l'impiété systématique* (1855); Anon. [Guynemer],
Dictionnaire des incrédules (1869); E. Vacherot, *La Religion* (1869); J. F. Nourisson,
Voltaire et le voltairianisme (1896); Robert van der Elst, *La Popularité de Voltaire*
(1897); Eugène Dufeuille, *L'Anticléricalisme avant et pendant notre république* (1911);
Marcel Thiébaut, *Edmond About* (1936); Marcel Mery, *La Critique du christianisme
chez Renouvier* (1952); Albert Bayet, *Histoire de la libre pensée* (1959); Keith Thomas,
Religion and the Decline of Magic (1971).

destroyed. Jansenism was much more than this—it was also a source of individualism and of a certain kind of egalitarianism —but its moral rigorism undoubtedly had the effect of turning people away from church. It set up traditions of anticlericalism, and it was by no means a mere memory in the nineteenth century, for there were still Jansenist journals under Louis-Philippe and Napoleon III and the last Jansenist order, the Brothers of St. Antoine at Mandé, did not collapse till 1888.[1] There were regions, like Lorraine, where Jansenism did not produce a hostile reaction, but in others, like the diocese of Nevers (which became highly anticlerical), the clergy refused absolution and communion so systematically, and demanded penance and contrition over many weeks before yielding, that resentment built up against them. The confessional was an important cause of disaffection, because some clergy used it in a vain attempt to control sexual behaviour. They looked on desire for sensual pleasures as the main source of evil and they demanded that sexual intercourse should seek, as far as possible, only the procreation of children. 'The secret of love', as one priest wrote, 'is in the art of self-restraint.' Confession was seen as 'repressing' sensualism and showing men that life was essentially a painful business: 'without pain, there would be no Church'. This was at a time when people were trying to reduce the size of their families. The confessors not only condemned contraception and coitus interruptus, but urged wives to resist it. The Church, in its effort to uphold the traditional large family, thus made itself a threat to harmony in the family. The anticlericals attacked the clergy for talking about sexual matters, for asking detailed questions about what went on between husband and wife, and they denounced the confessors' manuals as books of pornography, which only put dirty ideas into innocent minds. Anticlericalism was thus two-pronged: on the one hand the masses adopted it because religion interfered too much in their lives—Proudhon said 'their instinct tells them that the only thing that stops them being happy and rich is theology'—but on the other hand the anticlericals' leaders were almost as puritan

[1] *La Revue ecclésiastique* (1838–48); *L'Observateur catholique* (1855–64); Augustin Gazier, *Histoire générale du mouvement janséniste depuis ses origines jusqu'à nos jours* (1922); Pierre Ordioni, *La Survivance des idées gallicanes et jansénistes en Auxerrois de 1760 à nos jours* (Auxerre, 1933).

as the Jansenists and were very far from wanting to open the
doors to sensuality or materialism. The leaders and the masses
were therefore at cross purposes, and once the anticlerical
battle was won, the theory of anticlericalism had to be overthrown in its turn. If one compares the moral textbooks
produced by the advocates of the 'lay school' with the Catholic
catechisms one quickly sees that all they were quarrelling with
the Church about was the theoretical question of whether
morals were of divine origin or whether they were self-imposed
and how they should be taught, but the precepts of conduct
were virtually identical. The Jesuits were singled out by the
anticlericals as the most dangerous enemies of the people, but
it was precisely the Jesuits who did most to adapt Catholic
dogma to changing times and who urged moderation on confessors. Anticlericals attacked the clergy for dogmatism but
they were themselves keen to preserve the social order, and
Marion, professor at the Sorbonne and one of their main moral
philosophers, warned teachers that children must not be
allowed to grow up into dangerous 'little reasoners': 'great
circumspection should be used in the choice of occasions
given to the child to use his judgement'.[1]

Anticlericalism, frequently, was the product of divergencies
of temperament. Sociologists who have tried to explain it have
been driven, after showing why it flourished in one village rather
than another, to assert that each had a 'character' which was
ultimately beyond explanation. Historians who have investigated why particular individuals became anticlericals have,
after going through all the intellectual arguments, often felt
that personal accidents were as important: thus Voltaire
emerges as the son and younger brother of Jansenists, against
whose severity and fanaticism he rebelled.[2] Anticlericalism

---

[1] Louis Bailly, *Theologia dogmatica et moralis ad usum seminarium* (1789, reprinted
twenty times 1804–52), the leading Jansenist moral textbook; P. Bert, *La Morale
des jésuites* (1880), which is based on P. Gury's textbook of morals; Ch. Bellet, *Le
Manuel de M. Paul Bert, ses erreurs et ses falsifications* . . . (Tours, 1882); R. R. Palmer,
Catholics and Unbelievers in 18th Century France (Princeton, 1939); J. J. Gaume,
Manuel des confesseurs (9th edition, 1865); Le Curé X, *Les Mystères du confessional par Mgr Bouvier* (n.d.); Abbé D. Léger, *Le Guide du jeune prêtre au tribunal
de la pénitence* (1864); G. Belot, *Questions de morale* (1900); R. Allier, *Morale religieuse
et morale laïque* (1914); T. Zeldin, *Conflicts in French Society* (1970), chapter on 'Confession, sin and pleasure'.

[2] René Pomeau, *La Religion de Voltaire* (1956); cf. Abbé Berseaux, *La*

was irresistible to inveterate enemies of authority and it was natural that it should have been embraced by the radical party of the *small man*.[1] Once people had taken sides, there was almost nothing they would not believe about the wickedness of their enemies: the Jesuits were accused of inventing instruments of torture to apply to the genitals of their recalcitrant pupils, while the freemasons were very seriously seen by Catholics as communing with the devil. In one of the greatest hoaxes of the century, a third-rate journalist, Léo Taxil, made a living exploiting this credulity, inventing absurd stories which the most respectable Catholics believed, until he revealed that it was all invention.[2]

Anticlericals certainly liked to get together and Freemasonry became their favourite society. Because the freemasons shrouded their activities in secrecy, all sorts of accusations could be made against them: anticlericalism was therefore associated with revolutionary conspiracies and backstairs political intrigue, and attacked as being in league with Jewish and Protestant influences; the subject has proved of inexhaustible fascination and in 1925 a bibliography listed no less than 54,000 titles of works on it. The Vichy regime confiscated the freemasons' archives in its desire to expose their machinations, but they only made it clear, at last, that there was nothing very dramatic to reveal. Freemasonry was not originally anti-religious: in the eighteenth century, priests had been members. Both Napoleons had given it semi-official status, so as to keep it under control. But under the Second Empire many lodges were infiltrated by republicans, and they, in 1877, won the movement over to free thought by ending the homage it had hitherto paid to the 'Grand Architect of the Universe'. In due course, nearly all lodges became affiliated to the radical party. The number of freemasons rose from about 10,000 in 1802 to 20,000 in 1889, 32,000 in 1908, 40,000 in 1926 and about 60,000 in 1936. This was the result of a conscious policy of democratisation. In the eighteenth century there were two kinds of freemasons: members of the upper class and middle-class

---

Voltairomanie (Laneuveville devant Nancy, 1865) and Mgr de Ségur, *Les Ennemis des curés. Ce qu'ils sont, ce qu'ils disent* (1875).

[1] E. Faguet, *L'Anticléricalisme* (1906) for a largely psychological interpretation.
[2] E. Weber, *Satan franc-maçon* (1964).

men who liked to ape them, to call each other chevalier and wear honorific regalia. In the course of the nineteenth century, the social composition was increasingly widened; in 1880, reduced initiation fees were offered to soldiers and *instituteurs*; and in the twentieth century policemen and workers from the Confédération Générale du Travail were recruited. Freemasonry appealed first of all to people who liked mystic ritual, esoteric symbolism and fancy uniforms, and to those who liked to have somewhere to discuss ideas and meet like-minded friends. Increasingly however it became an organisation which politicians used for electoral purposes and which civil servants joined in order to further their chances of promotion, which hotel-keepers found useful as a way of enlarging their clientele and where businessmen could make deals and find jobs for their sons. 'Fraternal groups' were set up in the prefecture of police, in journalism, in the gas and electricity industries, in medicine and education. Since most radical politicians belonged to it, and since for a long time its leader was vice-president of the Senate, it was believed that it ran the country, as well as being the principal source of materialistic and anticlerical propaganda. This was a vast exaggeration: certainly it lent its aid to the anticlerical campaigns, but it was hardly responsible for initiating them. Its intellectual level sank rapidly, and though it passed resolutions calling for such reforms as the introduction of income tax, it was perhaps most important as a social club, membership of which was seen as a way of getting on in the world, and in which one also got immediate advantages, such as ten per cent discounts in shops owned by freemasons. It organised a certain amount of charity, but even more mutual insurance.

In 1904 a great fuss was made because the lodges had been asked to collect information about the political affiliations of army officers, with a view to thwarting the promotion of right-wing ones. The enemies of the freemasons, who organised themselves into Anti-Masonic Leagues, replied by publishing lists of freemasons, as a kind of repertoire of dangerous men. Every parliamentary and judicial scandal inevitably involved freemasons and this added fuel to the polemic. However, at the provincial level, the masonic lodges were pretty insignificant. The lodge of Saint-Brioude (Haute-Loire) had only forty-four members in 1911, half of them civil servants, thirteen of them merchants, six *cafetiers* and two barristers. In Laval (Mayenne) the lodge was a small republican club seeking to depose the sitting conservative members of parliament, and occasionally falling apart from disagreements, as it did over the Boulanger Affair; its members were above all *instituteurs*, led by the inspector of primary schools. There was considerable variation in the atmosphere of different lodges: some emphasised ritual, some were musical, some favoured playing cards and dominoes; but all of them loved holding banquets 'resembling sessions of the Convention' with their speeches and toasts. Freemasonry was divided between the Grand Lodge and the Grand Orient (the former, unlike the latter, was on the side of the workers in industrial disputes and admitted worker members), and there were three other minor varieties. The interest in politics palled in due course and after 1945 it was largely expelled. The Grand Master of the National Lodge said in 1972: 'It is time that Frenchmen got into the habit of talking about things other than politics.'[1]

Anticlericalism was, to a certain extent, France's alternative to England's Nonconformist churches. It was no accident that Protestants took a leading part in the anticlerical movement. Protestantism had been largely stamped out by the combined persecution of Church and monarchy, and its revenge was therefore twofold. Protestants entered the civil service in a proportion which may well have been considerably larger than the 2 per cent or less of the total population that they formed. In 1900 there were probably less than 650,000 of them; when Alsace and Lorraine were recovered in 1919, there were perhaps 800,000. If they had had a proportionate share of state posts, they would have had no more than one or two prefects, and ten deputies at most. In 1899, however, there were said to be about ten Protestant prefects and over 100 members

---

[1] A. Lantoine, *Histoire de la franc-maçonnerie française*: vol. 3, *La Franc-Maçonnerie dans l'État* (1935); A. Lantoine, *Les Sociétés secrètes actuelles en Europe et en Amérique* (1940); M. J. Headings, *French Freemasonry under the Third Republic* (Baltimore, 1949); A. Mellor, *La Vie quotidienne de la franc-maçonnerie française du 18ᵉ siècle à nos jours* (1973); E. Gautheron, *Les Loges maçonniques dans la Haute-Loire 1744–1937* (Le Puy, 1937); André Bouton and Marius Lepage, *Histoire de la franc-maçonnerie dans la Mayenne 1756–1951* (Le Mans, 1951); D. Ligou, *Frédéric Desmons et la franc-maçonnerie sous la 3ᵉ république* (1966); Raymond A. Dior, 'La Franc-Maçonnerie', *Le Crapouillot* (Sept. 1938); Paul Nourrisson, *Le Club des Jacobins sous la 3ᵉ république* (1900); Jean Marquès-Rivière, *Les Grands Secrets de la franc-maçonnerie* (1935).

of parliament.[1] In 1924 Gaston Doumergue became the first
Protestant president of the republic. A Protestant, Louis Méjan,
was one of the principal architects of the law of the separation
of Church and state; and many of the politicians responsible for
wresting education out of the hands of the Catholics were
Protestants. The Protestants seemed to be capturing the state,
using it to attack the Catholic Church from above, while at the
same time undermining it from below by whipping up the
anticlerical movement to unprecedented levels. This is how it
seemed to the Catholics. In fact it was only a small minority
of Protestants who were involved in active politics, and these
formed a heretical group within the community. Protestants
were very far from having a united attitude on any subject,
even on religion. They were not only divided between Cal-
vinists and Lutherans (as well as a few thousand Methodists,
Baptists, Derbyites etc. produced by English proselytisation)
but they were also geographically differentiated between the
two main regions, the south and the east. In the 1890s, one-
quarter of all Protestants lived in the department of Gard.
In this period, Protestantism was still predominantly rural,
even though there were sizeable communities in Paris and
some other cities. The southerners were the descendants of the
Camisards, who had fought a guerrilla war against the monarchy
in the eighteenth century, and rebellion was a family tradition.
But by the end of this period the mountainous regions, to
which they had withdrawn, became depopulated, and the
influx into the civil service and the liberal professions transformed Protestantism into a nation-wide phenomenon, with a
few representatives in most regions. The Protestants thus
seemed to be powerful for different and changing reasons.
There were however quietists as well as activists among them,
Dreyfusards as well as anti-Dreyfusards; they were the inspiration of the Co-operative movement, but they also had notable
industrialists and bankers who linked them with capitalism;
and in the interwar years, some supported the communist
party. They could never present a united front, because their
modern history was one of constant internal dispute; but there
were enough of them prominent in left-wing politics, and there
was enough hostility towards them among the Catholic clergy—

[1] Ernest Renauld, *Le Péril protestant* (1899); id., *La Conquête protestante* (1900).

who became far more vigorous in areas with Protestant communities—for anticlericalism to be seen as a continuation of the wars of religion.[1]

Anticlericalism was, finally, connected with anti-Semitism because Catholics took a leading role in the stirring up of hate against the Jews. Anti-Semitism was not a central problem in France until the end of the nineteenth century. The traditional animosity of the Church towards the Jews was echoed in the vague hostility that the French generally felt for the Jewish minority among them, but there were very few Frenchmen who ever came into contact with Jews: in 1840 there were still only 70,000 Jews in France, two-thirds of whom lived in Alsace. Catholic journalists like Louis Veuillot could thus inveigh against Jews during the Second Empire while revealing extraordinary misapprehensions and ignorance about them. The emancipation of the Jews by the Revolution had made them legally equal, but socially they were still apart. However, the successes that, as a result, some of them were able to obtain in French life soon caused this emancipation to back-fire on them. Rothschild became the symbol of capitalism and it was the socialists who were therefore the first pioneers of anti-Semitism in its modern form. It was the Fourierist Toussenel who published the first major anti-Semitic book of the nineteenth century. The idea that all Jews were wealthy was of course a myth, and as late as 1870, over 60 per cent of them were said to have died paupers. It was no contradiction that, even if Fourierist socialism was anti-Semitic, the Saint-Simonian variety should have had Jews among its most celebrated adherents. For what distinguished the educated Jews in France was their relegation of their Judaism into a purely religious peculiarity and their desire to turn themselves in all other respects into fully-fledged Frenchmen. Many of them saw themselves as symbols of the liberal principles of the French Revolution, and in gratitude their patriotism, as the Grand Rabbi of Paris said, was of 'an extraordinary fervour'. Darmesteter, the director of the École Pratique des Hautes Études,

[1] Émile G. Léonard, Le Protestant français (1953) and id., Histoire génerale du protestantisme, vol. 3 (1964) which has a large bibliography. Cf. also Jean Seguy, Les Sectes protestantes dans la France contemporaine (1956).

argued that the French Revolution was the fulfilment of the Jewish ideas of justice and progress. By the end of the nineteenth century, assimilation even became the official doctrine of the organised Jewish community.

But because Jews therefore sided with the cause of liberalism, they came to be seen as increasingly dangerous enemies by reactionaries. There were two Jews in the government set up by the revolution of 1848: the barrister Isaac Crémieux, who became minister of justice, and the banker Goudchaux, who was minister of finance. Crémieux was minister again after the overthrow of Napoleon III and used the opportunity to give full French citizenship to the Jews of Algeria—which became one of the bastions of anti-Semitism.[1] The Reinach family was closely associated with Gambetta. Alfred Naquet, the professor of chemistry responsible for the law allowing divorce (1886) and therefore bitterly hated by Catholics, sat on the extreme left; the fact that he had married a Catholic and ceased practising as a Jew did not stop all the animosity this issue raised being directed against the Jews. The admission of Jews into the freemason lodges stimulated the belief that they were involved in a massive conspiracy against the Church. Brilliant examination successes in the state schools, the instrument of Jewish assimilation, exacerbated jealousy.

But what is interesting about the rise of organised anti-Semitism is that it had relatively little to do with the development of the Jewish community. Anti-Semitism was an expression of the ignorance of the modern world that the Church suffered from in the mid-nineteenth century rather than of close observation of it. The anti-Semitic work that the aristocrat Gougenot des Mousseaux (commander of the Order of Pius IX) published in 1869 was inspired by the belief that Jews were cabbalistic worshippers of Satan.[2] The first newspaper devoted specifically to attacking the Jews, *L'Anti-sémitisme* (1882), was founded by a priest, a canon of Angoulême and Poitiers, where there were virtually no Jews at all. The best-seller that turned anti-Semitism into a national movement, *La France juive* (1886), which sold 100,000 copies in its

---

[1] See chapter 4 for the situation in Algeria.

[2] H. R. Gougenot des Mousseaux, *Le Juif, le judaïsme et la judaïsation des peuples chrétiens* (1860).

first year, was the work of a young journalist, Édouard Drumont, who had tried his hand at historical novels, playwriting and gossip collecting, and who produced not a work of observation, but a mass of falsehoods, many of them plagiarised from previous works. He claimed there were half a million Jews in France, though official statistics registered only 68,000 (plus 44,000 in Algeria). But by combining political polemic (for one of the main targets was Gambetta, who Drumont said was really a Wurtemberger Jew called Gamberlé) with amazing would-you-believe-it stories, he provided an explanation of why the world was going to the dogs. His book was eagerly bought by Catholics. In 1895 Drumont's newspaper *La Libre Parole* organised a competition for an essay on how best Jewish power in France could be annihilated; the two prizewinners were Catholic priests, as were two of the runners-up. Drumont was also a palmist and spiritualist, always carrying a mandrake root with him. His own credulity was more than matched by that of his followers. No Jew bothered to answer him.

The Dreyfus Affair ranged the Jews more firmly than ever on the side of the liberal republic, and therefore against its enemies, the monarchists and the clergy. The Jews deliberately tried to move the issue away from that of anti-Semitism to the more general one of toleration and respect for the individual. But the Jews were now also becoming recognisable as a foreign minority, as successive waves of immigration swelled their numbers, above all in Paris. In 1870 there were 24,000 Jews there. The Alsatians raised this number to 40,000 by 1881. The Russians then arrived, followed after 1919 by other East Europeans, so that by 1930 there were 150,000. The vast majority went into the clothing trade and set up separate quarters in Paris. Many of them could not speak French, many of them did not want to be assimilated and stressed their separateness, to the dismay of the old-established Jews. A few hundred joined the communist party, and so strengthened the impression that they were a danger to the established order. The old or French Jews, anxious to dissociate themselves, formed a Jewish patriotic organisation, and even allied with right-wing patriotic organisations, including the Croix de Feu. This did not prevent the followers of Maurras from making anti-Semitism a basic part of their teaching, and under Vichy the Jews were finally excommunicated from membership of the nation. It was only the extreme nature of their persecution that at last aroused the conscience of the Catholics, and it was only under Vichy that a section of the clergy at last came out publicly against anti-Semitism.[1]

The history of religious practice and dispute in this period reveals most strikingly how people with broadly similar outlooks could, as a result of disagreement on secondary issues, become enemies so violent that they became quite incapable of understanding or sympathising with each other. Anger, and traditions of animosity, thus prevented the reassessment of differences with changing times; and political divisions became more historical than real. In nineteenth-century France Catholicism was largely a religion of aggression and of incomprehension, with too many enemies to allow its charity to be fruitful. Though it preached resignation, it did not practise it: it was a religion of anxiety. In the twentieth century, it gradually and increasingly altered its outlook so that it came to appeal to a different sort of person: the longing for national uniformity gave way to a much more individualistic emphasis, which was not all that far removed from what the founding fathers of the Revolution had envisaged. Catholicism became, indeed, a refuge from the pressures of mass civilisation, just as it had once itself been a source of pressure for conformity. That it took centuries of warfare to effect this transformation was due partly to successive governments exploiting it to further their own quest for power. Church and state were inseparable when both believed it was their function to control what men thought. Neither ever succeeded. But when they stopped their persecutions, and the infinite variation in ideas was allowed free expression, there were new pressures upon them. It is uncertain just how far the battle for free thought was won.

[1] B. Blumenkranz, *Bibliographie des Juifs en France* (1974); Robert F. Byrnes, *Antisemitism in Modern France* (Rutgers U.P., 1950); Michael R. Marrus, *The Politics of Assimilation. A Study of the French Jewish Community at the time of the Dreyfus Affair* (Oxford, 1971); Pierre Pierrard, *Juifs et Catholiques français 1886–1945* (1970); David H. Weinberg, *Les Juifs à Paris de 1933 à 1939* (1974); Pierre Aubert, *Milieux juifs de la France contemporaine à travers leurs écrivains* (1957).

7. Technocracy

THE year 1914 is usually held to mark the beginning of a new era of anxiety. It quickly became a commonplace to contrast the stability of the pre-war years with the chaos that the war inaugurated, and that the Peace of Versailles could not halt. This book has tried to show that the myth of the good old days should not be taken seriously, for the nineteenth century any more than for any other age. That century was very far from being either stable or simple to live in. It is true that it did diminish insecurity in one very important way. For the first time in history, famine ceased to be a threat: on the whole Frenchmen no longer needed to fear death by starvation. But men became more mobile, both physically and socially; the many new opportunities before them complicated the choices they had to make and created tensions as severe as have been experienced before or since. The nineteenth century may, for the sake of schematic convenience, be said to have been dedicated to progress, but it was also frightened by it and quarrelled endlessly about it. It was, quite as much, a century of doubt. Far from living contentedly in the long warm summers that survivors of it liked to remember, it was worried about the future in a very fundamental way, precisely because resignation was not one of its characteristics. One could buy state bonds that yielded regular interest, but one was also obsessed by the need to save, economising on today's pleasures to fend off the dangers of tomorrow and old age. There were no long wars, but there were numerous short ones and the size of armies grew relentlessly.

1914 has been seen as a break in history largely for the wrong reasons. The inter-war years are, at present, rather in the same state as the Second Empire was for some fifty years after its collapse. The reign of Napoleon III could not be judged fairly after the humiliation of 1870: it was almost universally condemned as a failure, an aberration, a contradiction of all the high values that decent men should cherish; the emperor was derided as a fool and it seemed inexplicable that a civilised country like France should have submitted itself to his tyranny, fought in his quixotic wars and participated in the fawning adulation of his pompous rhetoric and of his upstart hench-men. It was only when both those who had lived through his reign and those who based their lives on the rejection of the errors of his generation were dead that the Second Empire could be regarded with detachment. It is only just beginning to be possible to adopt the same attitude to the years since 1914. The diplomatic and military historians have, as usual, been the first to clarify the outlines. The capture of the archives of the Third Reich has, by a curious quirk, illuminated the tergiversations of the Vichy regime, so that it is better known than the twenty years preceding it, but the history of inter-war France remains far less documented than that of Germany in the same period. The memoirs of generals and politicians have been fairly numerous but the French national archives have only recently been (partially) opened to historians. There have therefore been comparatively few doctoral theses that go beyond the study of foreign or party policy. One of the most remarkable of these, by J. N. Jeanneney, submitted in 1975, has shown what a vast array of polemical accusations and mis-conceptions need to be discarded before even the basic events can be established.[1] It was only in 1965–75, with the publica-tion of Sauvy's four-volume economic history of the inter-war years, that the statistics of the period began to be subjected to critical reappraisal.[2] So it is only gradually that the per-spective that regards these years as ones of exceptional chaos and failure will recede and allow the changes that took place in them to be seen in a less negative way, and with some sense of what was permanent and what was superficial.

The period 1914–45 was one of anxiety to those who lived through it not least because they did not know where it was leading. A great many people behaved, even after the war of 1914 and even during the German occupation of 1940–4, as though nothing fundamental had changed. The politicians of these years were most of them men who had picked up their

---

[1] J. N. Jeanneney, *François Wendel en République. L'Argent et le pouvoir 1914–40* (Nanterre doctorat d'état, defended in 1975, published in 1976).

[2] Alfred Sauvy, *Histoire économique de la France entre les deux guerres* (4 vols., 1965–75).

ideas before 1914. The price of success in the war was that the old leaders survived and the war could therefore be interpreted as no more than a severe illness or stroke, suffered by a middle-aged man, but one which was overcome: the republic was able to devote its remaining days to trying to regain the vigour of its youth. The battles of the politicians, the rise and fall of ministries, tell one about day-to-day preoccupations, but that is only one level of history.

At another level, one can see three major changes occurring in these years which transcend the bitter quarrels, which were abetted by politicians of almost all parties, and which place the details of events in a different light. The capitalist system, first of all, received a fatal blow in 1914, at least in the form in which it had existed in the nineteenth century. Its death throes may be regarded as a central theme of the next thirty years. After that, the economy was run on radically different lines and the state, which hitherto had limited its interventions to a comparatively small segment of life, emerged vastly more active, and very much transformed. The rise of an expansionist France in the 1950s, based on a 'mixed economy' and welfare benefits, cannot be understood without going back to these years. The peace of 1919, by returning Alsace and Lorraine, made France a great economic power. From this point of view, one could see the years 1871–1914 as in some sense an interlude. After 1919 the traditions of the Second Empire, stressing material prosperity, were revived. The full fruits of France's revenge were not immediately seen, because the country's expansion was held back by lack of labour and by a muddled fiscal policy. But the rapid development of new industries and the considerable prosperity of the 1920s showed that a path had been opened up. The great Wall Street crash and all the disasters that followed should not cause the promise of the 1920s to be confused with the gloom of the 1930s. Moreover, just as the First World War made Frenchmen say that they would never fight again, so the economic calamities that followed it made them determined not to suffer unemployment again. The end of insecurity in employment—or at least the establishment of insurance and compensation for unemployment—was worked out in these years, and greatly increased the role of the state in the economy. The constitution of 1946 accordingly laid it down that 'everyone has the duty to work and the right to have a job'. This represented the fulfilment of the demand for the Right to Work that the utopians of 1848 had dreamed of. It took a century to bring about; it was probably one of the most important achievements of universal suffrage; it was the state that undertook to guarantee it.

Paradoxically, however (and this is the second transformation that occurred in the period of the World Wars), the state became the supreme guide and director of the nation at the very moment when, from the international point of view, it lost its power of independent action. France had a population of only 40 million, in a world of 2,000 million. It was no longer able to defend itself on its own. Its foreign policy was dominated henceforth by a desperate search for alliances to compensate for its weakness, and by a very gradual realisation that it would have to find security, and a guarantee of its freedom, by co-operating with the rival nations it feared. It discovered that its economic problems, which hitherto it had palliated by customs protection, could not be solved by independent action, but was unable to accept this blow to its pride. The fierce reassertion of French values was the swansong of nationalism.

These were such revolutionary changes that it was difficult for people to adapt to them quickly, or indeed to comprehend them. They stimulated a dual reaction: an effort to ignore or stop change, or, alternatively, vigorous debate about the implications. These years were thus, thirdly, ones of intense intellectual activity, such as had not been witnessed since the early nineteenth century, when socialism was being concocted. However, thanks to the growth of education, intellectuals were far more numerous, and they occupied a less peripheral position in society. They now took a direct part in politics, as they had not hitherto done, and these were critical years in the history of their influence. The results of their activities were indecisive. They were not obviously successful, and they discredited each other also by their profound internal divisions; but they nevertheless continued to be as vocal and as self-confident in the guidance they claimed to offer to the country. This concealed the fact that they had lost their bid for power. A breach between intellectuals and technocrats—a breach which did not exist in the days of Saint-Simon—appeared in

these years. It was the technocrats who established themselves
in the positions of real power, in the civil service and in the
management of industry, while the intellectuals deceived themselves with verbal roles in political parties. The outcome would
become apparent only in the 1960s.

In 1914 the state was already the country's largest single
employer, and its activities had already gone beyond administration into direct industrial and commercial enterprise. Since
1674 tobacco had been a state monopoly but the trade in
tobacco was not carried out by state officials: a 'mixed'
compromise between state and private enterprise had already
been adopted, whereby the retailers were private individuals,
enjoying privileges, but not paid by the state. In 1889 the
state took on the direct manufacture of matches and the provision of telephones (which had hitherto been run by both the
state and a private company) and in 1908 the state bought the
bankrupt Western Railway. The radicals were attracted by
this extension of state activity, despite their attachment to
private property, because they hoped the profits would obviate
the need for higher taxation, and because they valued the
patronage that went with it. Unfortunately for them, the state
did not make much profit: it was claimed that the state's profits
from the manufacture of tobacco were only half of what England raised from its taxes on tobacco. In 1914 the state was
engaged in the following business activities (the turnover, in
millions of francs, is given in brackets):

> Military catering and clothing manufacture (564), post office
> (362), shipbuilding (216), munition and cannon manufacture
> (188), building roads and ports, restoring old monuments etc.
> (175), tobacco and match manufacture (140), gunpowder
> (77), savings banks (62), aeroplanes (49), horse-breeding
> (38), insurance (27), forestry (27), porcelain making at
> Sèvres (17), map making (1·6), newspapers (1·5).[1]

Much of this was in competition with private industry.

But the war of 1914 extended the sphere of state activity to
the control of the economy as a whole. Freedom of commerce
was limited, in that the state tried to fix prices, limit profits,
requisition and share out essential products. Labour was

---

[1] Adolphe Delemer, *Le Bilan de l'étatisme* (1922), 14.

allocated to industries by the selective release of soldiers from the front. Agricultural land left uncultivated could be requisitioned.[1] Food rationing and the granting of allowances to soldiers' families placed the whole population in much more direct subordination to the state. The state did not nationalise the war factories, however, nor did it institute industrial mobilisation for civilian industry (as Germany did). It worked through the capitalist system. Even for the import of raw materials, it preferred to get the businessmen concerned to combine into consortia which were given official status, but were run as private companies. The history of these consortia, of which there were fifty by the end of the war, provided a most instructive lesson. On the one hand, some hitherto conventional politicians came to think that the extension of state control over the economy should be retained and developed in peace time. The minister of commerce from 1915 to 1919, Étienne Clémentel (notary and mayor of Riom, an amateur opera librettist, playwright and artist) was galvanised by the delights of power and the revelation of chaos that office gave him into urging the establishment of a state department for economic planning: it would 'indicate to industrialists and businessmen . . . the general plan by which their efforts should be directed, so that the actions of individuals would help rather than hinder the interests of the state. A nation, like a business or an industry, must have an economic programme, a plan of action. Until now, nothing like this has ever been done in France.' Traditional methods, like customs regulations, no longer sufficed: 'government and industry must form an alliance to search for raw materials at the lowest possible cost, to plan for the intensive exploitation of all our natural resources and to determine the price of articles which must be manufactured by methods of mass production'. He considered that industry should form regional consultative groups, so that the state could negotiate with it on an adequate geographical basis. His experience of obtaining raw materials in war-time convinced him that international co-operation would be necessary to regulate trade and credit in peace-time and he urged the formation of an 'economic union of all free peoples' (meaning Western Europe and the U.S.A.). Jean Monnet, who forty years later organised

[1] Law of 6 October 1916.

the European Economic Community, was on Clémentel's staff.
The roots of the Common Market and of the French state
planning system go back to these experiences.

Not surprisingly, however, the war of 1914–18 did more to
discredit than to encourage immediate action in this direction.
The practical difficulties of mixed economic control were more
obvious than its advantages. The effect of the consortia was to
destroy many middlemen, but it also provided the businessmen
whom the state enrolled into them with undreamed of opportunities for profiteering, even though the consortia were
ostensibly designed to control this. The profits of importers
involved in the consortia were limited by law to 6 per cent.
The consumer did not obtain all the benefit from this, for the
state kept prices high enough to rake in very sizeable profits
itself: it was the largest profiteer, for example, in the Vegetable
Fats consortium, from which it made 16,000,000 francs, and in
the Petrol Consortium, which yielded it 25,000,000 francs'
profit in a mere nine months. In addition, however, businessmen in the consortia were able, by the astute manipulation of
privileges, to make a great deal of money also, as for example
Rocca of Marseille did out of agricultural oil-cake. Industrialists
quickly became skilful at exploiting government regulations,
which therefore had to be constantly altered. Some used
government institutions to break their rivals: thus the National
Dye Company was set up with state assistance, by a group of
industrialists and bankers, to challenge the Saint-Gobain
Company, which for its part used the war to extract subsidies
from the government, enabling it to re-equip at very little cost
to itself. One armaments manufacturer, Louis Loucheur,
got himself appointed minister of armaments and then, after the
war, minister of industrial reconstruction. This did not guarantee industry against excessive state interference, but on the
contrary increased it, for Loucheur quickly turned from poacher
into gamekeeper, and did much to increase state control; but
his activity showed how biased such control could be, benefiting
some firms and harming others. A considerable number of
businessmen entered the war ministries: this set up precedents
for the interpenetration of government and industry, but also
revealed its dangers when private interests were involved.[1]

[1] Jean Galtier-Boissière, *Histoire de la grande guerre 1914–18* (1959), 293; Albert

The proliferation of regulations and officials did little, in the end, to prevent vast profits being made, in a perfectly legal way, out of the war. The Aciéries de France's profits rose from 2,743,000 francs in 1913 to 11,000,000 in 1915; those of the Chambon-Feugerolles Steel Company from one to ten million. An investment company was formed which offered subscribers a return of their capital through dividends within six months and profits greater than the capital every six months. Manufacturers of shells, at least at the beginning of the war, were able to make profits of between 50 and 75 per cent. But it was not only Renault, making tanks, or Boussac, selling the state cloth for its aeroplanes, who did well. The milkmen were able to buy supplies at 17 centimes from farmers and sell them in Paris for up to 60 centimes, and greengrocers to sell Rhône peaches for *fifty* times what they had paid for them. Of course, it was not only the French state which could be exploited: the British and American armies made the fortune of tradesmen wherever they went (notably Rouen and Tours). But the French state's economic activities were publicly discredited by some notable scandals, which distracted attention from its less dramatic but ultimately more important innovations. The expenditure of 203,000,000 francs on setting up an arsenal at Roanne, which never manufactured more than 15,000,000 francs' worth of armaments, showed how the state could plunge into an appallingly expensive mess of mismanagement and inter-ministerial rivalry, beneficial only to the contractors who fed it with useless equipment. The plan to introduce profit-sharing and productivity bonuses, and to run the arsenal with a board of directors consisting both of bureaucrats and of private industrialists indicated, however, the direction that state intervention would ultimately take. There were occasions when the state did benefit the consumer in an easily visible form, as for example when it produced the National Shoe (a simple form of footwear, at half the normal price, to counter the shortage of shoes), but the manufacturers whom it commissioned to make this were reluctant to co-operate, and the comparatively small numbers that were produced quickly got into the hands of black-market profiteers. There were more examples of failure

Aftalion, *L'Industrie textile en France pendant la guerre* (1925), 113–14; G. Perreux, *La Vie quotidienne pendant la grande guerre* (1966), 169–76.

than of success. The symbol of all this planning was perhaps the scheme making schoolchildren collect horse-chestnuts as a substitute for cattle fodder, which produced only great rotting piles at village halls, with no one to take them away.[1]

The state's new role during the war was not the result of any doctrinal or political inspiration, but gradually adopted by force of circumstance, and implemented by conservative politicians. Its whole interventionist apparatus was dismantled after the war, but again a series of crises led to the revival of parts of it and the invention of new forms. The growth of the state's power was, with only a few exceptions, not due to socialist ministries or even to socialist pressure, which is one reason why the political history of these years is so misleading. The political parties were not the forces behind the gradual transformation of the country's economic organisation that took place between the wars. It was under a conservative government that the law of 9 September 1919 laid it down that in future all concessions of mining rights to private companies should involve a share of all profits earned being paid to the state, with a share being reserved also to the workers. It was the same government which in 1919–20 decided that the state should use the ships it had bought in the war, or obtained in reparations, to start a state merchant navy. But this was mismanaged so scandalously that it was disbanded in 1921, at a loss of some 300,000,000 francs.[2] Before the war, the state had given subsidies to encourage shipbuilding; it had distributed over 600,000,000 francs between 1881 and 1914, but France had nevertheless fallen from second to fifth place among the world's merchant navies; and until 1902 these subsidies were given preferentially for the construction of sailing boats, in the belief that there was still a great commercial future for them. After the war, however, the state demanded more than prestige in return. In 1920 it turned the Compagnie des Messageries Maritimes into a mixed company, whose

[1] J. F. Godfrey, 'Bureaucracy, Industry and Politics in France during the First World War' (unpublished doctoral thesis, Oxford, 1975); G. Olphe Gaillard, *Histoire économique et financière de la guerre 1914–18* (1923); Raymond Guildhon, *Les Consortiums en France pendant la guerre* (1924); M. Veissière, *Les Transformations du commerce français pendant et après la guerre* (1921).

[2] M. Roubion, *La Flotte d'état en France* (Paris thesis, 1923); L. Roux, *La Marine marchande française* (Paris thesis, 1923).

losses would be guaranteed by the state, but which would yield 80 per cent of its profits to the state, if it made any. In 1933 the state took over the Compagnie générale transatlantique (founded by the Saint-Simonian Péreire in 1861) which, carried away by its prosperity in the 1920s, had committed itself too optimistically in new ventures rendered ruinous by the Great Crash. The *Île de France* (1927), on which the most famous people in the world crossed the Atlantic, was a magnificent ship, but it now lost money, as did also the company's tourist and hotel subsidiaries, premature heralds of an industry stifled by the depression. The state became the majority shareholder, but in co-operation with the private shareholders who still nominated to one-third of the seats on the board. The state subsidy system, which made possible the *Normandie* (1935, the largest and fastest ship ever built), was thus, in part, rationalised; and the state ensured, in return, that the company paid wages approved by it and by the trade unions.[1] The law of 1922 organising the country's electricity distribution system provided that the state should pay for the strategically important network, but that the cost of the remaining lines should be shared roughly equally between it and private industry; the concessions to companies, however, would be for a limited period and would revert to the state. The basis of a nationalised industry was thus laid down very early. The state discovered that it could get very considerable control over industry and very sizeable profits from it without actually having to buy more than a minority share in it, and this is what it set about doing. Thus the Compagnie française des pétroles was set up between 1924 and 1931 with the state buying only 35 per cent of the shares, but getting 40 per cent of the votes on the board and the additional right to nominate two government commissioners to sit on it, with a power of veto on its decisions. The state got a larger share of the company's profits than its contribution warranted (following the precedent set by the law on mining concessions) and it also had a right to buy up to 80 per cent of the company's petrol if it so desired.[2]

[1] Edmond Lanier, *Compagnie générale transatlantique* (1962); R. Matignon, *La Compagnie générale transatlantique depuis la guerre* (Bordeaux thesis, 1937); G. Fabry, *De l'intervention directe de l'État dans les compagnies de navigation maritime* (Paris thesis, 1934).

[2] Edgar Faure, *La Politique française du pétrole* (Paris law thesis, 1938); Jean Rondot, *La Compagnie française des pétroles* (1962).

Long before the formal nationalisation of the railways, the state had virtually turned them into a public service, by forcing its own tariff policy on the companies, which meant that the state cheapened certain forms of transport, effectively lowering the price of certain goods and stimulating the growth of commuter suburbs. The railways had of course been built partly with the aid of government grants or guarantees, and the state was expecting to recover ownership of all the lines between 1950 and 1960. It already enjoyed free transport on the railways for its own employees and the army. In the inter-war years, however, it made the railways into a formal model of a 'mixed economy' company. In 1921 a Conseil Supérieur des Chemins de Fer was established to unify the policies of the seven railway companies and to share out operating losses between them; in 1933 the government obtained the right to nominate two of the directors in each company; and finally in 1937 the Société Nationale des Chemins de Fer was founded which established a single national system. But this represented neither confiscation of the companies' assets (which the socialists, and notably Jules Moch, advocated on the ground that they had failed to provide adequate services), nor buying them out (which would have cost the state a vast amount, and would have freed the companies of their debts to the state), but a compromise. The SNCF was a private company, in which the state was given 51 per cent of the shares. The companies remained in existence as shareholders of remaining stock. The thirty-three directors of the SNCF were to include twelve representatives of the state, twelve of the companies, four of the staff, three *ex officio* and two 'eminent' men nominated by the government. The employees of the railway thus did not become civil servants, but it was planned that the companies would gradually be bought out and that the state would acquire full control in 1982.[1]

In 1934 a law on road transport ensured that lorries should not compete too freely against the railways: the carriers were subjected to state control and required to reach an agreement with the railways to share the available traffic while the railways

[1] G. Pirou and M. Byé, *Les Cadres de la vie économique*, vol. 3: *les transports* (1942), 41–62; P. Espaillac, *La Réorganisation du régime des chemins de fer français* (Toulouse thesis, 1939); J. Laffite, *La SNCF* (Paris thesis, 1939).

were to close their smaller, unprofitable lines.[1] In under-populated regions, however, bus companies had since 1908 received subsidies, which in 1930 ran at 6,500,000 francs a year. Competition from cars was influenced by the taxes on them and, even more, on petrol (nearly 60 per cent of the price of which consisted of taxes), but the car industry, thanks to its prosperity, was the most notable example of old-fashioned private enterprise among the new industries.

Air transport had started in the same way: there were eleven companies in 1920 and the service between Paris and London was provided by three different rivals. But the principle of state subsidy quickly entered the air industry and in the 1920s three-quarters of the income of the five companies that survived this competition came to be provided by the state. As a result, they were amalgamated in 1933 as Air-France, in which the state was allocated a 25 per cent share. The state did not prohibit other private companies from flying, but it undertook to subsidise only Air-France. In 1940 there were still five independent air companies, but all of them had a special relationship with the state. Air Bleu was saved by a contract to carry the country's internal mail. Air Afrique was founded in 1933 as an experiment in full state ownership. Air-France-Transatlantique (1937) was established jointly by Air-France and the Compagnie générale transatlantique. Air-Malgache (1937) was set up by the government of Madagascar. Aéro-Maritime was the only really independent and unsubsidised firm, owned by shipping interests, but it was subject to government supervision of its route to West Africa. Commercial aviation illustrates well the many varieties of 'mixed economy' evolved in these years. The Vichy regime tried to codify these with a view to strengthening the state's control.[2] This was the prelude to full-scale nationalisation which took place in 1945.

It is interesting that the economist who made himself the theorist of these changes, Brocard of Nancy, saw this increase in state activity as only a function of the state's duty to encourage the development of industry, and as only carrying out one step in the transition from a local to an international economy.[3]

[1] Eugène Harter, *Les Chemins de fer français devant la concurrence de l'automobile* (Aix thesis, 1936).   [2] Statut de l'aviation marchande, 19 September 1941.
[3] L. Brocard, *Les Conditions générales de l'activité économique* (1934).

There is no evidence, however, that there was any coherent plan behind the successive *ad hoc* arrangements made with individual firms and industries. Many state take-overs were unwilling ones, designed to avert a crisis, as those of the Alsace-Lorraine and B.N.C. banks in 1930. Only rarely did the state seek complete ownership: the Alsace Potash Mines, ceded by the Germans, were an exception, and an exception also in the sense that they made large profits. The state was generally saddled with the ailing or experimental part of the economy. The nationalisation of the armaments industry in 1936 was, it is true, aimed at ending the profiteering of the 'death merchants'. The vast increase in municipal services was also largely inspired by socialist doctrines, for the socialists had a far greater hold on the country at a local level. Hitherto the Conseil d'État had opposed the efforts of town councils to take on tasks which private enterprise had carried out, but these legal barriers were broken down between the wars, and municipal transport, swimming baths, wash-houses, and even cinemas and groceries, were set up. Industry and commerce were still largely in private hands in 1939, but the state intervened far more than ever before and public control was extending to actual management in many spheres. The nationalisations of 1944–6 were thus not revolutionary.[1]

Private property no longer enjoyed the sacred status it had had in the nineteenth century. The Declaration of the Rights of Man proclaimed it to be inviolable. The state, since then, considered it to be one of its main functions to protect private property, and individuals seemed to make the accumulation of private property one of the main purposes of their lives. That public interest could override the inviolability of property was acknowledged in the law of 1841 which allowed expropriation for urban development, but the assumption still was that the individual had rights of paramount importance and the juries set up to assess compensation were composed of ordinary local people who were very generous in the sums they awarded. The courts limited expropriation to what was strictly necessary: a house had either to be positively and irremediably insalubrious[2] or actually in the path of a new street

---

[1] B. Chenot, *Les Entreprises nationalisées* (1956).
[2] Law of 13 April 1850.

for it to be possible to expropriate and demolish it. In 1918, however, a new law allowed whole zones to be expropriated, the amount of compensation was considerably limited, and the state began levying a capital appreciation tax on surrounding properties which benefited from works constructed by it.[1] Before the war, the landlord of a house could rent and evict as he pleased. Now tenants were exonerated from carrying out their contracts with him, they were given security of tenure and their rents were fixed by law, at levels far lower than had hitherto prevailed. Even tenants of furnished accommodation were given protection, provided they were permanent residents and declared that they could find nowhere else to go. Only 'luxury houses' were exempted.[2]

Increasingly large portions of people's private wealth were demanded in taxation. The land tax, which had been 3·2 per cent in 1890, rose to 12 per cent in 1920 and 16 per cent by 1939. The tax on industrial profits, which had been inaugurated in 1917 at 4·5 per cent, rose to 9·6 per cent in 1924 and 15 per cent in 1927. The tax on dividends, begun in 1872 at 3 per cent, reached 10 per cent in 1920, 18 per cent in 1926 and finally could in some cases be as high as 36 per cent. When one sold property in the nineteenth century one had to pay the state a tax of 5·5 per cent; in 1905 this was raised to 7 per cent, in 1920 to 10 per cent, and by 1939 it was 14·6 per cent. The inheritance of property was no longer principally a family matter, for the state made itself part-heir of every estate, and by the Second World War its share could be as high as 25 per cent when the property devolved to a child, but when it went to very distant relatives the state could receive as much as 80 per cent.[3] In 1913 the share of the national income collected in taxation was 8 per cent, but in the inter-war period it was between 12 and 15 per cent.[4] There were of course loud protests against this. The increase in taxation did not represent a greater sense of community. On the contrary, the effect of

[1] Jean Nory, *Le Droit de propriété et l'intérêt général* (Lille thesis, 1923); Auguste Étienne, *La Notion d'expropriation: son évolution* (Montpellier thesis, Nîmes, 1926); Louis Boudet, *De l'expropriation conditionnelle* (Toulouse thesis, 1926).

[2] Paul Muselli, *Du Conflit entre propriétaires et locataires et de sa réglementation dans la législation et la jurisprudence actuelle* (Aix thesis, 1928).

[3] Camille Roser, *La Fiscalité française devant l'opinion publique* (1940), 67–72.

[4] A. Sauvy, op. cit., vol. 4 (1975), 100.

the increase was to stimulate ingenuity among taxpayers in avoiding their obligations. The high rates were tolerated because they remained largely theoretical. In 1937 only 1,652,537 people in fact paid income tax, even though the country had 11,000,000 electors. Most of these taxpayers had been declared by their employers and so could not avoid paying; the self-employed got away more lightly: only one-half of the liberal professions paid income tax. The extreme complexity of the tax laws and the very unequal way in which they distributed the burden produced an almost universal feeling that the taxes were unfair and avoidance of them justifiable.[1] However, direct taxation was still much lower in France than in the rest of Europe.[2]

The important innovation of this period was the taxation of companies. This took two forms. In 1917 the turnover tax was invented, and transformed in 1936 into the production tax (which differed in that it was levied only once on each product). This is the ancestor of the value-added tax which was to become so popular with governments in the next generation. The second way in which money was levied from businesses was through the taxation of profits and dividends. The tax on dividends in 1913 had represented only 3 per cent of all the taxes levied by the state but by 1938 provided it with one-eighth of its income. By 1930 the capitalist had to pay 15 per cent tax on his dividends, and then 18 per cent income tax, plus duties when he bought or sold his shares, and altogether he could expect to keep no more than about 60 per cent of his income. Dividends moreover failed to keep up with the cost of living. In the chemical industry between 1913 and 1930, the changing distribution of income may be seen from this table:

Wages rose from	46·98 to 56·79%
Taxes rose from	6·23 to 18·27%
Dividends fell from	47·77 to 24·92%

This, of course, did not mean that capitalists necessarily became poorer, for all sorts of strategems were invented to conceal profits. It was in this period that businesses began to spend

[1] François Pietri, *Justice et injustice fiscale* (1933).
[2] It accounted for about one-sixth of all taxation in 1913, and about one-fifth in 1938.

lavishly on luxurious offices, with desks covered in morocco leather, standing on fine oriental carpets. Profits were used to set up subsidiary companies, yielding rich fees to the directors. In the 1920s about a thousand firms issued multiple-vote shares which turned them into family fiefs.[1] But all this meant that saving, which had been the foundation of nineteenth-century economics, was no longer possible in the old, simple way.

By far the heavist tax of all, and the greatest obstacle to saving, was, however, inflation. Between 1913 and 1948, whole-sale prices rose 105 times, and the price of gold 174 times. As against the dollar, the franc was worth in 1939 about one-seventh of what it had been in 1913.[2] Nothing like this had been known since the Revolution of 1789, whose soon-worthless paper money (*assignats*) had left a profound mistrust of all alternatives to gold. The effect of inflation now was rather more complex, because it was difficult to understand what was happening, and the same people could both benefit and lose by it. The first cause of inflation was government borrowing to pay for the First World War, but the press generally attri-buted inflation to foreign speculators. Successive governments showed themselves equally bewildered, and took totally opposed measures to cure the trouble, even though they were the main beneficiaries. Devaluation, deflation, reflation, confidence, stabilisation, the destruction of the *Mur d'Argent* (the mysterious financiers who seemed to be capable of deciding whether the state should be bankrupted or not) were formulae that econo-mists applied like desperate doctors dabbling in miracle cures. Thought on the matter was dominated by a desire to return to the good old days, when exchange rates were stable, and prices remained fixed for years on end—or so it (falsely) seemed in retrospect. In 1925 a subscription was opened to save the country by voluntary contributions, as though the state was an old man come on bad times, and in need of charity. Virtually no one saw that the state had never been so rich.

[1] Jacques Launey, *L'Évolution comparative des charges de l'industrie française* (Paris thesis, 1931), 249, 337; Désiré Dhamelincourt, *L'Accroissement des charges fiscales en France depuis la guerre 1914–18* (Lille thesis, 1939), 271.

[2] 1913 = 5·18 francs to the dollar; 1921 13·49; 1922 12·33; 1923 16·58; 1924 19·32; 1925 21·23; 1926 31·44; 1927–32 25·50; 1933 20·57; 1934 15·22; 1935 15·15; 1936 16·70; 1937 25·14; 1938 34·95; 1939 39·83; 1940–3 43·80; 1944 44·80; 1946–7 119·10; 1948 308·47. See André Bisson, *L'Inflation française 1914–1952* (1953).

In 1914 it was in debt to the tune of one year of national income. It had paid for the war by borrowing and so in 1921 its debt was two and a half times the national income. But inflation reduced this back to the 1914 level by 1929. It did not have to resort to any drastic socialist measures like capital levies but this in effect was what inflation achieved. Between 1914 and 1929 the state made a profit of about 1,000 million francs, which meant the transfer to it of three years and four months of national income at 1929 levels. The share of private incomes in the national income fell by about one-half. The state held its expenditure steady and indeed slightly reduced it between 1930 and 1935, but it was then able to increase it by almost 60 per cent in the years 1935–8.

Despite inflation, the national income rose between the wars by 0·9 per cent per annum on average, that is 20 per cent in all. Inflation was a disaster only to some people. The real earnings of labourers were 46 per cent higher in 1939 than in 1914. People with mortgages, once obsequious debtors, were turned into property owners. Though the state did best out of inflation, its gains were obscured by the fact that senior civil servants, by contrast, had their real earnings cut by 34 per cent. The worst losers of all were those who had lent the state money, the *rentiers*. They did even worse with their foreign investments, which were in some cases (notably Russian ones) complete losses. Shareholders in French companies lost about 43 per cent in the 1930s alone. Because prices were rising, investment had to become more speculative, with a view to capital appreciation rather than dividend income, and the speculation inevitably produced great losses as well as great—if impermanent—gains. The majority of the country was probably more prosperous, but this redistribution of wealth, on principles which were more mysterious, arbitrary and uncontrollable than ordinary taxation, made adaptation difficult.[1] The state had once been the protector of the saver, and though the *rente* did fluctuate 20 per cent up or down in the course of the nineteenth century, it was possible to rely on the state for a regular income from one's savings.[2] The state did not wish to

---

[1] A. Sauvy, op. cit. (1965–75), 1. 291; 2. 406–8, 418; 4. 173.

[2] P. Soulaine and L. Deneri, *L'État et l'épargne 1789–1919* (1919) gives the annual price of state bonds.

abandon the saver now, for it generally agreed with him that devaluation was equivalent to national bankruptcy, shameful as well as impolitic, but in practice it sacrificed him, rather than itself. It was in this period, therefore, that the state ceased to regard the preservation of acquired wealth as one of its major functions.[1] This did not mean, as many people believed, the end of the influence of the middle classes, though it did involve a change in their way of life. The radical *Dépêche de Toulouse* declared in 1926 that the cause of the disarray was 'love of lucre', but also 'prodigality'. People were spending more easily, bargaining less, thinking less about economising. The radical leader Herriot sent a circular to teachers urging them to drink less strong coffee and to put less sugar in it, but he was preaching against an inexorable tendency.[2] Inflation meant people had to earn more and spend it while their money was still worth something. This was one of the roots of the expansionist economy that was ultimately adopted. The middle classes made a new kind of deal with the state to achieve this.

Instead of dedicating itself to the preservation of private property, the state began to provide pensions, as an alternative form of security for old age. The law of 1910[3] had made a start, but in so hesitant a way, demanding such small contributions and guaranteeing such totally inadequate pensions, that though 3,430,000 people had entered the scheme by 1913, only 1,728,000 were left in 1922 and these quickly diminished. Old-age insurance schemes run by employers had also generally been regarded with disfavour by the workers, because they were not infrequently used as a way of blackmailing them into obedience, whereas the whole point of saving was that it made one independent of one's boss. The question was debated in parliament from 1924 to 1930, by which time objections to compulsory contributions had virtually disappeared. The law passed in 1930 guaranteed old people 40 per cent of their wages and in 1941 a uniform fixed pension of 3,600 francs was introduced. The retiring age was set at sixty, the lowest in Europe, but this was more a way of combating unemployment

[1] André Bouton, *La Fin des rentiers* (1932).
[2] M. Perrot, *La Monnaie et l'opinion publique en France et en Angleterre de 1924 à 1936* (1955), 169, 172.
[3] See Zeldin, *Politics and Anger*, 345.

than an institutionalisation of the middle-class ideal of early
retirement. Since the number of people over sixty in France
had increased between 1881 and 1941 by 25 per cent, the
problem of the old had taken on new importance. The pension
scheme—a compromise between the English and German
systems—was run partly by the state and partly by professional
bodies, but because contributions were fixed at a low rate,
serious problems of financing would soon arise; and moreover
only about half of the working population was affected: peasants
and artisans, as usual, resisted these new-fangled ideas.[1] In
1938, likewise, accident insurance, which a law had first sought
to encourage in 1898,[2] was made compulsory for all employees,
and rates of compensation were substantially raised. It was
recognised that accidents at work produced casualties almost
as heavy as those sustained in war: between 1920 and 1938
50,000 people were killed and 150,000 permanently incapaci-
tated in this way. The state left it to private insurance companies to provide the cover, before taking on the burden itself
by nationalising these in 1945. All these forms of insurance had
been pioneered by capitalist employers, as a way, some workers
argued, of shielding them from the influence of the revolutionaries; the employers' schemes had been resented, and the
state emerged as the impartial guarantor: but this only had the
effect of making the masses, in various degrees, civil servants.
This was seen most noticeably in the expansion of family
allowances. By 1932 virtually all large and middle scale
companies were paying these, and they were then made
compulsory, but always at the expense of the employers. In
1938 however the state began participating financially in these
allowances. The Vichy government so increased the rates that a
worker with a large family could get more in family allowances than he earned in wages.[3] The theory developed that a
man was entitled to a minimum living wage, a professional
wage which recognised his skill and thirdly a wage to maintain
his family. What he actually did at work was only part of the

[1] P. Waline, *Législation sociale appliquée* (1943), 135–89; Henri Hatzfeld, *Du
paupérisme à la sécurité sociale 1850–1940* (1971), on the ideological debates.
[2] See vol. 1, 667. The law of 1898 was extended to cover commerce in 1906,
forestry in 1914, agriculture in 1922 and domestic servants in 1923.
[3] The 1941 rate meant that a man with five children received 120 per cent of
his salary in family allowances.

reason why he was paid, and when he was out of work, his allowances continued to be paid.

The theorists wondered whether this would mean that people would work less hard. The Vichy regime had just rather optimistically made the cult of work one of its principles. It would take another generation before the implications of this were realised.[1] The problem of why a man should work at all, particularly when he was offered only dull and repetitive work, if he could find charity or the state to support him, could not be raised in this period. The workers, since 1848, had demanded the right to work: they had not been interested in unemployment insurance, except on the basis of mutual aid amongst themselves. Full unemployment insurance was therefore instituted only in 1958; but in the inter-war years the state took unemployment relief out of the hands of private charity. The municipal *bureaux de bienfaisances* were expanded (by decrees of 1926 and 1931), so that the state subsidised them to the extent of between 60 and 90 per cent on what they paid out to the unemployed. In addition the state gave subsidies to a host of union and mutual societies which also helped those out of work. Its intervention was thus cloaked in the garb of favouritism and influence, that characteristic of the Third Republic which perpetuated the arbitrariness of the monarchy.[2] Assistance in illness likewise involved a compromise between free medical treatment and the traditional capitalist system. There was free medicine in the railways and mines, but the doctors disliked this, wishing to keep their status as a liberal profession, and their ability to fix their fees in each case. The law of 1930 instituted a system whereby patients could choose their own doctors, and then get reimbursed by the state. The reimbursement returned roughly half of the fees paid and only 20 per cent of pharmaceutical and hospital expenses. The law covered only ten million people, excluding the self-employed. All this had to be paid for ultimately by taxation, and it was largely through increased charges on employers that the costs were met.[3]

[1] 'Jeunesse en rupture', *Autrement* (Jan. 1975), especially 58–67.
[2] Claude Lasry, *Lutte contre le chômage et finances publiques 1929–1937* (1938).
[3] Henry C. Galant, *Histoire politique de la sécurité sociale française 1945–52* (1955); P. Waline, op. cit. 115–38; G. N. Pipkin, *Social Politics and Modern Democracies* (1931), vol. 2.

It may seem contradictory that this was achieved despite all the obstacles the Third Republic supposedly raised against reform. There are two complementary explanations. On the one hand, this social legislation was pushed through by the determined efforts of a few men, who showed the power that the civil service could exert. It was Millerand who originally got the discussions going, after being impressed by a German insurance scheme he saw functioning in Alsace, and he got the Alsatian deputy Jourdain to produce a bill in co-operation with Georges Cahen (who was in charge of pensions at the ministry of labour) and with Antonelli, a professor of economics who was also a deputy. Together these men proposed a very wide-ranging plan of insurance, embracing all aspects of life, and foreshadowing the grandiose plans of the post-1945 era, which, like it, were the result of the combined efforts of professors, civil servants and technicians. The great problem was to get agreement from vested interests. This was achieved through the efforts of Raoul Péret, who was minister of justice under Tardieu but also president of the Mutualists Organisation, and Gaston Roussel, who was in charge of the Mutuality Department in the ministry of labour. The Mutualists were determined not to lose their dominant position in insurance. Roussel got them to sign an agreement, at the ministry of labour, with the Confédération Générale du Travail for a division of spheres of influence. The employers, through their spokesman Robert Pinot, declared that the proposals of the bill 'tend to nothing less than a modification of the traditional physiognomy of French society in its most characteristic traits' and that 'a totally different mentality would arise' if it was passed. The ministry got them to agree by withdrawing proposals for the equal representation of employers and workers in the management of the insurance scheme and by a reduction of the employers' contributions. The agreement of the peasants and doctors was moreover obtained by various compromises. The law of 1930 was a triumph of negotiation under the guidance of the civil servants.[1]

The second reason why the insurance scheme was introduced was that the 1920s enjoyed exceptional economic prosperity,

[1] René Hubert, 'Histoire philosophique de l'institution des assurances sociales en France', *L'Année politique française et étrangère*, vol. 5 (1930), 273–315.

comparable to that of the 1850s, and producing a new faith in prosperity through expansion. The basis of this revival was, first, the reconstruction in the territories damaged by the war and secondly the development of a number of new industries. The revival was very uneven, affecting only some sections of the economy.

Growth of Industrial Production 1913–29 (%)

Textiles	−8
Paper	+6
Leather	+19
Mines	+23
Building	+23
Metallurgy	+29
Mechanical Industries	+57
Rubber	+761

Coal production rose by 35 per cent (1913–30), though productivity per man-hour fell by 7·7 per cent. In the iron mines, however, productivity per man-hour rose by 41 per cent. Steel production trebled, making France the largest producer in Europe after Germany, and the equal of England: Schneider of Le Creusot modernised its equipment, diversified into ship-building and armaments, expanded into Czechoslovakia (Skoda), Hungary (petrol), Romania (aluminium), Poland and elsewhere. The French car industry became the largest in the world after that of the U.S.A. The electrical industry stimulated the growth of a whole variety of new enterprise, significantly organised in large firms and cartels with international links, under the dominance of the American G.E.C.[1] Though the textile industry as a whole failed to adapt itself to new conditions, the rayon industry (which owed its inception to a Frenchman, the comte de Chardonnet, a graduate of the Polytechnic and the École des Ponts et Chaussées who founded the first rayon factory in 1890) grew very fast in the 1920s, when over twenty firms were established to produce 'artificial silk'. In this decade, world production decupled, but France competed successfully, reducing its prices by 70 per cent,

[1] Cf. Robert Lecat, *L'Industrie de la construction électrique en France* (Aix thesis, 1933).

emphasising cheapness rather than quality and seeking large-
volume production; it was only after 1932 that it ceased
expanding and was overtaken by its rivals.[1] The chemical
industry, though not as insignificant before 1914 nor as dependent on Germany as is usually believed (it was in dyes that
the French were weak, and to a certain extent in pharma-
ceuticals, but not in electrochemistry or in the soda industry),
not only expanded in scope, but increased its productivity per
man-hour by about 60 per cent. Saint-Gobain, once a glass
works, became a giant international concern, with subsidiaries
in Germany and Italy, producing a wide variety of chemicals.
France became Europe's second-largest producer of aluminium. Its banks, which before the war had preferred to
finance foreign governments, now gave considerably more
backing to domestic industry. The Crédit National founded in
1919 (on the model of Napoleon III's Crédit Foncier) to
finance the repair of war damage, added an element of state
sponsored and directed industrial investment.[2] The result was
that exports of industrial products doubled in volume and the
national income increased twice as fast in the 1920s as in the
decade before the war.[3]

The most outstanding representative of the new industrial
management that was responsible for this was perhaps Ernest
Mercier (1878–1955). He had the typical antecedents which
made him a favourite of the regime: his grandfather had been
a Protestant republican who had emigrated during the Second
Empire, to found a pharmacy in Algeria; his father was mayor
and a leader of the radical party in Constantine; he himself
married the daughter of an anticlerical senator and, secondly,
the niece of Captain Dreyfus. He was educated at the Polytechnic, but left the state's service to enter private industry.
In course of time he became managing director of France's
leading electrical supply company, and later president of the

---

[1] Léon Robert, *L'Industrie de la rayonne en France* (Paris thesis, 1943), good graph,
p. 138. Cf. Pierre Clerget, *Les Industries de la soie en France* (1925).
[2] H. Laufenberger, *Enquête sur les changements de structure de crédit et de la banque*:
vol. 1, *Les Banques françaises* (1940), 225; Jacques Alexandre, *Les Grands Établissements financiers et le trésor public de 1919 à 1941* (Montpellier thesis, published Toulouse, 1942).
[3] A. Sauvy, op. cit. 1. 259–74; Claude Fohlen, *La France de l'entre-deux-guerres*
(1966), 71–83.

Compagnie française des pétroles. It was indicative of new trends that this child of the republic should have preferred industry to politics or literature. In 1925 he visited the U.S.A., as a guest of the General Electric Company, and was deeply impressed both by American prosperity and by the prestige that businessmen enjoyed there. He made himself the advocate of national reorganisation, in a style which was called neo-Saint-Simonian. He founded a movement Le Redressement français (1927), which won about 20,000 influential subscribers and which produced a host of pamphlets urging the modernisation of industry by the concentration of firms, standardisation in manufacturing, the stimulation of both higher productivity and higher consumption. French individualism, Mercier declared, was very pleasant, but obsolete. He hailed the election of Hoover to the presidency as a sign of the times: 'the most powerful people on earth, the American people, have elected an engineer as their leader'. He argued that government could no longer be left to politicians who spent their time arguing over ideology: more power must be given to the president and he should rely more on experts and technicians for advice. The efficiency of Henry Ford was the best way to triumph over Marx. The workers should be made happy not by giving them equal wealth, but by the possibility of self-realisation: new forms of industrial relations, rule by an élite of managers, rather than more democracy, was the answer. Mercier denounced fascism as giving too much power to the state. Corporatism he at first thought impractical because the workers were too attached to the class struggle, though he later saw virtues in its aim; but his ideal was an economy based on 'collaboration between producers and the state' and relying on planning by consent. He was an ardent European in the 1920s, and became president of the French Pan-Europe Committee, though he maintained that France would always have a special role to play as a nation, exercising its 'moral mission'. Mercier, however, was too obviously a rich man (his annual income in the 1930s was on average 2,500,000 francs) for him not to be regarded as primarily a defender of the interests of big business. Léon Blum denounced his doctrines as 'industrial Bonapartism'. Mercier's sponsorship of a war-veterans' journal *Nos plaisirs* and a workers' sports magazine *Le Muscle*, and his use of money in elections, even though he claimed to be above party, made the charges against him plausible. In fact big business was far from being united behind him, as the perfumer Coty's attacks on him publicly revealed. The variations in emphasis among industrialists, in their attitudes to the state and to democracy, were very considerable. Mercier's own views were probably more liberal than those of many of his supporters. His committee included Marshal Foch, Clémentel and Giscard d'Estaing but also Alibert (minister of justice in 1940), Hubert Lagardelle (minister of labour in 1942) and Lucien Romier (adviser to Pétain). His importance, however, lies not in the precise detail of his doctrine, but in the publicity he gave to the idea of technocracy. His daughter married Wilfred Baumgartner, who became governor of the Bank of France and minister of finance in the Fifth Republic. That was when his hopes, in modified form, became realities, when technocracy found a *modus vivendi* with parliamentary government.[1]

Three different attempts were made, by political methods, to bring about a new relationship between the state and society: Tardieu's 'politics of prosperity', Blum's Popular Front and Pétain's Vichy state. They were quite different in their ideological inspiration and in their character; all three of them failed; but they can be seen in retrospect to have the common element that they all sought to give a new role to the state and to modify, though not altogether or immediately to abolish, capitalism. Their ideas, and their failure, contributed powerfully to the formation of Gaullist France, which was in some ways a compromise between them.

André Tardieu (prime minister 1930–2) was intellectually one of the most brilliant figures of the Third Republic. He won the highest success in every field he entered. He came top in the *concours général*, top in the entrance examination to the École Normale (which he took because it was 'reputedly the hardest'), top in the entrance examination to the foreign service and then in that to the ministry of the interior. He became political secretary to the prime minister at the age of twenty-three and two years later one of the country's highest-paid journalists,

[1] Richard F. Kuisel, *Ernest Mercier, French Technocrat* (Univ. of California Press, 1967).

with regular columns (in the *Figaro* and then *Le Temps*) which had an international reputation and influence. He published a book on contemporary affairs almost every year. He combined with all this professorships at the École des Sciences Politiques and at the École de Guerre, and a guest lectureship at Harvard (for which latter job he learnt English). During the war, he was the main civilian adviser of the commander-in-chief Joffre and after it, he was Clemenceau's right-hand man in the making of the peace treaty; he showed his administrative ability also as High Commissioner in the United States. The legends about his amazing industriousness, fluency and quickness of mind are innumerable: he was 'the most perfect intelligence I have ever known' said General Gamelin. Everything he wrote, he wrote straight off without corrections: it was even reported that when he was in Washington, in an oppressively hot summer, 'though he dozed off from time to time, his hand went on writing'. Clemenceau said to him: 'You are a Napoleon'. Tardieu had thought at first that he could exercise power best behind the scenes, arguing that the real force in democracy was not the government but public opinion, and he would specialise in organising and expressing it. He never claimed or even wished to be original. His gifts were for efficiency, hard work, action, and that is why he had such an admiration for the Americans, in whom he saw these qualities cultivated and valued. However, frustration at the obstacles imposed by parliamentary routine led him, inevitably, to seek ministerial office. After holding a succession of portfolios in the 1920s, he came prime minister, the first one of the inter-war years who did not represent continuity with the pre-1914 era. He announced his policy as being the inauguration of a new era and as facing up resolutely to the future.

His policy had two sides to it. First, it sought to get the reforms that had been trailing for years in endless discussion—sent back and forth between the two houses and their committees —passed rapidly. There was no innovation involved here, only more efficiency. He told the radicals, to whom he had vainly offered a large share of the posts in his cabinet, not to shoot him 'when I come before you bearing your children in my arms'. By fifteen laws and fifty decrees, he did indeed dispatch a lot of business rapidly, most notably the social insurance scheme and free education in the bottom form of the *lycées*. Though classified politically as moderate right wing, he carried out, like a punctilious civil servant, the policy of the moderate left which had the majority in the country. Secondly, he proposed a 'plan of national re-equipment' based on unprecedented state investment: the modernisation of agriculture by rural electrification, reafforestation, an institute of agronomic research, credit facilities and a radio network for the countryside (1,750 million francs); the improvement of health to combat depopulation and the stimulation of research and technical education (1,450 millions); the improvement of roads, ports, and transport (1,797 millions); and the development of the colonies (3,600 millions). This was his 'policy of prosperity', which aimed both to make the country richer and to yield such increased revenue for the treasury that no further taxation would be needed to pay for it. On the contrary, he capped his programme with tax reductions of 3,340 million francs. There was virtually no section of the community whose interests he did not promise to advance: he held out the prospect of increased production, profits and wages. This was the expression of the euphoria that the prosperity of the 1920s had created. It was ironical that Tardieu came to power just as the depression set in; but Tardieu's was also a policy to combat the depression, for he declared that 'the old and noble doctrine of *laissez-faire* . . . confronted with the present concentration of capital, size of firms and internationalisation of business, is no longer adequate. Whether we like it or not, the state must henceforth intervene where formerly it did not, it must take charge of things it used to ignore.' He wanted political reform to follow, to concentrate more power in the executive: 'the state must resume consciousness of its duties and of its rights'. The popular will must be given fuller expression by the use of referenda and by the institution of women's suffrage. Civilisation was in crisis and 'to defend our civilisation, France must be in good working order'. For a time Tardieu was able to galvanise parliament into action: he got it to agree to meet three times a day, even including Sundays, but he had to ask for votes of confidence sixty times to force compliance. He failed to win genuine backing for his policy in parliament. He spent too much time abroad, in discussion with the leaders of other nations. He was unable to create the institutions needed to give his policy a chance of success, or to overcome the republic's built-in suspicion of power.[1]

However, though Tardieu was a failure in parliamentary terms, important new developments began to take place off the political stage, and it is behind the scenes that new forces were being created for change. Lucien Romier, the historian whose *Explanation of Our Times* (1925) provided a breviary for the frustrated critics of French conservatism, pointed out that power would increasingly rest not with politicians, but with the civil servants and the administrators. Now some of these began to become more conscious of their role and to exert a new influence in economic affairs. While the parliamentary debates concentrated on the problem of military security and reparations, the inspectors of finance came to realise that their apparently routine functions could provide the basis for new methods in the formulation and execution of ministerial policy. Inspectors of finance, whose original function had been to audit state accounts, had gradually seen the scope of their activities widened to include private firms in receipt of state subsidies; as early as 1855 the railway companies had been subject to their investigations. They were not numerous (there were about seventy or eighty of them at any one time) but promotion was rapid since they were recognised as an élite corps, and inspectors in their thirties could hold very influential positions. About a quarter of them resigned to go into private industry (in the 1890s a half of them), and they came to constitute a kind of freemasonry which extended equally over the civil service and the largest firms in the country. 'It is to them', wrote one of them, 'that is due that sort of loyalty, that discipline and cohesion of a large part of private finance towards the directives and policy of ministers.'[2] Their importance was increased when for the first time in 1926 parliament

[1] Rudolf Binion, *Defeated Leaders* (New York, 1960), 197–337; Michel Missoffe, *La Vie volontaire d'André Tardieu* (1929); Louis Aubert et al., *André Tardieu* (1957); Louis Guitard, 'Portrait sentimental d'André Tardieu', *Les Œuvres libres*, no. 184 (Sept. 1961), 79–96; Marcel Prélot, 'La France en 1930 et 1931', *L'Année politique française et étrangère* (1932), 68–123; André Tardieu, *L'Épreuve du pouvoir* (1931), *La Réforme de l'état* (1934), and *La Révolution à refaire* (2 vols., 1936–7).

[2] François Pietri, *Le Financier* (1931), 85.

began the practice of delegating 'full powers' to the executive, and when in 1932 an under-secretary of state was appointed with the task of co-ordinating economic policy and seeking ways of expanding the economy. The civil service began organising itself for economic planning.[1]

The ideas which inspired it, however, came from outside, and mainly from the graduates of the Polytechnic. In 1930 Jean Coutrot founded the Polytechnic's Centre for Economic Studies with about seven or eight others, and by 1937 it had 1,200 members, 'comprising almost all those in France with economic expertise'. The meetings were originally held at the home of Yves Bouthillier (an inspector of finance who became a minister under both Paul Reynaud and Pétain) but later in the Polytechnic itself and sometimes in the great amphitheatre of the Sorbonne. Members of this centre were to be found as advisers to almost every government from the 1930s to the 1950s. Coutrot himself was brought into the Popular Front government as head of a committee to reorganise labour relations, but he turned up again as an adviser in the Vichy government; he was present in the room when Laval offered Belin (the trade union leader, who also attended these Polytechnic meetings) the ministry of industrial production. Charles Spinasse (originally a professor at the École des Arts et Métiers) became Blum's minister for the national economy, and in daily conferences brought together several others from the same group; Branger, who was still a young student at the Polytechnic, was brought in as adviser on transport policy and Alfred Sauvy, a young graduate of the school, as head of a new information section. It is true that most of the ideas of these men in Blum's government were challenged by the young lawyers whom Blum's radical allies brought into the ministry of commerce: the achievements were very limited. In 1942 Bichelonne, who had been the top graduate of his year at the Polytechnic, succeeded Belin as minister of industrial production, with Gérard Bardet (one of the earlier organisers of the Polytechnic Centre) and Henri Culman (an inspector of finance, who had been a *chef adjoint de cabinet de ministre* in the Popular Front, and whose writings made him one of the theorists of the Vichy regime's economic policy) as particularly influential

[1] Jean Meynaud, *La Technocratie. Mythe ou réalité* (1964).

civil servants behind the scenes. The importance of this Poly-
technic group was due not to its advocacy of a particular
doctrine but to the new approach to government that it caused
to be adopted. It contained many different shades of opinion:
Jacques Rueff, who was an upholder of classical liberal economics and who served as Laval's adviser in 1934, Roland
Boris, the president of the group, later adviser to de Gaulle and
Mendès-France and brother of Blum's minister, and Pierre
Massé, who became a commissioner for planning in the Fifth
Republic. Coutrot introduced the method of research by teams,
each specialising in one aspect of the economy; and this was
gradually adopted as a method for the formulation of government policy. These men differed about details but they were
agreed that economic planning had to play a key role in the
future. Coutrot's friends, the Guillaume brothers, produced
one of the earliest theoretical treatises on economic forecasting
and the use of mathematical techniques.[1]

Jean Coutrot was one of those men who exerted a great
influence on his contemporaries without ever attracting public
attention; even if he had not committed suicide in 1942, he
would probably have remained a source of inspiration rather
than become a public figure. Coutrot believed that France
needed a thorough reassessment of its whole way of life: 'we
need to rethink our epoch, to understand it and to create it'.
The reassessment must extend to the questioning of all accepted
notions, which had not been attempted since the Saint-
Simonians. There was much in his movement which recalled
these utopian thinkers and industrialists, many of whom had
also been graduates of the Polytechnic. Had Coutrot lived to
work out his ideas, he might perhaps have won a place in the
history of thought as important as theirs, for the range of his
interests was unusually wide and he attempted to stimulate a
new synthesis that incorporated the latest findings of the new
sciences. He followed up the creation of his group by establishing a 'centre for the study of human problems'. This
brought together a dazzling collection of thinkers: the political
scientist André Siegfried, the jurist Marcel Prélot, the psychiatrists Henri Wallon and Georges Matisse, the sociologists
Celestin Bouglé, Hyacinthe Dubreuilh and Georges Friedman,

[1] Philippe Bauchard, *Les Technocrates et le pouvoir* (1966).

the trade unionist Robert Lacoste, the industrialist Detoeuf; and Aldous Huxley, whose visions of the future excited them, was also present at their meetings. Coutrot was keen that a new body of technocrats, independent of big business and concerned only with the public welfare, should be formed to plan the new society, and that their efforts should be directed to all 'indispensable' spheres of activity. Though the stress of the Polytechniciens was on economics, in this second group it was more on psychology. The problem of hunger was in the process of being solved; the next obstacle was hate and fear. There should be no more talk about liberty and justice, which were too vague, but rather of concrete difficulties in human relations. These should be seen as having two sides, psychological and social. The time had come to plan for a better kind of human; the emotional development of man was lagging far behind his material progress. The frequency of neuroses showed that the 'equilibrium of the individual' needed much more attention: sexual relations needed to be understood better, to discover whether the sexual act should be dissociated from its sentimental and moral concomitants, so that it would be like a 'sporting match'; the effect of professional specialisation on human nature needed to be investigated, for what was economically progressive was not necessarily emotionally beneficial. He asked whether the family still had a value 'in times like ours, of rapid transition'. Psychology and genetics seemed to hold out the hope of control being achieved over men's sensibilities and internal energies. It would then be possible either to diminish men's need to hate, or to divert it against physical rather than human enemies, or to confine it to an internal struggle against certain aspects of one's own nature. He believed that until personal and national egoisms had been resolved, it was no use founding bodies like the League of Nations, because egoisms could not be reconciled. Contacts between classes would have to be increased, and the new methods of communication, including television (he foresaw its power), needed to be used beneficially so as to mitigate these egoisms. Coutrot wanted much more planning than France has adopted. But he did leave room for private property, arguing that the state should intervene only to prevent the abuse of property rights. As the lawyers pointed out, the courts had already refused to recognise absolute property rights. Coutrot was still in favour of individualism, but 'co-ordinated individualism', not 'anarchic' or 'corporalised' individualism. He gave a lot of attention to economics, but he called his book *Economic Humanism*. He was never precise about what this meant. His life is interesting for the trends of thought it reveals rather than for clear ideas.[1]

The planners of the Polytechnic were still very much a minority. The mass of French economists were opposed to the idea of a planned economy, as they affirmed at their congress in 1933. The tradition of economics teaching in the universities was essentially liberal. It is true that Professor Charles Gide (whose *Principles of Political Economy*, translated into fifteen languages, was said to have been the most successful economics book after Adam Smith and Marx) devoted his life to the co-operative movement.[2] But François Simiand argued that economic progress came from alternate phases of prosperity and depression and that it was wrong to try to abolish the depressions, which, like the floods of the Nile, could be put to good use.[3] The economists claimed that the country lacked the statistics which would be needed as a basis for an economy directed by the government—which was true enough—and that state intervention only caused even more chaos, as recent experience showed. They preferred to maintain their role as critics and analysts of the eclectic school. Gaetan Pirou and Roger Picard, leading economists at the Paris faculty of law, were above all enemies of dogmatism. French economists have been reproached for being ignorant of the work of Keynes, but wrongly so. Keynes, as the author of *The Economic Consequences of the Peace*, had long been unpopular in France, whose claims for reparations he had attacked. In 1938, within two years of the publication of Keynes's *General Theory*, Blum's second government was already incorporating its ideas into its programme. But French economists were faced by a deluge of other theories which kept them fully occupied. Their general attitude was one of suspicion of new-fangled ideas.

[1] Jean Coutrot, *Entretiens sur les sciences de l'homme* (1937), *De Quoi vivre* (1935), *L'Humanisme économique* (1936).

[2] G. Pirou, *Les Doctrines économiques en France depuis 1870* (4th edition, 1941), 208.

[3] F. Simiand, *Le Salaire, l'évolution sociale et la monnaie* (3 vols., 1932).

It was only in the 1950s that they began to train their pupils to assume a directing role in the economy.[1]

In 1904 Veblen argued that the important division in society was not between rich and poor but between the scientists and the defenders of the old rites. He saw in the engineers the representatives of the former, concerned only with efficiency, while businessmen were the conservatives and it was they who, absorbed by the desire for profits, were preventing mechanisation from yielding its full benefits. The engineers of France did indeed begin to see themselves in something like this light in the inter-war years. Apart from the few hundred graduates of the Polytechnic and the other prestigious *grandes écoles*, engineers as a whole still had a humble status. Industrialists treated them as little better than foremen, and even the more advanced ones valued only the engineer who specialised in the commercial side of business. Despite their qualifications, most engineers were subjected to the same factory discipline as workers: they had to clock in four times a day, they had to make excuses as to why they were late to the porter, just like the workers, and in their presence; they were forbidden to wash their hands in the last fifteen minutes of the working day (on the ground that they could not do anything useful with clean hands in so short a time); they had to wear numbers on their coats and have their briefcases searched when they went home. Despite the increasing specialisation of science, they were often unable to use their training, because industry hesitated to employ them, and they were forced to take jobs in any technical capacity that was offered, not necessarily their own. They received wages which were not much higher than those paid to foremen. However, their numbers were increasing. In 1934 the title of *ingénieur diplômé* was created and by 1938 ninety-three different schools were able to confer it. The domination of the Paris schools was not threatened, but there were now also institutions, variously called Engineering Schools (Marseille) or Technical Schools (Strasbourg) or Polytechnics (Institut Polytechnique de l'Ouest), all over the provinces, as well as specialised ones

[1] G. Pirou, *La Crise du capitalisme* (2nd edition, 1936); Bernard Lavergne, *Essor et décadence des idées politiques et sociales en France de 1900 à nos jours. Souvenirs personnels* (1965), memoirs of a professor of economics; Louis Baudin, *Le Corporatisme* (1942), on the 1936 economists' congress.

like the Institut électro-Technique de Grenoble or the École Supérieure d'Aéronautique. By 1938 between 2,500 and 3,000 engineers were graduating every year.[1] They began to demand a higher status. The graduates of the new schools began to question the superiority of the Polytechnic and to criticise it for being too theoretical, for not training its graduates in administration or in industrial relations, for teaching too much mathematics and not enough physics or chemistry. The Paris Chamber of Commerce established a School of Management which used the Harvard Business School's case-study techniques and which gave the ambitious engineers who attended it new pretensions.[2] Henri Fayol, a graduate of the École des Mines of Saint-Étienne who rose to be head of several mining and metallurgical companies, published a treatise on industrial management, which encouraged the engineers in their belief in their own importance.[3] The engineer, it was now said, ought to be the pivot of the new industrial system, the mediator between workers and capitalists, the organiser of wage agreements, the person who could distribute responsibilities and run nationalised industries. He should no longer be seen simply as a technician but as the main component of the new managerial class, the *cadres*. The *cadres*, wrote one of these engineers in 1943, were the new aristocracy, but they were at the same time rebels, rebels against conformity and routine; they were distinguished by the desire to command and to assume responsibility. After 1918 they did indeed begin to organise themselves into trade unions which argued that they were qualified to put France into better order, but were being excluded from making the important decisions.[4] In 1937 they combined into a single Federation of Engineers (F.N.S.I.) with 23,000 members and were able to conclude over thirty collective agreements with their employers within a year, which considerably improved their financial position. This however had the effect of keeping them cut off from the employers. They still had an

[1] In 1970 the figure was 7,500.

[2] Pierre Jolly, directeur du centre de perfectionnement dans l'administration des affaires, *L'Éducation du chef d'entreprise* (1931), and *Joie au travail et réformes de structure* (1938).

[3] H. Fayol, *Administration industrielle et générale* (1917).

[4] Syndicat des Ingénieurs chimistes (1918); Syndicat des Ingénieurs électriques (1919); Union des Ingénieurs français (1920), etc.

inferiority complex towards the Polytechniciens and the Inspectors of Finance, and they were mistrustful of the bankers whom they accused both of running and of emasculating industry. These animosities were superficial and gradually disappeared with the widening of the idea of the *cadres* after the Second World War. However the engineers were far from all being dynamic and progressive, just as their accusations against their employers were indiscriminate. The inter-war period, which saw their rise, also filled many of them with a deep desire for security; and the nationalised industries would find ready recruits among them.[1]

These developments were, to a certain extent, superficial, in that they did not alter the attitude of the workers towards the state: but that is what did change during the Popular Front. The trade union movement, as has been seen, was traditionally hostile to all governments and to political parties in general, and sought the liberation of the worker by his own efforts. From 1914 onwards the union leaders co-operated in the drafting of social legislation, participated in some government consultative councils and to a certain extent made the unions instruments of government policy.[2] But this did not mean that the masses as a whole ceased to look on the state as an enemy. In 1936 however the possibility that this might change was glimpsed, though briefly. The advent of the country's first socialist government created a sense of euphoria and liberation among the workers, a feeling that they could at last express themselves freely, in a way hardly ever before experienced. The importance of the Popular Front, on the psychological plane, can be compared only to the revolution of 1848 and the 'events' of 1968: in the reaction it stimulated among conservatives, it was like the Commune of 1871. The spontaneous occupation of factories by workers, which showed how fragile the rights of property owners were, was deeply unnerving and shocking to the rich. All the supporters of the Popular Front remembered this among the most moving experiences

[1] Henri Château, *Le Syndicalisme des techniciens en France* (Paris thesis, 1938); Pierre Alamigeon, *Les Cadres dans l'industrie et notamment dans la métallurgie* (Paris thesis, 1943, published Bar-sur-Aube); Yvon Gattaz, *Les Hommes en gris: ingénieurs, cadres, chefs d'entreprise* (1970); cf. W. H. G. Armitage, *The Rise of the Technocrats* (1965).   [2] See Zeldin, *Ambition and Love*, 275-6.

of their lives, and rightly so. For the first time workers and employers met, at a national level, more or less as equals, and for the first time the influence of the government was openly on the side of the workers. The euphoria expressed itself in an atmosphere of carnival, which the grim factories had never produced before. But something of a myth has, as a result, grown around this. Just as important as the occupation of the factories was the fact that in no case was this followed up by a demand for their confiscation or nationalisation. Everywhere the workers took care not to spoil the equipment and machines. In the Galeries Lafayette, the occupiers abstained from using the beds or blankets for sale and slept on the floor. Hierarchy and property were thus only partially transformed; but they were transformed. The workers did not challenge legal owner-ship, but they acted as though the factories belonged to them also, in the sense that their labour gave them rights in them. What they demanded was greater respect as humans, a better wage as workers and not least security in their jobs, for part of the purpose of the occupations was that they prevented the employers from taking on other 'yellow' workers, which a simple strike would have allowed. Blum's government re-ceived all the workers' delegations which came to see it, even to the extent, on one occasion, of interrupting a cabinet meeting to do so. The most important result of the Popular Front was that it established the principle that the workers had a right to express their opinion on all matters concerning them: many consultative councils, of which their representatives were members, had been in existence since the turn of the century, but henceforth consultation of the workers became a necessary part of government. This was a radical change in the way the state functioned. But it took a little longer for the employers to recover from the shock they had received and adjust themselves to a new form of relationship with their employees. The workers for their part were so used to passive obedience to their bosses that they sometimes obeyed the shop stewards they now had to elect in just the same way, without argument. Democracy was not yet introduced into industrial relations.

The main institution which altered the situation was the system of collective bargaining. The state henceforth could impose minimum wages on industry. These wages were agreed by the main trade unions and employers, but the state could apply their agreement to all firms, even when they had taken no part in the negotiations. In cases where agreement could not be reached, the unions and employers could appeal to an arbitrator, but it is significant that the panel of arbitrators they agreed on consisted entirely of civil servants (councillors of state, judges, professors etc.), as did also the Superior Arbitration Court, established in 1938 to reconcile inconsistencies among arbitrations.[1] Workers and employers seldom could agree and the result was that in practice the state imposed its decisions on them. The institution of the *office du blé* (1936–9) enabled the state, also, to fix the price of wheat at rates which would reconcile the interests of producers and consumers, at the expense of hoarders and speculators. Never before in peace-time had it attempted to end the system of free market competition, on such a scale. A law tried, in addition, to prohibit price increases in other goods, 'unjustified by rising costs'. The state's long history of interference in conditions of work was now crowned by the laws instituting two weeks' compulsory paid holiday, and reducing the working week to forty hours. Its control over the Bank of France was greatly strengthened, not by nationalisation, but by abolishing the rights of the 200 largest shareholders, and replacing the plutocratic Regents by a council nominated by the state, who would be mainly civil servants. The influence of civil servants was further increased by the invention of the *loi-cadre*, by which parliament legislated in principle only, outlining a framework (*cadre*), but left the details to be worked out by the administration. Within the administration, Blum tried to impose greater cohesion, by taking no ministerial portfolio himself, and by establishing a secretariat charged with co-ordinating policy, so that the conflicts between ministries, and the delays this produced, should be minimised. Formerly, the ministry of finance almost had a *de facto* veto on reform; this new policy was an attempt to make government more coherent; but it had only very limited success. Everything that has been said about the increase in state power must be qualified by the proviso that bureaucracy, with its rivalries and red tape, had great difficulty

[1] J. Brissaud and T. A. Gueydan, *L'Évolution sociale et la pratique de l'arbitrage* (1939); D. Sarrano, *La Cour supérieure d'arbitrage* (Paris thesis, 1938).

in using that power. The larger the number of regulations forced through its machinery, the more frequent were its attacks of constipation.

The Popular Front is still a living memory and the least criticism of its work still arouses sensitive reactions from its surviving participants. These survivors see themselves as inaugurating a new era, whereas the historian sees precedents, continuities and limits to what was achieved in practice, which make the experience appear less heroic than it was to those who lived through it. In economic terms, the Popular Front was largely unsuccessful. The much-decried deflationary policy of the conservatives (1932–5)—which showed that conservatives also resorted to using state power to influence the economy—had produced a marked revival of production. The Popular Front gave the workers wage increases of unprecedented magnitude—amounting in all to 35 per cent and in some cases up to 50 per cent—but this was accompanied by inflation of 27 per cent within a single year, and by May 1938 workers' real wages were back to what they were in May 1936. Pensioners and civil servants, however, were left about 20 per cent poorer. Despite the shortening of the working week, unemployment fell at a slower rate in France than in neighbouring countries. Whereas elsewhere the depression was lifting, in France it was accentuated: production fell by 6 per cent, whereas it had increased by 8 per cent in the year before Blum came to power. Devaluation, which the workers had long, rather uncomprehendingly, opposed, was eventually forced on Blum, but he carried it out at too low a rate, so that it failed to make French goods competitive again. Blum had postponed it partly because he wished to obtain international agreement to it: he saw his negotiations as heralding new methods in the co-operative regulation of the world's finances. A young socialist, André Philip, declared that this episode had a decisive influence on his life, because it showed him that France was no longer able to solve its economic problems independently of other powers; reforms on a national scale were thus no longer possible. But this was not a lesson that was generally drawn, any more than, in the atmosphere of hostility and recrimination, it was seen that there were narrow limits to what a government could achieve without the full support of public opinion. The Popular Front represented only half the nation. Though it claimed to represent the poor against the rich, and though it is true that most of the rich were against it, there were people of all classes behind the opposition. So long as the state did no more than interfere in the working of the capitalist system, without really controlling it, it was dependent on the good will or 'confidence' of the capitalists. The fundamental change that was to make possible a much greater influence of the state on the workings of capitalism was the policy of planning, which, in effect, bribed the capitalists by financial inducements to invest in a way the state approved. The idea of co-operation based on self-interest—since moral consensus was absent—was a post-war invention.

To criticise the Popular Front government for not doing more is, however, to ignore the limitations within which it had to work. It was not a socialist government, as Blum was at pains to point out. The socialists were asked to form the ministry because they won most seats, but they had to share power with the radicals, and to rely also on the votes of the communists. The radicals remained by far the largest party in the Senate, so that full approval of all legislation had to be secured from them. In due course they overthrew Blum by refusing to allow him to increase taxation: even at modest rates that seemed too socialist for them. The Popular Front had as its policy the implementation of the moderate common programme of the left: it must be judged therefore for the way it achieved this. Its importance should be measured less in terms of legislation than in the emotional impact it had. It represented the revival and reunification of the left. Blum abandoned his reluctance to take office without a majority largely because of the threat of fascism. One of the first laws he passed dissolved the paramilitary 'fascist' leagues. Like the occupation of the factories, directed partly against 'yellow' workers, the socialist occupation of power was designed to keep the fascists out and to save democratic institutions. But it produced reactions of terror on the part of many conservatives who were in no way fascist. It was not a formula which worked, therefore, first because it immediately created antagonisms based on fear, and second because it involved the resurrection of old labels to solve new problems. The experience of the Popular Front showed that the idea of the left, however powerful emotionally, was in practical terms sterile: from the right wing of the radicals to the left wing of the communist party was too long a road. There was perhaps no other formula available, given the backward-looking character of politics, but, revolutionary though the Popular Front seemed, it was not revolutionary enough to find an alternative.

And yet Blum must be considered one of the most impressive statesmen of the Third Republic. No politician—apart from Gambetta and Jaurès—has been so admired and loved, though it is true none has been more hated and insulted. He was France's first Jewish prime minister but he received none of the tolerance that Disraeli was allowed in England. Anti-Semitic insults of the most vulgar kind were shouted at him while he made his speeches in parliament. On one occasion he was physically assaulted and beaten up: it is this kind of atmosphere that explains why the Popular Front seemed obviously neces- sary. Blum was proud of being a Jew; he believed that Jews had a special role to play in the revolution, because, he claimed, they were practically critical, rationalist and above all devoted to justice. His mother, he said, 'carried the sentiment of justice to such melancholy extremes' that when she gave him and his brother apples for a snack, she cut two apples in half and gave them each one half from each apple. Justice and Judaism, he argued, were one and the same thing: it was no accident that both Marx and Lassalle were Jews. But Blum was not a practising Jew and if he fitted into any stereotype himself, it was rather into that of the typical French intellectual. His father, who was of Alsatian origin, had built up a successful wholesale business in silk ribbons, but Blum never showed any interest in commerce and turned instead to literature and social life. He quickly established a considerable reputation as a literary critic on *La Revue blanche*, championing young writers systematically, arguing that each generation must protest its originality against its elders but also display a wide tolerance to different schools of writing. However, he took a particular interest in seeking out the ideas in literature, equating beauty with truth, and he liked clarity, sincerity and disinterestedness above all else. He won admission to the École Normale Supérieure, but left after a year, having found its work un- congenial and having failed in his examinations. He then gained entry into the Conseil d'État (by competitive examination, at his second attempt) and for twenty-four years he combined his writing with service as a member of the country's highest administrative judiciary, specialising in disputes between the state and the individual; he participated in the process by which, on the one hand, the public interest was gradually allowed to override the sanctity of private contract, and on the other, the administration was forced to account for abuses of its power. At the same time, he took an interest in politics at the theoretical level; and he helped finance the socialist paper *L'Humanité* and Péguy's bookshop, where many socialist academics and writers met to discuss the renovation of the world. Blum led a sociable and varied life. He hated specialisation. He declared that science could no longer be considered the key to the future, because it had become too specialised, and, besides, it increased suffering and injustice even if it also created new wealth. He rejected both the Tolstoian solution of sacrifice and all appeals to violence. He was hostile to simple formulae. His own temperament and talents inclined him to the conciliation of contradictions and animosities. That is what attracted him above all to Jaurès, who had the same inclinations and with whom he formed a deep friendship. It was only a feeling of obligation to carry on Jaurès's work after his death that persuaded Blum to enter active politics himself. Socialism, for both Jaurès and Blum, was a kind of religion, an expression of their character, rather than an economic analysis of society. Blum was even less of a Marxist than Jaurès. He said that Marx was a 'mediocre metaphysician', whose economic doctrines were increasingly outdated every day. Blum's own socialism was much more an extension of the ideas of the eighteenth-century *philosophes*; it was, he said, the result of a 'purely rationalist conception of society' seeking to reduce 'the obscure and evil forces which resist clarity of mind and the action of will based on reflection'; its aim was justice and happiness. He did believe that the collectivisation of property was the fundamental solution, but he was against achieving this by violence, arguing that the revolution should come only when the time for it was ripe. The real revolution was education, which transformed men's minds, not *coups d'état*: the Bolsheviks had confused ends and means and their seizure of power was a fraud. He was against minorities arrogating rights of dictatorship to themselves; he wanted socialism to triumph only when men saw that it was that was best for them, that it was in their own interest. This, however, did not make him a reformist. He argued that reformism and revolution were not alternatives but appealed to different people, depending on how far ahead they were disposed to look: reforms should not be thought of as likely to satisfy the masses and put them off revolution, at least if revolution was understood in his way, as the culmination of change. This is an example of the way Blum reconciled opposing tendencies among socialists; and it was, in large measure, due to his conciliatory efforts that the socialist party was, after the breach with the communists, expanded until it became the largest party in parliament. Blum was accepted as the party leader because he was recognised as having the subtlest brain in it, the greatest skill in developing its policy and enunciating its attitudes to the issues of the day. The result was that French socialism remained above all a humanistic creed, placing its major emphasis on the fulfilment of the individual.

Blum was a man of exceptional sensitivity, whose gentleness and kindness won him deep affection from all those who worked for him, just as his natural authority, firmness and ability to understand complicated problems quickly commanded respect. The preservation of individual liberty remained the foremost aim of the party. To such an extent was Blum attached to parliamentary government, as the indispensable guarantor of that liberty, that, though he saw the need for it to be made much more efficient in France, he was extremely anxious that the strengthening of the executive should be done in a way which would not jeopardise the system. He proposed changes therefore not in the parliamentary system, but simply in the techniques of government. Though he urged nationalisation, he wanted nationalised industries to be run as autonomous institutions, working for the public interest but largely independent of the government. Though he believed that capitalism had failed, in that its crisis was due to its inability to create enough purchasing power among the masses to buy the goods it produced in increasing quantities, he did not propose to overthrow capitalism, but rather to induce it to increase that purchasing power by raising wages. He kept his party out of office, so long as it did not have a majority, being determined that it should not become contaminated by power; he considered it his duty to pass on its doctrines unsullied to succeeding generations; and when in 1936 he did take office, he limited his ambitions precisely to the execution of the common programme of the left—which did not involve the establishment of socialism. The point on which he was most vulnerable was his foreign policy, for the socialists were by tradition pacifists and the menace of Nazism left them perplexed and indecisive. After 1945, Blum thought that he had made a mistake and that he should have supported a war against it, to destroy it before it caused further trouble. He had, however, seen the dangers inherent in Hitler's rise to power more clearly than most. Blum's enemies were blinded by passion, therefore, when they saw him as a dangerous and fanatical threat to French society as it existed. In many ways, he gave expression to the very generosity, rationality and moderation which that society cherished. But he illustrated also the limits of its rationality. He was no more able to understand his opponents than they to understand him. For all the acuteness of his sensibilities, his imagination was not broad enough to comprehend the reasons, for example, why the anti-dreyfusards persisted in denying the evidence of Dreyfus's innocence. He was, even as a very young man, remarkable for his awareness of the need for people to find satisfaction for the different sides of their personalities, physical, intellectual and sentimental, but he ultimately considered that the rational side should be dominant, and he could not help thinking that it could be made dominant by the use of rational argument. The weakness of socialism was that it remained fundamentally a doctrine for intellectuals.[1]

Technocracy made further headway under the Vichy regime. But that regime was also a manifestation of the survival of gerontocracy, and it is this that now requires explanation.

[1] Gilbert Ziebura, *Léon Blum et le parti socialiste 1872–1934* (1967); William Logne, *Léon Blum, The Formative Years 1872–1914* (North Illinois U.P., De Kalb, 1973); James Joll, *Three Intellectuals in Politics* (1960); Joel Colton, *Léon Blum, Humanist in Politics* (New York 1966); *Léon Blum, chef du gouvernement 1936–7* (Cahiers de la fondation nationale des sciences politiques no. 155, 1967); Georges Lefranc, *Histoire du Front Populaire* (1965).

8. Gerontocracy

NOSTALGIA was more widespread than optimism. The forces resisting change were more powerful than those which accepted or welcomed it. The years after 1914 therefore need to be looked at also from the point of view of those popular reactions which were fundamentally conservative, even when they assumed apparently revolutionary stances. It has been suggested[1] that the division of French politics into left and right was ultimately more confusing than useful, and at no time was this more obviously revealed than in this period. The men who opposed change, or who continued to repeat traditional gestures, were to be found in almost all parties, both left and right.

The reason for this must be sought, first of all, in the effect of the Great War. The war brought revolution to the three great kingdoms of continental Europe, but not to France. Yet this was the war that produced the heaviest loss of life France had ever sustained. One million four hundred thousand French soldiers were killed, i.e. 17·6 per cent of the army (compared with 17·1 per cent killed in the Austrian army, 15·1 per cent in the German and 13 per cent in the British). In economic terms this represented the disappearance of 10·5 per cent of France's active male population (compared with Germany's loss of 9·8 per cent and Britain's 5·1 per cent). The recovery of Alsace and Lorraine was not enough to compensate and the French population fell from 39·6 million to 39·12 million.[2] Though victorious, France was severely mutilated; and just as the defeat of 1871 had produced a conservative reaction, so in 1919 a conservative parliament was elected—the first right-wing majority since the foundation of the republic. The restoration of the pre-1914 world was not only felt as

---

[1] See Zeldin, *Politics and Anger*, ch. 1. The opposite view is taken by François Goguel, *La Politique des partis sous la 3ᵉ république* (new edition, 1958); this remains an indispensable source, but it should be remembered that it was written in 1942–5.

[2] Germany's population fell from 64·9 to 59 million; Britain's rose from 45·4 to 47·9. Cf. Michel Huber, *La Population de la France pendant la guerre* (1932).

a need, but became an obsession. So many young people were killed in the war that the old politicians were able to survive with less opposition than they might otherwise have encountered, and old ideas were thus given a new lease of life. Resentment was a legacy of the war, more than hope. Three million soldiers were wounded: 1,100,000 suffered permanent disablement. Ex-servicemen's organisations, incapable of forgetting the past, became an important new power in the land.

The experience of the war was of such a nature that it encouraged the desire for revenge rather than for a new start. Sixteen per cent of the population (6·5 million) suffered from occupation by the enemy. Ten departments on the eastern frontier spent most of the war under German rule or served as a battleground: the war on the western front was fought almost entirely on French territory. In 1918 the population of this area had been reduced by 2,880,000 people (44 per cent). The department of the Aisne lost two-thirds of its inhabitants, those of the Marne and Meuse one-half. There were three types of victims: those who fled, those who remained under German rule, and those whose possessions were devastated by battle. About 1,500,000 left their homes at the approach of the German armies and spent the war as refugees. The government attempted to distribute them evenly over the whole country, but many preferred not to move too far away: the population of some departments was swollen by 10 or even 15 per cent. The fate of the occupied regions was more tragic. Some villages, anxious to avoid all provocation, spontaneously handed in their guns to the *mairie*. But during the invasion, whole villages were annihilated when the Germans felt their advance was endangered or resisted by the civilians. German atrocities became a subject of vigorous propaganda and German barbarism in this war was declared to exceed even that of the Thirty Years War. Once the front was stabilised, however, the Germans sought to exploit rather than punish. Military control was firmly established over all economic activity: the occupied regions were organised to produce food and other goods for the benefit of Germany. Forced labour was used to build and maintain the roads, railways and forests and to work the armaments factories. In the villages all were compelled to work in the fields. Men were requisitioned for special jobs by the army through the mayors (for the Germans kept the French administration under their military rule); they were usually allowed to go home in the evenings if their jobs were not too far away; but some were enrolled into the Z.A.B. (Civilian Labour Battalions) which were virtually military and sometimes worked at the front. Dependence on the whim of the commanders, reinforced on occasion by the taking of hostages, maintained a constant state of anxiety. Billeting of German troops, curfews, the confiscation of cars, bicycles, cameras, the imposition of heavy fines for a large number of new offences, compulsory 'loans', taxation and exactions of various sorts, strict control of all travel, the gradual closing of most shops and taverns, the halting of commerce and the disappearance of most fairs, the replacement of money by barter, the prohibition of correspondence with France— all this turned the occupied region into something resembling a vast concentration camp. In Belgium, at least most of the agricultural produce was left to the inhabitants; but France was treated with greater severity by its invaders: after 1915 almost all food was removed. The large towns could obtain neither eggs, nor meat nor milk for three years. Famine was averted by the Americans, working through the Red Cross and through a Committee for the Feeding of the North, to which the Germans readily and naturally gave every facility. An elaborate rationing system was instituted, which provided less than an adequate diet, but enough to sustain life. The death rate rose from 27 per cent in 1915 to 41 per cent in 1918 (compared with 21 per cent in Brussels in 1918). Tuberculosis and malnutrition affected the children in particular.[1]

In the final stages of the war, the Germans systematically destroyed all the steel mills and textile factories and 80 per cent of the mines, after having stripped them of useful machinery. As they retreated, they evacuated and razed the land so as to leave it completely empty. Soissons, twice occupied and twice razed, the scene of fighting for thirty-two months, had by 1918 only 500 of its former 15,000 inhabitants. Reims retained only 15 per cent of its population, who survived in underground caves, where the public authorities, schools and

[1] Paul Collinet and Paul Stahl, *Le Ravitaillement de la France occupée* (1928), 152–3.

churches continued to function. In the sizeable area devastated by battle, the work of many generations was almost
completely annihilated, the land rendered unfit for agriculture;
half the farm buildings were destroyed, three-quarters of the
farm implements lost, most of the animals killed.[1] The actual
damage and suffering inflicted was exacerbated by propaganda
about German atrocities. This probably produced an even more
long-lasting legacy of hate. The most distinguished scholars
contributed to the vilification of the enemy. A pamphlet claimed
that phrenological study showed that the Germans' brains
lacked the organ of comparison, which explained not only the
Germans' inability to make reasonable judgements, but also
the depression in their skulls, which made room perfectly for
the visor of their helmets. One whole floor of the *Maison de la
Presse* was given over to the manufacture of false photographs
showing horrible mutilations. The Catholic Church had a
propaganda association under Mgr Baudrillart, rector of the
Catholic Institute of Paris, which spread rumours of atrocities.
The French were particularly forceful and imaginative in their
invention of these horror stories, which is why the Germans, who
engaged less successfully in the same kind of propaganda,
emerged as the criminals.[2]

It took about a dozen years for the physical damage of the
war to be repaired. There was an opportunity for the building
of a new France. Indeed, a compulsory national town-planning
law (14 March 1919) required every city of over 10,000 inhabitants to make plans for improvements within three years, and
every town or village which had been damaged, irrespective
of size, to produce a reconstruction plan within three months.
An expropriation law (6 November 1918) allowed the state
or a municipality to expropriate for public use a whole zone
and not just the land immediately needed. Every new building
in the devastated regions had to conform to public sanitation
laws; thatched roofs were forbidden, even on barns; measures
against damp were required, the ventilation of kitchens, the
compulsory installation of water-closets in all new lodgings
with two rooms or more, a minimum size for windows; no

[1] George B. Ford, *Out of the Ruins* (New York, 1919), 1. 57.
[2] J. M. Read, *Atrocity Propaganda 1914–1919* (New Haven, 1941), 24, 142–4,
with a good bibliography.

new building was to be higher than the street was wide.[1]
But the financial provisions for the reconstruction encouraged
profiteering rather than the modernisation and re-equipment
of industry. The state undertook to indemnify all losses sustained through enemy action but it offered overwhelming
financial inducements to rebuild in the same region. An owner
could take his money and not rebuild, but in such a case he
would receive only the value of the property in 1914. If he rebuilt, he would get a sum three or four times larger, to compensate for the increased post-war cost of rebuilding—but he had to
rebuild in the same commune, or at least within a radius of fifty
kilometres of the original site, provided always this was inside
the 'devastated battle zone'. This reflected a natural fear that
otherwise a whole region of France would remain a desert,
but it resulted in the guiding principle being the reconstruction
of the France of 1914 in almost identical shape. No attempt
was made to consider the national economic interest, to decide,
for example, whether a destroyed sugar factory should be replaced by another one, rather than something else. No distinction was made, in allocating compensation, between productive
re-equipment and the reconstitution of consumer assets.
Twenty-nine milliard gold francs were distributed in war
compensation, which was obviously an exaggerated sum, for
it was equal to one-tenth of the total private wealth of France
in 1914. The idea was that German reparations would pay for
it. The committees which assessed damages were therefore
generous in their estimates, if only from patriotism; and in
addition some found scope for fraud or embezzlement. Germany of course did not pay. Instead of levying a tax on property
throughout the country, to share the burden, the state therefore
raised the money by loans. The money market was unable to
withstand this, and by 1925 the state was virtually bankrupt.
Inflation meant that the victims of war damage were replaced
by victims of the collapse of the franc.[2]

The French had been exceptionally resourceful in meeting
the challenges presented by the war. The population in the
unoccupied regions was kept well fed at little below pre-war
standards; military supplies were, after initial chaos, produced

---

[1] Ford, op. cit. 145, 153–4.
[2] Edmond Michel, *Les Dommages de guerre de la France et leur réparation* (1932).

in adequate quantities; and the war was won without any real crisis and without revolution. This very success, however, was to be a principal cause of the failure to reform either the political or economic mechanism when peace came. The success was, of course, to a certain extent illusory, because the French made up the deficiencies of their production by borrowing. The payment of the price of victory was postponed till after peace was made: the crisis came then, rather than during the war. Some people lost all they had, but a great many more survived fairly comfortably and some even prospered in the war. Thus though the peasants suffered enormously in terms of war casualties—673,000 were killed and another half a million were seriously wounded, out of about eight million— the survivors were able to pay off their mortgages, thanks to inflation, and the labourers were able to command much higher wages. Though agricultural production fell drastically during the war, there were large profits to be made, despite the government's efforts at price fixing. In particular wine-growers did well because the army bought up one-third of their production, at prices three times higher than those prevailing in 1914. The peasants were the principal bene-ficiaries of the black market created by food rationing (which really hit only the towns), and though they complained about billeting and the destruction of crops, they made enormous profits from the troops, and foreign ones most of all. The war therefore did not turn the peasants into revolutionaries, but confused their thinking about their situation. While despair or ambition continued to drive large numbers to the towns— so that the number of peasants fell by 14 per cent between 1919 and 1930—the land continued to be a refuge for those who had still not come to terms with the modern economy. Though large farmers increased production—total food production rose by 3 per cent in these years, despite the fall in the agricultural population, and productivity per person rose by 19 per cent— France could no longer claim to be self-sufficient in food, and the peasants were subjected to ruinous international competition.[1]

[1] Food consumption (%):

	1910–13	1923–31
from metropolitan France	85·1	74·8
colonies	6·8	9·5
foreign countries	8·1	15·7

Prosperity alternated with crisis: in 1930–5 it was agricultural prices which fell more than those of any other commodity, despite protection; but in the next four years, peasant incomes rose by over a half. Though it is now argued that too many people were trying to live off the land, there were many who were still preaching a return to the land, and that was official policy in 1940–2. Far from higher productivity being the obvious solution to the peasants' problems, governments urged them to reduce production in the 1930s. The confusion resulting from these apparent contradictions prevented any general acceptance of 'modernisation' as the answer. The attempts to establish large-scale co-operative farms under the pressure of war in 1914–18 had failed completely: one near Toulouse, which had received a loan of three million francs interest free from the government failed to make any profits. The co-operative of the Forez lost four million francs. Ministerial exhortations and circulars had no practical results. There was no new or general sense of direction in agriculture, beyond the desire to keep France a predominantly rural nation.[1]

Nostalgia was only one form of conservatism. Another kind of resistance to change came from ignorance about the changes that were taking place, and the inability to understand them. What people thought was happening was, in some ways, as important as what actually did happen. The inability to judge events was partly a question of slow psychological adaptation, an inevitable tendency to find what one was looking for, but partly also a result of the inadequacy of information about the economy. France's statistical service in this period consisted of 120 men, at a time when even Czechoslovakia employed 1,198 in its similar service and Germany 2,358. The cost of living index was compiled on the basis of the retail price of only thirteen articles, ignoring, for example, the cost of clothing and rents. Whereas in the 1920s most countries in Europe established institutes to study the economy, on the model of the Harvard Economic Service, France did not do so.

[1] M. Augé-Laribé, *L'Agriculture française pendant la guerre* (1925), 62; A. Sauvy, *Histoire économique de la France entre les deux guerres* (4 vols., 1967–75), 1. 239–58, 2. 128, 137, 293; G. Perreux, *La Vie quotidienne des civils en France pendant la grande guerre* (1966), 146–7.

In 1938 no one knew, for example, what the national production of chemical products, or agricultural machines, or textiles
was. It was only in that year that a decree-law[1] ordered a
survey of production and distribution. The result was that
Blum was unable to see the damaging effects of the forty-hour
week on the economy. The politicians had to work largely in
the dark. There was no obstacle therefore to bogy men ob-
sessing them and, even more, the public.

Probably the most worrying of these bogy men were the
industrialists and bankers, who moreover did their best to
conceal the facts about themselves. They had only themselves
to blame if their activities were construed in the most un-
favourable way. The phenomenon which attracted particular
attention was the concentration of business into larger units.
The number of firms fell by 35 per cent between 1906 and
1926, which meant that artisans were going out of business.
The number of firms employing between 21 and 100 workers
increased by 60 per cent and those with over 100 workers by
50 per cent.[2] The number of people employed in factories with
over 500 workers doubled between 1900 and 1931 to reach
almost one and a half million. However the proportion of
firms which could be considered large-scale was still small. In
1931 only 13 per cent of the industrial work force were employed by firms large enough to put the bulk of their workers in
factories of 100 or more men. In 1939 there were still 151,044
family firms against 43,080 limited liability companies, even if
the total capital of the latter was larger. Cartels in particular
attracted attention. Much was made of the fact, also, that by
1936 the three largest car manufacturers had won 75 per
cent of the national market, whereas in 1913 they had only
29 per cent (a rather untypical situation). The difficulties of the
economy were thus blamed somewhat uncritically on big
business without a proper appreciation of its real, and rather
limited, role. Battles were fought against imaginary enemies,
or at least enemies whose might and whose unity were grossly
exaggerated.[3] To what extent employers were 'malthusian'

[1] A decree issued by the government, without a parliamentary vote, but having
the force of law.   [2] G. Pirou, *Les Cadres de la vie économique* (1940), 1. 143.
[3] M. Lévy-Leboyer, 'Le Patronat français a-t-il été malthusien?', *Le Mouvement
social* (July–Sept. 1974), 3–49, which contains a valuable bibliography of recent
work on industrial developments in the inter-war years.

in these years, and impregnated by the 'Maginot Line' attitude, is debatable, and the tendency, now that more research is being done on employers, is to argue that these accusations cannot be applied indiscriminately to them: neither the government nor the masses had adequate information about their policy. Many employers had great difficulty in understanding the effects of devaluation on industry and on exports, so that they took the most contradictory action.

The workers, for their part, were confused about their own situation by inflation, which made impartial calculation difficult. During the First World War, their real wages had risen considerably, particularly among the poorer paid; 413,000 workers were brought back from the front to the factories, where they earned high civilian wages while the peasants fought and died for a private's pittance. The French workers did much better in the war than the German ones, who, because of industrial mobilisation, had their real wages reduced by 42 per cent in 1914–16, and who had still barely returned to 1914 levels in 1918.[1] The improvement in the French workers' position continued between the wars, and even in the 1930s their real wages rose by no less than 25 per cent: they were the beneficiaries of the collapse of food prices.[2] However, whereas in May–July 1917 96 per cent of strikes were totally or partially successful, the strikes of 1919–20, which many thought might be the presage of revolution, were disastrous failures and, as has been seen,[3] the workers' relations with their employers remained bitter and antagonistic. Though the Popular Front was immensely important in revealing what the workers could achieve by spontaneous action, it was also immensely disappointing: the large gains in wages were quickly cancelled out by price rises; paradoxically 1937 and 1938 were the years when the workers' standard of living did not rise. Unemployment for French workers never rose very high in official figures (which gave a maximum of under half a million unemployed, i.e. 5 per cent of the industrial and commercial work force) but short-time

[1] W. Oualid and C. Picquenard, *La Guerre et le travail. Salaires et tarifs* (1928); G. D. Feldman, *Army, Industry and Labour in Germany 1914–18* (Princeton, 1966), 117, 472. Cf. the play *Les Nouveaux Riches* by Abadie and Cesse, first performed at the Sarah Bernhardt Theatre in Paris on 1 March 1917.

[2] Sauvy, op. cit. 2. 25, 406.   [3] See Zeldin, *Ambition and Love*, 274–82.

work, which probably affected one-fifth of workers, was a source of profound demoralisation throughout the 1930s, for France was slower to recover from the depression than other countries.[1]

Most of the politicians of the inter-war years offered the country virtually the same programme and solutions that their predecessors had done in the nineteenth century. Indeed most of them had established themselves as ministers long before 1914, and since they continued to win elections, the mass of the people accepted and probably shared their traditional attitudes. Thus it was generally agreed, even by his enemies, that Poincaré, whose life almost spanned the whole Third Republic (1860–1934), owed his success to his being particularly representative of that regime's ideals. Poincaré consciously sought to give expression to these ideals in his policies. He could be attacked for identifying himself, and France, with the middle-class savers, the *rentiers*, and to devoting his life to rescuing them from inflation; but he was proud to acknowledge this as his ambition and he did not consider that this meant he was selfishly serving the interests of a minority class. It is true there were only about 510,000 *rentiers* who owned state bonds.[2] But Poincaré saw them as only one section of the rather larger group of people who had invested their savings in other securities, and of the even wider community which believed in saving. The savers were, to him, the motor force of French society, just as to the socialists the workers were. French society was based on ambition, the ambition to make money, to become educated and to rise in the social scale. It was a society that worked because it kept the road to *embourgeoisement* always open, and leadership was constantly renewed by new recruits, who rose to comfort or eminence on the basis of their savings, usually amassed slowly through several generations. Ambition, Poincaré thought, was a good thing

---

[1] C. Gide and W. Oualid, *Le Bilan de la guerre pour la France* (1931); Arthur Fontaine, *L'Industrie française pendant la guerre* (1925); G. Olphe Gaillard, *Histoire économique et financière de la guerre 1914–1918* (1923); A. Sauvy, op. cit.; C. J. Gignoux, *L'Économie française entre les deux guerres 1919–39* (n.d., about 1940); E. Dussauze, *L'État et les ententes industrielles* (1939); J. Tchernoff, *Les Ententes économiques et financières* (1933–7).

[2] This is the 1911 figure.

because it stimulated progress and the spirit of invention, but also thrift and prudence. Poincaré's dedication to this ideal shows that when Guizot had held up the motto 'Get Rich' to his countrymen, he had found a response and Poincaré indeed repeated Guizot's famous dictum, while modifying it slightly: 'Help yourselves,' he said, 'and the state (which is not Heaven) will help you later, if it can'. He was not as opposed to state interference as Guizot; though he remained basically a liberal, he thought the state should prevent the growth of monopolies and 'capitalist concentration' because these blocked the road of the rising small entrepreneur (failing to see that the large firms were offering the middle classes an alternative method of advancement and a new form of power). He was against the state taking over the role of providence and distributing favours and subsidies to its protégés, but he believed that the state should express the pride and self-satisfaction of its members by an active foreign policy. Nationalism, as his brother-in-law, the philosopher Boutroux said, was not incompatible with liberalism because it represented the reaction of the individual against 'the increasing obliteration of man by impersonal science, matter and chance'. Poincaré saw in the cult of the fatherland a way of reconciling reason and sentiment, self-interest and altruism. He was the heir not only of Guizot but of Thiers also, for whom a strong state, in the monarchical tradition, was necessary both for the dignity of Frenchmen and for the security of their property. Poincaré was, however, profoundly devoted to the republican regime and he never even toyed with possible alternatives. This was partly because he was a lawyer with a deep respect for legality—he was horrified, for example, that the Bank of France should have secretly engaged in financial manipulations which were not entirely legal—and partly because, as a minister, he considered himself a servant of the regime, with a duty to defend it. Honesty was for him one of the very basic virtues. He practised what he preached, moreover, and he owed his long tenure of the highest offices to the respect he inspired as incorruptible. Honesty meant that if ever he asked a civil service messenger to run an errand for him on a private matter, he would pay for it personally. He abandoned politics for a decade in order to make a fortune at the Bar, so that he could be financially independent; and he then used up his savings as president of the republic, refusing to do more than receive his salary. He rejected the offer of a lucrative sinecure which might suggest he was using his political influence for personal benefit. He had no doubts about what was right and wrong. Legality, justice and morality were all one to him. He was not interested in innovation, or in trying to solve insoluble problems. He was content to be the common denominator of his countrymen.

Poincaré was cold, timid, unattractive, unemotional. 'A head of state in the exercise of his duty', he said, 'has not the right to have tears in his eyes.' He was neither loved, nor admired, but he was respected. He was frequently referred to as France's lawyer, employed to get it its rights. Authors like Giraudoux were appalled that a lawyer, concerned above all with the past, quarrelling endlessly with the Germans about money, should claim to personify France, and be widely accepted as doing so; but the preoccupation with money was undoubtedly one national obsession. Poincaré was in fact also a man of considerable culture. He had been more attracted by literature than law in his youth; he had written no less than four novels, never published; he was elected to the French Academy and he always enjoyed the company of writers and artists more than that of politicians. But he had very few friends. He was representative of the tradition that regarded emotion as a private matter, and life as essentially serious, demanding, above all, hard work. He worked twelve hours a day and seldom accepted social invitations; he wrote all his letters by hand even when president of the republic; he answered his correspondence promptly and was always efficient. He concentrated on finance because he believed that sound finances were the essential foundation for an ordered society, and the state's main function (he quoted Thiers on this) was finance and defence. He was not therefore a party man; he offered himself as an arbitrator, a conciliator, who could fulfil national ambitions. He was not entirely conservative in the way he interpreted these. His talent had been recognised when he was still very young and he had first been drawn into a government as early as 1886, as a *chef de cabinet* on a minister's staff; and he became a minister in his thirties.

The ideas that guided him in the 1920s had been acquired forty years before. Poincaré was thus a staunch enemy of socialism, to the extent of voting against Waldeck-Rousseau who had been so rash as to admit a renegade socialist into his ministry. He had started his life as an admirer of Méline. He had opposed even pensions for railway workers. He always saw the reduction of government expenditure as a major objective, and budget deficits as the source of most evils. But in 1899 he had broken with Méline, arguing that anti-socialism could not be the entire programme of a politician. He eventually came to accept the idea of an income tax, provided that the traditional secrecy of business profits and family affairs was respected. He accepted insurance, provided it was run on mutual principles (not by the state). He thus typified the conservative who gradually came to accept that times were changing, and who belatedly adopted ideas that had been fashionable a generation earlier.

Poincaré's greatest achievement was to make the conservative *rentier* come to terms with the fact that his savings had been irrevocably lost in the chaos of the war and its aftermath. Poincaré took a very long time to admit this himself. He had always worked to give the country its rights and he believed in firmness in the exaction of those rights. In 1912–14, as prime minister and then president of the republic, he had not flinched from the idea of a war against Germany, if that was the price that had to be paid for the recognition of France's rights. After the war, he had supported the declaration of German war guilt and the exaction of large reparations. He had demanded the annexation of the Rhineland; and when Germany defaulted, he ordered the occupation of the Ruhr. Whereas Millerand, who had spent his life making compromises, wanted to do a deal with the German industrialists, to establish a Franco-German iron and steel compact, Poincaré insisted on the German state meeting its obligations. British and American historians have generally condemned this attitude as a refusal to face the economic realities, but French ones have maintained that France had a strong case and was shamefully and selfishly let down by its allies. The French middle classes could not see why, in the conflict of interests, they should be the ones to make sacrifices. They were in no mood for sacrifices; they felt their very existence was at stake, and so it was if their aristocratic pretensions—to live off accumulated capital rather than from daily work—were considered an essential part of their values. They gave way only because in 1925 they seemed threatened by total bankruptcy. Poincaré devalued the franc to four-fifths of its pre-war level. He accepted the Locarno treaty which put an end to the policy of sanctions against Germany. He carefully fixed the devaluation at a figure high enough to avoid unemployment and social unrest, but low enough to make French exports very competitive in world markets. In the process, he saved the parliamentary institutions of the republic; and he gave the traditionally influential classes a further lease of life. He did not stop negotiating with the Germans about reparations, and even if no money could be extracted from them, his supporters could still cherish their mistrust or hate of the Germans for another generation. Poincaré for many years collected material for a biography of Thiers, whom he greatly admired. He and Thiers stood in the same tradition, and together they show the continuity of the liberal, chauvinistic, cultured, basically self-satisfied core of middle-class families, who would not admit change unless absolutely forced to.[1]

This was only one kind of conservatism. Another was less readily identifiable, because it called itself radicalism. But in these years radicalism for the first time admitted that the most dangerous enemy was communism, and for the first time it ceased to pay lip-service to all 'advanced' ideas. This was a belated recognition that the radical party had matured into a network of families who, by temperament and tradition, were still hostile to capitalism and Catholicism but who, in practice, had won their place in the world as they found it, were proud of their achievement and thought that it was enough if arrangements could be made for others to follow in their footsteps. They would never proclaim themselves satisfied, but, provided they could criticise, they were. They did not believe in the redistribution of wealth, but only in making it easier for more

[1] Marguerite Perrot, *Le Mode de vie des familles bourgeoises* (1961), for the effects of inflation; Pierre Miquel, *Poincaré* (1961); Fernand Payen, *Raymond Poincaré; l'homme, le parlementaire, l'avocat* (1936); Raymond Poincaré, 'Vues politiques', *La Revue de Paris* (1 Apr. 1898), 638–58; id., *Idées contemporaines* (1906); id., *Au service de la France* (memoirs, covering the years 1912–18, 10 vols. 1926–33).

people to acquire it, in moderate quantities. Their doctrine ultimately reduced itself to the worship of moral virtues, just as the conservatives' did, though they saw salvation through education rather than religion. This enabled them to live on two planes—to be highly critical of society in their speech, but to be highly representative of the virtues of that society and to lead conformist lives according to its rules. France was thus held steady by this central core of people who, though they toyed with ideas, and often accepted that change was desirable, always found good reasons for postponing doing anything about it.

It has been suggested that in these years, the middle class in France divided into two components—the small capitalists (who lived off their private incomes) and the wage earners—and that the socialists gradually drew the latter group away from the radicals. Radicalism was thus left with an essentially conservative clientele, attached to private property and public order, hostile to big business but not to small savers.[1] In several other countries the petty bourgeoisie would have been tempted by fascism. In France the radical tradition prevented this: its stress both on rationalism and on prudence kept them loyal to the republic. But they did not use their influence in the cause of reform. This was partly because they were deeply divided. The radical party included both Clemenceau and Caillaux who advocated diametrically opposed foreign policies, to the extent that the former had the latter arrested and charged with treason. There were at least four major cliques within the party after 1919, grouped around the personalities of Herriot, Daladier, Chautemps and Sarraut, who took different lines largely for reasons of temperament. It was rare for them all to vote in the same way. Once their programme of anticlericalism, parliamentary government and educational opportunity had been achieved, the radicals became, in the inter-war years, essentially the party that acted as the middleman in politics, keeping the system going by arranging compromises, mitigating the effect of inevitable legislation or economic crises. Even their attitude to big business' was ambivalent. They received election funds from the insurance companies and most

[1] J. P. Florin, 'Le Radical-socialisme dans le département du Nord 1914–36', *Revue française de science politique* (Apr. 1974), 236–77.

of their newspapers were taken over by press magnates. They held directorships in powerful capitalist companies. They gave protection to financiers who could oil the wheels of government, even to the extent of allowing the famous crook, Stavisky, immunity to pursue his swindles. Though they made electoral alliances with the socialists, they were very reluctant to share power with them and the collaboration of the Popular Front was unpleasant to them, because they were, ultimately, unwilling to launch a serious attack on capitalism: they agreed to participate in Blum's government 'from pride, fear and ignorance'. In 1938 they finally adopted anti-communism as the main plank of their programme. At the same time the new generation of their members formed a group *Jeunesses Radicales*, which made Order, Authority and Nation its motto. They turned to the empire as holding out the hope for a new patriotic salvation. It was not surprising that in 1940 they voted in large majority for Pétain. However, the radicals had room within their ranks for men like Mendès France and Jean Zay whose reforming zeal was unquestionable and genuine.[1] The explanation of this is to be found less in political terms than in character. To explain why so many different kinds of people were radical is like explaining why they got married. One can see this by looking at the radical leader, Herriot.

Édouard Herriot (1872–1957), like Poincaré, lived almost right through the Third Republic and he was one of its heroes. He owed his ascendancy, however, to totally different qualities. Whereas Poincaré was moved by duty, Herriot needed above all affection. He was the leader of the radicals because he exuded fraternity. He was always jovial, hearty, friendly; he was a brilliant and insatiable conversationalist; he loved making emotional speeches and these were so eloquent that even political audiences shouted 'encore' at the end of them. He was deeply sensitive, easily hurt by the least criticism and in constant need of applause, and of a reciprocation of the flattery he showered on all with whom he came into contact. There was no malice in him; but, as he himself said, he was a spoilt child. He was a scholarship boy who had won every academic success and ended up a university professor of literature at Lyon. He was a literary man, who wrote more than

[1] Peter J. Larmour, *The French Radical Party in the 1930s* (Stanford, 1964).

thirty books, and whose first attraction was to beauty rather
than to philosophical systems. His conversation was studded
with literary quotations; he did not go into politics because he
liked arguing, but because he liked the human contact, mutual
stimulation, but most of all agreement with others. Even his
youth was marked by no political enthusiasms, but rather by a
series of rejections: he lost his faith without realising it 'as one
loses one's hair'; he was repelled by socialism, in the excessively Germanic form, as it seemed to him, that it was
developing; and the doctrines of Maurras also appeared too
harsh. Herriot would have liked politics to be based on sympathy, and he even tried to apply this to international relations.
That is why his heroes were the utopians of the 1840s and
particularly Constantin Pecqueur.

That is why, also, he wrote his two theses about women of the
eighteenth century: he adored women who won sympathy by
their charm, who were intelligent enough to converse but
who acquiesced in male superiority. He would have liked
international relations to be based on the same principles of
human attraction and was dismayed when dour politicians like
Ramsay Macdonald did not respond. Under Herriot's leadership, the radical party became a great club, where a good time
was had by all, but whose members were puzzled that not
everyone wished to join. Eloquence, said Herriot, was man's
beauty. The radicals were content to limit strife to verbal
gymnastics. That was to raise an enormous barrier against
action or change.

This did not mean that Herriot opposed the reforming ideas
of his time. On the contrary, he understood them as well as
anyone. He was immensely learned and widely read. In 1919
he published a two-tomed study of the reforms that France
needed to undertake: he was very radical indeed in his recom-
mendations, demand nothing less than 'a total transformation
of our habits and institutions': 'the time has come', he said,
'to found a Fourth Republic'. His review of detailed problems,
with long and comprehensive bibliographies, made his book
appear an impressive political treatise. He seemed, moreover,
to be in favour of rapid modernisation. He praised the Americans for their dedication to productivity, and combining this
with the radical cult of education, he coined the slogan 'to

understand and to create' (creation meaning producing, in the widest sense). Technical education should be advanced and scientific management and research encouraged. He embraced Taylorism as a new application of Cartesianism. Despite his own absorption in literature, he proclaimed that science contained the key to the future, and traditional culture should serve rather as a resource for factory and office workers in monotonous jobs. Foreign policy must be based on an acceptance of greater interdependence between nations. There was no real difference between socialism and radicalism, according to Herriot, except in the way it was implemented; radicalism did things more gradually and opportunely. However, though Herriot sometimes said he was an ordinary man (*peuple*)—and he was indeed popular because he was unpretentious—he also said that he was a bourgeois. When it came, therefore, to the question of who would carry out these reforms, Herriot was considerably less conciliatory. He was suspicious of 'technicians' and denounced the Polytechnic as the 'only theology faculty that has not been abolished'.[1] Though he castigated the big capitalists, he was frightened by them. He resigned in 1925 rather than fight them. He declared his ministry had come upon an impregnable *Mur d'Argent*, which stood as an obstacle to progress. That defeat was a traumatic experience, to which he often referred with horror. People accused him of lacking the courage of his convictions, for he could not bring himself to impose an income tax that really worked, that was not the subject of fraud and evasion. But he was restrained by a deeply ingrained liberalism. The prospect of another battle with the capitalists made him unwilling to co-operate with the socialists, and he liked finance ministers to be moderate men who commanded the confidence of the bankers. He was not willing to push his belief in equality beyond equality of opportunity, because he thought (like Poincaré) that individual effort should be recompensed by individual reward and social promotion. He said he deplored the material poverty of the workers less than their spiritual poverty. He was all for female rights, but argued that women were not ready for more than the municipal vote, and though he advanced equality of educational opportunity for girls, he was suspicious of too much 'intellectual

[1] E. Herriot, *Notes et maximes inédites* (1961), 40, 46.

excitement' for them, which could produce 'disequilibrium'.[1]
He was not anti-religious, but he could not abandon the
traditional anticlericalism of his party, and so he roused much
animosity, even though it was his ambition to reconcile Frenchmen. He said he was shocked by a notice he once saw reading:
Restaurant ouvrier, cuisine bourgeoise.[2] Yet there was the same
contradiction within him. Though he was a most amiable,
intelligent and friendly man, he was also very difficult to
get on with as a colleague. He was ready to rally in times of
national crisis, but when it came to taking action, he insisted
on formal procedures being adhered to, on parliament debating
the matter at length, and he staunchly resisted the right to
issue decree-laws being given to governments. He was in
favour of European unity, but his sympathy with other nations
was superficial: he was sure the French were the most intelligent people in the world.[3] The radical party's support was
virtually indispensable to every government, though it was
not large enough to form a ministry by itself: the radicals
were like the feathers on a duck's back; they kept France
warm and caused all reforms to run smoothly off.

This is not to say that the *Mur d'Argent* was entirely a myth
and that big business was not also a powerful conservative
force, but it was probably less of an obstacle to the radicals than
their own hesitations. How the capitalists used their money to
influence politics can be seen by taking the case of François de
Wendel. He called himself, not without some plausibility,
France's leading industrialist. He was the symbol of plutocracy
(as Caillaux called him) and of the occult power of international
finance, to the extent that an assassination attempt was made
on him, with the aim of avenging the shooting of Jaurès.
His family's factories were for a time partly French and partly
German, as a result of the loss of Alsace and Lorraine, and he
was therefore accused (falsely) of putting pressure on the
government to avoid damaging his firm's property in Germany
during the war. Wendel's position astride the frontier in fact
made him not a partisan of co-operation with Germany, but

[1] E. Herriot, *Créer* (1919), 1. 9, 2. 227.   [2] E. Herriot, *Jadis* (1948), 1. 146.
[3] M. Soulié, *La Vie politique d'Édouard Herriot* (1962), 121; P. O. Lapie, *Herriot*
(1967).

violently hostile to it. If there was one motive behind his political life, it was his fear of Germany. His *bête noire* was Caillaux, whom he might have approved of for his orthodox views on finance, but whom he detested because Caillaux favoured peace with Germany. Caillaux said to him: 'I am a man from the West. I see the Anglo-Saxon danger more.' Wendel preferred Poincaré who was an easterner, a 'man of the frontier'. Wendel was thus firmly opposed to the Vichy government during the war: he thought the main value of Nazism was that it revealed Germany in its true light. He always considered the national interest and foreign policy more important than the defence of the social order at home. He was attacked in the press, nevertheless, as being anxious not to offend Hitler, since the Wendels owned mines in Germany. It was significant that the newspaper which waged this campaign against him was subsidised by another section of the French plutocracy, notably Ernest Mercier and the electrical industry. The first thing that emerges from a study of the plutocracy is its profound divisions, its inability to act in unison and its failure therefore to make much impact on the course of events. Wendel's private papers show him to have been in almost constant disagreement with the Comité des forges, even though he was its president and even though he contributed 20 per cent of its budget: the interests of its members were too diverse to make a concerted policy possible. In the Bank of France, of which he was a governor, he was likewise at odds with many of his colleagues, because there was a long-standing breach between the bankers and the industrialists. The personal friendship of Wendel and Rothschild cut across this division, but the bankers were themselves divided between those who wished to rescue the small savers and those who were willing to borrow more from America and make a new start, based on a great export drive. The crisis of the franc in 1924–8 has long been regarded as proof of the ability of the Bank of France's governors (the cream of the plutocracy) to dictate to the state. Wendel was determined to get rid of Herriot and considered himself the representative of those who were panic-stricken by the advent of the radicals; he was keen to use his power to save the country from the reds. However, closer examination of the negotiations between the

Bank and the government reveals that it was mainly the government's hesitations that allowed the Bank to appear as an obstacle.

A more accurate accusation is that the plutocrats used their money to finance newspapers and pseudo-fascist movements. The perfumer Coty was particularly active in this way. But the case of Wendel, which has been carefully studied, shows that though a lot of money did change hands, it probably had very little effect on politics. Wendel bought *Le Journal des Débats* and he collected subscriptions from large firms to keep *Le Temps* as a conservative paper; but after a time Rothschild discontinued his contribution saying that it was a waste of money, since these papers made very little difference to public opinion. Wendel did give Pierre Taittinger's Jeunesses Patriotes 50,000 francs; but he was suspicious of anti-parliamentary groups, because he subsidised a parliamentary party himself, the Union des Républicains Démocratiques. This party also received funds from the Union des Intérêts Économiques, an organisation to distribute the political funds of big business, as well as 150,000 from Tardieu when he was prime minister (but Tardieu had himself received donations from the Comité des forges). However, Wendel had a lot of trouble in his own party and at one point found himself in a minority of fifteen out of about a hundred: the party's other leader, Louis Marin, was a *petit bourgeois* who was essentially a nationalist, and not pro-capitalist. Millerand used to be the Comité des forges's attorney, but when he became president he shunned Wendel, determined to show his independence. Wendel indeed found himself discounted and avoided, precisely because he was rich and people were anxious not to appear to be in his pay. He lacked the personal qualities needed to exert a real influence in politics. He said that since he did not have a stable of race-horses or play baccarat, he felt he could afford to pay for the luxury of having an independent opinion. The money he spent in this way reinforced the view that the plutocracy stood in the way of change. Wendel certainly had no developed ideas for reform and he criticised the Vichy government for trying to establish a 'New Order', when it would be better to 'save and defend the old one'. He believed that men were always the same, and nothing would improve them. The traditional organisation of society was therefore best. It is possible that many who were not plutocrats thought the same.[1]

The Vichy regime (1940–4) does not fit into the traditional dichotomy of left or right. It is generally classified as reactionary and backward-looking. It was this; but it was more than this; and it is its complexity that makes it important. If it had simply been a tool of the German conqueror, these four years could perhaps be considered (and some have argued that they should be) as an awful nightmare, to be forgotten as quickly as possible, and 'to be expunged from history'. But the 'National Revolution' it inaugurated represented a genuine attempt at reform, which needs to be taken seriously despite the confusions in it and despite its disastrous failure. It gave expression to a widespread determination to create a new France. The Third Republic had identified progress with parliamentary government and liberalism. Once people took the advantages of these for granted, they became increasingly critical of the concomitant inconveniences. About half the nation always had doubts about the prevailing system. So in 1940, it was not the Germans who overthrew the Third Republic. Parliament voluntarily abdicated and voted all its powers to Marshal Pétain, without reservations. This was an acknowledgement of impotence. It was not, therefore, just the right-wing opposition to the republic which thus gained office. Representatives of virtually all parties, abandoning their old attitudes, sought to co-operate in establishing a new order. For a time, Pétain's government enjoyed a popularity which was perhaps more widespread than that of any previous government.

The basis of the Vichy regime was both hope and despair. There was no need for the French to stop fighting, and a small minority argued that the battle could be continued, if necessary by withdrawing from the mainland to the colonies. But only about 35,000 took this view, or believed it strongly enough to join General de Gaulle's resistance movement in its early, lonely days. The vast majority of the nation was not willing to repeat the traumatic experiences of 1914–18. About ten

[1] J. N. Jeanneney, *François Wendel en République. L'Argent et le pouvoir 1914–40* (1976).

million people fled before the invading Nazi army in the greatest exodus the country had experienced, creating unprecedented conditions of chaos: they did not believe they could stop the Germans and they had no wish to die, heroically or otherwise. The armistice that Pétain signed was therefore greeted with almost universal approval and relief. Pétain believed that France's defeat had been caused not by military mistakes but by moral collapse. It was therefore no use fighting. The defeat should be used as a basis for a complete overhaul of the country. Guilt and shame inspired a search for refuge in traditional values as well as a desire to deny and break away from the immediate past. The depth of this feeling can be judged from the unprecedented powers that parliament voted Pétain, greater than any absolute monarch had enjoyed. All authority was vested in him, without limitation of time, and without responsibility to anyone. Pétain was eighty-four years old. The faith placed in such an old man was a sort of reversion to childhood by the nation, an abandonment of critical faculties and of responsibility brought on by mortal terror.[1]

Pétain was a soldier, not a politician. The Vichy regime was run by soldiers, civil servants and experts, not by politicians, who were largely discarded and some of whom were even put on trial on the charge of being responsible for the disastrous war.[2] Pétain's ministers were mainly civil servants who had already helped to run the country from behind the scenes under the Third Republic and who were now given greater, and visible, power. Inspectors of finance, councillors of state, Polytechniciens were in particular evidence, and they far outnumbered the visionaries and romantics. When Admiral Darlan became prime minister in 1942, he advanced technocracy even further. So though there seems little continuity between the Third and Fourth Republics on the political level, there was in fact an underlying one, because most senior civil servants survived through all these changes. Something like 98 per cent of those who served Vichy remained in state employment under the Fourth Republic. Their experiments

[1] Robert O. Paxton, *Vichy France* (1972); Robert Aron, *The Vichy Regime* (1958); Richard Griffiths, *Marshal Pétain* (1970); Stanley Hoffmann, *Decline and Renewal, France since the 1930s* (1974), 3–60.

[2] On the role of soldiers, see R. O. Paxton, *Parades and Politics at Vichy* (Princeton, 1966).

with the organisation of the state were decisive for the future character of French society.

They were far from being united in their views, and so their influence was not obvious. Bouthillier, the inspector of finances whom Pétain appointed minister of finance (1940–2), was imbued with what have been called typical middle-class ideas: a suspicion of the state and of bureaucrats, for even bureaucrats were self-deprecating, but he was also proud of the independence his status conferred on him, and he bitterly resented the suggestion that the inspectors of finance were tools of capitalism. He thus had a two-sided attitude to the state: he was opposed to the state running everything (*dirigisme*) but he criticised the business classes for behaving like the parlements of the *ancien régime* and he declared that capitalism was not basic to French civilisation. He was orthodox in his financial ideas, but he also wished to end the class struggle and to force the capitalists to give the workers more power in the economic field.[1] By contrast his successor Bichelonne had much less concern for human considerations. He was regarded as the Polytechnic's most brilliant graduate, with a 'prodigious intelligence' but one which saw all problems in their technical aspect. Bichelonne believed that economic planning by the state was not just a wartime expedient, but a permanent necessity. He has been remembered by supporters of Vichy as a hero, and he was indeed the incarnation of the technocrat of those days: 'effervescent, always late, always running, always sweating, jostling people out of the way, his arms always loaded with files, his desk covered with large piles of them, behind which he disappeared. He was a little too keen to show his talents to all who approached him.'[2] Pétain's ministers of education were university professors and his ministers for industry people with experience of industry.

Pétain's ideal was that he should give orders in a military fashion to a few ministers, who would pass them on to their subordinates, and so on down the chain of command. He thus had only a small inner cabinet, and met his ministers as a body infrequently. He had been given virtually absolute power, for it

---

[1] Yves Bouthillier, *Le Drame de Vichy* (1951), 2. 264, 274–5, 293, 303, 379.

[2] *Le Gouvernement de Vichy 1940–2* (colloque de la Fondation Nationale des Sciences Politiques) (1972), 207.

was limited by no institutions: he was given the right to promul-
gate a constitution as he pleased, and he never bothered to
do so. His speeches were studied as though they were holy writ
and collected as the embodiment of the principles that should
guide the nation.[1] His speech writers were, however, numerous:
some had an Action Française background; others were
Personalists or Corporatists. Pétain was moreover surrounded
by a sort of royal court in which obscure men, appointed to
positions in his household for accidental reasons, wielded
considerable influence. The only minister who was admitted
to Pétain's intimacy was Alibert, a megalomaniac professor of
constitutional law who was put in charge of justice, and who
ironically had no scruples about increasing the arbitrariness
of the regime. But Pétain was brought into power by the
politicians of the Third Republic, and Pierre Laval (his deputy
prime minister, July to December 1940 and prime minister
April 1942 to August 1944) carried many of the attitudes of that
regime into Pétain's. Pétain hated Laval but also felt he needed
him: that was another of the complex alliances of Vichy.

Laval's father had been a butcher and innkeeper with a few
acres of land. He himself had all the qualities of the tight-
fisted, astute Auvergnat peasantry. He got himself a job as an
usher in a *lycée*, took a degree in science, determined to be more
than a schoolmaster, became a lawyer, offered cheap consulta-
tions, made a name as a negotiator who could settle cases out of
court and ended up as one of the most successful barristers in
the country. He joined the socialist party. He acquired some
fame for defending trade unionists who were prosecuted
for violent agitation or strike action, proclaiming himself a
'manual lawyer' in the service of 'manual labourers'. In 1914 he
was elected to parliament as the youngest socialist deputy. But
when the socialists and communists split after the war, he would
not choose between them and became an independent socialist.
'My socialism', he said, 'was much more a socialism of the heart
than a doctrinal socialism. I was much more interested in men,
their jobs, their misfortunes, their conflicts than in the digres-
sions of the great German pontiff.' He did indeed have an
uncanny skill at understanding men. He had extraordinary
charm. His external appearance, it is true, was unprepossessing

[1] Maréchal Pétain, *La France nouvelle, principes de la communauté* (1941).

and suspicious: even as prime minister he still looked, it was said, like a chestnut vendor in his Sunday best. But he could quickly win sympathy and confidence in tête-à-tête conversation. He has been called one of the most persuasive and plausible people of his day. He was no orator; he could not write well; he lacked elegance; he had no gift for rousing the masses; but he was a master of individual seduction and backstage politics. He never became pompous and always kept his old socialist habits of camaraderie and *tutoiement*. For twenty-one years he was mayor of Aubervilliers where he raised to a fine art the business of doing favours: he handed people who came to his political surgery their letters of recommendation at once, so that they could post them themselves. He bought up two newspapers and a radio station to support him and turned them into profitable enterprises as well. He bought a 300-acre farm in Normandy and made it pay; he acquired the château of his native village, exploited the mineral spring in it and got all the railways to use his bottled water. He became a rich man but kept his simple habits. He had no taste for night life; he went to bed at nine; his wife who spent most of her time at home had the reputation of having only one dress. Laval was one of the few politicians of this period not to be smeared by financial scandal. He had no idealism, but it is perhaps too much to say that he was moved simply by ambition, for there was a strong element of self-defence in his search for power. He never dreamt of becoming a dictator. He knew his limitations and his qualities too well. He was no intellectual. He was guided by his native wit and he confirmed his hunches by consulting an astrologer.

Laval had no illusions about France either. His crime to his countrymen, a generation later, was his pessimism. 'We shall always be thirty-eight to forty millions', he said, 'compared with (Germany's) sixty to seventy millions, and we have a common frontier. Do you know the Arab proverb: If you cannot kill your enemy, give him your daughter in marriage?' His character made it impossible for him to place faith in the League of Nations: he preferred individual bargains with nations. He thought he could apply his skill at personal negotiation to international diplomacy. He had no scruples about dealing with dictators, for he considered that democracy was out of date. 'We are paying today', he declared, 'for the fetishism which chained us to democracy and delivered us to the worst excesses of capitalism, while around us Europe was forging without us a new world inspired by new principles.' Bolshevism was the great danger to him, Russia the main threat to France, and Germany the best safeguard against it. He feared England as a traditional enemy. He was willing to collaborate with Germany, to remodel the French constitution on fascist lines, because otherwise Germany would force a much more unpalatable domination on France. He did not believe that Hitler intended to crush France. Whatever happened, France would inevitably have, because of its sheer size, an important part in a European federation. He believed he could play off Germany and Italy to his own advantage. But he destroyed what popularity he had by saying too bluntly, 'I desire the victory of Germany'.

Laval's defenders have hailed him as a forerunner of Franco-German co-operation and a United Europe. They quote his statement to the American ambassador: 'My policy is founded on reconciliation with Germany. Without this reconciliation I can see no hope of peace, whether for Europe, France or even the world. I am certain that the Germans will be victorious but, even if they were to be defeated, my policy towards them will be the same, because it is the only one which is in the interests of ultimate peace.' His view of Europe had much in common with de Gaulle's, except that he did not wish it to extend to the Urals, for he hated Russia, while on the other hand he was always very favourable to the United States. The trouble with Laval however was that he was too clever, or too simple. He admitted: 'I have always had simple ideas in politics.' He misjudged Hitler and failed to see that co-operation with him on equal terms was impossible. He disregarded the warnings of his wife (who was Jewish) that agreements with Hitler were not worth the paper they were written on. He ended up an intriguer who was duped; a representative of the Third Republic's skill at compromise (a significantly ambiguous word) who carried it to disastrous extremes.[1]

[1] Geoffrey Warner, *Pierre Laval and the Eclipse of France* (1968); Hubert Cole, *Laval, a Biography* (1963); Alfred Mallet, *Pierre Laval* (2 vols., 1955); Georges Saint-Bonnet, *Pierre Laval, Homme d'état* (1931); Maurice Privat, *Pierre Laval* (1931).

Pétain protested that what Laval lacked was 'spiritual values'. This summarises the ambiguity of the Vichy regime. It was an attempt to raise the country's moral level, but never was morality more controversial. It will be a long time before historians are able to disentangle the many different levels of consciousness at which people behaved in these years. The aspects of character brought out by the strains of war and occupation gave life the appearance of being lived under bright stage lights, both distorting normality and revealing its frailty, enabling people to shut out from their vision what they preferred not to know. The Vichy regime has been called the triumph of the *ratés*, the failures, and the revenge of the minorities. It is true that it brought to power many of the right-wing groups that had been excluded from the Third Republic, and that a surprisingly large number of second-rate and dubious people suddenly came into prominence. But this happens with most regimes that follow predecessors who abdicate or collapse. The Bonapartists likewise appeared to be nonentities, vastly inferior in culture and status to the Orleanists they replaced, but the Orleanists had originally been upstart journalists and professors when they seized power. The originality of the Vichy regime was that it was supported not only by failures, but also by some very successful people. The evicted politicians of the Third Republic were replaced partly by men who had hitherto kept out of politics, but who had managed important sectors of the economy or of government. The regime revealed the contradiction that had existed in the Third Republic between the façade of authority and the realities of power behind it. 1940 was one of those revolutions (1848 was another) when the sudden disappearance of a government has the same effect as clothes being torn off a person, revealing in nakedness all the muscles, blemishes, scars and eccentricities that are normally concealed. That is why it cannot be considered an unfortunate lapse, a gap in history, best forgotten.

The political theory of the Vichy regime was thus many-sided and even more at variance with its practice than is usual. To talk about the regime as a coherent entity is misleading. However, beneath the variety, there does seem to have been a common search to 'rediscover the mission' of France, to find its 'true identity'. Christianity, first of all, was considered

an essential part of this. In these four years, the Catholic part
of the nation was reintegrated into it, after over a century of
persecution. This took place, significantly, not only as a result
of the policy of the Vichy government, but also in the Resistance movement, in which practising Christians played a role
side by side with the communists. After the liberation, the
Catholics were at last able to share power on equal terms with
other parties. The Vichy regime ended the prohibition against
religious orders; church property seized in 1905 and still
unsold was restored to the Church; subsidies were given to
church schools and optional religious instruction allowed in
state ones. The government made the Catholic ideal of the
large, hierarchical family its own; it limited divorce; it greatly
increased family allowances, and encouraged mothers to
remain in the home. It was significant that Pétain, who was
himself childless and married to a divorcée, should have led
this campaign, which resembled a confession of guilt and a
renunciation of the individualist values of the Third Republic.
This did not express simply an ephemeral mood. Despite all the
anxiety caused by the war, it was in this period that the French
birth-rate suddenly began rising, and the new attitude to
children was maintained in the Fourth Republic. The Church
gave Pétain its blessing and support, but there was no widespread religious revival, for this altered behaviour was not
specifically religious in origin. The Church was soon disillusioned by the regime when it saw that Pétain had other
allies who were barely compatible with itself. Its harmonious
relations with him were damaged by his persecution of the
Jews, though there were those who defended anti-Semitism
as being in the tradition of Christianity.[1]

The ambiguous relations with the Church illustrated what
varied interpretations were placed on morality. There was
constant talk about the need to strengthen morals. The firmly
established belief in education was not weakened. However,
because the Third Republic's schools had claimed to be
creating a new kind of citizen, they were blamed for all the
disasters that had befallen the country. The Vichy regime,
nevertheless, saw the answer only in more education. It

[1] Mgr Guerry, *L'Église en France sous l'occupation* (1947); Jacques Duquesne,
Les Catholiques français sous l'occupation (1966).

attacked 'easy-going' teaching methods, which assumed that children were naturally good and needed simply to be left to grow with the minimum of constraint. It argued that such an attitude left most people without a clear purpose in life, and certainly without a moral one, and that was why France had collapsed in 1940. It wanted discipline to be instilled as an end in itself, and patriotism to be taught without reservations. The family, rather than the individual, should be the basic unit in society, so in the schools it wanted the cultivation no longer of individual critical powers but of the team spirit: 'Learn to work together, to think together, to play your games together,' said Pétain. 'Bookish learning' was discredited, as was the ideal of education as an impartial search for truth: 'Life is not neutral: it requires one to take sides boldly,' declared the Marshal. However, since he was deeply suspicious of the state's teachers, who had the reputation of being impious and rebellious, he sought to create the new moral generation not so much in the schools, which were vexed with controls rather than developed, but in independent youth organisations. His policy was in some ways a development of tendencies in Catholic education, stressing character training above scholarship. Youth movements were given a large amount of encouragement, but because the old-established ones were unwilling to lose their identity, they were allowed to survive and no unified moral doctrine was preached throughout all of them. The nearest the regime came to establishing an original youth organisation of its own was its Chantiers de la Jeunesse, a civilian replacement for military service. Here young men of twenty-one spent eight months partly in forestry work (producing much-needed fuel) and partly attending classes on morals and history, based on Action Française textbooks. It is unlikely that this had any effect in so far as indoctrination was concerned; but the stress on physical effort and on sport did. Sport, as has been seen, expanded enormously during this war and its development as a mass activity for children dates more from Vichy than from the Third Republic. Sport, of course, did not make the French either more moral, or more Christian. The new generation, as a whole, was not affected by this proselytising, any more than it was subdued by the discipline. To control the rebelliousness of youth, or as one participant in the effort put it, to end the war between the family and the school, was a very ambitious aim. Even the schools for training leaders (*écoles de cadres*) evolved along different lines, showing how consensus was a vain dream.[1]

Pétain did not try to establish a totalitarian state. He was not a fascist. There were fascists who supported his régime, but they were not given important positions of power, except on the propaganda side. The fascists were to be found in Paris much more than in Vichy. Their violently phrased newspapers gave the regime a veneer of fascist verbiage, but the reality was different. Pétain was opposed to the extension of the power of the state. He condemned socialism and liberalism equally. He had a certain admiration for Salazar, but he was too much of a French peasant to be interested in copying foreign models. The political and economic doctrine which enjoyed greatest favour under his government was corporatism. This was an adaptation of the Social Catholic ideas of La Tour du Pin[2] which sought to combine social justice with the preservation of hierarchy, to keep capitalism but to get rid of ruinous competition, to replace both the class struggle and state intervention by self-governing professional and regional corporations.[3] Corporatism was in some ways a new form of solidarism,[4] and like it an attempt to avoid the dilemmas of modern life. There were people who stressed the traditionalist aspects of corporatism, and thought it meant the revival of the medieval corporations. Pétain indeed promised to restore the provinces of the *ancien régime*. But though a commission was appointed, under the historian Lucien Romier, to prepare a law on the subject, nothing was in fact done.[5] The nearest Pétain came to implementing corporatism in anything like its full sense was in agriculture, where it was shown that it was much more subtle than simple reaction. The Peasant Charter organised the rural population into 30,000 local syndicates, united them

[1] J. Hervet, *Les Chantiers de la jeunesse* (1962); Janine Bourdin, 'L'École de cadres d'Uriage', *Revue française de science politique* (Dec. 1959), 1029–45; on the educational policy, see the forthcoming work of W. D. Halls and J. Long's Oxford thesis.

[2] Marquis de la Tour du Pin, *Vers un ordre social chrétien* (1907).

[3] M. H. Elbow, *French Corporatist Theory 1789–1948* (New York, 1953).

[4] See Zeldin, *Politics and Anger*, ch. 8.

[5] Pierre Barral, 'Idéal et pratique du régionalisme dans le régime de Vichy', *Revue française de science politique* (Oct. 1974), 911–39.

into a hierarchy of regional and national institutions and so
for the first time gave the peasants a chance to speak with one
voice. It forced the peasants to produce leaders from within
their own ranks and these leaders were to survive into the
Fourth Republic, when the peasant pressure group was as a
result far more powerful. The corporation was supposed to
enable the peasants to manage their own affairs, to regulate
production and sales. In the eyes of Louis Salleron, the principal theorist behind this reform, the corporation was both
an attack against individualism and a liberation from state
power. In practice, however, the state appointed the leaders and
used the corporation as an instrument for the implementation
of its own policies.[1] The results were thus confused: the tendency
towards state control was accentuated; the traditional cry of
'back to the land' was given official patronage and the maintenance of a large peasant population remained a strong ideal;
but the peasant corporation leaders evolved in the course of
these years and by 1944 were talking about combining the
preservation of peasant values with modernisation and higher
productivity.[2]

The introduction of corporatism into industry likewise both
strengthened traditional forces and opened up new possibilities. An attempt was made to save the artisans from extinc-
tion by industrialisation. The old Compagnonage was revived.
Industry in general was required to organise itself into groups,
so that each branch of it could allocate raw materials amongst
its members and manage its own affairs. Eventually 321
comités d'organisation were set up (about ten times as many as
had been intended, for particularism proved to be strong).
To a certain extent this meant that the cartels and trade
associations that had developed before the war were now
generalised, so what was established was not so much self-
government, but government by big business, for it was the
large firms which dominated the committees. But there were
civil servants (like Laroque, a councillor of state specialising in
industrial relations) who thought big business employers were

[1] Louis Salleron, Naissance de l'état corporatif. Dix ans de syndicalisme paysan (1942).
[2] G. Wright, Rural Revolution in France (Stanford, 1964), chapter 5; André
Bellesort et al., France 1941: la révolution nationale constructive. Un bilan et un programme
(1941).

unfit to be given such a large share in managing the economy; and the government commissioners who sat on each of these committees used their very considerable powers to the extent that they were accused of autocracy. Here too, therefore, supposedly autonomous institutions were turned into instruments of state control. The hostility of the smaller firms to this was exacerbated by the policy of allocating raw materials in proportion to the size of firms in 1938, so calling a permanent halt to competition or expansion. In 1942, however, Bichelonne changed this rule and created a new criterion, that allocations should be in accordance with a factory's productive efficiency and the quality of its work. This did not always change things, but it did encourage the growth of a new concern with productivity among the smaller employers. Planning took on far more sophisticated forms than in the Third Republic. All firms were required to send in monthly statistics, and to reply to questionnaires asking between 150 and 320 different facts. Punch card machines were installed in a central Paris office to process this information; general production plans were made by industries, standardising and rationalising output (shoes, for example, were to be made in only thirty-seven types, and there was an effort to improve the distribution system for them). A Ten-Year Plan for National Equipment was drawn up by François Lehideux (Renault's nephew and sometime managing director), who was minister of industrial production. The result of this was to stimulate the growth of several new kinds of technocrats. The officials of the old trade associations used to run small offices with tiny staffs. Now they multiplied, acquired far greater importance, and that was the basis of their great power after the war. The state, for its part, increased the number of civil servants at a faster rate than ever before. It sent out commissioners and inspectors to control the activities of business. At first industrialists were hostile to them, rejecting all idea of state control, and speaking contemptuously of the 'insolent and ignorant excise officers' who poked their noses into their affairs. But in time these were replaced by 'distinguished and educated gentlemen' whose inspection of the books could be helpful, and who were often relied on for advice, not only in interpreting regulations but also in improving management. This experience of close state supervision (made necessary by war rationing and price controls) did not win businessmen over to *dirigisme*, which remained a bogy, but it did show them that the state could be used to mitigate the worst horrors of competition. Employers saw that the men in the ministry had a lot in common with them, particularly as it was increasingly the same men who moved in and out of jobs in the public and private sectors indiscriminately. It was on the basis of the mutual confidence that was gradually built up in this way that the planning of the post-war period was developed.

The problem of the relation between employers and workers was, however, not solved, and this was the weakest point in the Vichy economic system. Corporations in theory should have had representatives of workers and managers on the committees that ran them, but the trade unions were virtually abolished, because contaminated by socialism. *Autogestion* (which was one of the ideals of the regime) was a farce and the 'mixed social committees' which replaced the unions were forbidden to discuss wages. The authoritarianism of big business was thus even reinforced. It was no accident that the vast majority of employers sided with the Vichy regime and in the Fourth Republic (for hardly any of them were purged as collaborators) they resumed open battle with the workers. But a new generation of employers, the *Jeunes Patrons*, made their appearance, discontented with the domination of large firms, and willing to buy co-operation from their workers by higher wages, improved conditions and more humane treatment.[1]

Though there were thus important ways in which trends of the inter-war years were developed under Pétain, to be continued in due course by the republics which followed, the regime was a failure because it did not remain faithful to its aim of uniting the nation. In 1940 it had quite exceptionally wide support. But its doctrines involved the eradication of so many elements of French society, which it condemned as pernicious, that its base grew narrower and narrower. The politicians

[1] Paul Leroy, *L'Industrie de la chaussure: économie libérale, économie dirigée* (Nancy thesis, 1943), one of the best descriptions of the detailed working of a *comité d'organisation* by a shoe manufacturer; H. W. Ehrmann, *Organised Business in France* (Princeton, 1957), 58–100; Bernard Mottez, *Systèmes de salaire et politique patronales. Essai sur l'évolution des pratiques et des idéologies patronales* (1966); E. Dussauze, *L'État et les ententes industrielles* (Paris thesis, 1938).

were the first victims. There was widespread disillusionment with them. But when they were put on trial as criminals, they were turned into martyrs. The purge of local councillors hurt the pride of a large number of notables. Pétain's declared aim of replacing hierarchies of birth and wealth by one based on 'merit'—an élite drawn from all classes—was never given the institutional embodiment he promised: the provincial assemblies never materialised; and his own absolutism was maintained. The Jews were quickly singled out as enemies, long before the Germans expressed any desire that the 'final solution' should be applied to France. The Jews were, however, slow to react, because official French anti-Semitism, as introduced by the law of 3 October 1940, simply excluded them from government service, and exempted Jewish war veterans from these discriminatory measures. A sort of apartheid system was envisaged, by which the Jews, distinguished by a yellow star on their clothes, should form an autonomous corporation or ghetto. It was only gradually, as increasingly fanatical racists were placed in charge of Jewish affairs, and only in 1942, when systematic deportation began, that the French Jews were doomed to extermination.[1] In fact most of those deported (about 65,000) were foreigners: only about 6,000 French Jews went to the German concentration camps; about half of these never returned; about 20,000 were interned in French concentration camps. Though various ministers and officials claimed that they tried to minimise the effects of this organised brutality, and though Frenchmen did indeed suffer less from it than other Europeans, the damage it did to the plausibility of the regime was far greater than the cheap popularity it attracted. Equally futile was the regime's war against the freemasons, to whom it attributed absurd machiavellian intentions and vastly exaggerated power.[2] Most dangerous of all was its persecution of communists, which nullified any pretence that it was well disposed to the workers. All this created too many enemies, too many Frenchmen who were not recognised as such.

[1] Xavier Vallat, *Le Nez de Cléopâtre* (1957). For the way the anti-Semitic policy affected one Jewish girl, see Georgette Elgey, *La Fenêtre ouverte* (1973), an outstanding piece of autobiographical writing.

[2] See the vast number of publications on freemasonry in this period.

These atrocities might have been condoned if the country as a whole had benefited from collaboration with Germany. Pétain honestly believed that by making an armistice, he was saving his countrymen from a much worse fate: the preservation of human life was his aim in 1940 as it had been at the battle of Verdun in 1916. But Paul Reynaud, who riposted that the Germany they had to deal with was led not by William II but by 'Genghis Khan', was proved to be right in his argument that France would simply be manipulated by its conquerors. The advantages of the armistice were indeed short-lived. Germany exacted, under the euphemism of 'occupation costs', between a fifth and a third of France's national income. Virtually one-half of public expenditure went to Germany each year in this form. In addition, about 40 per cent of industrial production went to Germany; over half the French labour force was employed on German contracts. Between 1,300,000 and 1,400,000 French workers were transported to Germany to work in factories there, so that one-tenth of the total active labour force in Germany was French. The effect on the French economy was, first, a trebling of the paper money; secondly, a great decline in productivity (partly from lack of labour and raw materials, but partly also from resistance by French workers to German orders); and thirdly a fall of one-third in food consumption. France, as it turned out, was hungrier and colder than any other country involved in this war.[1] Pétain did not dupe his enemy.

But collaboration with Germany had wider implications. There were those who believed that France could no longer survive as an independent nation, that it must make common cause with the victorious Reich and so win for itself a privileged position in a united Europe, that peace was unattainable except by European unity—the League of Nations having failed so miserably—and that Germany was offering Europe a chance not only of unity but also of prosperity. Many collaborationists saw themselves as men of advanced, progressive ideas, as idealistic visionaries, or alternatively as realists accepting the inevitable. The collaborationists came from all parties: their attitude was a matter of temperament,

[1] Alan S. Milward, *The New Order and the French Economy* (Oxford, 1970), 63, 272–88.

an indication of the quality of their optimism. Some were seeking revenge for the lack of recognition they had suffered under the Third Republic; some rejoiced in the collapse of France because they thought that only from death could it be resurrected (as Drieu La Rochelle saw it); some were fanatics to whom the violence of Nazism was intoxicating; some were inspired by a hatred of Jews and of communists. There were groups, parties and militias which made collaboration an organised activity, but these were numerically insignificant. Collaboration was more widespread in a more subtle way, in daily life. Not infrequently it could be combined with resistance.[1] At the liberation, over 100,000 were gaoled for collaborating. There were rumours that as many were killed in private revenge by men of the Resistance who had suffered at the hands of the collaborationists, though only 4,500 murders of this kind seem to be authenticated.[2] The division of France into collaborators and resisters made the liberation, in part, also a civil war. The bitterness that these divisions bequeathed took a whole generation to lose its sharpness. It is still not possible to discuss this period in France with total equanimity.

If the Germans had won the war, the collaboration would now be presented as a sign of the impending collapse of French patriotism. This would be in keeping with the normal tendency to give history the appearance of a great river, always flowing in one direction. The Second World War certainly brought home to more Frenchmen what some of them already began to realise in the First World War, that their national independence was no longer viable in the old way. But it was very difficult to adjust mentally to the implications of this, and people came to accept the different implications at different speeds. That had been the cause of the failure of inter-war diplomacy. There had been men like Briand who saw the solution in European reconciliation. He had shown early on in his career that he was not simply a verbose idealist: in the

---

[1] Michèle Cotta, *La Collaboration 1940–1944* (1964).

[2] Marcel Ophuls, *Le Chagrin et la pitié* (film, 1972), and the analysis of it by Stanley Hoffmann, op. cit. 45–60; Peter Novick, *The Resistance versus Vichy* (New York, 1968); Louis Noguères, *Histoire de la Résistance* (1967); S. Hawes and R. White, *Resistance in Europe 1939–45* (1957); Robert Aron, *Histoire de l'Épuration* (1967); H. Michel, *Bibliographie critique de la Résistance* (1964); and H.R. Kedward's important *Resistance in Vichy France* (Oxford, 1978).

dispute over the separation of Church and state, he had carried a policy which had not ended the deep animosities but which had been decisive in enabling the two parties to live henceforth with increasing tolerance of their differences. In 1929 Briand had proposed a European federation, with economic co-operation as a first stage. Both Tardieu and Herriot had talked about establishing an international army. But the desire to extract reparations from Germany, the fear of German rearmament, the apparently conflicting interests and unreliability of allies and the precariousness of the balance of power diplomacy, had confirmed traditional attitudes. The feeling remained that France must use its power—or what was left of it—to get its way. But people were becoming increasingly unsure whether they wished to fight simply for prestige. The divisions during the Vichy regime reflected the country's tension between patriotism and despair.[1]

Inevitably this bred anger, which was indeed the emotion most prominent at the end of this period. The history of anger has yet to be written. The Resistance movement provides a good angle from which it may be approached. Roderick Kedward has shown how anger was one of the major factors that lay at its roots. The angriest people of all now were the communists, who regarded Vichy as the revenge of the rich for the Popular Front, and as an intensification of the class war: they were just as angry with the government as with Germany. Journalists who were censored, teachers who resented aid to the rival church schools, freemasons and Jews who were persecuted, all had immediate cause to be angry, but what is notable is that very frequently, it was often only when they became personally involved that their anger led to action. Anger needed to be shared to express itself, and it became more powerful when it was.[2] Anger was the stimulus behind the desire for a new order, but also the obstacle to seeing clearly the implications of the survival and decay of the principle of gerontocracy.

[1] For a guide to inter-war diplomacy, with an up-to-date bibliography, see J. Neré, *The Foreign Policy of France from 1914 to 1945* (1975, French edition 1974).
[2] H. R. Kedward, 'Anger in the Resistance' (unpublished paper).

9. Hypocrisy

FRANCE is supposed to be a country where the intellectual enjoys great prestige and influence. This is true in so far as a large number of people like to think of themselves as intellectuals. A sample survey in the 1950s revealed that 30 per cent of insurance clerks considered themselves as belonging to the intellectual class; and even 20 per cent of typists in another survey described themselves in the same way. This is partly a relic of the age when everybody with a university or school diploma regarded himself as being raised above the masses by that very fact; this is what the Russians meant when they invented the word *intelligentsia* in the 1860s. The definition that every person whose work involves more mental than physical labour is an intellectual was adopted by the International Confederation of Intellectual Workers at their fifth congress in 1927, and following that the French census of 1954 counted 1,100,000 people as intellectuals, including in this category army officers, priests, lawyers, doctors, engineers, teachers and booksellers. The number would have been even larger if students were added. The fact that bodies like the Music Hall Singers' Trade Union and the Association of Stenotypists demanded to be classified in this way shows that the term has won approval beyond literary circles. It is not just that it enables marginal groups to avoid the dilemma of admitting that they are workers, or that they are bourgeois; nor that education gives status. Literature has been highly respected in France as an essential national activity. Literary men have been called to high public office simply because of the prestige their books have given them. Writers moreover have taken to debating publicly about almost every aspect of human affairs, so that they have constituted themselves into a kind of national consultative council, self-appointed, but taken almost as seriously by the press as they take themselves.

The term 'intellectual' has been popular perhaps also because it has been both a term of abuse and a source of pride.

An intellectual was sometimes defined as a person with highly developed critical faculties. He was associated therefore with the left. This was the case at the end of the nineteenth century, when the word was first adopted in France. The literary supporters of Dreyfus, who signed a manifesto in his favour, were heralded as 'the intellectuals' by Clemenceau. Conservatives replied by attacking them as the pretentious, half-baked inhabitants of libraries and laboratories who claimed to be supermen, who sought to raise writers and professors into a new noble caste, proud that they did not think like ordinary men. Cleverness, the intellectuals were told by those on the right, was not everything and certainly not as important as practical experience, character, judgement or will-power. Nevertheless the right wing produced its own intellectuals also. In 1913 Agathon's inquiry at the Sorbonne showed that the students there were attaching themselves to ideals of chivalry and chauvinism which were just as critical of the *status quo* as those of the left.[1] The Camelots du Roi (founded in 1908 to demonstrate, often with violence, in favour of a monarchical restoration) were mainly students, and between the wars the right-wing Action Française was described as 'the party of intelligence', opposing that of the professors. The French Academy and many learned societies were bastions of conservatism and in 1935 Henri Massis was able to collect 850 signatures from intellectuals of the right approving Mussolini's invasion of Abyssinia. The Vichy regime had the support of many intellectuals. It was only because these men were discredited by collaboration with the Germans, and disappeared into obscurity, that, after 1945, intellectuals appeared to be predominantly left wing. But this was a short-lived illusion. The Semaines des écrivains catholiques (an annual congress) now renamed itself the Semaines des intellectuels catholiques. By 1968 it was clear that university professors were not predominantly left-wing—that was a reputation which a vocal and distinguished minority in the faculties of letters and science gave them; but medicine and law were mainly conservative. It is true that attacks on intellectuals came most powerfully from the right— the Poujade movement of small shopkeepers in the 1950s was particularly hostile to them—but in 1956 a member of the

[1] Agathon, *Les Jeunes Gens d'aujourd'hui* (1913).

socialist party could still complain that even among socialists 'there is no more opprobrious epithet than that of intellectual'.

Intellectuals may, paradoxically, perhaps be distinguished less by their intellectual opinions than by their emotional attitudes. They often described themselves as people whose primary concern was with truth and with knowledge, who regarded thought as the most superior form of activity, and who held disinterestedness, originality and critical power in the highest esteem. But precisely because they have been so critical, they have not spared themselves, and every one of these definitions has been attacked by them. They have been in disagreement amongst themselves on almost every subject. However, they have, despite their search for originality, generally shared three characteristics of personality. They have been above all self-conscious, and life for them has had two parts, experience and meditation on experience, with the latter usually taking more time than the former; almost invariably this has meant that they have been personally ill at ease in the world. Secondly, they have been people who have been unable to tolerate the contradictions of life: they have devoted themselves to resolving contradictions and to reducing complexity into simplifications. They have been inventors and adepts of systems and formulae. But they have been more than just followers of a religion or a creed, because, thirdly, they have not normally been concerned simply with their own salvation or welfare, and they have sought solutions of universal scope, and of an abstract nature, applicable to all men. They were not necessarily highly educated, or academics; on the contrary the autodidact, the party militant, the book-loving artisan, the village pharmacist were much more typical examples of rank-and-file intellectuals. Intellectuals were essentially abnormal in their attitudes. Until the twentieth century thinking was regarded as a painful and even dangerous activity and a *Treatise on Nutrition* in 1907 still argued that the energy of the brain had no connection with the other energies developed by the body: it was only later that the processes by which the blood circulated in the brain and oxygen was used by it were established.[1] Intellectuals were

---

[1] Aron Bacicurinschi, *Contribution à l'étude de l'alimentation des intellectuels* (Paris medical thesis, 1936).

eccentrics, who suffered a special kind of tension as individuals in society. The irony of their situation was that the solutions they proposed often only reinforced the contradictions of which they felt themselves to be the victims. This is what emerged with particular force in the inter-war period.[1]

The idea that intellectuals have been increasingly influential has gained currency mainly through frequent repetition, rather than as a result of any careful analysis of their power. This book has attempted to show that their power manifested itself mainly in the way people looked at the world's problems. The intellectuals raised disagreements on to the abstract plane of principle and so consolidated differing opinions, formulated issues and categorised people in ways which they might not have chosen for themselves and which were not necessarily accurate. In particular, they interpreted history and in doing so greatly simplified it. It is impossible to study the past without being influenced by their interpretations, which have been like rose-coloured spectacles placed on every schoolboy's nose. Their simplications have become a part of national culture; they continue to influence politics; and they are therefore themselves an important part of history. Inevitably, the intellectuals attributed to themselves great influence on the course of events, but in a way that is considerably exaggerated. French history and French life therefore have to be studied on two levels; what happened and what people thought was happening were often very different. The explanation of change in terms of the relatively small set of ideas that interested most intellectuals at any particular time has meant that large segments of life have been ignored as trivial or vulgar, simply because they could not be fitted into the common thought patterns of intellectuals. This book has tried to show that education, which was one of the main ways intellectuals exercised their influence, met with much resistance despite the material benefits it could confer, and that traditional mentalities survived to counterbalance the attitudes that the schools propagated. There was much behaviour intellectuals were unable to alter, or even to touch.

[1] 'Les Intellectuels dans la société française contemporaine', special issue of the *Revue française de science politique* (Dec. 1959). Cf. Richard Hofstadter, *Anti-Intellectualism in American Life* (1962), and R. Pipes, *The Russian Intelligentsia* (Columbia U.P., 1961).

Intellectuals were therefore in an ambiguous situation, and that is perhaps why their view of themselves alternated so dramatically between arrogance and despair. On the one hand, they sometimes claimed to be the new spiritual leaders of the world, replacing the clergy. It has been seen how the 'genius' emerged in the early nineteenth century, challenging traditional hierarchies, seeing himself as destined to be the guide of the masses.[1] Intelligence, it was claimed, gave those who were gifted with it a mission of leadership and the rights of an élite. As one author said in 1855, those who expressed the results of thought—writers most notably—were not 'jugglers with words', but 'flagellators of vice and glorifiers of virtue'. They had to assert themselves as the judges of mankind, and not tolerate being looked on as simply 'literary clowns who are paid to facilitate the digestion'. The trouble was that they were often greedy; they sought reward in easy money rather than in high respect, and debased themselves by writing about sex and crime ('brothel and prison literature').[2] Balzac said that a writer was a prince because he shaped the world; Vigny declared that intellectual deeds are the only great deeds and dreamt of an aristocracy of the intelligence. This was not an exclusively French phenomenon: Carlyle, for example, wrote of the Hero as Man of Letters and (for a time) thought of him as 'our most important modern person'. But the man of letters has become an obsolete category in England, where intellectuals have generally been much more self-effacing. In France, by contrast, the political regime was dubbed in 1927 the *republic of professors*, and the ruling radical party was considered the representative of the 'provincial idealist' who maintained the superiority of spiritual over material values.[3] Education was one of the Third Republic's main obsessions. So French intellectuals have been distinguished by close association with political power. It has frequently been pointed out how large a number of graduates of the École Normale have played a central role in politics. But, at the same time, the intellectuals had much to complain about on the subject of the way they were treated. The U.S.A.,

[1] Volume 1, chapter 16, 'The Genius in Politics'.
[2] Alexandre Weill, *L'Homme de lettres* (1855), 68; cf. Jules Brisson, *De l'influence de l'homme de lettres sur la société* (1862).
[3] Albert Thibaudet, *La République des professeurs* (1927).

supposedly anti-intellectual, was far more generous financially
to its authors than France was.[1] Very few French writers were
able to live off their books, let alone become rich. The re-
wards of authorship were always very modest, and remain so,
apart from a few exceptions.[2] So, as well as calling themselves
demi-gods, intellectuals also lamented that they were a proletariat.

In the mid-nineteenth century, theirs was a proletariat of
bacheliers (secondary-school leavers); in the twentieth century
it was a proletariat of university graduates, who were unable
to find jobs to match their exceptional qualifications. Intelligence alone was not enough to obtain employment in a society
controlled by family networks. The problem of the over-
production of intellectuals arose very early, but it developed
in a cyclical rather than in a gradual way. The first crisis
occurred between 1840 and 1870, when the number of secondary-
school graduates doubled: it was no accident that the republican party of the Second Empire was swollen by so many
frustrated young men. In the Third Republic, the expansion
of education was roughly matched by an expansion of career
opportunities in the civil service and commerce. But between
1900 and 1939, the number of students in the faculties of letters
increased sixfold. This was a symptom of prosperity (in that
these were largely the children of well-to-do parents), but also
a cause of hardship, for there was no way that all these lovers
of literature could put their energies to satisfying use. The
number of candidates for posts as teachers of literature rose
from 837 in 1922 to 2,067 in 1935, for a roughly constant 180
vacancies a year.[3] In the inter-war years unemployment became a problem, however, not just for students of the arts, but
for professional people in general.[4] These years were ones of
unprecedented intellectual ferment not only because there were
more potential intellectuals than ever before, but also because

[1] Robert Lévy, *Le Mécènat et l'organisation du crédit intellectuel* (1924) complains
that only 0·5 per cent of the 1923 French budget was spent on subsidising the arts
in all their forms.

[2] Édouard Gaède, 'L'Écrivain et la société'. Unpublished report on an inquiry
into the opinions of over 300 living authors (2 vols., University of Nice, 1972).

[3] Ronald Weil, *Le Chômage de la jeunesse intellectuelle diplômée* (Paris law thesis
1937), 119.

[4] Victor Rousset, *La Condition économique et sociale des travailleurs intellectuels*
(Paris law thesis, 1934).

the problem of the place of the intellectual in society presented itself as an urgent one in practical terms. In 1914 the
intellectuals were described as men who aroused jealousy or
hostility, in reaction against their arrogance and their claim to
be more knowledgeable than their fellows, but it was pointed
out that they were men who were also constantly humiliated
by their own inadequacies. They were themselves among the
victims of the war against respect that they waged; they were
too unsure of themselves to act decisively; and though they
were attracted by the company of other intellectuals, it was
ideas, rather than real friendship, that held them together:
they were unsociable, lonely people.[1] The interest of the inter-
war years is that intellectuals now tried to escape from this
situation.

A sociologist has laid it down as a general rule that the
influence of intellectuals depends on the attitudes of people
towards intellectual culture.[2] This is either a tautology or not
wholly true. It is possible for intellectuals to be influential
without the masses being aware of their influence, and without
them approving of what the intellectuals stand for. The same
sociologist believes that the influence of intellectuals increases
with the spread of education. This is likewise too simple, for
education is concerned not only with the spread of knowledge,
but also with the classification of people (creating both failures
and an élite) and with separating them into different kinds of
specialists, who can be more conscious of what divides than what
unites them. The notion that education encourages dedication
to ideas, rather than to material goals, was an illusion only
intellectuals suffered from. The first step in any investigation
of the influence of intellectuals must be of the varieties of
intellectuals, and of the way they influence each other, before
they can influence others. Intellectualism (this book has argued[3])
is closely linked with individualism. If intellectuals are self-
conscious people, the growth of self-awareness is the basis of
their importance. Literature seems to have been a principal
factor in the development of self-awareness. Literature in this

[1] A. Cartault, *L'Intellectuel: étude psychologique et morale* (1914), 249, 300, 310.
[2] Edward Shils, *The Intellectuals and the Powers and other essays* (Chicago 1972),
155.
[3] Chapter 2 on Individualism.

period was concerned above all with revealing the nature of man and with seeking ways by which he could express his individuality. Intellectuals have therefore been the great enemies of hypocrisy, if by hypocrisy is understood not only the pretence to virtue, but the all-pervading need to play a role. Intellectuals rebelled against the tolerance of contradictions and of compromises that role-playing involved.[1] They made an issue of the difficulties of living. They therefore confirmed themselves as outsiders, and that greatly limited their influence. They influenced each other most of all.

A heretic breed of intellectual developed in the form of technocrats and technicians. These men relegated principle to a secondary place and raised the efficient management of society into a sufficient activity. By concentrating on action, they won a directing position in both the political and economic spheres. The distinction between intellectuals and technocrats was a subtle one; the two were not always mutually exclusive. Just as the intellectual rejected the narrow specialisation of the academic, so the technocrats aspired to the same kind of universal competence or outlook that the intellectuals claimed. Indeed the technocrats carried this eighteenth-century tradition of the *philosophes* further, for whereas the intellectuals often came to despise the practical, the technocrats claimed to be inspired by theory and to be practical at the same time. An inquiry in 1963, asking technocrats what qualities they thought made them successful, revealed that 75 per cent of them placed the major emphasis on 'general culture' and only 25 per cent on technical knowledge.[2] The intellectuals were the guardians of this general culture, even if they were often superficially, also, its most vociferous critics. The technocrats were their pupils, as were all educated men. The intellectuals therefore did indeed, in some ways, occupy a position in society similar to that of the clergy, and their jargon was popularised in the same way that lip-service was paid to Christian morality. But that did not mean that their ideas ruled the country, any more than the fact that most Frenchmen got married in church meant that Christianity ruled their lives. It was always

[1] Cf. André Malraux, *Antimémoires* (1967), 13.
[2] F. Bon and M. A. Burnier, *Les Nouveaux Intellectuels* (1966, new edition 1971), 106, 107 n.

even more difficult to measure the influence of intellectuals than of priests, and that is why intellectuals could entertain illusions about their own importance. But their position was far weaker than that of the Catholics, because they were much more elitist, constantly witch-hunting, refusing to recognise as one of themselves those with whom they disagreed. Anarchy reigned amongst them, and that was not the least of their torments.

In the inter-war years Julien Benda, in a celebrated book, *The Betrayal of the Intellectuals*, attacked them for abandoning the high realms of disinterested, abstract speculation and for descending from their ivory towers into the market-place.[1] Their justification, he argued, came from their dedication to rational, universal values. Once they started participating in daily politics, they became victims of passion, they compromised their ideals, they lost the prestige that came from maintaining that their kingdom was not of this world. Benda was correct in his observation of the new practical concerns of intellectuals, but he was in a minority when he deplored this. The interest of these years is that the intellectuals now for a time had a central role in national life, because they sought practical solutions to their dilemmas.

The communist party was the creation of intellectuals, and it showed how much they could achieve, but also how far they were from being able to win control over those who were attracted by their ideals. By 1945 over a quarter of the electorate was voting communist. The party became the largest in the country, overtaking the socialists in 1936.[2] But 1947 marked the peak of its influence, and it was never able to expand beyond this minority position, formidable though it remained. The ultimate failure meant that for a whole generation a very sizeable portion of the intellectuals, who were intensely attracted to communism, were kept in permanent opposition, with very important consequences for their status and their own image of themselves.

[1] Julien Benda, *La Trahison des clercs* (1927).
[2] Party membership 1921 109,000; 1923 55,000; 1930 39,000; 1933 28,000; 1935 86,000; 1936 280,000; 1937–8 320,000; 1945 387,000; 1947 907,000; 1956–66 just over 400,000.

The failure was not the result of accident, or of tactical mismanagement. The communist party appealed to a wide variety of people, from almost every class. It represented the revival of the traditional French revolutionary ideal but also an abandonment of methods hitherto tried. The failure of the general strike of 1920 showed the need for alternatives and the Russian model, the only successful one in the world, was irresistible. To be a communist meant first of all to accept the leadership of Russia, to see radical change as obtainable only through a global revolutionary movement. The party remained obedient to the directives of Moscow throughout this period, because Soviet achievements were immeasurably more impressive than anything French revolutionaries had been able to do. To be a communist involved a measure of humility. In 1920, 110,000 out of the 180,000 members of the Socialist party broke away to form a separate communist party. Their decision was based on considerable ignorance about Russia. The Syndicalists, who formed a major portion of the new party, imagined that the Russian revolution had been a victory for their doctrines, because it had begun with a strike and had led to the establishment of workers' soviets. Those who negotiated the adherence to the Communist International thought that Bolshevism was not basically different from Jaurèsism, only covered with *sauce tartare*. Léon Blum protested in vain that Bolshevism was autocratic and that he would ultimately prefer France as it was than France run by a disciplined, authoritarian party, that denied both democracy and liberty. The Russians however were at first careful to show great moderation, so that joining the International appeared to involve only a minimum of obligations. These misunderstandings soon came out into the open. The 'Bolshevisation' of the party (1920–4), when dissident and anarchist elements were expelled, led to a loss of one-half of its membership. The abandonment of the tradition of the unity of the left, and the denunciation of the socialists as the prime enemy, led to the loss of half of the remaining faithful in the years following. The party thus came to be a small sect, with little influence on the country at large: nineteen out of its twenty-six deputies in 1924 were elected in the Paris region. However, this contraction enabled it to build itself up in a thoroughly original way, as a disciplined, hierarchical organisation, based on cells which had no means of influencing policy, the orders coming from a virtually self-perpetuating leadership, controlled by emissaries from Moscow. A party school at Bobigny trained the functionaries who ran the system; subsidies from Russia paid their salaries.[1] In the 1930s future leaders were sent to the International Leninist school in Moscow for a course lasting two and a half years, which completed the acceptance of Marxism as an instrument of revolution that transcended national boundaries and traditions.

The domination of Russia was not easy to achieve and in the inter-war years the rate of elimination of members of the central committees for deviations of various kinds was about 50 per cent and only one-tenth of the leading militants survived successive purges to get appointed to the committee four or more times. The long tenure of power by Maurice Thorez contrasted sharply therefore with the instability of his subordinates: his control of the party was accordingly enhanced. Thorez epitomised the originality of the communist party organiser. Whereas in all other parties parliamentary office came as the crowning of an interest in politics that began on an amateur and part-time basis, Thorez was a professional politician all his life, being appointed a local party functionary at the age of twenty-three and head of the national party at thirty-two. The party functionary's task was not to make policy in the way the political leaders of other parties had to, because communist policy was decided in Moscow, and the party's theoretical doctrine had been more or less fixed once and for all. He had no worries therefore about carrying out contradictory orders, even if they involved complete volte-face, because he recognised these as tactical manœuvres, not to be confused with the ultimate principles the party stood for, but which prudence occasionally required it to conceal or gloss over. Communists elected to parliament were bound by written undertakings they had to give in advance, to resign if called upon to do so by the party; they had to give the party a portion of their salaries; they accepted that they were responsible not to their electors but to the central committee. The communists were

[1] Annie Kriegel, *Aux origines du communisme français 1914–1920* (1964) and Robert Wohl, *French Communism in the Making 1914–1924* (Stanford, 1966) are the two excellent standard works on this early period.

not weakened therefore by the friction between the deputies and the constituencies which so hampered other parties, or by compromises other deputies got into the habit of making with their opponents. Thorez was able to remain supreme over the party members not only because he enjoyed the confidence of Moscow, but because he embodied the virtues the party admired. He was, by origin, a genuine worker, the son and grandson of miners, who had gone into the mines himself at the age of twelve; but he had come top in his primary school and, always regretting that he had not had a better education, he was an autodidact intellectual, the kind that the workers respected. He taught himself German in prison so as to be able to read Engels, Goethe and Heine in the original; he learnt not only Russian but also Latin in his efforts to become a cultivated person. He was not tormented by the problem of asserting his individuality or of differentiating himself by originality: he represented the workers' desire to achieve dignity, to overcome their sense of being inferior, to obtain more responsibility. One of the great attractions of communism was that it treated the man who joined the party as the member of an élite, destined to lead his fellows to better things. The result was, however, that the atmosphere in the party was one of comradeliness, rather than of personal friendship. Thorez was admired for his solidity, his dynamism, his oratorical and polemical skill; but it was not held against him that he was secretive, ruthless, hungry for power, unhesitating in abandoning colleagues who were guilty of deviation, however long or close their collaboration had been. The cult of personality was applied only to one leader. This meant that even if everyone else in the party could consider himself something of a political theorist—and all were expected to study Marxist theory—that status did not involve individualistic illusions. There was no room for eccentrics or anarchists. Collective action was the basic creed.

To the party leaders, abrupt changes of tactics were acceptable because, as Maurice Thorez said, their principle was that 'one cannot be tied by a formula or a resolution'; they were 'realists' who 'demand only what is possible in the conditions of each moment'.[1] The balance of idealism and

[1] M. Thorez, *Fils du Peuple* (1960 edition), 46, 128.

practicality was one of communism's major preoccupations. But the changing tactics appealed to different clienteles and the party's membership therefore constantly changed also. To appreciate the appeal, one should add to its membership figures the large numbers who passed through it, leaving disillusioned. In this period, communism was a two-faced phenomenon, presenting a frightening monolithic organisation to its opponents, but internally racked by tensions, exactly like the respectable marriages of the bourgeois society it denounced. This was partly because the relics of various national traditions remained a powerful influence within it. The communist party aimed to be a workers' party. In 1926 it claimed that only 5 per cent of its members were middle class. This was probably inaccurate: in the Limousin region, out of 3,100 members, only 600 were workers, 2,000 were peasants and 500 were small proprietors and artisans. In 1929 four-fifths of the party were said to be workers. It is certain that it obtained massive support from workers in the metal industries (who in the Seine comprised one-third of its total membership) and in state and railway employment. The party never gained many adherents in the private sector of industry as a whole. Its working-class element diminished steadily and in 1959 only 40 per cent were industrial workers.[1]

It was no accident that an increasing proportion consisted of civil servants, given the regimentation that members had to accept. But in the course of these years, a considerable variety of classes were incorporated into the party, so that communism came to mean different things in different parts of the country, beneath its apparently uniform structure. In 1934 the party did a roundabout turn, ceased to consider democratic socialism as the prime enemy and offered itself as the bulwark against fascism. It dropped its internationalism for a fiery patriotism, and claimed to be the most national of French parties, giving asylum to the middle class as well as to the workers, assuming in effect the mantle of the Jacobins. It was thus able to be the principal beneficiary of the enthusiasm engendered by the Popular Front.[2] By refusing to take

[1] M. Perrot and A. Kriegel, *Le Socialisme français et le pouvoir* (1966), 202–8.
[2] Daniel R. Brower, *The New Jacobins. The French Communist Party and the Popular Front* (Cornell U.P., 1968).

office with Blum it remained a party of opposition and was unsullied by the failure of his government. It made the reunification of the left its major objective and when that unity was achieved, it emerged as the leader of the left because it had the best organisation available, to incorporate the mass of hitherto unpolitical workers who flocked into the trade unions. Having won this hold over the workers, it spread its influence into agriculture during the Second World War. Despite the complications caused by its support for the Soviet–Nazi pact, which temporarily put it out of harmony with public opinion, it was able to make enormous gains by then taking a leading part in the Resistance, making itself the champion of patriotism as well as of the poor. Between 1937 and 1945 its membership in industrial regions rose only by about 50 per cent but by three and a half times in rural areas, so that for a short time the peasants comprised over a fifth of the communist electorate. The communists appealed to the industrial workers of the north and to the peasants of the Massif Central and the Mediterranean for rather different reasons, which were very similar to the reasons for the success of the Guesdists before the war in these contrasting situations.[1] The peasant communist was, as the Guesdist ones had been, above all heir to the traditions of the revolution of 1789. He was not interested in the subtleties of Marxism, but voted communist, paradoxically, simply to assert his independence.

There were villages like Épagny (Aisne) which in 1946 gave 60 per cent of its votes to the communists; but this was a purely theoretical protest by the rural proletariat, for in the local elections, not a single communist was put on to the municipal council, which was predominantly conservative, and the largest gentleman landowner continued as mayor without significant opposition. The way communism inherited the traditions of radicalism could be seen in the village of Saint-Pierre-Toirac (Lot) whose smallholders in 1945 abandoned radicalism for communism, but the superficiality of their change was shown a decade later when half of these new communists transferred their vote to Poujade's *small man* movement. Personal considerations could make peasants vote communist, as it could make them vote anything else. Samazan

[1] See Zeldin, *Politics and Anger*, 381–8.

(Lot-et-Garonne) elected the first peasant communist to parliament as far back as 1920: Renaud Jean, who became the party's expert on agricultural affairs, was mayor of this village, but he did not turn it into a model soviet: the co-operatives all failed, because, as he himself said, the peasants were too individualistic for such things; and the achievement he was particularly proud of, which his political position had won the village, was not only to have had a school established in it, but also to have obtained for it its own village priest.[1] In urban regions, by contrast, an important attraction of communism was that it provided every kind of social facility for its members, curing the very 'alienation' it was supposed to represent. The party's slogan was 'You have to be a communist twenty-four hours a day'. It created organisations to cater for every recreational need, to provide every form of leisure activity; it had its own newspapers and collections of books for members to read, just as the parish libraries kept the Catholics in a separate intellectual world. It not only ensured that the welfare of its members was always looked after; it provided not just clubs for them; it also held out the hope of an alternative career, for the successful militant could become a paid party functionary.

Paradoxically, therefore, communists were frequently people who were not interested in politics, and for whom membership involved abstention from discussion with their opponents. (In the rural south, it was different: communism appealed to political animals, who liked arguing, but who were not necessarily particularly interested by Marxism.) The result was that the revolutionary character of the party was somewhat deceptive. What it demanded from its members was conformity. It did not have the stimulus of youthful radicalism, because it denied that there could be such a thing as a conflict of generations: its attitude to the young was that they should be initiated into the party by a sort of apprenticeship in youth organisations, and there was no question of these challenging the orthodoxy of the leadership. A survey carried out in 1949 among the readers of L'Humanité showed that they had almost exactly the same possessions and habits as the readers of France-Soir, a popular non-communist paper: the only difference was

[1] Gordon Wright, *Rural Revolution in France* (1964), 187–208.

that the readers of *L'Humanité* were far less frequently subscribers to the telephone.[1] The high ideals of the party were matched by a concentration on winning practical material advantages for its members. It was concerned much more with happiness than with liberty. In the popular mind, as public opinion polls revealed, it was generally considered the party which was most concerned with improving the workers' wages (just as Gaullism was regarded as aiming above all at the glory and economic prosperity of France).[2] The party's supporters found in Marxism an explanation of why their wages were low, and how their exploitation could be ended; they found in the party the only organisation that seemed really interested in their well-being and that offered them comradeship and a sense of being appreciated. But their votes were very far from being inspired by mainly materialistic aims. Only a small minority of the communist voters were party members. Most of these voters were expressing protest at the established system, which meant that they retained their sense of independence against all organisations and institutions. Surprisingly, when questioned in the 1950s, only 14 per cent of industrial workers said that the workers were happiest in the Soviet Union, whereas 54 per cent said they were happiest in the U.S.A. Faith in Russia survived this, and this assertion often went hand in hand with the statement that the workers were slaves of capitalism in the U.S.A. Truth had many purposes, and many faces. It required a special mentality—or rather mentalities—to vote communist. Only a quarter of Frenchmen in the lowest income groups voted communist at the height of the party's popularity.[3]

The position of intellectuals in a party which, on the one hand, was so bureaucratic and, on the other, was a coalition of such disparate elements, could not but be difficult. Yet the party became increasingly attractive to intellectuals and the communist temptation was an experience that a large number of them went through. Opponents of the party have tried to dismiss this as an essentially emotional or neurotic infatuation,

[1] Annie Kriegel, *The French Communists: Profile of a People* (Chicago, 1972), 23, 58, 172.

[2] *Les Communistes en France* (Cahiers de la Fondation Nationale des Sciences Politiques no. 175) (1969), 270.

[3] Hadley Cantril, *The Politics of Despair* (New York, 1958), 112.

in which the convert 'systematically deceives himself' about his motives and pretends to himself that he is moved by rational arguments.[1] It is true that Marxism became the subject of serious study only after 1929 when the first French periodical devoted to it, the *Revue marxiste*, was founded; and that it was only in 1934 that the philosopher Henri Lefebvre published his *Selected Texts from Marx*. It was only then that Marxism began to alter the direction of philosophical thought in France, and so of the schoolboys who studied philosophy. By 1945, however, one-quarter of the students of the École Normale Supérieure were party members; and though a decade later this proportion had fallen to only 5 per cent, one-quarter of the students of the Cité Universitaire still voted communist in 1956.[2] The reasons that led so many inquiring and sensitive minds into the party were too numerous and complex to be summarised by any simple explanation. The physical horrors of the Great War filled some with such a violent hate of the generation and the civilisation that had produced it, that they could see hope only in total reconstruction, and the Bolshevik Revolution set a clear example of how this could be attempted. Communism offered the chance of putting dissatisfaction to positive use. The surrealists led the way in transforming the intellectual's individual and largely literary revolt into a search for a more total liberation, which Marxist revolution seemed to offer: this, they hoped, would 'change life' and 'transform the world'. There were those who joined simply because they wished to identify themselves with the Russian Revolution, for even if they knew little of its doctrines, it seemed to be the herald of a new age of justice and of fraternity. Believers in the need for a radical alternative to the *status quo*, or in the need for violence to change it, found in it the exhilarating prospect of unselfish action and dedication.[3] 'We were in search of a mystique' said Froissard, talking of the generation that emerged from the war.

But it was more than that, as the case of Paul Nizan illustrates. He was the son of a bourgeois, but the grandson of a

[1] J. Monnerot, *Sociology and Psychology of Communism* (Boston, 1953).

[2] David Caute, *Communism and the French Intellectuals 1914–60* (1964), 29: a key work for understanding the history of this period.

[3] Nicole Racine and Louis Bodin, *Le Parti communiste français pendant l'entre-deux-guerres* (1972).

railway worker. Nizan was tormented that he could not call himself the brother of the workers: he was tormented by guilt that his family had deserted the class from which it had sprung. He went to the École Normale, but hated being part of a 'factory to produce élites', entrusted by the bourgeoisie with the task of justifying its domination. He revolted against the philosophy professors whom he accused of turning out watch-dogs for the *status quo*, of making philosophy synonymous with understanding, so that it did not require one to do anything about the evils of the world; professors simply brain-washed their pupils—defenceless youths exhausted by examinations—and taught them to play intellectual tricks with words. Nizan fled to Aden in disgust, becoming tutor to the family of Antonin Besse (a French merchant-millionaire who later founded St. Antony's College, Oxford).[1] But he could not escape from his anxieties. He abandoned teaching to work for *L'Humanité*. He saw in Marxism a doctrine that gave 'satisfaction for all the appetites of human nature'. The Communist Manifesto was, in his view, the proclamation that 'man is love and that he is prevented from loving'. Communist literature should therefore 'denounce the scandal of the conditions imposed on man'; it must be responsible, committed, suggesting solutions and not mere reflection; above all it must 'give men self-consciousness', which was how Marx defined philosophy. Nizan illustrated the feeling of intellectuals who were dissatisfied simply with thinking: 'a thought', he said, 'has a desire for something, it wants a purpose'. He hoped to find it in the party. But in 1939 he resigned from the party over the Russo-German pact. He had not ceased to be a patriot. Thorez claimed Nizan had been a police spy all along. This denunciation was typical of the slurs the party heaped on those who broke with it—a practice which was a factor in keeping its relationships charged with high emotion. This explains, in part, why some of those who deserted communism ended up at the opposite extreme of politics, collaborationists with the Germans under Vichy, persecuting their former friends.[2]

In 1945 the pupils of the École Normale explained in a series

[1] Another tutor later employed by Besse was Jacques Le Goff.

[2] Paul Nizan, *Intellectuel communiste. Écrits et correspondance 1926–40*, ed. J. J. Brochier (1970).

of public letters what it was that drew them to the party, even if they did not always join it. Marxism, they said, gave them a sense of lucidity, above the contradictions of society: it satisfied their need for coherence and their refusal of passive resignation before the world's problems. It offered optimism, but of a severe kind, based on facts and capable of being translated into daily action. It made sincerity possible, that is to say, the cohesion of thought and action, the abolition of hypocrisy. Some thought disputation and criticism in the way that other parties allowed. In 1924 Rosmer (he adopted this pseudonym from Ibsen's character who could not stand hypocrisy) was among those who complained about the party's excessive discipline: 'It produces a cascade of marching orders to which it expects obedience without understanding and above all without a word of reply except to murmur the sacramental: Captain, you are right! A secret society mentality is being created and the methods of N.C.O.s are being established . . . Soon the party's bureaucracy will surpass that of the French state.' The party replied that intellectuals could not understand how a single ideology could be imposed in a party formed from varied schools of thought, but that the working class was instinctively hostile to the survival of the old intellectual traditions. There followed a period of systematic anti-intellectualism, or rather of opposition to the notion that intellectuals had a special role to play in the party. Ordinary party members thought of themselves as intellectuals of sorts, and they resented the claims of bourgeois intruders (like the surrealists) to a privileged position, or to a special competence. The demands made on intellectuals who joined the party therefore required exceptional sacrifices, which gradually led to accepting that individualism was only a sign of useless pride and that it had had its day: the need now was to seek salvation by collective means. The Second World War had shown the incompetence of the ruling class, but it had failed to dislodge it from its privileges. Only the workers could be creators of a new era: the party offered intellectuals a chance to get away from their isolation, to overcome their guilt about it, to express their longing for greater fraternity, for the communist party seemed the only one which had won genuine enthusiasm among the workers. Some were attracted by the party's 'extraordinary dynamism', its 'idealism, appetite for efficiency, discipline and success', by its determination to do something positive and at once, by the feeling that to be a member was an adventure. Some joined because it became fashionable to do so, just as others abstained because they wished to show that they could resist fashion. Catholic beliefs did restrain many students from taking the final plunge, but not infrequently the temptation of Marxism remained powerful and even obsessive.[1]

There were many intellectuals in the party at its foundation, and they were quickly made aware that it would not tolerate deviations. But after 1936 the party adopted a new line, of welcoming anybody of the left who would join, of infiltrating non-political groups and capturing them for communism. It sought to win prestige by obtaining the adhesion of great names. It had a charming second-rate poet, Paul Vaillant-Couturier, in charge of its relations with intellectuals: he brilliantly combined a concern for the problems that interested intellectuals with an easy-going, eclectic and modest approach to life, being always good-humoured, loving good food, popular songs and revolutionary hymns, aviation, archaeology, hunting and fishing, travel.[2] So Picasso could say that he found in the communist party 'a homeland', and Aragon talked of it as *la famille*. There were intellectuals who claimed that belonging to the party influenced their whole lives, including their physics (as Langevin claimed), but that was not borne out by the way they in fact continued to keep their work and their politics separate. Leger insisted that his art should remain in a distinct compartment when he joined the party. The party, at this stage, turned a blind eye to these heresies. It was only after 1945 that it began to demand a more total obedience of its directives and the production of a special kind of literature and even a special kind of science. It was this tolerance that made possible its popularity among such marginal but important groups as the teachers. In 1955 Raymond Aron launched his attack on communism as the *Opium of the Intellectuals*, deploring that its adherents could not argue without hate and that they

---

[1] Enquête sur le communisme et les jeunes, *Esprit* (1 Feb. 1946), 191–260.

[2] André Wurmser, 'Paul Vaillant-Couturier', *Europe* (15 Nov. 1937), 396–8; *Vaillant-Couturier. Écrivain*, ed. André Stil (1967); P. Vaillant-Couturier, *Enfance* (1938), illustrated by the author.

saw in argument the 'secret of human destiny'. That probably marked the end of the honeymoon period in the relations of the intellectuals and communism.[1]

In the communist party, the intellectuals tried to lose themselves in a working-class movement. At the same time, other intellectuals, in the so-called right-wing movements, frontally attacked many of the values traditionally sacred to those who believed in the culture of the mind. At the very time when the power of the intellectuals seemed to be higher than it had ever been, they appeared to be bent on suicide. This was a period of exceptionally vigorous intellectual debate, but never perhaps did confusion hold more sway in the minds of intelligent men. Opinions were held with dogmatic violence, until they were discarded like burst balloons. Some intellectuals were attracted, in varying degrees, by fascism, though few were well informed about its development in Europe, and they generally talked of it vaguely as an 'aesthetic' or an 'ethic'. 'We do not know what we ought to do', wrote Drieu La Rochelle, 'but we are going to try to do something, no matter what.' The fascist sympathisers had a longing for action, like the communists, but their view of action was unashamedly romantic: they claimed to wish to overthrow all idols, to shock the society that made them uncomfortable, but they were also deeply attracted by the old French nationalist traditions, even more than by foreign example. They raised physical courage into a fetish and held up youth as the ideal state: they saw themselves as the representatives of a new generation. 'Thanks to us,' wrote Paul Marion, who became Pétain's minister of information, 'the France of camping, of sports, of dances, of travel and of group hikes will sweep away the France of aperitifs, of tobacco dens, of party congresses and of long digestions.'[2] It is important to understand why so many intellectuals came to despair of intelligence.[3]

[1] Henri Lefebvre, *La Somme et le reste* (1959); Paul Langevin, *La Pensée et l'action* (1964); R. Aron, *L'Opium des intellectuels* (1955); J. Touchard and others, 'Le Parti communiste français et les intellectuels 1920–1939', *Revue française de science politique* (June 1967), 468–544; and the forthcoming history of the French communist party by Edward Mortimer.
[2] On Paul Marion, see the unpublished thesis by G. M. Thomas (Oxford 1970).
[3] Raoul Girardet, 'Notes sur l'esprit d'un fascisme français 1934–9', *Revue française de science politique* (1955), 529–46.

Intellectuals had an inheritance of gloom that went back at least to the late eighteenth century. Though they rebelled against Catholicism, they also developed and expanded the pessimistic strand in its teaching which saw the world as the home of sin and corruption. Disenchantment with progress occurred almost as soon as the faith in it arose. The intellectual, as an individual, was assailed by solitude, boredom, dissatisfaction with himself, and guilt, all of which were accentuated because he set himself impossible goals and because the distractions with which he tried to appease his worries—love, glory, travel, religion—never quite satisfied him. Rousseau has been called the father of this *mal de siècle* and Baudelaire is supposed to have reformulated it, as a consciousness of the inescapable solitude of man, tortured by his vices.[1] But, as has been seen, it required more than fashion or the influence of writers to produce it. Already in 1860, at the height of the Second Empire's prosperity, a liberal writer asserted that the pessimists were outnumbering the optimists.[2] The intellectuals were perhaps inevitably prone to pessimism, because while they held out new hopes before mankind, they were particularly sensitive to the conflict of the individual and society and they saw themselves as a minority battling against vulgarity and the errors of the masses.[3] There were those who protested that the French nation, as a whole, 'the nation of wine-drinkers', was essentially gay and vivacious; but even its prosperity was declared to be a sign of decadence: Bergson said that 'humanity groans, half crushed under the weight of the progress it has made'. The intellectuals were nearly always moralists who were worried by pleasure.[4] They had need of heroic measures to extract themselves from their despondency.

The cult of the irrational became, paradoxically, one of their solutions. Bergson (1859–1941), the country's leading philosopher, seemed to have made this respectable. Bergson was, in politics, a moderate liberal, and he was horrified by the conclusions people drew from his philosophy, but misunderstanding was the price he paid for his fame. He was an

[1] Ch. Dédéyan, *Le Nouveau Mal de siècle de Baudelaire à nos jours* (vol. 1, 1968).

[2] Charles de Rémusat, 'Du pessimisme politique', *Revue des Deux Mondes* (1 Aug. 1860), 729–31.

[3] G. Palante, *Individualisme et pessimisme* (1913).

[4] K. W. Swart, *The Sense of Decadence in 19th Century France* (The Hague, 1964).

immensely impressive lecturer and a fluent writer, and his
ambition was to produce a philosophy that everybody could
understand. He did not in fact invent a great deal. He probably
owed his instant success (and his later, almost total, eclipse)
to the fact that he combined a number of ideas current in
his youth into a general synthesis. He made them more convincing by appearing to base them on the latest scientific
discoveries: each of his books dealt with a philosophical
problem, in relation to biology, psychology, physics and
anthropology. The philosophers Ravaisson, Boutroux, Cournot
Fouillée, Guyau had not made much impact outside academic
circles. Bergson borrowed from them, but by making himself
also a populariser of science, while at the same time vindicating
spiritual values against the menace of mechanistic determinism, he was able to provide every man with a new justification for the urges created by emotional hunger. Bergson
was not anti-rationalist: what he did was rather to deny that
reason necessarily produced clear results, or that emotion was
necessarily a source of confusion or obscurity. He gave a new
status to the 'inner life', which science appeared to have
explained as an amalgam of physical stimuli. Science, he argued,
could not penetrate beyond time and space to *la durée*, the
permanent core of individuals, built up with memories, known
through introspection, and which language was unable to
describe. The individual was in a constant state of creativity.
His inner life was the source of his liberty. The best reason for
action was not to have a reason, but to act 'because it is me'.
The *élan vital*, which was a development of the eighteenth-
century Montpellier medical doctrine of vitalism (Bergson's
science was not always the most modern), became the symbol
for a new kind of emotional dynamism. *Bergsonisme* was vigorously denounced as mysticism by many intellectuals, but it
was for that very reason attractive to others. It was not surprising that on his death-bed, Bergson (born a Jew) declared
his acceptance of Catholicism, refusing to join the Church
only because such a course might seem an abandonment of the
Jews in their hour of persecution. Bergsonism was not a Christian
doctrine, but it seemed to destroy materialism and was therefore
a source of inspiration for the religious revival.[1]

[1] H. Bergson, *Œuvres* (ed. Robinet, 1959); C. Péguy, *Note sur M. Bergson et la*

Mysticism was particularly acceptable now, partly because, in reaction against the aridity of science and the failure of positivism to provide adequate emotional sustenance, Catholicism found a new appeal among writers and students. This was by no means wholly an emotional revival: Jacques Maritain, basing himself on a new interest in St. Thomas Aquinas, led a movement which was vigorously intellectual. Others found in Catholicism a religion of expiation and sacrifice: Huysmans had died refusing all pain-killing drugs, wishing to suffer for others, to expiate the sins of mankind. The fascination with suffering can be seen in the work, for example, of the painter Rouault; the obsession with guilt in the poetry of Claudel; the rejection of contemporary society in the colonial adventures of Psichari, the grandson of Renan; the rebellion against individualism in Alphonse de Chateaubriant, who became a Nazi because he somehow saw it as the logical conclusion of his Catholicism. Religion was far from pushing people into reactionary or extremist political stances, but it did provide a stimulus for the rejection of materialism, for the acceptance of discipline, for the condemnation of the idea of life as a simple search for happiness. Thus Saint-Exupéry (1900-44) ended up appearing to be a reactionary mainly because of his silences: he was not interested in ideologies, but in self-abnegation. He declared himself in favour of liberty: liberty however meant not doing what one wanted, but 'fulfilling a destiny', 'finding one's way to God'. His cult of the heroic qualities of leadership could easily be debased from the selfless ideals he held dear into sadistic exploitation. Saint-Exupéry's message was ambiguous: he approved of air pilots being punished for mistakes they had not committed, because that would reinforce discipline. It needed the horrors of the Second World War for Catholicism to shake itself free of its traditional sympathies for hierarchical and authoritarian political systems.[1]

---

philosophie bergsonienne (1914); A. Thibaudet, *Le Bergsonisme* (1922); J. Chevalier, *Bergson* (1926); V. Yankélevitch, *Bergson* (1931); B. A. Scharfstein, *The Roots of Bergson's Philosophy* (New York, 1943); M. Barthélemy-Madaule, *Bergson adversaire de Kant* (1964) and *Bergson* (1967); 'Hommage à Bergson', *Bulletin de la société française de philosophie* (Jan.–Mar. 1960); T. Hanna, *The Bergsonian Heritage* (New York, 1962); A. E. Pilkington, *Bergson and his Influence* (Cambridge, 1976).

[1] H. Stuart Hughes, *Consciousness and Society* (1959) and *The Obstructed Path* (1969); Richard Griffiths, *The Reactionary Revolution: the Catholic Revival in French*

Georges Sorel (1847–1922) had very little influence in France, and not much elsewhere, but he illustrates how widely intellectuals were now straying from traditional paths. He adopted in turn the causes of revolutionary syndicalism, royalism, fascism and Bolshevism. Though he cared nothing for the contradictions in his writings, there was a logic behind this, for the one thing he was certain about was that democracy had failed, most of all because it had led to a collapse of morals: 'France', he wrote, 'has ceased to believe in its principles.' He was at bottom an old-fashioned moralist. His early works had been about the Bible. He considered chastity to be an indispensable ingredient of the ethical rejuvenation he wished to bring about. But all the methods so far tried he condemned as hopeless: education simply obscured the issues in 'the verbosity of professors'; peaceful revolutions preserved too much of the past; socialism was a new form of careerism; the bourgeoisie were cowards. Sorel urged the proletariat to revolutionary violence, not because he admired them—he had no illusions about the common man's virtues—but simply because they were the only group powerful enough to change things. He was not clear what he would put in the place of what was overthrown, for he despised utopias. He wanted a revolution not to capture power—that is what he criticised all other revolutionaries for—but to rouse the bourgeoisie from their slumbers, to give an opportunity for heroic action, for fervour and grandeur. Violence, as he preached it, did not mean force (which simply establishes a new power): violence abolished power and brought about a new 'sublime' situation, a new morality. This had to be achieved without the aid of intellectuals, whom he also despised as idle exploiters of other peoples' labour. Sorel was not a practical revolutionary: he spent the first half of his life as a road and bridge engineer in the civil service, and then lived in quiet suburban retirement, with the peasant girl whom his bourgeois family dissuaded him from marrying. The engineer came out both in his quest for 'order' and in his paradoxical disregard for material prosperity. Sorel was significant because he emphasised the

Literature 1870–1914 (1966) and Micheline Tison-Braun, *La Crise de l'humanisme. Le conflit de l'individu et de la société dans la littérature française moderne* (2 vols., 1967) are invaluable guides, with good bibliographical references.

importance of myth and irrationality in behaviour. He shows
how disillusionment with the established order had gone so far,
that its destruction was preached, simply in the hope that somehow, out of the chaos, a new romantic heroism would emerge.[1]

The various tendencies came together in the Action Française movement, which, more than any other, gave expression
to the anxieties of intellectuals in the inter-war years. The
Catholic historian Daniel-Rops wrote: 'Action Française is
incontestably the only great party of our day that has a place
for intelligence in its programme. In the ranks of that party,
an intellectual, far from feeling suspect as he would be in the
midst of the parties of order, will feel respected. Communism
is less systematic about finding a place for intelligence.'
Action Française was an essentially middle-class organisation,
characterised by a Belgian newspaper as 'a bizarre mixture of
intelligence and vulgarity, science and stupidity'. Its newspaper, which reached a circulation of about 100,000 copies,
was read by Proust, even though he was a Dreyfusard, because
it was so well written, providing 'a cure by elevation of the
mind'. Several of its leaders and supporters were elected
members of the French Academy. It included among its
founders the scientist Quinton (grand-nephew of Danton)
and Fagniez (the co-founder of the 'scientific' *Revue historique*);
it numbered an exceptionally large proportion of doctors
among its members, as well as teachers, librarians, lawyers,
clergy, army officers and noblemen. It flirted briefly with the
working class, but failed to have much appeal for it, even though
Léon Daudet (one of its most popular writers) believed anti-
Semitism was the way to attract it. University students joined
it enthusiastically, and combined with its brigades of thugs to
beat up hostile professors, break up lectures and unpatriotic
or immoral film shows, fight with opposing groups, and sell
the movement's newspaper in the streets. It established an
Institute, with professorial chairs named after its heroes—
Barrès, Comte, Sainte-Beuve, Louis XI, Pius IX. It was very
much an intellectual movement, financing itself to a not

[1] James H. Meisel, *The Genesis of Georges Sorel* (Ann Arbor, 1951); Richard
Humphreys, *G. Sorel, prophet without honour* (Cambridge, Mass., 1951); P. Andreu,
Notre maître, M. Sorel (1953); G. Sorel, *Les Illusions du progrès* (1968), *Réflexions sur
la violence* (1908).

inconsiderable extent from the sale of its publications, though even more from funds provided by Léon Daudet (to whom the fortune of the sugar-refining son of Baroche, Minister of Napoleon III, had passed, by a complicated route) and by the wife of a director of the Creusot steel works.[1]

Charles Maurras (1868–1952), the movement's main leader, was a bitter, deeply disillusioned man of letters. Having lost his father at the age of six, and gone partly deaf at fourteen, he lost his religious faith, adopting a tragic view of life, obsessed by death and the helplessness of man. He continued to value Catholicism as a symbol of national unity, as an institution that offered order and beauty: religion was good for others. But Maurras had no real interest in the masses, opposing education, even primary education, as giving them excessive conceit. He rejected almost every ideal of his time: he dismissed the class struggle as an invention of intellectuals, though he never bothered to learn much about the working class, or about economics. He developed hatreds which nothing could assuage; he resented ever having to admit he had made a mistake; he revelled in slandering his enemies. He saw enemies, indeed, on every side: Jews, Protestants, foreigners, politicians, intellectuals (there was plenty of self-hate in him too). All his life he imagined plots and conspiracies everywhere. He decided that the problems of men could not be solved by reason. There were only two paths of escape from the 'world of darkness man carries in him': one was will-power, discipline, revolt and violence against society as it existed; and the other was a return into the womb of tradition. Feeling humiliated by France's poor showing at the Olympic games of 1898 he declared his conversion to royalism. Monarchy, he said, had made England great; monarchy was also a symbol, and France had need of symbols, as opposed to the abstract ideas with which its republican leaders had bemused it. He turned liberty upside down, demanding not liberty for the individual but for the government, liberty for fathers to dispose of their property as they pleased, liberty for the old provinces to be reconstituted. He was deeply attracted by the 'order' and stability he imagined to have existed in the medieval world

[1] Eugen Weber, *Action Française. Royalism and Reaction in Twentieth Century France* (Stanford, 1962) is the best and fullest guide.

and urged a reconstruction of many of its institutions. But he
was using monarchy only as a tool: though he attracted many
aristocratic supporters, the Pretender was always ill at ease
in his relations with Action Française and ultimately condemned it. Likewise, his alliance with the Catholic Church
was essentially too cynical and compromising to be successful.
Maurras undoubtedly made himself into a political figure,
whose writings gained far more attention than the number of
votes he might have been able to win would have justified.
But his power remained essentially verbal. He could not pass
from polemic to action. In the crisis of February 1934, when the
demonstrations of his supporters seemed to open up the chance
of overthrowing the republic, Maurras dissuaded them from
carrying their violence to any conclusion: he busied himself
writing his editorial for the next morning's issue of his newspaper. It became uncertain whether Maurras really wanted
to change things. After the defeat of 1940, he objected both to
collaboration with the Germans and to resistance against
them, because that would damage the unity of France. His
steady support of Pétain, who acknowledged him as an inspiration, proved sterile.[1]

The consequences of such doctrines did not seem contradictory, because the intellectuals who followed Maurras
believed that they were giving life its full meaning: instead of
trying to repress violence, it should be accepted, just as the
passions in general should not be repressed; they saw themselves
as raising these passions to a higher level, accepting the nasti-
ness of life but finding a place for heroism in it all the same.[2]
That they did have some echo outside their own ranks was
seen in the success of the political language which blossomed
in this period as new alternatives to the political parties,
offering demonstrations, uniforms, physical fitness and sometimes violence as substitutes for old-fashioned verbal debate.
These were able to draw on a whole variety of forces for which

[1] C. Maurras, *Enquête sur la monarchie* (1900–9); *L'Avenir de l'intelligence* (1905);
H. Bordeaux *et al.*, *Charles Maurras*, *Témoignages* (1953); Leon S. Roudiez, *Maurras
jusqu'à l'Action Française* (1957); R. Havard de la Montagne, *Histoire de l'Action
Française* (1950). Mr. Victor Nguyen is writing a doctoral thesis on Maurras and
is the editor of an illuminating new series *Études maurrasiennes*, published by an
Institute to study Maurras, founded in 1973.
[2] E. Berth, *Les Méfaits des intellectuels* (1914).

the parliamentary regime did not cater. Thus the Jeunesses
Patriotes (founded in 1924) combined Bonapartist tendencies
with the organisation of a youth movement. Its president,
Pierre Taittinger, deputy for the old Bonapartist fief of Charente-
Inférieure, was assisted by a student of the École Normale,
Henri Simon; its demonstrators were partly provided by the
Phalanges Universitaires. It claimed a quarter of a million
members and obtained one ministry and three under-secretary-
ships of state in Tardieu's government of November 1929. But
its increasing concentration on parliamentary elections led to its
losing its appeal for the young and the impetuous. Georges
Valois's Faisceau or Blue Shirts (1925), who claimed to be the
first French fascists, was a break-away from Action Française,
seeking to win the support of war-veteran organisations to carry
out Maurras's programme. Valois believed that Maurras had
provided the ideas but could not carry them out. However,
Valois had no special political skills either: he ended up disillusioned with fascism, as he had been with royalism and
syndicalism, and he died, accused of Gaullism, at Belsen concentration camp.[1] Jacques Doriot's Parti Populaire Français
(1936) tried to bring together socialists and nationalists, who
were disillusioned with the traditional parties: by being at
once anti-capitalist, anti-bolshevik, anti-Semitic and revivalist,
by having as its leader a genuine worker with considerable
demagogic skill, who managed to give the impression that he
would produce a clean sweep of the old order, this party,
which was as near as France came to having a fascist party,
appealed to many intellectuals on the one hand, but also to
workers, clerks and artisans, and it got some rich financial
backers too. Doriot was the man whom the author Drieu La
Rochelle (1893–1945) hailed as 'the good athlete . . . our
champion against death and decadence', a leader, at last, who
was not 'a fat-bellied intellectual'. Drieu La Rochelle joined
this party because he hated 'the old *gaga* world of left-wing
intellectuals' who lived off a 'rationalist conception of life',
ignoring the 'bodily self-expression that is the main need of
contemporary man'. Drieu thought he wanted action rather

[1] G. Valois, *La Monarchie et la classe ouvrière* (1909), *L'Homme qui vient* (1910),
Intelligence et production (1920), *L'Homme contre l'argent* (1928), *L'Homme devant
l'éternel* (1947).

than words; because he was attracted by too many ideas, he rebelled against them, mixed them up and sought an escape from his agitation, and from the real world, in heroism. Doriot tried to rule the tortured or frightened men who followed him in the manner of the fascist dictators, but he did not have their stamina. By becoming an all-out collaborator with the Germans, he undermined his nationalist base. He probably never had more than 60,000 active members and his sympathisers probably did not exceed 300,000.[1]

More important was Colonel de la Rocque's Parti Social Français, which in 1940 claimed three million supporters and may well have had two million, enough to be offered a seat in Paul Reynaud's war cabinet. La Rocque was the son of a general, who sought to express his military ideals, after his own retirement from the army, by forming an association of decorated veterans, the Croix de Feu. This grew from a small sect into a para-military league and then into a political party designed to reconcile Frenchmen in yet another combination of nationalism, social reform and heroism. La Rocque was a reserved man, as were his lieutenants, and his originality has not been fully appreciated because of his superficial fascist links. He was both a woolly idealist, a believer in dedication to the public service, and an astute politician, willing to play with fire but cautious about it. His refusal to seek power himself, or to attempt violent revolution, became an important source of strength. He was an advocate of European union, but thought this would come about only under the threat of the 'Asiatic danger'. He carefully kept religion out of politics; he was respectful towards the Catholic Church and he rejected anti-Semitism. He was not extremist enough for the intellectuals, but he was probably more effective in popularising a mishmash of their doctrines for mass consumption. He lacked the stature of de Gaulle, but he was in some ways a precursor of him; and he might perhaps have become a powerful figure had war not broken out. As it was, he quarrelled with Pétain, and was finally deported by the Nazis.[2]

[1] Paul Serant, Le Romantisme fasciste (1959); J. Plumyène and R. La Sierra, Les Fascismes français 1923–63 (1963); D. Wolf, Doriot (1969); M. Winock, 'Gilles de Drieu La Rochelle', Le Mouvement social (July–Sept. 1972), 29–48.
[2] Lt.-Col. de la Rocque, Service public (1934); id., Au service de l'avenir (1946); Henry Malherbe, La Rocque (1934); François Veuillot, La Rocque et son parti comme

The 1930s, in some respects, resembled the 1840s, and they ended as tragically as the great optimist rising of 1848 did. These were the years when intellectual debate assumed exceptional proportions. The intelligent young men of the 1930s were permanently marked by their youth, as the men of 1848 were by theirs: both remained clearly recognisable. The two periods had this in common, that the established order appeared intolerable, unjust and corrupting to a large number of the rising generation of educated men. Rejecting money-making or pure literature, they sought not just political solutions for their distress, but total solutions, which were ultimately moral, religious or quasi-religious. They did not just give themselves up to talking or writing, though they did a great deal of this, with a seriousness that made their elders and their successors appear quite frivolous, but they were also willing to act. They believed themselves to be on the threshold of great transformations, and they were confident that they could not only influence them but direct them. Never were ideas, as such, more respected, or so freely produced. Within the established political parties, youth movements blossomed to challenge traditional orthodoxy; new parties were founded; little groups of people, publishing their programmes in numerous ephemeral reviews, made the intellectual and political world very conscious of its ferment. Introspection ceased to have any more attraction, still less did gerontocracy, both of which had failed to produce sustainable ideals.[1]

The intellectuals were, nevertheless, no more successful in 1939 than they had been in 1848. Their internecine strife was part of the explanation. This took on new dimensions of violence. People now condemned each other to death because they did not share opinions. Political dispute ended in civil war, in 1944 as it had done in 1849. The search for national

---

je les ai vus (1938); Edith and Gilles de la Rocque, *La Rocque tel qu'il était* (1962). For petit bourgeois opinion, cf. Hubert Ley, *L'Artisanat entité corporative* (1938). For right-wing movements, Malcolm Anderson, *Conservative Politics in France* (1974).

[1] J. L. Loubet del Bayle, *Les Non-conformistes des années 30* (1969); J. P. Maxence, *Histoire de dix ans 1927–37* (1939); Pierre Andreu, 'Les Idées politiques de la jeunesse intellectuelle de 1927 à la guerre', *Revue des travaux de l'académie des sciences morales et politiques* (1957), 2ᵉ semestre 17–35; Jean Touchard, 'L'Esprit des années 1930', in Guy Michaud, *Tendances politiques dans la vie française depuis 1789* (1960), 89–120.

reconciliation, or rejuvenation, produced, once more, a division of the country into uncompromisingly opposed factions. So just as the 'sentimentals' were discredited after the fiasco presided over by the poet Lamartine, so the intellectuals of the 1930s found themselves either cast into opposition as communists, into obscurity as fascists, or into disillusionment by the collapse of their ideals. What they had shared was a faith in the importance of commitment. Some continued to preach this, reinforced in their faith by the experience of the war. But this did not enable them to escape from their isolation: they remained a group apart, essentially ill at ease, because of the complexity of their temperaments. They wished to simplify the options before men, but in doing so they ignored the problem of how to deal with those who would not agree with them, who could not fit into their systems. They did not find a remedy for the vicious circle of revolution being followed by reaction. They were not as revolutionary as they thought, for their practical proposals usually remained institutional, even though the faults they wished to remedy were essentially moral, in the sense that what they cared about most was how the individual behaved. But once they placed their faith in institutions, these were taken over by experts in the running of institutions, who perpetuated the old bureaucratic traditions and who were inevitably corrupted by power. In this, the intellectuals made the same mistake as the Catholic Church had done, of believing it would be strengthened by political support. The revolutionaries of 1848 had been as ambitious as their successors of 1930 but their attempt to improve human behaviour by a vague emotional appeal to fraternal instincts could not last more than a few months, if that. Society continued to live with its contradictions and to use hypocrisy as its method of diminishing friction between humans.

The intellectuals had always found this intolerable. They had previously coped by cultivating detachment, but that was something they now found intolerable also. After so many years of critical activity, they wished to escape from the lonely position they had adopted, and which a few of them, like Julien Benda, still urged them to maintain. The crisis in Europe was in any case too grave to allow them to remain aloof. But commitment and detachment were not as incompatible as they believed. Commitment meant that they took themselves with deadly seriousness. They ceased to be able to look dispassionately at themselves. Independence of mind, rather than abstention from worldly concerns, had always been their most valued contribution to society; when expressed as humour, it was one of the ways that they found an echo in the masses; some intellectuals, like Valéry, still appreciated the virtues of this approach. But these years generally appeared too sombre; the mirrors became too darkened for most people to see their own reflections, still less to laugh at them.

If the quality of human behaviour, which was the concern of intellectuals, had not been much advanced between 1848 and 1945, it was perhaps because its history was still being regarded as the record of crime and folly. People had not yet come to see it rather as the record of illusion and weakness, with illusion being understood to involve dreaming as well as miscalculation, and weakness being seen as including sympathy, and stemming from fear. The intellectuals of 1848 were too naïve, too generous in their interpretation of human behaviour. Those of the 1930s were often that also, but they were generally too angry, too tormented themselves to provide the leadership for those who did not share their preoccupations, and who did not feel understood by them.

Conclusion

WHAT then does French history add up to? I began this book by asking how much truth there was in the traditional generalisations made about France, whether there was a common core of attitudes which Frenchmen shared beneath their endless arguments and what indeed these arguments signified. My answer is that it is not enough to make either of the personifications of France on which conventional wisdom has agreed. It is not enough to select a certain number of achievements by Frenchmen, notably in political theory, the arts and literature, and maintain that France represented 'culture', that it stood for spiritual values, for human dignity and for taste. These were, without doubt, the reasons why Paris could claim to be the capital of the world in this period. France, though financially not richer than other nations, did seem to have greater resources of sympathy and to care more passionately about more universal problems. The France of these years will always remain memorable for the brilliance of its writers and its artists, for the vivacity of its social life, for its inexhaustible curiosity and versatility, for its ability to enjoy life even while it was aware of all that was bitter in life. Its unique combination of intelligence, style and feeling more than compensated for its self-satisfaction and obstinacy and for the qualities which foreigners found ridiculous or disagreeable.

However, such a view categorises a whole nation on the basis of the characteristics of a tiny minority, and it ignores all that could contradict it. The majority of Frenchmen were in fact peasants who cared little for these artistic ideals and who themselves admitted that they were egoistic, rapacious and mistrustful. The bourgeoisie, which claimed to incarnate the nation's values, was also held to symbolise selfishness, philistinism and complacency. The French produced lofty principles and ideas, but they could be brutal and violent and they prided themselves on being a military nation. Their economic and political organisation was chaotic, and even the brilliant writers were continually lamenting the country's decadence.

It is not enough, either, to see France's historical importance in its pioneering role in the establishment of democracy. It was indeed the first country to adopt universal manhood suffrage. It shook the whole world with its declaration of the rights of man, its repeated use of revolution to overthrow arbitrary or unpopular governments, its triple principles of liberty, equality and fraternity and its opening of careers to talent. Its history was therefore of interest not just to its own children, but was inseparable from that of modernisation in every corner of the globe. No nation, no democracy can write its own history without acknowledging some debt, or some indirect influence to France. French history will always remain of universal historical significance. There is no doubt, however, that French society, as it emerged from these revolutions, has increasingly ceased to be a model. Repeated political crises have suggested that democracy, in France itself, has been a failure. The diversity of opinion and interest seems to have ended in stalemate. Social privilege has not been eliminated. There are numerous flagrant contradictions between the high principles the French have proclaimed and the way they have behaved in practice.

There is always a demand for simple answers to large problems, for the chaos of daily life to be given meaning. Intellectuals have derived much of their influence from their specialisation as suppliers of formulae which do just that. Their explanations have not only enabled people to make sense of the world around them but have also determined in large measure what they see around them. They have, as it were, provided the glue that makes events hold together. The first aim of this book has been to separate the glue from the events, the myths from the reality, to distinguish what was said from what was done, to contrast what actually happened with what people thought was happening. Once the facts are allowed to come loose, it is possible to think again about the patterns into which they might fall. There is no reason why historians should accept the frameworks that have been bequeathed to them, or why they should continue to use traditional categories. Old myths, of course, are not to be simply discarded as useless dross: on the contrary, they provide invaluable clues for the understanding of social unity and consensus; but they are misleading because they inevitably see problems from one point of view and their authors usually attribute too much importance to themselves. I have not followed the politicians in thinking that history can be summarised in a series of reforms, for people's lives were not as fundamentally altered by institutional and legislative changes as the politicians believed or hoped they could be.

Because of the way French history has been written, there have been two myths which I have particularly investigated: that of *la France bourgeoise* and that of the political cleavage of Frenchmen into left and right. I approached these notions by pulling them apart, by pointing out the difficulties they caused and how they were created precisely to conceal these difficulties, to give an appearance of coherence. Six case studies of particular sections of the bourgeoisie, and detailed analysis of the divisions and subdivisions of the various political parties, led to the conclusion that it would be useful to put aside these general labels and start again. Rather than begin with preconceived views about the groupings one should use to study men, I have used as my point of departure the individual and the attitudes with which he faces the world. That is why this book is divided into six sections—ambition, love, politics, intellect, taste and anxiety—which are six different ways of looking at the individual. The book thus starts, as a first step, by reducing history into a kind of *pointillisme*, and reducing complex phenomena to their most elementary forms. This serves the purpose of disengaging the facts from what holds them together and making one conscious of the independent existence of interpretations placed on facts, in the way that space between objects can be seen not as a blank but as having a character and colour of its own, apart from what surrounds it. But the more individual people are studied in detail, the more complex do they reveal themselves to be. So I have not sought for a single key to explain their behaviour. Other disciplines may develop 'general theories', but historians fool themselves if they try to do this. Historical theories indeed have always been simplifications, and they need to be revealed as such. Historical analysis inescapably finds the individual the object of many different pressures and often presenting a different face to each of these; he can behave, depending on the circumstances in which he finds himself, in ways which may appear contradictory, and he hardly ever becomes quite predictable. From *pointillisme*, therefore, I have gone on to attempt a portrait of the individual simultaneously from several different sides, as though I were painting not just the obvious face, but the back of the head also, and the features rearranged so that they may all be seen at once. I have been hesitant about claiming to see causal relationships, which historians tend to imagine too freely. To talk of causes means to talk of proof and it is difficult to prove motives, character or interpretations. I prefer juxtaposition, so that the reader can make what links he thinks fit himself. This limitation has the advantage that I can show the whole complexity of each factor, without having to suppress all those that do not fit into the causal pattern. Chronology is the most primitive causal pattern imposed on events: I have sought to avoid its tyranny too, and to show time moving at different speeds in different compartments of life. I have been interested in change but equally in continuities and survivals. I have not sought to prove that change in one sphere necessarily influenced other spheres. I have found all sorts of obstacles that prevented clocks from harmonising: the country was full of stuck barometers and thermometers out of order. People's ability to adapt to change superficially, while preserving their deeper attitudes, has been seen over and over again.

I started the book by probing into the ambitions of Frenchmen as individuals, because that showed how they saw both their present and their future. Superficially, their ambitions seem to have merged into a common obsession with social mobility. The French Revolution established not so much equality, as the principle of equality of opportunity, which meant that competitiveness was raised into a virtue. But competitiveness did not take the same form as it did in America, or at least as legend associated it with America. France was not united by this cult, nor by the optimism it could have engendered. There were always those who had strong doubts about the wisdom of ambition, fearing the conflicts it produced, and maintaining a preference for the traditional idea of following in one's father's footsteps, or using his influence to establish one's own career. There was no one universal ambition. Glory, money, happiness, security, influence were rival attractions. Different occupations led to one or other of these, and when a choice between them was made, it implied also the choice of a distinct way of life. Men were thus separated by their jobs into private worlds, with different aspirations. This fragmentation was seen not only among the bourgeoisie, but also among the peasants and the workers. A psychological study of the ambitions of French people today has confirmed that this fragmentation continues. They are still divided as to what they hope for. Thus 89 per cent of the sons of teachers and of people in commerce admit to being ambitious and 80 per cent of sons of clerks, soldiers and policemen, but the average of all the occupations is only 55 per cent. The nature of ambition in fact varies: on average three-quarters of the population believe that hard work is the way to success, but only one-third of intellectuals and artists think this, and less than half of lawyers: there are those who believe they have a right to get to the top, because they have superior gifts. Manual workers are exactly divided on this subject, hope and despair being equally balanced. Sixty per cent of the sons of soldiers have as their ambition the desire to devote themselves to an ideal, rather than to making money, but only 21 per cent of the population as a whole share this attitude. By contrast 77 per cent of the sons of merchants hope to do well through the influence of their families and parents; whereas the nation as a whole is equally divided on just how much nepotism can achieve.[1] Different social groups thus clearly cultivate different aims; it is not possible to link pressure for change with a whole class. On the contrary, for those groups which are most ambitious are bitterly hostile to each other. Thus teaching, the army and commerce have been the three major avenues for social climbing. Far from being allies, however, the members of each of these professions have held the other two in contempt. France has not entirely thrown off privilege, and the cult of equality is balanced by jealousy. Perhaps it was because rising in the social scale still remained very difficult that rivalry was so pronounced; perhaps it was because there were so many failures, that the success of others was resented as much as it was applauded as proof of the principle of equal opportunity.

The importance of the family, as the basis of French civilisation, was another widely acclaimed myth. People felt so strongly about family life because they experienced its benefits comparatively rarely and they therefore dreamt of it as an ideal. It has

[1] C. Lévy-Leboyer, *L'Ambition professionnelle et la mobilité sociale* (1971).

been shown that, around 1900, 45 per cent of marriages lasted less than fifteen years; to be an orphan, to be illegitimate, to be abandoned or sent away to wet-nurses in one's infancy was a common experience. Nearly 40 per cent of women worked (not all that much less than the 68 per cent of men who did) and so the idea that the wife's place was in the home was something many people could long for, without having known it.[1] How to make family life more satisfactory, for those who did lead such a life, was a source of much worry. Contradictory solutions were proposed. The relations of husband and wife were clearly often unsatisfactory. The two belonged to opposing cultures, and were educated differently. The conflict about religion was partly a conflict between the sexes. The fact that there was no strong feminist movement indicated not that the situation was harmonious but rather that each sex had successfully built up defences around itself, and that it was holding its own in the war between them. In 1960, only a tiny minority found friendship with members of the opposite sex possible. The respectable façade of marriage was maintained only by a well-organised system of prostitution. The relations of parents and children were far from being ones of authority and respect that every generation likes to imagine once existed. The rebellious child was already a problem in 1848, just as the 'permissive society' was. Love was the revolutionary factor in social relations, as 'ideas' were in politics, and love was also counter-revolutionary. Some parents reformed the family by introducing more affection into it, but the affections of father and mother were not necessarily of the same kind. Control of children, and particularly of daughters, was what mothers struggled for, but the over-possessive mother was already being complained about in the Second Empire. Fathers, for their part, had difficulty in expressing their affection, for it did not combine easily with the obedience they also demanded. Love and ambition often conflicted. Parents keen to get on in the world made demands on their children which placed great strains on them: the coldness of the aristocracy towards its children was copied by some members of the petty bourgeoisie, in the hope of instilling the virtues that led to success. In the 1950s, a majority of parents still believed that more severity was needed in bringing up children.

[1] Volume 1, 315 and 351.

Love and discipline thus continued to be alternative and conflicting bases of the family, but family instability did not just reflect political conflicts in general, for the family was, also, to some extent, at war with society. Parents appealed to the schools to establish harmony between the generations. But the educational system they set up developed its own independent ideals. It told parents that they were incapable of giving children an adequate upbringing, that the defects children suffered from were indeed largely due to the laziness, ignorance or faults of parents themselves. However, a conflict between schools and children soon also became evident, and the schools were no more successful than parents in making the young behave as they were told. The children played off school against parents and developed defence mechanisms of their own to counteract both. With the lengthening of the schooling period, and the ending of child labour, children became almost a separate class in society. This was only very vaguely perceived. In the inter-war period, adolescents were declared to have 'special psychological problems', which was the beginning of the recognition of their autonomy, and of the inability of their elders to understand them, let alone control them. So, even if there was more love in the family at the end of this period, love had also set up tensions of its own. It was a disruptive factor, cutting across all other divisions, as well as the source of conciliations. Shame, or hypocrisy, prevented an acknowledgement of these difficulties and it was only in 1968 that the conflict of generations was finally recognised as a major political problem, but that problem had long been in existence. The Saint-Simonians had been rebels not just against the political and economic order, but against its emotional bases also: they included a large number of orphans or children of irregular upbringing. Jules Vallès openly stated that he participated in the rising of the Commune partly to obtain revenge for the cruelty he had suffered as a child at his father's hands. The relationship between family and politics will, however, always remain obscure, because there is no way of assessing the precise influence of family background, but it may be that those who engaged actively in politics will be seen as sharing certain emotional characteristics, as much as dedication to the public good.

The cult of the intellect was another of the pillars of French civilisation. This period was distinguished by the enormous efforts made to spread that cult and to develop a uniform way of thinking among a population which was only just emerging from illiteracy. This was, again, another kind of revolution, which created new forms of prestige and privilege. The state, partly in order to counteract its rival the Church and partly to 'moralise' the masses, embarked on a programme of education which undoubtedly strengthened nationalist sentiment and participation. The influence of Paris was greatly increased; provincialism and patois were cowed into admission of their inferiority; the favours of the state went to those who could pass examinations, showing that they had learnt to admire a select number of literary gods and could more or less imitate their speech and their style. But the uniformity thus created was superficial. The state found that, with the school system, it had brought into being a monster it could not control. The schools developed values of their own, which were not in harmony with those of society at large. They preached admiration of the great minds of the past and rejected the commercial, industrial world as corrupting and base. Like the Church, they saw their role as the protection of children against adult temptations; they felt unappreciated and therefore fell on the defensive. Like the bureaucracy, they did not just serve the state but made their own preservation and expansion a primary goal. They were moreover divided amongst themselves and so instead of producing pupils with equal chances in life or ones who accepted the same values, they created a series of élites, separating secondary and primary pupils into two distinct worlds. They made it easier for people to rise in the social scale, but only marginally, for education could not override the influence of the family. Examinations opened the road to success for some, but damned others as failures. The cult of intelligence was corrupted by facile verbalism, by mediocre imitativeness; for many, it meant not acceptance of spiritual values but a way of getting a job and more money. But it also led to the growth of a large class with a vested interest in respect for the intellect, which became a power to be reckoned with, though inevitably it also aroused opposition as well as admiration.

The admiration, and the resistance, could be seen in the country's taste. Books and newspapers, like trains, greatly increased the possibilities of communication, and therefore of uniformity. Science and literature combined to offer people similar experiences, and to give equality probably more practical meaning than politics did. They greatly increased optimism, and intellectuals became the leaders of society in the sense that they formulated its hopes. But they also found that their exhortations were very often shed like water off a duck's back. The literature that gained the widest audience was not always that which seemed to deserve admiration: the masses welcomed books that fitted in with their traditional preoccupations and with their desire for escapism, and they found food for their imagination in trashy novels and popular journalism. To 'elevate' their taste became the intellectuals' hopeless mission. They encountered a further obstacle in the fact that taste got confused with imitation: the furniture the peasants began to fill their houses with, the clothes they ordered from the department stores were parodies of the artistic creations on which they were based. A contradiction between the aims of artists and the tastes of the masses, which refused to be shaped by them, was revealed. Artists became concerned with giving expression to their individuality; only rarely did that result in work with a universal message; artists therefore withdrew into a more or less private world of their own.

The masses did not show themselves receptive to intellectual or sensual originality, first because they had more pressing problems connected with their mere survival, and secondly because beyond that, getting on in the world became a matter not only of acquisition, but also of appearance. In taste, social mobility involved showing off one's wealth, which meant modelling appearances, as far as possible, on those who were better off. This turned into the imitation of mediocrity; but this imitation was not entirely voluntary, and certainly not spontaneous. The role of intermediaries was probably decisive: the masses bought what goods they could. Merchants and manufacturers decided what should be sold and these hidden arbiters of taste were not as responsive to demand as they might claim. Just as in politics, the people got less of what they wanted, in return for their taxes, than the politicians promised them, so the search for cheapness and for profits distorted the benefits that were derived from both artistic and industrial production. Democracy was still in its infancy and it was no more able to express its desires clearly than a child at a fair. It stared with awe at the intellectual jugglers; it envied them their verbal skills, but it was not on the whole attracted by the intellectual way of life, which was too narrow for it. It undoubtedly found the stalls of the materialists, hawking comfort and property, more attractive. But it is wrong to say that it was seduced by them. This was not a materialist society, and not just because it was too complex to have any such simple attachment. It has been shown how the desire for immediate pleasure was firmly repressed in many sectors, how it was the industrial workers, with no hope of rising out of their class, who were willing to spend their money freely, above all on food and entertainment, as soon as they got it; but peasants and clerks preferred to save, in the belief that there were more permanent satisfactions. There was little popular demand for the social benefits that governments organised, like sanitation or cheap housing estates, which segregated the poor. The standard of living was raised not just by pressure from below, for the workers were as interested in independence as in prosperity. The bureaucracy expanded not because it was overworked but because it searched endlessly for more to do. Government expenditure, or inflation, ultimately made saving impossible for the small man, and the consumer society thus became a necessity. Industrialists, for their part, produced goods for the masses less to 'meet demand' than to increase their profits. They were slow to see the need to raise wages if they were to find more buyers for their goods. The expansion of industry led to a reduction in the hours of work, or rather a reorganisation of work, so that work became distinct from leisure. All this proceeded in a very haphazard way: it was certainly not a sign that the masses were able to reorganise their lives according to their taste. They had more money to spend, but they also had more demands on them. Their lives could be far richer, but boredom was also a larger menace in many trades. But if things were not as they would have liked them, they bore with them because they had a large arsenal of defence mechanisms, of which humour was not the least powerful. They were involved in far more defensive battles, of this private nature, than in occasional open rebellion.

The injustices of politics and economics were not their only source of worry: in private anxiety men had to cope also with their own selves. This was a period in which self-awareness increased enormously and the discovery of the individual was as revolutionary as the extension of his physical power through industry. Here again intellectuals led the way, analysing their loneliness, their guilt, and the conflicts of their emotions. They showed how education and the cultivation of sensibility did not necessarily increase happiness. As physical diseases were gradually conquered, nervous maladies proliferated to take their place. Individualism did not lead to a demand for more liberty, for it also made many of those who were affected by it turn for comfort and support to other sources: it revealed that fraternity was a principle even more difficult to implement than equality; and the intellectuals who pondered it were too torn within themselves to offer acceptable solutions. The doctors acted as advisers and consolers, but though they won much influence as a result, they offered palliatives, not solutions. Anxiety therefore split the nation along other lines. The discipline the army offered young men who were compulsorily passed through it was shrugged off, and military ideals remained the private code of an isolated, professional group: it never succeeded in exerting much influence outside times of war. Catholicism, to which the nation nominally adhered, was the object of the century's most vigorous quarrels, concentrating the animosities produced by other disputes too; it has only recently ceased being a source of division, and instead it has become the creed of another minority. Thus society was fragmented by yet another cell. And on its fringes, the criminal world had its own mysterious laws. The fall in population gave the impression that anxiety was sapping the nation's vitality, but that was to measure vitality unfairly: and besides it was not every couple who started having one child only—the nation was divided here also, and there was still a large group who produced large families. There was no one attitude even in the face of death.

Politics reflected these various pressures inadequately. It tried to simplify life by dividing Frenchmen into supporters of left and right. There is no doubt that to a considerable extent it succeeded. These labels have been immensely powerful influences and to that extent they do represent a very definite bifurcation, which makes it almost impossible for people on opposite sides of this barrier to co-operate. To Frenchmen this is something inescapable. No account of politics which does not base itself on it can make sense to them. But to outsiders, who have not been involved in the almost religious emotions this breach has produced, it appears not simply as a distinction between supporters and opponents of change (valid both on the theoretical and traditional levels) but also as a basic source of confusion. Because of it, Frenchmen have been unable to see just how much unites them, or they have tried to fit disagreements into this stereotype which distorts the realities. They have, of course, been partly conscious of this, and the division of left and right has in practice been attenuated by various modifications. The left has had to be split into two, to accommodate the communists, and the right has been forced to recognise as its illegitimate offspring such hybrid forms as Bonapartism or Gaullism; a blind eye has had to be turned to all those politicians who climbed into power on a left-wing programme, only to behave in office indistinguishably from their right-wing opponents. It is legitimate to classify politicians according to the principles they appeal to; but it is equally necessary for historians to judge them by what they do as well as by what they say.

The first step is to differentiate between political philosophers, governments, party militants and the masses. With political philosophers, ideology is all-important; but ideologies are notoriously ambiguous. One cannot divide Frenchmen, for example, into followers and opponents of Rousseau or Proudhon, because they have been interpreted in radically different ways and have been claimed as the founding fathers of both libertarian and totalitarian systems. There are, it is true, clear friends and enemies of Marx, but Marx, as has been shown, was mixed up with so much other ideology, that there are profound and fundamental divergences between those who admired him. Every ideal—democracy, liberty, or socialism—has been twisted into too many shapes to have a clear significance. The clash of theory and practice has confused matters further still. It has been shown how French politicians tacitly divided themselves into those seeking ministerial office and those content to act as middlemen. Those who entered governments very seldom escaped being corrupted by the fascination of power. Their history has to be written in terms of the use they made of the state, which still had many of its *ancien régime* characteristics, and which was almost constantly strengthened, irrespective of the political theory that was supposedly being implemented. This century may be remembered as the great age of liberalism, but the bureaucracy all the same trebled in size. Clemenceau, the staunch radical fighter for liberty, and for long the representative of the individual against authority, was in office as fierce an upholder of governmental power, as ruthless a repressor of trade unions and of strikes, as the dictator Napoleon III, and indeed whereas Clemenceau carried out a certain amount of nationalisation, Napoleon III's was paradoxically one of the rare governments to reduce state regulation of industry and trade. Waldeck-Rousseau, because he was associated with the anticlerical campaign and with the law enfranchising trade unions, has remained a hero of the left, but he despised left-wing politicians, he disliked the revolutionary trade unions, hoping to win the workers away from them; he had little of the left wing's optimism, still less its faith in education: he was a jumble of prejudices, with an authoritarian personality that saw fraternity in distinctly theoretical terms. By contrast, Léon Blum, who terrified the bourgeoisie because he was a socialist, was one of the most sensitive politicians to hold high office, one of the most warmly attached to humane values and indeed the least willing to use violence to enforce his programme, insisting that socialism could work only when everybody was ready for it and accepted it. To suggest that politicians should be distinguished by their temperaments, by their sensibility or their style of behaviour, is not to minimise the importance of ideology, but to place this in a broader perspective, as part of a whole personality and a total situation, and not to see it just in terms of theory.

These confusions were exacerbated by the 'notables', the party militants and those for whom politics was a way of life. At this level, doctrinal issues were constantly invoked and passionately debated. But these men had three different roles: to spread consciousness of general interests and so make the masses as a whole participate more actively in the national community, to act as the intermediaries who arranged the compromises and the deals between government and people, and to fight amongst themselves for power. Whereas the most famous politicians generally had the ambition to overcome national divisions, to go beyond party, and win the approval of all Frenchmen, political divisions were stressed by the local militants, for whom the exclusion of their enemies was always a major preoccupation. Politics had several faces: it showed the general significance and importance of apparently minor disputes, but it also provided a means by which the authority and favours of the state could be used to win personal battles. All sorts of animosities therefore came to group themselves under the banner of lofty principles, which helped to make sordid ambitions respectable. Village rivalries were thus consolidated; family feuds grew into impregnable traditions; people often forgot what they had originally quarrelled about, but they were certain they had to go on fighting. Politics in France was particularly intertwined with history because of this: old divisions were perpetuated even though new solutions had arisen. It was long impossible for left and right, embittered by the anticlerical war and by memories of mutual persecution, to face up to the fact that the redistribution of real economic and political power was making nonsense of many of their prejudices. The masses were not as interested by politics as legend has it, and just how superficial their adherence to the parties was became evident from time to time, when they emerged from their lethargy to show enthusiasm for 'saviours' like Napoleon III, Boulanger or Pétain. The extreme left wing was not so much a party as an opting-out of the party system; syndicalism, and then the 25 per cent communist vote showed how widespread this attitude was. *Apolitism* has been somewhat confused by the fact that some parties have emerged, like Bonapartism, or Gaullism, as the avowed representatives of the 'silent majority'. They have claimed that there was a national consensus, which was concealed by party strife, and to which they could give expression. This was only partly justified, though it was perfectly true that there were many issues on which the people would have agreed, if only party considerations had not stopped them.

It would be more accurate to say that the country was divided between those with a partisan mentality and those with a consensus mentality. The 'national' movements were not truly national, because they appealed only to the latter, and they obtained their cohesion partly by attacking the former: they too always had enemies. It should be possible, however, for the historian to see, with hindsight, what both these mentalities had

in common, apart from the difference in temperament. Religion
is a good example: this was what divided people as much as
anything: but on the practical level, that is to say, on the level
of morality, clericals and anticlericals were not really divided:
being both puritan, they believed in avoiding temptation, and
in seeking spiritual as opposed to material satisfactions. The
masses were unable to express their own opinions on this matter
in a clear way, but it is certain that they did not share this
puritan philosophy, or at the very least that they were divided
about it. The issue of the consumer society, and of pleasure while
one could get it, was never put before them, and yet this was
perhaps the most fundamental question raised by industrialisation and urbanisation. Democracy therefore only went a certain
way: it offered the masses a certain amount of choice, but the
choices were not necessarily formulated in a way to allow them
to express their aspirations in their entirety. The power of the
intellectuals, who formulated the choices, was based on this. But
it has been seen that often more portentous choices were forced
on the people by the facts of economic life: here it was a different
set of men who both offered the options and limited them.

Technocracy was an attempt to produce a compromise between the various pressures in this society, and some coherence
between them. It was the old monarchy's benevolent despotism,
modernised by meritocracy, democratised by the public opinion
poll and a broadened social conscience, but remaining firmly
seated in the old traditions of centralisation and bureaucracy.
However, even its all-seeing efficiency could not cope with the
multitude of human tensions and diversities that could not fit
perfectly into its programme of political stability and economic
prosperity. It had, besides, no consolations to offer in times of
depression, and no emotional attractions to win it forgiveness
when it made mistakes. It did not solve the problem of democratic participation. But neither had the traditional form of
government it ultimately replaced, or rather absorbed. Gerontocracy had survived so long because it had found subterfuges to
absorb the conflict of generations, allowing superficial political
changes to mask underlying continuity. The movement of
parties to the left gave scope to youthful opportunism, while a
compensating institutional conservatism and historical attitudes
minimised the consequences and preserved the system as a

whole. However, education so strengthened those sections of the community which had hitherto been excluded from political power—women and children—that the hypocrisy about the difficulties of family life could no longer be maintained, and gerontocracy collapsed with it.

The conclusion need not necessarily be, as some political analysts have argued,[1] that this was a 'stalemate society'. It appears so only if one holds up certain liberal ideals to it and wonders why it has failed to meet them. By this criterion, some people were indeed frustrated, but one should not assume that participation or efficiency were universal aspirations, nor that Frenchmen as a whole knew what it was that they wanted, even if the political system had allowed them to achieve it. If one wishes to characterise this society with a label of this sort one could call it rather a cellular society. The occupational, ideological, regional and social groups of which it was composed absorbed themselves deeply in sectional interests, and developed ways of life which made these groups as near as possible private worlds, each with its own satisfactions. Artists, businessmen, teachers, soldiers, each pursued different goals; people grouped themselves in family and client networks; mentally, they functioned at different times rationally, emotionally, superstitiously, humorously. The frustrations of national politics were thus made more remote. Tocqueville's idea of the Frenchman as an isolated individual, helpless before the centralised state, and the modern sociologists' vision of him as tormented by alienation, were true only if one ignored whole aspects of his life, in which he found ample scope to express himself and to make something even out of his misfortunes. He may not have been able to attain his ideals, but he found many substitutes for them. It is legitimate to show in what respects the political system did not work, but one should not forget also that in practice, somehow or other, people managed. How they did says as much about their culture as their ideals and their institutions.

These six different approaches to life have shown divisions cutting across Frenchmen in so many ways that there were an almost infinite number of permutations. If enough aspects of

[1] See the suggestive writings of S. Hoffmann, *In Search of France* (1963) and *Decline or Renewal?* (1974).

their lives are taken into account, Frenchmen cannot be classified or categorised. The political and economic myths which
sought to make common action possible or to give them the hope
that there was a universal solution for their troubles were too
partial, too restricted to a limited range of problems, to dominate general behaviour and attitudes. What this book has tried
to show is that the individual had not learnt to cope with himself, let alone with the political and economic institutions surrounding him; the emotional stability was lacking to make these
work as the theorists planned. The problems of human relations,
of dealing with family, friends and strangers, were baffling
because self-knowledge was still in a very primitive stage.
Frenchmen were not short of ideas, nor of banners behind which
they could march, but they were short of mirrors in which they
could see themselves. The mirrors that existed were generally
misted up by the fog of principles which made it difficult to see
the realities, and in any case people looked at their mirrors
through coloured spectacles, having chosen a colour to suit them
in early youth and seldom changing. The compartmentalisation
of society meant that, in addition, people were fitted with
blinkers. The nineteenth century opened up new opportunities
for everyone, but people seized them with caution. They bol-
stered themselves up by playing roles, which simplified things
in some ways. But this meant also that new barriers were raised
up between men, for specialisation affected not only their jobs,
through the division of labour and the rise of the professions, but
life in general. The young and the old began to split off as
separate classes. Male and female maintained separate ideals.
The twentieth century's answer to this was to seek an escape
from these barriers through distractions, entertainment, leisure.
But the growth of leisure only created a new compartmentalisation in that work and leisure were now separated too. Durkheim
thought the answer to the dissatisfaction which this was causing
was to strengthen the institutions of these small worlds, but that
would only have accentuated their isolation and would have
done nothing to improve communication between them.

The problem that remained unsolved at the end of this period
was how individuals could escape from their private worries,
transcend the specialisation that industrialisation and technocracy demanded, and acquire some detachment from pressures

upon them. They could not obtain that mastery of the environment that the scientists promised them, nor even that control over their own destinies that the politicians claimed universal suffrage gave them, until they had ceased to be slaves of their history, their self-deceptions, their passions and their worries. It is in this sense that the political, economic, social and moral strands of the history recounted in this book converge: each of them forced the individual to define himself in his allegiance, his specialisation and his tastes. I have shown how people got round the inconveniences this caused, but they found only palliatives for the pressure that they should be consistent and predictable. The search for prosperity was necessary and inevitable, but the preoccupation with it allowed people to forget what their goals were, or to avoid asking the question. At the end of this period, Frenchmen still had not worked out clearly where their priorities lay.

So one cannot sum up modern French history simply by talking about democracy and art. One can, alternatively, see it as being dominated by competitiveness and anxiety. To do this is to distinguish between two kinds of history, between the spoken and the unspoken, between the way people liked to see themselves, and the side of them they preferred to keep quiet about. That is what I have tried to do in this book. I have tried to show that if one ceases to look on Frenchmen's actions simply through the categories which they liked to employ, then the inspiration of their daily lives turns out to be also the bane that tormented them. Competitiveness distracted them from the principles they preached; it often became a partial substitute for those principles; but it opened the door only to new worries. This has therefore been a history of an infant democracy, characterised by confusion about its direction, and with a tendency to get lost in conflicts whose meaning often became obscure. It has also been a commentary on the difficulty, for a nation, of making choices, of forging its identity and of finding the detachment to judge what it is doing.

This book has been not quite a post-mortem examination of French nationalism, but rather a summing-up of its achievement as it reaches the age for retirement, or as it prepares to merge itself in a new European nationalism, whose character is even more uncertain. Europe will undoubtedly inherit an ambivalent legacy from it. The nationalism of France was based on a euphoria which gave people the illusion that they had found a purpose, but the closer examination of that purpose, attempted here, suggests that the choices were only dimly beginning to be seen. The euphoria was, to a certain extent, artificially stimulated. It undoubtedly made possible the achievement of noble and plausible goals, but it also diverted a great deal of energy into sterile pursuits. French nationalism in this period, though it was progressive and liberal, was still the child of the monarchs of the *ancien régime*; it was obsessed by power and vanity. Its ambitions were constantly disrupted by emotion, because it had only a limited understanding of the individual imagination: it placed its faith in laws and institutions. Individuals learnt to shrug these off, and this, as much as the efforts of the politicians, explains why France was, to a certain extent, or sometimes, a free country.

In writing this book, I have seen my main purpose as one of clarification. I have tried to do this not by simplification—for the problems dealt with have shown themselves to be more complex as they are more deeply pursued—but above all by distinguishing between different levels of historical reality— ideological, social, institutional, emotional. The way to get a picture of the whole wood, while surrounded by a mass of trees, is to learn how to see it in different ways, to allow the light to illuminate different aspects, and so to become aware of its changing, complementary and even contradictory variety.

Every generation is confused by its past and uncertain about the significance of its own times. The historian questions the generalisations that have become current about the past and its relations with the present. He tries to discover what people have been trying to do, which is not necessarily what they said or thought they were doing, and to show why plans went astray, why situations no one wanted came about. Historical study is a necessary preliminary to an understanding of the choices that each generation has to make, and to a reordering of the priorities it must have before it. The historian is not a soothsayer, he cannot tell what is going to happen next; but he may perhaps have some use all the same, in the sense that he can be a kind of court jester. He cultivates detachment. Humour, as has been shown, is one form of detachment. The historian tries to interest and entertain, but also to say what his readers may not wish to hear.

For myself, not the least reward for having devoted twenty-one years to research on this subject, is that I do not feel that I have ceased to be concerned with the universal by studying the ideas, manners and achievements of France in such detail. France has always had something interesting to say about virtually every aspect of life; I have found it an unfailing source of stimulation. So, though I have not hesitated to paint a true likeness, as I see it, warts and all, this is a work composed with affection. It is offered to its sitter, in all modesty, with gratitude.

BIBLIOGRAPHY

PRESSURE of space makes it impossible to place here bibliographical references additional to those in the footnotes: since these will be of interest only to specialists, they can be reserved for a separate volume. This note will simply indicate how the reader can find out more on particular topics.

Books published in France have been listed since 1811 in the *Bibliographie de la France. Journal officiel de la librairie*. From 1934 *Biblio* has performed a similar function. These, however, are not as convenient to use as Otto Lorenz (a German who became a naturalised Frenchman), *Catalogue général de la librairie française*, which first appeared in 1867 with four volumes covering the years 1840–65; it continued to come out every decade or so after that; but unfortunately stopped in 1925. The great merit of this work is that it has a subject index, which must be the starting-point of every piece of research. To supplement it, one should use the catalogues of the Bibliothèque Nationale, though that again is complicated. The author catalogue was started in 1896 and has now reached the letter V. This means that twentieth-century books published by an author whose name begins with a letter from the beginning of the alphabet are not to be found in it. Books published after 1960 have, however, separate published catalogues. For the gap left in this way, a visit to the B.N. is indispensable, to consult its card catalogue. The unpublished subject catalogue in the B.N. is invaluable (for books published after 1882). The general rule is in fact that a bibliography for research on France can only be properly compiled by a visit to Paris, not only for this unpublished subject catalogue, but also for those to be found in other, specialised, libraries. A descriptive list of these can be found in *Répertoire des bibliothèques de France* (new edition, 1970). For example, the Bibliothèque Marie Durand is where everyone wanting to work on women's history must go; subject catalogues on cards in the Institut Pédagogique and the Musée Social are indispensable for research on education and social questions; the library of Nanterre University has a collection on the First World War and politics and economics since then, which is unrivalled.

When it comes to discovering what articles have been written, things are much harder. Simply to know what periodicals existed, one needs to visit the B.N. to consult its *Catalogue collectif des périodiques conservés dans les bibliothèques de Paris et dans les bibliothèques universitaires de province,* which lists those that came out before 1939. Three volumes of this catalogue have been published; the final volume (A–C) is awaited. For more recent periodicals, H. F. Raux, *Répertoire de la presse et des publications périodiques françaises* (1958, new edition 1961) lists 15,000. The *Annuaire de la presse* (1878, annual) is also useful. But there is no full index to articles in periodicals, and indeed few periodicals printed indexes. The *Revue des Deux Mondes* is an important exception. *Le Monde* is being indexed at the moment and the years 1861–80 have so far been done. This is the nearest there is to an equivalent of the index of the London *Times,* which can be useful for France; but the most important indexes to French periodicals are to be found on a single shelf in the Salle de bibliographie of the B.N. There is no alternative but to leaf through periodicals and newspapers, which is always rewarding, even if time-consuming. An additional snag is that many newspapers, particularly provincial ones, are kept at Versailles, and have to be ordered in advance for consultation in Paris.

For the more straightforward kinds of history, there are the historical bibliographies. These began with the *Catalogue de l'histoire de France* (1885–95) in twenty-two volumes, listing the B.N.'s holdings, by subject. (This is continued on card indexes in the basement of the B.N.) Then came G. Brière and P. Caron, *Répertoire méthodique de l'histoire moderne et contemporaine de la France 1899–1906* (1907); P. Caron, *Bibliographie des travaux publiés de 1866 à 1897 sur l'histoire de France depuis 1789* (1912) and P. Caron and H. Stein, *Répertoire bibliographique de l'histoire de France* (1920–9). The Comité Français des Sciences Historiques published a good guide to *La Recherche historique en France de 1940 à 1965* (1965). Since 1953 there has been an excellent *Bibliographie annuelle de l'histoire de France,* which has sections on political, institutional, economic and social, religious, colonial, 'civilisation' and local history. This gives obscure articles as well as virtually all significant books. But one needs to supplement it by investigating what unpublished memoirs and theses have been produced. This can be done in part by consulting the lists published in the *Revue historique* and more systematically by going through the universities' official catalogues of theses, *Catalogue des thèses de doctorat soutenues devant les universités françaises,* another time-consuming activity, since they are arranged not by subject but by faculty. For work in progress, there is the *Répertoire raisonné des doctorats d'état, lettres et sciences humaines, inscrits d'octobre 1970 à mai 1975* (1975), which is published by the Fichier Central des thèses at the University of Paris X—Nanterre, a visit to which is also desirable, since they keep a useful subject catalogue. For masters' theses, there is no real substitute for personal contact with the supervisors, because many of them used to be kept by the supervisors and never found their way into any library.

The specifically historical bibliographies should be supplemented by others, whose great value is not sufficiently recognised. A. Grandin, *Bibliographie des sciences juridiques, politiques, économiques et sociales* (1926), published in three volumes, and supplemented with annual volumes which take it up to the end of the war, is particularly useful for references to law theses and to official publications. There are interesting subject classifications in Otto Klapp, *Bibliographie der französischen Literaturwissenschaft* (Frankfurt am Main, published annually since 1956) and René Rancoeur, *Bibliographie de la littérature française moderne, 16e-20e siècles* (1962 onwards). The third volume of Hugo P. Thieme, *Bibliographie de la littérature française de 1800 à 1930* (1933) is a subject catalogue on 'Civilisation', but this work is also very valuable for the lists of books and articles written by and about all the major and many minor 'literary' authors. It was continued by S. Dreher and M. Rolli, *Bibliographie de la littérature française, 1930-9* (Geneva, 1948), and then by M. Drevet for 1940-9 (1954). The fullest literary bibliography is H. Talvant and J. Place, *Bibliographie des auteurs modernes de langue française 1801-1927* (started in 1928 and reaching volume 21, letter M, by 1975). Other useful specialised bibliographies have been given in the footnotes of this book. Among the fullest ones for recent work are the *Répertoire général des sciences religieuses* (1950 ff.) and the *Bulletin signalétique du C.N.R.S.* which since 1956 has had a series on the human sciences. Léon Vallée, *Bibliographie des bibliographies* (1883) and L. N. Malclès, *Manuel de bibliographie* (1963) and *Les Services du travail bibliographique* (1950-8, four volumes) can give further guidance. One can often find unexpected information in such specialised works as J. Leguy, *Catalogue bibliographique des livres de langue française sur la musique* (1954); the *Bibliographie géographique internationale* (1931 ff.) which used to be a supplement to the *Annales de géographie française* (1893-1930) and which is particularly useful for local and economic history. For science, see F. Russo, *Histoire des sciences et des techniques. Bibliographie* (1954), and the bibliographies in R. Taton, *Histoire générale des sciences* (1957 ff.) and M. Daumas, *Histoire générale des techniques* (1962 ff.). For medicine, the best thing to do is to go to the library of the Paris faculty of medicine, which is full of curious things. Medical theses are a vast untapped source, and rather difficult to get hold of: they have to be ordered in advance at the B.N.: A. Hahn, *La Bibliothèque de la faculté de médecine de Paris*

(1929) and *Table des thèses soutenues devant la faculté de médecine de Paris* (1939) may help.

The best encyclopedia to start one off on research is P. Larousse, *Grand Dictionnaire universel du 19ᵉ siècle* (1866–76, fifteen volumes and two supplements), as fascinating as the early editions of the *Encyclopaedia Britannica*. Several more recent editions are of varying quality and depth. A. de Monzie and Lucien Febvre, *Encyclopédie française* (1937) is the most instructive for the early twentieth century, and it also has long bibliographies. There are some good religious encyclopedias, notably A. Vacant, *Dictionnaire de théologie catholique* (1903–50, thirty volumes); A. Baudrillart and R. Aubert, *Dictionnaire d'histoire et de géographie ecclésiastiques* (1912 ff.); J. Bricourt, *Dictionnaire pratique des connaissances religieuses* (1925–33, seven volumes), and G. Jacquemet, *Catholicisme* (1947 ff.). To discover quickly what a place is like, consult P. Joanne, *Dictionnaire géographique et administratif de la France* (1890–1905 in seven volumes), or his one-volume *Dictionnaire géographique, administratif, postal, statistique, archéologique de la France, de l'Algérie et des colonies* (second edition, 1872), which is an indispensable reference work; to bring it up to date, there are the *Dictionnaires des communes*, which however are far less informative. For urban history, see P. Wolff and P. Dollinger, *Bibliographie d'histoire des villes de France* (1967). There are a large number of local bibliographies, which need to be supplemented by leafing through local periodicals: here again nothing can replace a visit to the local departmental or municipal libraries, from which one always emerges with new ideas.

For political history, M. Block, *Dictionnaire de l'administration française* (third edition, 1891) and *Petit Dictionnaire politique et social* (1896) are useful for the definition of terms and the details of laws. Legislation needs to be looked up in J. B. and J. Duverger's *Collection complète des lois, décrets etc.* (annual), but a visit to the library of the faculty of law in Paris will always prove useful: there is virtually no law which has not had some commentary written upon it by a law student, and the encyclopedias there show one further complications and links. The parliamentary debates are easily followed both in the *Moniteur universel*, later the *Journal officiel* (which also published laws and decrees), and in separate series, one for the lower and one for the upper house, variously entitled *Compte-rendu des séances du corps législatif* and *Procès-verbaux des séances du corps législatif* for 1852–60, *Annales du Sénat et du Corps législatif* 1861–70 and *Débats parlementaires* for the Third Republic. For diplomatic history, see D. H. Thomas and L. M. Case, *Guide to the Diplomatic Archives of Western Europe* (Philadelphia, 1959).

France is poorer in biographical dictionaries than other countries. The *Dictionnaire de biographie française* (started in 1933 by J. Balteau and continued by Roman d'Amat) had by 1975 reached the letter F. It is indispensable and also has bibliographies, but needs to be supplemented by A. Robert and G. Cougny, *Dictionnaire des parlementaires français 1789–1889* (five volumes, 1889–91), continued by J. Jolly, for the years 1889–1940, in a series which started in 1960 and is not quite complete. In addition, L. C. Vapereau, *Dictionnaire des contemporains* (third edition 1865, sixth edition 1893, the different editions all remain valuable); Nath Imbert, *Dictionnaire national des contemporains* (1936); E. Bénézit, *Dictionnaire des peintres, sculpteurs, dessinateurs et graveurs* (eight volumes, 1955–61). There is a full list of all these biographical dictionaries in J. Auffray, 'Bibliographie des recueils biographiques des contemporains aux 19e et 20e siècles' (unpublished mémoire, Institut National des Techniques de Documentation, 1963). The I.N.T.D., which trains people to produce bibliographies, has a large number of unpublished ones in its library, on the most diverse subjects, compiled by students as part of their course, and many are extremely interesting. For almanacs, beginning with the major political one which lists all office holders, *L'Almanach national* (annual, called *l'Almanach royal* or *Impérial* at different times), see G. Saffroy, *Bibliographie des almanachs et annuaires* (1959).

The information to be found in manuscript and in archival depositories is only very partially catalogued. The *Catalogue général des manuscrits des bibliothèques publiques en France*, which was started at the end of the nineteenth century, is of little use for this period except in its very latest volumes, which means that there is no ready way of discovering, except by direct inquiry, what manuscript collections are to be found in most provincial towns. The Bibliothèque Nationale's *Nouvelles Acquisitions du département des manuscrits* (issued every few decades, starting 1891) is important, but it needs to be supplemented by the latest catalogue in the manuscript reading room itself. The largest depository of manuscripts is of course the Archives Nationales. The collections in Paris include the papers of parliament and the ministries, divided by series. The most important ones for this period are: F1 Administration in general and personnel; F1c Elections, including prefects' reports on public opinion; F1D decorations; F2 and 3 local administration; F4–6 administrative accounts; F7 police; F8 sanitary control; F9 military; F10 agriculture; F11 food supplies; F12 commerce and industry; F13 public buildings; F14 public works; F15 poor assistance; F16 prisons; F17 education; F18 printing and bookselling;

F19 religion; F20 statistics; F21 fine arts; F22 labour and insurance; F23 extraordinary services in war-time; F30–4 finance; F35 state industries; F36 economic affairs; F70 Minister of State; F80 Algeria (but most archives concerning it are in Aix-en-Provence); F90 posts and telegraphs; C election results and frauds; O5 Napoleon III's household; AJ5–10 inter-war reparations; AJ12 Panama Company; AJ13 Opéra (but see also those in the Opéra's own library, and those in the Bibliothèque de l'Arsenal); AJ16 Academy of Paris; AJ17 Imprimerie Nationale; AJ21, 24 and 25 economic reconstruction after World War I; AK Cour des Comptes; AM Cour de Cassation. The BB series of the Ministry of Justice is important: 1 and 5 personnel, 6 files on magistrates, 7 files on tribunaux de commerce, 8 juges de paix, 9 solicitors, auctioneers and huissiers, 10 notaries; 11 naturalisations, 11 and 12 changes of name; 15 dispensations for marriages; 2 and 16 civil division; 17 Minister of Justice; 3, 18 and 19 criminal division, 20 assize courts, 21–4 pardons, 31 Alsace-Lorraine in 1871. Printed public documents are to be found in the AD series, arranged by ministry. The archives of the former ministry of the colonies are very rich; the records of the navy, which are incomplete but contain much still untouched, are partly in the National Archives and partly in its own archives; those of the army are in the Château de Vincennes where the Service historique de l'Armée is situated. Just as the navy has interesting information on the colonies, so the army's archives are indispensable for French political history.

The archives of local government are divided into the following series, situated in the provincial *départements*' capitals: M politics, P finances, R army, S public works, T education, U justice, V religion, X poor, Y prisons, Z miscellaneous and with all sorts of interesting things in it. The archives of the communes are some-times in the departmental archives and sometimes in the *mairie*. In local research one needs to discover how much has been destroyed by enemy action during wars, or simply lost. Only a small part of the collections are catalogued. See the A.N.'s publications: *L'État des inventaires des archives nationales, départementales, communales et hospitalières au 1er janvier 1937*, with supplements since then.

M. Rambaud, *Les Sources de l'histoire de l'art aux archives nationales* (1955), supplemented by periodical reports on further acquisitions, is indispensable. For the theatre, the Bibliothèque de l'Arsenal is a starting-point; for music halls the Collection Gustave Fréjaville. For music see C. Pierre, *Le Conservatoire national de musique* (1900), and the archives of the institution, and J. Chailley on 'Recher-ches musicologiques' in *Précis de musicologie* (1958). For literature,

D. Gallet-Guerne, *Les Sources de l'histoire littéraire aux archives nationales* (1961). For social history in general, Colloque de l'École Normale Supérieure de Saint-Cloud, *L'Histoire sociale, sources et méthodes* introduced by E. Labrousse (1967); J. Le Goff and P. Nora, *Faire l'histoire* (three volumes, 1974). For statistics, B. Gille, *Les Sources statistiques de l'histoire de France* (1964) which unfortunately stops at 1870, and for the way to use them, see the works of A. Daumard; also C. Legeard, *Guide de recherches documentaires en démographie* (1966). For trade union history, R. Brécy, *Le Mouvement syndical en France 1871–1921, essai bibliographique* (1963). The *Annuaire statistique* (annual since 1878) is a mine of curious information, and a starting-point for using the larger, full series of official statistical publications.

Private papers are harder to find than they are in many other countries. There is no central register. But the Archives Nationales now has four important series: AB xix for private documents it has acquired by extraordinary means, AP for private papers bought or donated; AQ for business archives and AS for archives of associations. It has published a catalogue of these, but again a visit is necessary to secure more up-to-date information.

Finally, P. Guiral, R. Pillorget and M. Agulhon, *Guide de l'étudiant en histoire moderne et contemporaine* (1971) lists the most important standard works, major articles, textbooks and reference books, as well as containing much useful general advice. It is worth looking too at similar works on other branches of study, such as those on sociology, philosophy, literature, etc.

All this may seem somewhat chaotic, and so it is, but then finding one's way through the chaos produces a good part of the pleasure of writing history.

GUIDE TO FURTHER READING

THERE is a mass of interesting histories revealing the mental torments of the French people in this period, but they are hardly ever looked at, because they have the outward appearance of obscure technical works. The doctors who wrote them, however, were often elegant and perceptive authors and sometimes extraordinarily gifted men. I particularly recommend, for a start, J.E.D. Esquirol, *Les Maladies mentales* (1844), of which an English translation was published in 1845; P. Briquet, *Traité de l'hystérie* (1959); A. Brierre de Boismont, *Du suicide* (1856) and *Des hallucinations* (1862); V. Magnan, *De l'alcoolisme* (1874); J.M. Charcot, *Clinique des maladies du system nerveux* (1893); P. Janet, *Les Obsessions et la psychathénie* (1903) and *De l'angoisse à l'extase* (1928); R. Laforgue, *Psychopathologie de l'échec* (1941). Useful books on the history of psychiatry include A. Hesnard, *De Freud à Lacan* (1970), H. Baruk (born 1897), *Des hommes comme nous, mémoires d'un neuropsychiatre* (1976) and *La Psychiatrie française de Pinel à nos jours* (1967) which contains valuable guides to further reading. On Charcot, there are two biographies in English, by A.R.G. Owen, *Hysteria, Hypnosis and Healing* (1971) and by G. Guillain, *J.M. Charcot* (1959). On Janet there is a book in English by a Swede, Bjorn Sjovall, *Psychology of Tension* (1967) and Claude M. Prevost, *Janet, Freud et la psychologie clinique* (1973).

The novelists provide an alternative approach to the history of anxiety. The works referred to on page 412 will direct the reader to the innumerable general histories of literature, which can help him choose among their writings; among the most recent guides and references books are: Maurice Bruézière, *Histoire descriptive de la littérature contemporaine* (1975); P.O. Walzer, *Littérature française, 20ᵉ siècle* (1975); Jacques Brenner, *Histoire de la littérature française de 1940 à nos jours* (1978); Claude Bonnefoy, *Dictionnaire de la littérature française contemporaine* (1977); Yves Olivier-Martin, *Histoire du roman populaire en France* (1980); Michel Ragon, *Histoire de la littérature prolétarienne* (1974); Marc Soriano, *Guide de la littérature pour la jeunesse* (1975), François Caradec, *Histoire de la littérature enfantine en France* (1977). Recent biographies, and studies around individual literary figures, include: Arlette Michel, *Le Mariage chez Honoré de Balzac: amour et féminisme* (1978); Linda Orr, *Michelet* (Cornell, 1976); José Cabanis, *Michelet, la prêtre et la femme* (1970); Joanna Richardson, *Victor Hugo* (1976) and *Zola* (1978); Curtis Cate,

George Sand (1975); Jonathan Culler, *Flaubert, The Uses of Uncertainty* (1974); Maria Paganini-Ambord, *Flaubert, la présence de l'écrivain dans l'œuvre* (Zurich, 1974); Alex de Jonge, *Baudelaire, Prince of Clouds* (1976); A.W. Raitt, *Prosper Mérimée* (1970); Michael G. Lerner, *Maupassant* (1975); Fernande Zayed, *Huysmans, peintre de son époque* (1973); Claude Martin, *La Maturité d'André Gide 1895–1902* (1977), which goes beyond Jean Delay, *La Jeunesse d'André Gide* (1957) and P. de Boisdeffre, *Vie d'André Gide* (1970); Claude Sicard, *Roger Martin du Gard* (1976) and René Garguilo, *La Genèse des Thibault chez R. Martin du Gard* (1974); Curtis Cate, *Antoine de Saint-Exupéry, His life and times* (1970).

Modern reflections on the work of the novelists are to be found in Roger Sayre, *Solitude in Society, A Sociological Study in French Literature* (Cambridge, Mass., 1978); René Demoris, *Le Roman à la première personne du classicisme aux Lumières* (1975); Jean Deprun, *La Philosophie de l'inquiétude en France au 18ᵉ siècle* (1979); Michel Raimond, *La Crise de roman des lendemains de naturalisme aux années vingt;* M. Mansuy, *Positions et oppositions sur le roman contemporain* (1971); J. Bellemin-Noel, *Psychanalyse et littérature* (1978); Charlotte Wardi, *Le Juif dans le roman français 1933–48* (1972); Fernande Gontier, *La Femme et le couple dans le roman 1919–39* (1976); Paolo Solinas, *Le Roman patriotique français de 1870 à 1914* (Cagliari, 1970); Pierre Labracherie, *La Vie quotidienne de la bohème littéraire au 19ᵉ siècle* (1967). But one should not neglect the old masterpieces of criticism, like the very sharp book by H. Taine, *Les Philosophes français du 19ᵉ siècle* (1857), which is much broader than its title suggests, or P. Bourget, *Essais de psychologie contemporaine* (1885).

The starting-point for the study of religion is G. Le Bras, *Études de sociologie religieuse* (1955), and F. Boulard, *Problèmes missionaires de la France rurale* (1945). For detailed application of their methods, see G. Cholvy, *Géographie religieuse de l'Hérault contemporain* (1968) and Y.M. Hilaire, *La Vie religieuse des populations du diocèse d'Arras 1840–1914* (Lille, 1977). On anticlericalism see T. Zeldin, *Conflicts in French Society* (1970). On Protestants, Jeanine Estèbe, *Les Protestants* (1980). On Jews, Michael Marrus, *The Politics of Assimilation* (1971) and the book he will shortly publish in collaboration with R. Paxton on the Jews during World War II. On Freemasons, J.C. Faucher, *Histoire des franc-maçons dans les Deux Sèvres* (1977). On population problems, Francis Ronsin, *La Grève des ventres. Propagande néo-malthusienne et baisse de la natalité en France 19–20ᵉ siècles* (1980); Colin Dyer, *Population and Society in 20th century France* (1978); Peter Stearns, *Aging in French Culture* (1976) and P. Aries, *L'Homme devant la mort* (1977).

To understand the political mind one can look at the works of Stanley Hoffman, *In Search of France* (1963) and *Decline or Renewal* (1974), and Robert Paxton, *Vichy France* (1972), the biographies by J.N. Jeanneney, *F. de Wendel en republique* (1976); Pierre Miquel, *Poincaré* (1961); P.O. Lapie, *Herriot* (1967); G. Warner, *Pierre Laval* (1968); J.C. Allain, *Joseph Caillaux* (1978); J. Lacouture, *Léon Blum* (1979); Philippe Bauchard, *Léon Blum* (1976); Fondation Nationale de Science politique, *Édouard Daladier, chef de gouvernement* (1977); R. Remond, *La France et les Français en 1930–39* (1978); J.P. Cuvillier, *Vincent Auriol et les finances publiques du Front populaire* (1978). To place politics in a wider European context, see Robert Wohl, *The Generation of 1914* (1980) and Charles Maier, *Recasting Bourgeois Europe* (Princeton, 1975). For the political reactions of individuals in times of crisis, R. Kedward, *Resistance in Vichy France* (1978). On the problems of technocracy see A. Peyrefitte, *Le Mal français* (1967); R.F. Kuisel, *E. Mercier* (1967); Phillipe Bauchard, *Les Technocrates et le pouvoir* and the unjustly neglected works of Jean Coutrot, which deserve reprinting; also G. Thuillier, *Bureaucratie et bureaucrates en France au 19ᵉ siècle* (1980). On new forms of organisation, Isabel Boussard, *Vichy et la corporation paysanne* (1980).

New books on thinkers include F. Bon and M.A. Burnier, *Les Nouveaux Intellectuels* (1966, new edition 1977); R.L. Nichols, *Julien Benda and Political Discourse* (Kansas, 1979); Jack J. Roth, *The Cult of Violence: Sorel and the Sorelians* (University of California Press, 1980); Paul Mazcaj, *The Action Française and Revolutionary Syndicalism* (Chapel Hill, 1979) to add to the standard work of Weber; D. Desanti, *Drieu La Rochelle* (1978); S. Petremont, *Vie de Simone Weil* (1978); H.R. Lottman, *Albert Camus* (1978); André Thirion, *Révolutionnaires sans révolution* (1972). Serge Berstein, *Histoire du parti radical* (1980) is now the standard work on its subject. On the communists, see in addition to the books by Annie Kriegel and Robert Wohl, the new study by Edward Mortimer (1980), A. Harris and A. de Sédouy, *Voyage à l'intérieur du parti communiste* (1974), and Jacqueline Mer, *Le Parti de Maurice Thorez ou le bonheur communiste français* (1977). For fascism, see A. Deniel, *Bucard et le francisme* (1979). For royalists, Henri de France, Comte de Paris, *Mémoires d'exil et de combats* (1979).

One can pursue the quest for the military mind in R. Girardet, *La Société militaire* (1953); Alistair Horne's trilogy on modern French wars; M. Howard, *The Franco-Prussian War* (1961); J.J. Becker, *1914: Comment les Français sont entrés dans la guerre* (1977); Guy Pedroncini, *Les Mutineries de 1917* (1967); Jacques Meyer. *La Vie quotidienne des soldats pendant la grande guerre* (1966); D.B. Ralston, *The Army of the Republic 1971–1914* (Cambridge, Mass., 1967); Robert J.

Young, *French Foreign Political and Military Planning 1933–40* (Cambridge, Mass., 1978); Charles de Gaulle, *Mémoires de guerre* (1954–9) and *Mémoires d'espoir* (1970).

For colonial adventure start with R. Girardet, *L'Idée coloniale* (1972) and *Les Temps des colonies* (1979); C.A. Julien and C.A. Ageron, *Histoire de l'Algérie contemporaine* (1979, 2 vols); F. Renaudot, *Histoire des français en Algérie 1830–1962* (1979); C.A. Julien, *Une Pensée anticoloniale 1914–79* (1979). There are numerous good books in English on the colonies, referred to in the footnotes, to which may be added J.P. Spagnolo, *France and Ottoman Lebanon* (1978) and Jacques Thobie, *Intérêts et impérialisme français dans l'empire ottoman 1895–1914* (1977).

Finally, for the collapse of one of the pillars of the old civilisation, Theresa McBride, *The Domestic Revolution: The Modernisation of Household Service in England and France 1820–1920* (1976).

INDEX